Transition to Neo-Confucianism

Shao Yung on Knowledge and Symbols of Reality

Transition to Neo-Confucianism
Shao Yung on Knowledge and Symbols of Reality

Anne D. Birdwhistell

Stanford University Press · Stanford, California · 1989

Stanford University Press
Stanford, California
© 1989 by the Board of Trustees
of the Leland Stanford Junior University
Printed in the United States of America

CIP data are at the end of the book

· · · · · ·
To Ray

Acknowledgments

My study of Shao Yung began more than ten years ago, after I had completed my dissertation on the early Ch'ing philosopher Li Yung. I realized then that I did not satisfactorily understand the philosophical problems and arguments of the early Ch'ing period, an age very critical of Sung philosophy. Thus I felt compelled to try to understand the beginnings of Neo-Confucianism.

The types of problems in which Shao Yung was interested and the enigma that he has posed for over nine hundred years contributed to my choice of which Sung philosopher to examine. As I became familiar with Shao Yung's thought, my initial conception of his philosophical system was rudely altered by the ideas themselves. Shao Yung was by no means an unknown philosopher, but he was, I contend, often misrepresented and not well understood—either by his contemporaries or by posterity.

I hope that my analysis and the perspective that I offer will contribute to a better understanding of Shao Yung's thought. Given the historical treatment of Shao Yung, I suspect that some of my interpretations, like those of others before me, will be open to serious dispute. I do realize, moreover, that I have not quite followed the sagely advice of Ch'eng Hao, Shao Yung's contemporary, who said that twenty years were required to understand Shao Yung.

Even though I have not spent the years Ch'eng Hao recommended, I have accumulated many debts in my search for understanding. Stockton State College, Pomona, New Jersey, provided funds for several summers of research and for a sabbatical that allowed me to write this book. My Stockton colleagues have given me support and encouragement, and I especially thank Allen Lacy, Joseph Walsh, and Margaret Marsh.

I began my study of China more than twenty years ago as an undergraduate at the University of Pennsylvania. The initial guidance and help of Derk Bodde and W. Allyn Rickett enabled me to develop my interests in Chinese philosophy and culture. As a graduate student at Stanford University, I studied with David S. Nivison, who directed both my M.A. thesis on the *Huai-nan Tzu* and my Ph.D. dissertation. During my graduate years, I further benefited from the teaching of the late James J. Y. Liu, who stimulated my interest in thinking about tradition.

More recently, I have received encouragement and help from Nathan Sivin, who has offered criticism on several of my articles. Fred Gillette Sturm has aided me with his comments on several papers that were preliminary pieces to this study. I am grateful to Nancy Cheng and her staff at the East Asian library of the University of Pennsylvania for their assistance over many years. The editorial assistance of Stanford University Press has been superb, particularly the help from John R. Ziemer. Above all, I thank my husband, Ray L. Birdwhistell, for his support and for our countless hours of discussion on the nature of theory and theoretical problems. The views and interpretations expressed in this study are my own, and I take responsibility for all errors.

A.D.B.

Contents

1 · Historical and Philosophical Contexts   1

2 · The Background   20

3 · Beginning a Theory   42

4 · The Theoretical Structure of Reality   66

5 · Concepts of Change: A Focus on Cosmology   95

6 · Concepts of Change: Human Beings and the Universe   124

7 · To Recognize a Sage   162

8 · To Become a Sage   179

9 · Within the Intellectual Traditions   197

10 · The Threads Running Through   227

Appendix A: The Charts and Diagrams   235
Appendix B: Selected Charts   237
Appendix C: List of Chinese Characters   247

Notes   257
Bibliography   291
Index   309

Transition to Neo-Confucianism
Shao Yung on Knowledge and Symbols of Reality

I
· · · · ·
Historical and Philosophical Contexts

> *Learning that does not end in delight cannot be called learning.*
> —*Shao Yung*[1]

Shao Yung (1011–77) was an extraordinary thinker who lived during an extraordinary age. Among the great thinkers of the Northern Sung (960–1126), Shao Yung was acknowledged a person of unusual knowledge and understanding. His philosophical importance was widely recognized, and his uniqueness was admitted unquestioningly. Other than the classical period of Chinese philosophy during the latter part of the Chou dynasty (1122?–256 B.C.), few periods in Chinese history have matched the achievements of this dynamic age. During the Chou period the foundations for Confucianism and the fundamental patterns of Chinese culture were laid. In the Northern Sung, cultural elements from more than a thousand years were combined into a new system, Neo-Confucianism. This form of Confucianism dominated Chinese thought and culture until the twentieth century.

Despite the acknowledgment of Shao Yung's importance by subsequent Chinese philosophers, his role in the development of Neo-Confucian philosophy has been greatly contested. Some of his contributions have been recognized, but others have been ignored or overlooked. Shao Yung has drawn strong praise and vehement criticism. Many scholars have admired him for the breadth of his knowledge and for his unusual interests. Still, the comments of

---

Unless otherwise indicated, all translations are my own.

critics, both friendly and unfriendly, often were based more on Shao's reputation than on a close familiarity with his thought. Shao Yung's thought was never well understood, and even today he remains one of the most famous enigmas in Chinese philosophy.[2]

As a thinker and as a member of society, Shao Yung was clearly a rebel intellectual. He was involved in questionable areas of thought, and he openly opposed social conventions and government policies. It would be hard, however, to find someone more representative of Chinese culture. This seeming anomaly of orthodoxy and rebellion makes him an intriguing example of the contradictions often found in Chinese history.

This study attempts to provide a perspective on the philosophical thought of Shao Yung. To understand his thinking, it is necessary to utilize a contextual as well as an analytical approach. The questions that he was addressing, the ideas that he proposed, and the implicit assumptions that he made must be examined. Also essential is a consideration of historical context—the philosophical tradition to which he belonged, the age in which he lived, and later philosophers' interpretations of him. My primary aim here is to analyze the structure of Shao Yung's thought and to show how it made sense intellectually. My efforts are guided, however, by the recognition that Shao Yung's philosophy cannot be separated from the historical and philosophical contexts.

The Historical Context

During the Northern Sung, the formulation of a number of talented thinkers resulted in the founding of a new philosophical system. The name eventually given by the Chinese to this system, which is known in the West as Neo-Confucianism, was "learning of the *tao*" (*tao-hsüeh*). This name explicitly signified a link with the ancient teachings of Confucius (551–479 B.C.) and Mencius (372–289 B.C.). At the same time, the name implied an identification that denied Taoist and Buddhist influence. Although agreement on the contributions of particular eleventh-century philosophers is not unanimous, scholars have long recognized the importance of five thinkers in the founding of this new learning: Shao Yung, Chou

Tun-yi (1017–73), Chang Tsai (1020–77), Ch'eng Hao (1032–85), and Ch'eng Yi (1033–1107).³*

The historian and philosopher Ssu-ma Kuang (1019–86) was originally included in this elite group, but by the late twelfth century, Chu Hsi (1130–1200), the great synthesizer of Neo-Confucian thought, had removed him from the orthodox line of the transmission of the *tao*. Although he questioned Shao Yung's role as well, Chu was never successful in obtaining a consensus on Shao's position. Nonetheless, Chu Hsi did go so far as to omit Shao Yung from the *Chin-ssu lu* (Reflections on things at hand), Chu's influential anthology of the sayings and writings of the early Neo-Confucians.⁴

Uncertain as some of the details of the early development of Neo-Confucian thought may be, its importance is hardly debatable. Confucianism and Neo-Confucianism are virtually synonymous with traditional Chinese culture. They are the cultural systems within which the government and society of China functioned from the Han dynasty (206 B.C.–A.D. 220) until the Ch'ing dynasty (1644–1911).⁵ Moreover, even in this century, remnants of Neo-Confucianism are embedded in Chinese culture and society.

The Northern Sung was important not only for its philosophical thought, but for advancements in many areas of scientific and technological knowledge. The economy, the political system, and the social structure experienced major changes, and developments in literature, art, and the writing of history kept pace. Printing, which had developed in the late T'ang dynasty (618–906), led in the tenth and eleventh centuries to publication of the Confucian classics, the Buddhist canon, and other major works. On the negative side, military weakness kept the Northern Sung from possibly greater accomplishments. Clearly, a strong foundation was laid for the far-reaching cultural developments of the Southern Sung (1127–1279).⁶

Several characteristics of Northern Sung philosophical activity are particularly relevant for understanding Shao Yung's thought. Competing traditions of learning, which had previously flourished, continued to survive, but in altered form. Some traditions developed,

---

*To avoid ambiguities, *yi* is used instead of *i* throughout.

others declined. The *Yi* learning (*Yi-hsüeh*), a tradition of knowledge based on the *Yi-ching* (Book of changes), was one area of philosophy that retained its vitality and importance even as it underwent significant change. Moreover, a new philosophical orientation began to emerge—an emphasis on moral philosophy.[7]

The *Yi* learning, which originally developed and flourished during the Han dynasty, combined various theoretical and practical interests. Although the *Yi-ching* was the central text in this tradition, other works were important too. Related texts ranged from the Confucian classics and important early philosophical works to non-classical, apocryphal texts devoted to esoteric knowledge associated with symbols, theoretical systems, and numerology, all of which could be applied in astrology, fortune-telling, and alchemy. After the Han, the *Yi* learning did not die out, but the general emphases of philosophers changed. Many of the esoteric aspects of the *Yi* learning were transmitted only in secret traditions, still largely unknown. During the tenth century, however, ideas from the *Yi* arcana began to spread to a broader intellectual audience.

By the Northern Sung, the *Yi* learning had divided into two major branches: *yi-li hsüeh*, which emphasized moral thought, and *hsiang-shu hsüeh*, which focused on cosmology and the functioning of the universe.[8] The second term, literally the "learning of the images and numbers," has sometimes been translated as "numerology." Although some aspects of this branch of *Yi* learning are strikingly similar to the concerns of the Pythagorean numerologists of early Greek philosophy, in particular, an interest in numbers and music,[9] the translation *numerology* is too limited. *Numerology* conveys nothing about the concept of the images, which were as important as numbers in *hsiang-shu hsüeh*, and nothing about the other ideas central to this learning.

The learning of the images and numbers, part of the esoteric tradition of the *Yi* learning, consisted of several theoretical systems that implicitly served as explanations of the patterns of change in the universe. It emphasized various symbols, the two most important of which were the images (*hsiang*) and the numbers (*shu*). The symbols differed in their level of abstraction or their degree of generality. The numbers, for example, were more abstract than the images. The levels of abstraction that the symbols represented were, in effect, grades of theoreticity, to use W. V. Quine's term.[10]

All the philosophical systems of the five founders of Neo-Confucianism were based on the *Yi* learning. Chou Tun-yi and Chang Tsai incorporated elements from both branches. The two Ch'eng brothers followed the branch of moral philosophy, and Shao Yung that of the images and numbers. Although Shao Yung thus differed from the others in not emphasizing moral thought, he was still within the broad current of the times. As the eleventh century unfolded, however, the gap between his thought and that of the moralists widened.[11]

Not only did the thought of these philosophers have much in common, but also, except for Shao Yung and Chou Tun-yi (who apparently did not know each other), their lives were closely intertwined.[12] Some were scholar-officials, and most spent significant portions of their adult lives in Loyang, a former capital and a seat of continuing upper-class wealth, power, and culture. In addition, as opponents of the political and economic reforms advocated by the "new" party of Wang An-shih (1021–86), these men sided with the more tradition-minded "old" party. Their political participation varied widely, however, ranging from the active, official involvement of Ssu-ma Kuang to the passive but sympathetic support of Shao Yung. Both politically and intellectually, these philosophers were not oriented toward radical change. Rather, their position echoed that of Confucius, who regarded himself as someone who believed in and loved antiquity.[13]

Along with developments in the *Yi* learning, Northern Sung philosophy was characterized by a revival of interest in Confucianism. The newly printed editions of the classics helped to stimulate a renewal of interest in pre-Ch'in and Han texts, and interest in these philosophical texts revived certain patterns of thought from early Confucianism. From the pre-Ch'in thinkers, Northern Sung thought absorbed an emphasis on practical political action and rationalistic thought, and from the Han thinkers cosmological ideas on the unity of the three spheres of heaven, earth, and humanity, as well as on correspondence, resonance, and order in the universe. Unlike some of his contemporaries, Shao Yung tended to be influenced more by Han, than by pre-Ch'in, thought.

The renewal of interest in Confucianism was accompanied by an explicit, if selective, rejection of Buddhism. The movement to revive Confucianism began in the T'ang dynasty and particularly gained momentum from the writings of the great essayist Han Yü (768–824) and his views on the concept of the orthodox tradition (*cheng-t'ung*). Applying the political concept of legitimate succession to other areas of the culture, Han Yü linked a Confucian renaissance with an overt rejection of Buddhism. By the Northern Sung, Buddhism was widely seen as alien to, and subversive of, Chinese culture and Confucian values. In particular, the supposedly pernicious effects of cultural pluralism were interpreted as being the result of Buddhist influences. The renewed interest in early Confucian texts and ideas thus was part of a broad movement that sought to preserve essential Confucian ideas and values.

An emphasis on comprehensive systems was another characteristic of eleventh-century intellectual activity. Although some scholars have interpreted this behavior as compensation for the Sung's military and territorial losses, in the realm of philosophy, at least, more plausible reasons can be found. In rejecting Buddhism, Northern Sung philosophers focused on pre-Buddhist thought, that is, on Han learning. Consequently, Han ideas on the unity of the realms of nature and of human beings and the belief that events in one sphere affected events in other spheres easily entered much of Sung philosophy.[14]

These ideas were accepted by Han philosophers as different as Tung Chung-shu (ca. 179–ca. 104 B.C.) and Yang Hsiung (53 B.C.–A.D. 28),[15] and they had an explicit basis in the *Yi-ching* and in the various Han commentaries and texts associated with it. These views were fundamental not only to Confucian thought, but also to Taoist thought and the related esoteric traditions, which included such works as Wei Po-yang's (fl. A.D. 142–67) *Chou Yi ts'an-t'ung-ch'i* and Kuan Lang's (3d century A.D.) *Tung-chi chen-ching*.[16] In addition, many Buddhist writings presented a comprehensive view of the universe.

In the Sung, philosophers were not the only ones to attempt a grand system uniting all of reality. Historians also specialized in synthesis and wrote comprehensive works, including some of China's most important encyclopedias and histories. The *Tzu-chih t'ung-chien* (Comprehensive mirror for aid in government) by Ssu-ma Kuang is, for example, one of the most famous works of this period.

These characteristics of Northern Sung thought constitute an important part of the background of Shao Yung's thought. Within this historical context, Shao Yung's general emphases and ideas were, on the one hand, neither unusual nor even idiosyncratic. He shared many tendencies and assumptions with his contemporaries. On the other hand, Shao Yung clearly was different. He utilized ideas from the entire range of the intellectual heritage, including some that had developed in the esoteric traditions and had not been public knowledge before. Other ideas were well-known ones that he used in new ways.

Shao Yung's uniqueness, however, did not result merely from the breadth of his thought or from his distance from the increasingly dominant emphasis on moral philosophy. Rather, it arose in large part from the theoretical problems that concerned him. He pursued questions and suggested answers that anticipated views of later philosophers, some even hundreds of years later. It is not surprising that many of his contemporaries claimed not to understand him.

The Philosophical Context

The philosophical context, especially some of the characteristics of the tradition of Chinese philosophy, offers another perspective on Shao Yung's thought. The absence of a tradition of metaphilosophy in premodern Chinese philosophy is particularly important. Simply stated, metaphilosophy is formal thought about philosophy aimed at making the rules and conditions of philosophical discourse explicit. It consists of the guideposts that aid one in understanding. Two important criteria for determining the presence or absence of metaphilosophy are the style of argumentation and the organization of philosophical writings.

Chinese philosophers rarely commented explicitly on what they or other philosophers were doing. With few exceptions, they did not systematically define key terms or openly state primary assumptions. In many cases, writers did not even state the philosophical problems they were addressing. From the Han to the Ch'ing, tightly organized arguments were uncommon. In the development and argumentation of ideas, Chinese philosophers seldom followed a linear pattern and rarely tried to show that alternative views entailed contradictions.

Although seldom, if ever, stated, the premises and rules of evidence were nonetheless present for those who sought them. These elements could have been stated explicitly had the philosophers wanted or felt the need to do so. However, explicitness of a degree expected by Western philosophers was not part of the Chinese tradition. The dominant mode or task of discourse was not an examination of the logical relationships between assumptions and conclusions. With the notable exception of the Ch'ing period, Chinese philosophers did not even stress new evidence.[17]

Metaphilosophical concerns were, by and large, seen as the responsibility of commentators and readers. Weighing and analyzing the elements of beliefs also became an important task for historians of thought. Readers were expected to know the philosophical problems and the implications of the different points of view. A writer presented his ideas to a public that he expected to be conversant with the ideas and the tradition of such writing.

One of the chief difficulties in deciphering Shao Yung's thinking lies in his method of presenting ideas. Numerous passages in his major philosophical work consist of correlations, which can be highly ambiguous unless one knows the theoretical meaning of the items correlated and the intent of the correlations. Shao's sets of correlations may be compared to graphs and tables without identifying labels. Fortunately, commentators have provided the information necessary for interpreting the correlations.

The lack of a metaphilosophical tradition poses difficulties in translating as well as in understanding. Translating such passages as the sets of correlations clearly presents special problems. Since more than the literal text must be taken into account to understand the ideas being presented, a word-for-word rendering is not very satisfactory and makes little sense. Moreover, even straightforward prose styles of argumentation provide unsuspected pitfalls. Like other philosophers, Shao Yung commonly used terms in more than one way; of course no warning was given to alert the reader to the different usages.

Unfortunately, such textual difficulties have often been coupled with imprecision in the use of Western philosophical terms. The result has been translations clearly inadequate from a philosophical perspective. Chinese terms have often been rendered into English without sufficient acknowledgment of the philosophical implications of the English terms or without clarification of the differences in meaning between the Western and Chinese philosophical idea. For purposes of philosophical analysis, unless one can read the original text, the technical vagueness of many English translations of Chinese philosophical texts makes them highly questionable.

The characteristic organization of Chinese philosophical writings further reflects the Chinese lack of interest in metaphilosophy. Many works are anecdotal, consisting of a series of loosely related sayings, notes, or conversations. Other works are commentaries on a classic. In structure, these works follow the organization of the classic. Although tightly organized essays were relatively rare after the Warring States period (403–222 B.C.), some works were written in this form. In general, however, the organization of written forms complemented the style in which ideas were argued: a series of discrete ideas was presented, with their connections left unstated but implied.

The conventions surrounding direct quotation also illustrate the lack of a metaphilosophical tradition. Chinese authors rarely indicated the source of a quotation, instead inserting quotations in texts without acknowledging either the act of quotation itself or the author. However, commentators invariably noted the sources of the views cited. Although these characteristics are not found in all Chinese philosophical works, they are part of the general absence of metaphilosophy, a characteristic deemed necessary in much of Western thought.

These characteristics of traditional Chinese thought pose problems in untangling the organization and presentation of ideas. Shigeru Nakayama has suggested that, from the Han dynasty on, Chinese philosophizing was carried on primarily in the "documentary" style,[18] a style that dominated Chinese learning in general. In contrast, much of Western thought is characterized by a "rhetorical" mode of learning, derived from early Greek philosophy, whose argumentative, or adversarial, style entailed the development of arguments based on an appeal to logical reasoning. Its discourse included and often depended on metaphilosophy, or formal thought about philosophy.

Although unusual, argumentation of ideas was not absent from Chinese philosophy. In a rare reference to such activity, Ch'eng Yi described Shao Yung as even better at arguing than Chou Tun-yi.[19] The aim, however, was not to discover contradictions in reasoning or to build up a position through logical reasoning. Rather, the philosophers emphasized the historical precedents for their views. Documentation, the keeping of records, and research on records were from early times a striking feature of Chinese scholarship. After Confucianism became the established orthodoxy during the Han dynasty, philosophers generally adopted the documentary style, with the result that much of their writing consisted of citations of already established data as support for particular views. Philosophers did not argue positions by appealing to logical coherence. Instead, since fidelity to truths was the issue at stake, they simply accumulated more data to buttress a position. The evidence characteristically consisted of passages from the classics or remarks of established philosophers and commentators. Clearly such writing was designed for a sophisticated readership.

Two other characteristics of the Chinese philosophical tradition are important for understanding Shao Yung. First, because philosophical activity was heavily oriented toward action, philosophers had little incentive to examine explicitly the logical structure of their beliefs. Beliefs were proposed or advocated. True, the pre-Ch'in philosophers of the School of Names (*Ming Chia*) did engage in argumentation that involved disputation, and their writings show evidence of some concern with logic, but the dominant form of philosophical activity stressed practicality rather than logical disputation.[20]

A final characteristic of Chinese philosophy relevant here is the conception of philosophical schools as bodies of knowledge built on truths contained in the classics. Thus, it made sense that much philosophizing occurred in the form of commentaries on the classics. Even when the form of writing was not strictly a commentary, the ideas presented were often interpretations of specific but unstated passages from the classics or from other important early texts. From the Sung to the Ch'ing, philosophizing was called "discussing learning" (*chiang-hsüeh*), an indirect acknowledgment that philosophy was a matter of learning, understood as both knowledge and knowing, and not an organization of an argument to be tested for logical coherence.

These characteristics apply to the philosophical traditions that originated in China. Buddhism, however, introduced into China a different set of assumptions about philosophical writing. Many of the early Buddhist works are rhetorical in style and follow a linear, and sometimes even explicitly stated, method of development. Often presenting a comprehensive view of the world as well as a set of instructions for the believer to follow, Buddhist writings provided an alternative standard for the presentation of philosophical views.[21] Some of these standards were gradually incorporated into Chinese philosophical writing.

The writings of the founders of Neo-Confucianism reflect the influence of both earlier Chinese and Buddhist styles. Their works are presented in such forms as recorded conversations, long and short essays, commentaries on the classics, and poetry.[22] Chou Tun-yi's *T'ung shu* (Explanatory text), Shao Yung's *Huang-chi ching-shih* (Supreme principles that rule the world), and Chang Tsai's *Cheng meng* (Correct discipline for beginners) exhibit certain characteristics of the Buddhist style. These works differ in form from many Confucian writings, in that they do not consist of sayings, conversations, or collections of notes. Although many of the ideas within these works refer to ideas in a Confucian classic, particularly the *Yi-ching*, they are not commentaries in a formal sense. Buddhist standards are further reflected in these works in the presentation of a metaphysical position along with moral and epistemological views.

Shao Yung's Writings

Shao Yung's ideas and his methods of presenting them set him apart from most other philosophers. Shao's answers to such disparate theoretical problems as nature and the universe, political history and society, personal behavior and morality, and ultimate wisdom and sagely knowledge were certainly unusual. Moreover, the form in which he presented his ideas was not conducive to easy understanding. Shao's use of prose discourse was conventional, but his charts and sets of correlations were uncommon ways of representing ideas.

Fortunately, Shao's known writings are extensive. However, any review of Shao as a person is limited by the lack in his extant works of personal writings, such as letters and notes, a source of information available for many other Neo-Confucians. Shao is mentioned in the notes of some contemporary and some slightly later philosophers, and many of Shao's poems and his essay "Wu-ming kung chuan" (Biography of Mr. No Name) contain autobiographical elements.

Shao's major philosophical work is the *Huang-chi ching-shih* (Supreme principles that rule the world). This work incorporates, in some form and to some degree, all his major philosophical ideas. Shao's other writings consist of *Yü-ch'iao wen-tui* (Conversation between the fisherman and the woodcutter), "Wu-ming kung chuan" (Biography of Mr. No Name), and a collection of poetry, *Yi-ch'uan chi-jang chi* (Collection of beating on the ground at Yi-ch'uan). These works supplement and expand on the ideas presented in his major philosophical treatise. (Some scholars have questioned Shao's authorship of the *Yü-ch'iao wen-tui*. However, since that work does not present any views not found elsewhere in Shao's writings, we need not take up that problem here.)

In the Chinese philosophical tradition, works consisting of conversations constituted one important style of writing. For those works identified in some way with Taoist thought, the early Taoist work the *Chuang Tzu* established the model. Shao Yung's *Yü-ch'iao wen-tui* is similar in form to many passages in the *Chuang Tzu*. Shao's title also echoes that of chapter 31 in the *Chuang Tzu*, "The Old Fisherman."[23] Works in this form typically give the impression that their ideas are not presented in a deliberate manner. Appearances to the contrary, however, in terms of the development of its ideas, Shao Yung's essay is deceptively well organized.

The *Chuang Tzu* contains many conversations involving artisans and workers, people who are clearly not literati. The knowledge of artisans was thought to differ in fundamental ways from that of the Confucians, who were concerned with governing the state and with regulating society and the family. Artisans and workers possessed knowledge not contained, indeed not containable, in words. It was believed that this Taoist type of knowledge was learned from nature and experience and not from books.

Shao's work may thus appear to be concerned with Taoist kinds of knowledge rather than with Confucian moral knowledge concerning society and government. Close examination reveals, however, that Shao's conversation deals with the same basic topics as his *Huang-chi ching-shih*. Both works emphasize Shao's ideas about the structure of the universe and about sagely knowledge. In addition, Shao's conversation includes Taoist ideas about such matters as the use of words and the implications of differing perspectives, as well as some Confucian ideas about morality.

In the "Biography of Mr. No Name," Shao Yung uses another form of philosophical writing, the short biographical essay. In both content and title, Shao's biography has Taoist associations. By playing on the double meaning of the word *name*, the title evokes Taoist associations with that which is ultimately nameless, such as the *tao* (the way), and the Taoist idea that the truly great man has no fame. The opening passage of the *Lao Tzu* (*Tao Te Ching*) states, for instance, that the way (*tao*) that can be named is not the eternal way and that the beginning of heaven and earth has no name. The *Chuang Tzu* says that the sage has no name (or no fame), and Ho Yen, a third-century Neo-Taoist, later evoked these ideas in the title of his essay "Wu-ming lun" (On the nameless).[24] In his "Biography of Mr. No Name," Shao Yung favorably compares his sagely subject (probably a reference to himself) with the nameless ultimate of the universe, the *tao* or *t'ai-chi* (Supreme Ultimate). Both the sage and the *tao* leave no traces, and both have no true name. Shao uses this work to address certain philosophical questions usually associated with Taoist thought, such as point of view and the use of names.

Poetry is yet another form Chinese philosophers used to present their ideas. The somewhat cryptic title of Shao's collection of poetry, "Beating on the Ground at Yi-ch'uan," alludes to a line in an ancient folksong.[25] Although the folksong had political implications, Shao's poems address many subjects. In addition to political opinions and comments on morality, they touch on his philosophical ideas in the areas of epistemology and the nature of the universe. Unlike his other writings, Shao's poems contain references to contemporary people and to specific situations calling for personal moral action. Shao's collection of poetry is particularly useful for indicating the range of topics contained in his philosophical thought.

The *Huang-chi ching-shih* is Shao's major philosophical work. The title alludes to a phrase in the "Hung Fan" (Great plan) chapter of the *Shu-ching* (Book of documents). It also broadly suggests that the subject of the work is the patterns of the universe.[26] Shao discusses, among other topics, his views on the fundamental characteristics of the worlds of nature and human society, on perception and knowledge, and on the capabilities of the sage.

The organization and the scope of ideas of the *Huang-chi ching-shih* are similar to those often found in Buddhist works and seldom found in Confucian or Taoist works before the eleventh century. The first half of this work, which is entitled *Kuan-wu nei-p'ien* (Perceiving things, inner chapters), consists of a systematic development of a comprehensive ontological (including cosmological) and epistemological position. Shao begins with the nature of reality (the universe) and concludes with the ultimate, perfect kind of knowing. This scheme follows the Buddhist assumption that one must understand the nature of reality before one can "know" it, that is, before one can reach enlightenment. In Buddhism, an intellectual understanding of the nature of existence is a prerequisite for the ultimate, mystical experience of knowing.

In contrast to this structure, which is also found in other Northern Sung works such as Chang Tsai's *Cheng meng*, Confucian works before Shao's time typically did not lay out an explicit ontological and epistemological position. However, as if implicitly affirming the Confucian basis of Shao's thought, the second half of the *Huang-chi ching-shih*, entitled *Kuan-wu wai-p'ien* (Perceiving things, outer chapters), consists of a form frequently found in Confucian writings and modeled ultimately on the *Analects* of Confucius. This section contains sayings of Shao Yung collected by his followers, arranged in an order that in general parallels the topics of the Inner Chapters. In effect, the Outer Chapters serve (in a most unusual way) as Shao's own commentary on his ideas in the Inner Chapters.

Thus, the very structure of the *Huang-chi ching-shih* provides mute evidence that Buddhist and Confucian assumptions were involved in the formation of Shao's thought.

Shao Yung's Thought

Given the lack of a significant metaphilosophical tradition in Chinese philosophy, commentators are especially important for interpreting a philosopher's ideas. For the *Huang-chi ching-shih*, the remarks of three commentators in particular are of great help: Shao Po-wen and Ts'ai Yüan-ting of the Sung period and Wang Chih of the Ch'ing period. Shao Po-wen, the son of Shao Yung, was the first commentator on the *Huang-chi ching-shih*. He offered a brief chapter-by-chapter explanation of the work and a longer summary of its main ideas.[27] Ts'ai Yüan-ting, a twelfth-century scholar, compiled the charts that now form the first two chapters of some editions of the *Huang-chi ching-shih* and made extended comments on the basic aims and concepts of Shao's thought.[28] Wang Chih (1685–?) added more charts to Shao's work, collected the comments of other commentators, and wrote an extensive summary of his own thoughts on Shao's work.[29]

These three scholars clearly understood the fundamental aspects of Shao's philosophical system in the *Huang-chi ching-shih*. They also clearly recognized the plan of organization of this work. Their understanding may seem a simple matter, but the extent of disagreement on Shao's ideas belies the belief that his thought is simply a matter of numerology, cosmology, divination, or some other similar area of knowledge. Where some have seen a proto-scientist, others have seen only a mystic or a bad astronomer. Regarded not simply as a philosopher, he also has been known as a poet, historian, fortune-teller, and political protester. Cross-temporal judgments in the past and cross-cultural judgments in this century have been equally diverse (see Chapter 9). For this reason, the views of commentators must be taken into consideration.

A realistic characterization of Shao Yung's thought would begin with a recognition of both its complexity and its theoretical emphasis. Shao Yung was, above all, concerned with the problem of change and activity in the universe. He described and explained many kinds of change, focusing on the patterns by which change was believed to occur and the systems of symbols that represented these patterns. These concerns led him to address important, related questions about the nature of reality and the nature of knowledge. He was interested in theoretical patterns, not in the particulars of everyday human experience.

The systems of symbols derived from the *Yi-ching* and indeed were the framework around which this classic was organized. The symbolic systems constituted theoretical levels of reality and were regarded by followers of the *Yi* learning as explanations of change in the universe. During the period of secret transmission from the third to the tenth century, however, many aspects of these symbolic systems had become obscured. Much of Shao's effort was devoted to elaborating on and clarifying aspects of these theoretical systems, which had long been believed to explain change in the universe. To appreciate the complexity of Shao's thought, it must further be recognized that many of Shao's ideas refer simultaneously to the various sets of symbols and to the *phenomenal world* of human experience.*

Although Shao Yung's philosophical system derived from the *Yi* learning, he was nonetheless a highly creative thinker. In his pursuit of the implications of given concepts, he went beyond the traditional confines of the *Yi* learning to formulate new concepts and to address philosophical problems that were unusual and sophisticated for his time. Although he phrased his thoughts in ways very different from modern philosophical discourse, the problems that concerned him are still of great interest.

The problem of the structure of events lies at the heart of Shao Yung's questions concerning the phenomena of change. I use the term *events* in its broadest sense, to refer not only to activities but also to particular things and to time. The central question for Shao was Where does one event begin and end? Where are its boundaries? How does one determine the shape or scope of an event so that one does not mistake a section of it for the whole? Shao Yung

---

*Throughout this study, I use the term *phenomenal world* to refer to the physical universe as it is experienced by human beings through their senses. I am not suggesting that there are other, intangible realities "behind" the sensible world. I use the term *reality* in a similar way to refer to the world of human experience.

applied this question to many kinds of experience, including the recognition of time and the understanding of behavior. (For Shao, "behavior" referred not only to the activities of humans and other living things but also to the movements of the physical universe. Moreover, time was—in a remarkably modern sense—not separable from behavior.)

In discussing the shapes of events and the drawing of boundaries, Shao Yung used various subjects to conceptualize the problem, such as the calendrical and cosmic cycles of the universe and the application of appropriate names and forced names. He was particularly concerned with the perspective from which one applied names and terms. Because perspective influences perception, he related his ideas on these matters to the question of the boundaries of an event. Shao's attention to behavior and to human perception and knowledge is further evidence of his concern with the problem of recognizing the beginnings and endings of events. He knew that too narrow a focus rendered one incapable of distinguishing aspects from wholes.

In stressing the pattern rather than particulars of events and behavior, Shao Yung assumed that the activities of both things and humans, including the human activity of consciousness, all followed (or operated according to) a single, basic pattern. Shao described this pattern as one of birth and completion. Not independent or discrete in themselves, the two events were aspects of another, larger event.[30] Shao extended this pattern of birth and completion to most kinds of events and behavior. He considered it to be the pattern of *yin* and *yang*, and he even applied it to political activities.

In dealing with the issue of the appropriate segmentation of time and events, Shao Yung recognized multiple levels of organization of reality. An event that was a whole on one level was only a part on another level and vice versa. Consequently, without reference to a context, no particular event could be labeled a whole or a part. In his "dialectic" in contrast to that of Hegel and Marx, Shao included both synthetic and analytic movement, that is, two becoming one and one becoming two. Shao also recognized that the entities on each level were related to those on other levels in specific ways appropriate to the level. Thus, for example, in terms of the proposition that individual people form families and families form states, the state was the whole, and its parts were families, not individuals.

Chapter 2 begins with the general intellectual and historical contexts of Shao Yung's thought, his family, his education, and his adult life. This chapter is designed to indicate the intellectual and social links between Shao Yung's thought and the thought of his predecessors and contemporaries. The six chapters that follow consist of my analysis of Shao Yung's philosophy. In Chapter 3, I identify and discuss the central focus of his thought: change and activity in the universe. To order and to make sense of his many ideas, I treat his thought as a theory of explanation. My discussion thus examines characteristics of theory in general and the necessary aspects of explanatory theory in particular. The second part of this chapter treats the conceptual tools that Shao assumed as givens and used to explain change and activity in the phenomenal world. These concepts are analyzed as constituting the ontology of his explanatory discourse. I also examine the logic of his philosophical system, or the proof structure.

In Chapter 4, I investigate Shao's views of the theoretical structure of the universe and the relationship between the realms of experience and theoretical structure. This chapter concludes with a discussion of Shao's use of numbers to make comparisons between non-numerical things. From a theoretical viewpoint, the abstract realm of the images and numbers serves as the domain of evidence in Shao's explanatory theory.

In Chapters 5 and 6, I examine the system of concepts Shao used to explain the various kinds of change and activity in the universe. Several critical features apply to Shao's thinking in general. One important characteristic is his use of a moving observational viewpoint to express his idea that all events must be viewed in terms of context and abstract patterns. Some scholars have described this as a concern with objectivity,[31] but I find this characterization misleading and beside the point.

In Chapters 7 and 8, I examine Shao's views on the sage. The discussion in these two chapters takes up the questions of Shao's views on knowledge in general, the particular characteristics of the sage, the unique kind of knowledge the sage has, and the method by which the sage achieves true knowledge. In the course of this discussion, I also examine such relevant topics as Shao's views on the process of knowing, his concepts of the self, and the unstated problem that he faced of finding appropriate words for experiences that did not occur on the verbal or conceptual level.

Chapter 9 consists of an examination of Shao Yung's thought in historical perspective. In this chapter, I am concerned with the theoretical question of how context influences perception. Also of concern is the question of how the judgments of scholars are tied to the standards and expectations of their own time. I discuss how later scholars, premodern as well as modern, assessed Shao's philosophy. Their comments clearly illustrate an idea Joseph Levenson so simply stated, "With the passing of time, ideas change."[32] I have included the opinions of other scholars as another way to help make sense of the complexities in Shao Yung's thought and in the philosophical and cultural traditions of which he was a part.

Chapter 10 brings together the major ideas of this study. I identify some of the threads that tie his ideas internally to each other and externally to his culture. I suggest the ways in which he participated in China's major intellectual trends—Confucianism, Taoism, and Buddhism—as well as his contribution to later developments in Chinese philosophy and culture. His thought was highly complex. In the judgment of Ch'ien Mu, the great Chinese scholar of this century, Shao Yung was like a stranger, from another time and place.[33] I hope that this study will provide some understanding of that stranger.

2

The Background

In brief, even in the formulation of concepts, the angle of vision is guided by the observer's interests. Thought, namely, is directed in accordance with what a particular social group expects.
—Karl Mannheim[1]

Although some of Shao Yung's ideas may appear today to border on the fantastical, his philosophy was an attempt to respond to issues and problems that were cultural concerns, not simply idiosyncratic interests. Despite differences in answers, other thinkers were, and had been, involved with similar questions. A common interest in certain cultural and philosophical problems made widely varying positions possible and plausible. Since general concerns were rarely stated explicitly, however, such concerns often appear elusive or vague to posterity, making it difficult to see that dissimilar philosophical positions often were different answers to the same problem. In the Chinese tradition, philosophers seldom explained in detail the nature of the problem being addressed. One became acquainted with the problems as one became educated and took one's place in society's elite, educated class.

Philosophical positions were thus, in part, answers to certain broad, but not necessarily stated, concerns of the literati. It is from this perspective that the social and intellectual context of Shao Yung's thought constitutes an important dimension of his thought. His family background, his education, his acquaintances, and the intellectual traditions in which he participated and with which he identified contributed to a set of assumptions and ideas at the heart of his explicit philosophizing. Whether openly stated or not, these assumptions and ideas formed the foundation of his thought.

The Shao Family

Shao Yung was the scion and progenitor of scholars.[2] He was born into a family that had belonged to the elite class for at least three generations and that was to continue unmistakably to belong for several generations after him. Like families in the British traditions of Oxford and Cambridge and like some of the aristocratic great families of China, his family had shared a scholarly tradition for generations.[3] The Shao family had focused on history and the classical texts. Shao Yung was thus heir not only to the general values and ideas of the literati class, but also to a family that had its own intellectual emphases. Shao Yung received the classical education of the Confucian scholar and potential official, but parental tutelage led him to develop an interest in subjects outside the areas of examination-oriented Confucianism.

Shao Yung's family maintained a relatively high level of social prominence for at least six generations, and perhaps more, since the records are not reliably complete. From his great-grandfather to his grandsons, Shao's family was outstanding enough to be mentioned in the major historical records. The fact that his great-grandfather, his son, and two of his grandsons were officials certainly contributed to the privileged status of the family. Although Shao Yung himself did not take the examinations, he was offered and declined two official posts. His younger brother, Mu, did obtain the *chin-shih* degree, the highest degree, but he died before he had a chance to establish himself.[4]

Shao Yung's ancestors came from the Yen region in the north, near present-day Beijing. In the distant past, supposedly because of a familial link to Duke Shao of the Chou dynasty, who had been enfeoffed in Yen, their surname had been changed from Chi to Shao.[5] The Shao family specifically identified as home a place called Fan-yang, but, apparently because of military disturbances, they relocated several times. For many years, the family lived in what is now the border area between Hopei and Honan provinces. Shao Yung's great-grandfather eventually established a home in Heng-chang, in northern Honan. There Yung's father was born and raised, but in midlife the father moved the family to Kung-ch'eng, also in northern Honan.[6] Shao Yung himself, at the age of 30, moved to a place near Loyang. Later, he moved again with his father, this time to Loyang. Shao Yung subsequently made Loyang his home for the rest of his life.

The story of the Shao family does not appear to be unusual. As a military officer, Shao Yung's great-grandfather, Shao Ling-chin, began the family's rise in fortune.[7] Shao's grandfather, Te-hsin, and his father, Ku, continued to maintain the family's status, but neither held an official post. Their non-participation in public life seems to have been the result of deliberate choice. Although Shao Te-hsin died young, when Ku was only eleven *sui* (years), Te-hsin was still able to influence his son. Thus, Ku was later praised for his filial piety toward his mother after his father's death. Shao Te-hsin is described as a scholar and a Confucian, but the records give no further information about him.[8]

More is known about Shao Ku, Shao Yung's father.[9] He had three children, two sons and a daughter. Yung was the older son, by Shao Ku's first wife, and Mu, Shao Yung's younger brother, was the son of Ku's second wife. According to the records, Mu was devoted to Yung, but unfortunately he died young. Nothing is recorded about Ku's daughter except that she married into a family named Lu.[10]

Shao Ku is described as a man who loved learning. Not wealthy, he lived by teaching the classics to village students. He was interested in the classics and in literature, and in the tradition of a philosophical Taoist, he liked to withdraw to the mountains and to the solitude of nature. His alternative names reflect this interest; his style was T'ien-sou, literally "old man of heaven" (or nature), and his courtesy name was Yi-ch'uan, which was the name of a stream that he often visited and by which he was buried.[11]

Shao Ku had much opportunity to pass on his interests to Shao Yung, since Ku lived a long life and had a close relationship with his son. Ku died in 1064 at the age of 79, when Shao Yung was 53. Moreover, they lived together for the last fifteen years of Ku's life. Thus it is not surprising that Shao Yung shared his father's literary and philosophical interests. Indicative of Yung's fondness for literature, for example, are the many poems in the *Yi-ch'uan chi-jang chi*. In the area of philosophy, Shao Ku was most interested in the *Yi* learning and, in addition, studied sounds, tones, and rhyme categories. Like many other Northern Sung scholars, he wanted to "rectify" the sounds, characters, and tones by re-establishing the ancient pronunciations.[12] Ku wrote a commentary on the *Chou Yi* (Chou Changes), in five *chüan*, entitled *Chou Yi chieh* (An explanation of the *Chou Yi*).[13]

The study of musical pitches and tones had been an integral part of the *Yi* learning since the Han dynasty.[14] The records indicate that Shao Ku was especially interested in the music-related aspects of the *Yi* learning, particularly the theories of correlation and resonance and the pitchpipes and notes. Shao Ku reportedly correlated the tones and musical pitches with such *Yi-ching* concepts as *yin* and *yang*, the hard and the soft (*kang* and *jou*), opening and closing (*p'i* and *hsi*), leading and following in harmony (*ch'ang* and *ho*), the four seasons, and the four cardinal directions.[15]

Since Shao Ku's commentary on the *Chou Yi* is no longer extant and the specific topics that he discussed are not recorded elsewhere, we can only surmise that the commentary contained ideas similar to these. However, the similarities between Ku's ideas and his field of knowledge and those of Shao Yung are undeniable. Both were concerned with the regularities of the universe and the correspondences between the realms of human society and of nature.

For example, the following passage, quoted by Wang Ying-lin (1223–96) and attributed to Shao Ku, clearly resembles passages in Shao Yung's writings.

In [the realm of] heaven there are *yin* and *yang*; in [the realm of] earth there are *kang* and *jou*; in [the realm of] the pitchpipes there are the opening and closing [*p'i* and *hsi*] [of holes]; and in [the realm of] notes there are leading and following in harmony.

When one *yin* and one *yang* intermingle, then the sun, moon, stars, and zodiacal space are completed. When one *kang* and one *jou* intermingle, then metal, wood, water, and fire are completed. When one opening and one closing intermingle, then [the four tones of] *p'ing*, *shang*, *ch'ü*, and *ju* are completed. When one leading and one following intermingle, then [the four sounds of] opening, flourishing, harvesting, and closing (*k'ai*, *fa*, *shou*, *pi*) are completed.

When the pitchpipes unite with the notes, then tones are produced. When the notes respond to the pitchpipes, then sounds are produced.[16]

Wang Ying-lin commented that

> the book of Perceiving Things [*Kuan-wu*, by Shao Yung] is based on this. It says that that which opens and closes imitates [the realm of] heaven, and that which is pure and muddy imitates [the realm of] earth. What is first closed and afterward open is spring. What is purely open is summer. What is first open and afterward closed is autumn. Winter then is closed and has no tones. *Yin** is spring's tone; *yang* is summer's tone.[17]

This quotation from Shao Ku expresses some of the ideas in the theory of correlation. Heaven and earth are opposing realms within the universe; groups of four are fundamental units; there are associations among the various kinds of reality. The interaction of *yin* and *yang* results in the four heavenly "images," *kang* and *jou* in the four earthly images, and so forth. These ideas are also found in Shao Yung's *Huang-chi ching-shih* and are presented in one of his charts.[18]

Shao Yung's family background contributed significant elements to the social context of his thought. First, in contrast to Shao Yung's great-grandfather, both his father and his grandfather chose not to participate in official life. Second, his father chose a life of simplicity and, if not poverty, certainly not a high level of material comfort. Throughout his life, Shao Ku was close to nature. Family practices thus made Shao Yung familiar with the kind of life that he himself later chose to live.

Although there is no necessary relationship between one's lifestyle and one's philosophy, there can be, and often is, a connection. As Neo-Confucianism developed, such connections did become important.[19] Choices about life course reflect personal values and external influences, either conscious or not. Moreover, different kinds of knowledge are stored in different places, or niches, in society and are transmitted in different ways. One's knowledge relates to one's place in society. Since Shao Yung's ties to certain popular bodies of knowledge and practices were often criticized, this phenomenon is important for understanding Shao Yung's thought. In

---

*Text mistakenly has *tung* (east) instead of *yin*.

making a distinction between his own concept of destiny (*ming*) and that of the masses, Shao Yung himself showed his awareness of the social location of knowledge. "If it is a matter of heaven-ordained destiny [*t'ien-ming*], then I do know it. But if it is what the masses call fate [*ming*], then I do not know it."[20]

One responsibility of scholar-officials was to maintain the classics and the traditions of knowledge and values associated with them. The ideal of passing the examinations, attaining the *chin-shih* degree, and serving in the bureaucracy was part of the literati's tradition. Other kinds of knowledge and related behavior belonged to other groups. Popular Taoist diviners and Buddhist monks, for example, had their own traditions. Even when different groups used the same texts, their interpretations and uses of the texts could vary widely.

The phenomenon of superficial, but misleading, similarities applies to numerous concepts as well. Close examination of some apparently similar concepts shows that they belong to different traditions of knowledge. Although similar (but not identical) terms are used, for instance, the Taoist adept's concept of nourishing life or his pursuit of immortality differed considerably from the Confucian's aim of moral cultivation. Shao Yung was, of course, not the only philosopher whose ideas, because of their similarities to other ideas, led scholars and philosophers to question his affiliation. Ch'en T'uan, a tenth-century precursor of Shao Yung, rejected the Taoist label given him. Claiming that it was a mistaken description, he even denied knowledge of Taoist matters.[21]

A third reason for considering Shao Yung's lifestyle is that Chinese philosophy was closely linked with action.[22] As Yang Hsiung, the Han philosopher who greatly influenced Shao Yung, said: "In learning, putting things into practice is foremost. Putting things into words is next, and teaching others is third."[23] Shao also said that actions were better than words.[24] The philosopher's duty was not merely to talk about his ideas; he was to implement them. Moreover, one's lifestyle carried with it implications concerning one's beliefs and the tradition of knowledge with which one identified. Behavior had social meaning.

Like his father and grandfather, Shao Yung became a recluse or scholar in retirement. He was a "hermit in town."[25] In this, Shao

Yung was following an ancient Chinese tradition of withdrawing from society. Early in Chinese history, reclusion became associated with righteous political protest and Confucianism. Gradually, although for different reasons, other groups adopted this ideal. For a Confucian official, such a lifestyle was a form of political or social protest against imperial actions that he judged immoral or harmful to society. From a Taoist viewpoint, however, life as a recluse implied a more sweeping rejection of society, including social conventions, material rewards, and honors, in favor of nature.

Shao Yung's reclusiveness appears not to stem from a single source. Given his family background, the severity of his withdrawal in his later years, and many of his philosophical and political ideas, it is clear that several motives were involved. He wrote several poems critical of governmental reforms, and there undoubtedly was a strong political component to his behavior.[26] In addition, various accounts tell of Taoist-like characteristics. He scoffed at the usual standards of etiquette, he had a relaxed and informal manner of behavior, and he showed no interest in taking the examinations and pursuing an official career.

The historical model for Shao's behavior may have been Ch'ü Yüan (338–278 B.C.), a poet and a high official in the ancient state of Ch'u. Legend portrays this ancient hero both as a nonconformist, eccentric, mad poet and as a cultivated, restrained, sober official who resigned in protest.[27] Although Shao Yung did not hold office, he could have done so. Moreover, he was a poet and unconventional.

Although some scholars have questioned the purity of Shao Yung's Confucianism (see Chapter 9), they have tended to do so not because of his lifestyle but because of the nature of his ideas. During the twelfth century, as the push for a Confucian orthodoxy became stronger, judgments of the purity of a person's thought became increasingly important. In that context, lifestyle was seen, to a greater extent, as indicative of philosophical position.

To complicate matters, the records are not unequivocally clear about Shao Yung's lifestyle. The distinguished Marxist historian Hou Wai-lu, basing his opinion on a Sung source, has suggested that Shao enjoyed a life of luxury and ease with his friends and did not accept office for fear of losing those benefits.[28] In the Sung, the practice in aristocratic families of supporting scholars would have made this possible. Other scholars, however, have claimed that Shao lived on the edge of poverty.[29] Shao himself said that his reason for not getting married at a younger age was poverty.[30] Apparently, Shao began to live in comfort only after he moved to Loyang, where he developed friendships with wealthy officials. Presently, the question of whether as an adult he lived a simple life by choice or by necessity seems unanswerable.

Relatively late in life, Shao Yung married and had two sons. His wife, who is described as very wise, was the younger sister of Wang Yün-hsiu, a classmate of Shao's friend, the official Chiang Yü.[31] One of Shao's two sons, Po-wen (1057–1134), became famous, but nothing is recorded about the life of his other son, Chung-liang.[32] While growing up, Shao Po-wen listened to the conversations of his father's friends and became quite familiar with the political affairs of the times. Shao Po-wen was recommended for office by Ssu-ma Kuang and subsequently held many posts in a long official career. He was also a prolific writer, and not surprisingly, his special field of knowledge was the *Yi* learning.[33] Shao Yung thus transmitted his intellectual inheritance to the next generation.

Shao Po-wen had three sons, P'u, Po, and Fu. Of these three grandsons of Shao Yung, his only known grandsons, two rose to high positions. Shao P'u, the oldest, held several official posts. Shao Po, the next brother and holder of a *chin-shin* degree, not only held office, but also was a writer.[34] With this generation, however, the Shao family disappears from the historical records.

Although meager, this material about the Shao family does indicate the intellectual and social traditions of the family. Shao Yung was raised in a family that, while paying scant attention to wealth, valued the Confucian classics and was dedicated to the service of society. It is significant that the one classic specifically mentioned in reference to Shao Yung's father was the *Chou Yi*. This classic, along with the *Ch'un-ch'iu* (Spring and autumn annals), formed the cornerstone of Shao Yung's own thought. The fact that Shao Ku wrote a commentary on the *Chou Yi* and expressed ideas similar to those of Shao Yung suggests a strong familial influence on Shao Yung. Although Shao Ku's interest in making correlations with sounds and tones was but one aspect of Shao Yung's thought, both emphasized groups of four as the basic framework for correlations.

Shao's life as a hermit in town followed the pattern of his father's and grandfather's lives. His inaction was an active response to a positive model. These familial characteristics unquestionably locate Shao Yung, both socially and intellectually, firmly within the Confucian-dominated, ruling, educated class of the Northern Sung period.

The Education of the Future Philosopher

Many elements contribute to the attainment of an education. Books are but one aspect. The conditions of the learning process and expectations concerning the eventual application of one's education are less tangible elements, but no less important. The characteristics of teachers and schools are also relevant. In order to appreciate fully how Shao Yung's educational background laid the groundwork for his future development as a philosopher, these and many other aspects should be considered. The historical records, however, omit many potentially important details. Nonetheless, enough is included in the records to permit discussion of what Shao Yung read, who taught him, and how he pursued his education, topics that will help uncover nonexplicit and implied aspects of his thought and the sources of the intellectual concerns to which Shao Yung was responding.

Shao Yung received the broad literary education of the Confucian scholar and potential official. He studied the Confucian classics and knew the ideas and values represented in them. He was also familiar with other well-known philosophical texts and thinkers.

Several points about the classics are important. The classics embody early Chinese philosophy and reveal the philosophical concerns and values of the literati class and the high culture of China.[35] Furthermore, they are the textual focus of the Confucian tradition and emphasize historical, philosophical, literary, and social knowledge. They include ideas about the natural and human worlds, historical records from the state of Lu during the middle Chou dynasty, various Chou documents and records, folk and court poetry, and comments on moral, social, and political values. Equally important in the Chinese tradition is that the texts were not allowed to stand alone. Commentaries on the classics were part of the classical tradition of knowledge, and periodically they themselves became the focus of intellectual discussion and disagreement.

Shao Yung certainly received instruction in the Five Classics: the *Yi-ching* (Book of changes), the *Shu-ching* (Book of documents), the *Shih-ching* (Book of poetry), the *Ch'un-ch'iu* (Spring and autumn annals), and a chapter in the *Li-chi* (Book of rites), the *Ta-hsüeh* (Great learning).[36] In his writings, Shao commonly referred to the first four as the *Yi, Shu, Shih,* and *Ch'un-ch'iu.* In addition, Shao Yung in his writings referred to such works as the *Chung-yung* (Doctrine of the mean), the *Mencius,* the *Hsün Tzu,* the *Chuang Tzu,* and the *Lao Tzu.*[37]

Shao Yung's grandson Shao Po wrote that, of the set of classics that his family had once owned, only one volume, the *Yi-li* (Rites), had survived destruction from war or fire. Shao Po also said that his grandfather had copied by hand the *Book of Changes,* the *Book of Documents,* the *Book of Poetry,* and the *Spring and Autumn Annals.*[38] Comments like these corroborate what is evident from Shao's writings—his great familiarity with the classics.

The twelfth-century Neo-Confucian commentator Chang Hsing-ch'eng noted that Shao Yung had studied the learning of the philosophers and the hundred schools (a reference to pre-Ch'in philosophy) and that Shao was familiar with the theories of Buddhism, Taoism, and the adepts.[39] Chang also observed, with relief, that none of these traditions of knowledge had deflected Shao's aim. Chang was saying in effect that Shao had some knowledge of all the major traditions of Chinese thought but had—fortunately—managed to avoid contamination from these other, unorthodox traditions. Supporting Chang's comment about the breadth of Shao's reading is Shao Po-wen's claim that "there are no books that my father had not read. However, he regarded the Six Classics alone as fundamental, for they captured the profound ideas of the sages."[40]

References and quotations that attest to Shao Yung's education abound in his philosophical writings and poetry. Sometimes he merely alludes to the works of previous writers; at other times he quotes them. Still other passages are so similar to passages in the writings of others that it looks as if Shao had copied them.[41] Shao mentions many philosophers by name, including Confucius, Mencius, Hsün Tzu, Lao Tzu, Chuang Tzu, Yang Hsiung, Wen Chung-tzu (Wang T'ung), Han Yü, Ch'en T'uan, the Buddha, and his own contemporaries.[42]

In speaking of his father's views of past philosophers, Shao Po-wen commented:

> He regarded Lao Tzu as knowing the essence of the *Yi*, and he regarded Mencius as knowing the application of the *Yi*. He discussed Wen Chung-tzu, who said that the Buddha was the sage of the western regions, and he [Shao Yung] did not regard this as wrong. He did not speak about the learning of Buddhism and Lao Tzu. He knew it, but he did not talk about it.[43]

Although the records do not explicitly state that Shao Ku taught his son the *Yi-ching*, they imply that he did so.[44] In any case, at about the age of 30, Shao Yung began intensive study of the *Chou Yi* under Li Chih-ts'ai, an official and a "great Confucian."[45] Apparently these studies were quite extensive, for the broader term "*Yi* learning" is used to describe them. This term refers not only to the core of the classic itself, the *Chou Yi*, and to the "Ten Wings" or appendixes, but also to all areas of thought, both in the classics and the apocrypha, related to the *Yi-ching*. The correlation theories involving numbers, musical pitches, the seasons, and the four directions mentioned above in connection with Shao Ku were, for example, part of this tradition of thought.

Shao Yung was clearly drawn to the study of several aspects of the *Yi* learning. Moreover, his interests developed beyond the confines of moral philosophy, which was becoming increasingly popular among Confucians in his lifetime. Soon after moving to the Loyang area, for instance, Shao developed an interest in divination.[46] Although his interest in popular lore concerning such subjects was to continue throughout his life, Shao viewed this association with ambivalence. He distinguished between what he regarded as genuine foreknowledge and the vulgar predictions of the popular diviners. Others, too, recognized a difference. They claimed that, in contrast to those who simply manipulated numbers, Shao followed the *tao* or *li* (principle or pattern).[47] In spite of Shao's mixed views on this association, the records contain many stories about his abilities at predicting and the unusual events in his life.[48]

The historical records leave little doubt about the extent of Shao Yung's education. From his own comments and those of others, we know that he was familiar with at least most of the major Chinese philosophical works. The texts that he read, however, were only one aspect of the context in which his thought developed. Other aspects of his education contributed to his philosophical system as well.

For some traditions of knowledge, the texts themselves are the object of study. In other traditions, however, the same texts are viewed as a repository of data on different aspects of the social and natural worlds. It is clear that the Chinese considered this distinction an important one because it involved basic values and primary intellectual orientation. Indeed this distinction seems to have been the central problem in evaluating Shao Yung's thought. In other words, since different traditions of knowledge used the same texts, it is not enough to discover what texts a person studied. Because perspectives and purposes varied, we must also know how the texts were taught and used.

Chang Hsing-ch'eng was aware of this problem.

The master [Shao Yung] studied the learning of the *Yi*, *Shu*, *Shih*, and *Ch'un-ch'iu*. He investigated completely the deep mysteries of [the learning of] ideas, words, images, and numbers. He understood the *tao* of emperors, kings, and hegemon. He wrote a book of over a million words. He studied the essences with utmost thought for 30 years. He contemplated the increases and decreases of heaven and earth, he extrapolated the waxing and waning of the sun and moon, he examined the periods of *yin* and *yang*, and he investigated the forms of the hard and the soft.[49]

In this passage, Chang was reviewing the subjects that Shao thought about and studied. After mentioning four of the classics, Chang identified the kinds of knowledge that occupied Shao Yung: images and numbers, the history of the Ch'un-ch'iu period, and knowledge about the universe, including time and earthly phenomena. In all these areas, Shao was interested primarily in theoretical structure and not in the pursuit of new empirical data.

Chang indicated that Shao also studied the traditions of commenting on the four classics mentioned. These traditions assumed that the truth had been known at some time but lost in later ages.[50] A primary aim, therefore, was the recovery of lost truths or original meanings. The corruption of texts was seen as contributing to this loss, and their "rectification" as necessary to the process of recovery. This kind of learning, or textual exegesis, emphasized the texts themselves as the object of study.

Chang pointed out that the objects of study of most concern to Shao were not the texts. Through his work on the *Yi*, Shao studied the fundamental natural forces of the universe, and through his work on the *Shu*, *Shih*, and *Ch'un-ch'iu*, political and social thought and the patterns of history. The objects of study were thus activity in nature and activity in the human world. The theoretical aspects on which Shao focused were assumed to be contained in these texts as well as in historical data. As Chang indicated, Shao Yung used his knowledge in all these areas to develop his own ideas.

Shao Yung was certainly aware of the difference between a textual and non-textual object of study, and he preferred the latter. Shao Po-wen used the phrase "explainer of life" from one of Shao Yung's poems to emphasize this direction of his thought.

Throughout his life he did not engage in the learning of textual explication, and he often said, "The meanings of the classics are clear by themselves; a wretched person will not understand them anyway. To build a house under a house or to set up a bed under a bed certainly stirs up doubts...." He was a so-called explainer of life.

Shao Po-wen continued:

Thus he had a poem that said, "To explain life, it is not necessary to boast." [51]

Shao Yung's orientation was directed toward knowledge about the world of experience, whether of the past or present, of human beings or nature. He was not interested in pursuing textual questions and commentary traditions. Although both kinds of knowledge were concerned with the world, their emphases were not the same. Stressing this distinction, Shao Yung said: "In learning, human affairs are most important. The classics of today are the human affairs of the past." [52] Shao's opinion is reminiscent of Chang Hsüeh-ch'eng's comment some seven hundred years later that "the six Classics are simply six kinds of history used by the sages to transmit their teachings." [53]

Shao Yung therefore received at least the basic elements of a Confucian education, which could lead to an official career. He studied the classics and the traditions of learning associated with them. As a mature philosopher, Shao differed from many other philosophers in neglecting textual explication. Unlike a text-oriented scholar, he emphasized the theoretical structure of the world of experience. Moreover, he regarded the classics as primarily a record of past human experience. He did, however, share with his contemporaries the view that one could discover by oneself, without the help of commentaries, the meaning of the classics.

Although he never sat for the examinations, the historical accounts do not indicate whether he ever studied specifically for them.[54] The contrary is strongly implied by Li Chih-ts'ai's comment to Shao, "You are not someone seeking the examinations."[55] By the time that remark was made, Shao was already at least 30 years old, an age when most aspirants to office were in the midst of the examination process. In any case, Shao Yung did not earn any official degrees through the examination system. His education was put to another use.

Given the emphasis on oral transmission as an essential aspect of teaching and learning, teachers were particularly important. A philosopher's identification within the intellectual tradition was determined to a great extent by his teachers. Teachers influenced access not only to professional and political opportunity but also to various kinds of knowledge, particularly those kinds not confined to texts. The transmission of ideas through texts was recognized as necessary and important, but often texts were supplemented with oral instruction. This method placed a high value on the teacher-student or master-disciple relationship. A reflection of this tendency is the Buddhist concept of transmitting the mind (*ch'uan-hsin*). Knowledge of alchemy, medicine, and much of what is called "religious Taoism" was transmitted in oral traditions associated with textual traditions.[56] Although this cultural pattern later changed radically with the evidential research movement of the Ch'ing period, during Shao Yung's time it was assumed without question.

For modern scholars studying the past, knowledge of a philosopher's teachers is a clue to the specific historical context and general orientation of that philosopher's thought. To reconstruct a system of thought, knowledge of the particular problems of concern is necessary. Fortunately, the Chinese themselves valued the study of origins and the lines of historical development. Although often not entirely accurate, the records are still of considerable use. Thus, the question of Shao Yung's teachers is an important one and one that the historical records have addressed.

The two most important teachers of whom we have knowledge were Shao's father, discussed above, and Li Chih-ts'ai.[57] Although we are not explicitly told that his father taught him, the similarities between Shao Yung's thought and that of his father indicate much influence. The records also mention a few other teachers: a Mr. Jen from Fen-chou, in modern Shansi province, who was a specialist in Yi studies, and a Mr. T'ang, with whom Shao is said to have studied divination.[58] At present, nothing further is known about these men.

Although Shao was already 30 when he began studying with Li Chih-ts'ai, Li strongly influenced Shao's thought. Li held the *chin-shih* degree and served in a number of government posts. He first met Shao Yung and began to teach him in 1041 in Kung-ch'eng. For three years Shao diligently studied with Li, even following him to his new posting in Ho-yang, northeast of Loyang in present-day Honan province.[59] In 1045, Li died. From all accounts, however, the shortness of the relationship did not reflect its importance for Shao. Li was knowledgeable about the learning of moral principles (*yi-li*), the learning of the principles of things (*wu-li*), and the learning of nature and destiny (*hsing-ming*), as well as the learning needed for the examinations.[60]

Li set for Shao a straightforward course of study that encompassed what was called the learning of the principles of things, or knowledge pertaining to the patterns of nature and the universe.[61] Li started with the *Ch'un-chiu*, because he believed that its ideas could be used to understand the ideas of the other five classics. He then taught Shao the other classics, ending with the *Yi*. Perhaps not surprisingly, the *Yi* and the *Ch'un-ch'iu* occupy fundamental positions in Shao's thought.

After Li died, Shao Yung composed this epitaph for his teacher's gravestone: "A gentleman, who searched throughout the world to hear about the *tao*, Master Li I regarded as my teacher."[62] These were words of highest praise.

Before studying with Li Chih-ts'ai, Shao Yung had had no permanent teacher other than his father. When younger, he had traveled around, studying with different people.[63] Although Shao's thought reflects the influences of both Shao Ku and Li Chih-ts'ai, Shao Yung's biographers generally fail to mention his father's role and instead emphasize Li. It seems clear, however, that both men played important roles in Shao Yung's education.

Although Shao did not pursue the examination route, he was not regarded as an idle or lazy student. The records stress his intense and persevering nature and his sincerity about his intellectual quests. The descriptions of him as a student often touched on his poverty, his persistence, and his travels.

Little is known about the details of his early education, but apparently even as a child he was recognized as unusually bright. It is even claimed that he was able to say the word for "mother" at birth. One account says that he first went to school in Chin-chou (present-day Chin-hsien, in Hopei province). Later, at Pai-yüan, at the foot of Su-men Shan (in modern Honan province), he seriously began his studies. There he studied the *Yi*. From the time he was young, Shao Yung was known for his energy, his ambition, and his unrelenting efforts to study history, or "the affairs of the former kings."[64]

Later, after Shao began studying with Li Chih-ts'ai, he became even more determined. Supposedly for three years he sat up day and night in deep thought! He even copied the *Chou Yi* by hand and pasted it on the walls of his room so that he could recite substantial portions every day.[65]

The young Shao Yung did not let poverty interfere with his studies. He went without a stove in winter, and he used the cooking oil as fuel for the lamp so that he could read at night. One day a high-ranking military officer saw Shao Yung and asked him, "Who studies with such hardship like a *hsiu-ts'ai*?" The officer then gave Shao a hundred rolls of paper and ten pens. Although hesitant at first, Shao finally accepted the gifts.[66]

As a young man, Shao Yung traveled extensively, primarily to learn from those reputed to have outstanding knowledge. Shao Po-wen wrote that his father had told him that his travels had been very difficult.[67] In traveling about to learn from others as well as from texts, Shao Yung was following a centuries-old intellectual tradition. Once, when praised for his rigorous habit of study, he

sighed and said, "Formerly men made friends of those in antiquity, and yet I still have not gone to the four corners [of the world]. Should I not hurry now?" Thereupon he went to Wu and Ch'u, passed by Ch'i and Lu, and visited Liang and Chin [i.e., he visited the boundaries of the civilized world, bypassing those areas nearer the center, where he lived]. After a long time he returned and said, "The *tao* is here [within me]." Then he began to have the idea of settling down.[68]

After this trip he returned to Kung-ch'eng and began his studies with Li Chih-ts'ai.[69]

In terms of Shao's intellectual development, this long trip in his twenties may be seen as symbolic of his transition from an unfocused, struggling young student to a developing thinker. He made no further trips to pursue knowledge. He had determined his intellectual quests, and he then pursued them with Li Chih-ts'ai.[70]

Just as Shao's travels were a crucial early step in his transition from student to philosopher, his marriage in his mid-forties was an important event in this process. In 1048, at the age of 37, Shao moved to Loyang. When he was still not married at age 45, he was persuaded by his friends Chiang Yü and Chang Chung-pin, both of whom were officials, that it was his moral duty to get married. Echoing the words of Mencius, who said that of the three unfilial things, the worst was to have no sons, they convinced Shao of the importance of marriage.[71] With Shao's consent, they then made the arrangements. With the birth of first one son and then another, Shao Yung had at last assumed this Confucian moral responsibility. In the context of Chinese philosophy and in his personal beliefs, Shao Yung's actions in this respect were indeed a philosophical matter.[72]

The records thus indicate that Shao Yung studied in order to learn and to satisfy his own interests. It does not appear that he studied in order to take the examinations. Enduring poverty as well as the hardships of traveling, he was relentless in his pursuits. His interests led him to concentrate on one area of the *Yi* learning, but not before he had gained a broad and thorough education. As a complement to his intellectual activities, he accepted the moral demands of Confucianism. That is, a superior man must be filial; and to be filial, one must marry and have sons.

Associations in Loyang

Shao Yung's adult life in Loyang—the conditions under which he thought, wrote, and taught—constitutes the third aspect of the intellectual and social context of his thought under consideration in this chapter. Two questions in particular are addressed here: Who were his intellectual companions and what interests did he share with them? By indicating how Shao's philosophical interests coincided with the intellectual interests of the educated elite, the answers to these questions will help to show how Shao Yung's thought fit into the context of his own time.

In contrast to his youthful years of hardship, Shao Yung led a rather comfortable life in Loyang. He was supported in large measure by wealthy and politically prominent friends. Wang Kung-ch'en, Fu Pi, Lü Kung-chu, and Ssu-ma Kuang were among those, for example, who supported him not only with a house but also with an elaborate garden. Shao called his residence Nest of Repose and Happiness (An-le wo) and called himself Mr. Repose and Happiness (An-le hsien-sheng). Though a recluse in terms of active political participation, Shao did not live apart from society. He had frequent contacts with his friends, and although he declined to serve, he was recommended for office several times. He was fundamentally a teacher, a writer, a philosopher, and apparently somewhat of an eccentric. He was known for liking to ride in a cart, the squeaking noises of which warned people of his approach.[73]

It was not accidental that Shao Yung chose to make Loyang his home. Since the T'ang period, Loyang had been a city of aristocratic power and influence, and during the Northern Sung it remained a flourishing cultural center.[74] The cultural aspects no doubt played a role in attracting Shao Yung to Loyang, particularly the strong base of *Yi* learning in Loyang.[75] Loyang was also the home of many Northern Sung officials and the city to which a number of "old" party members withdrew when they opposed Wang An-shih's reforms between 1069 and 1072. There they continued to live their lives of privilege and political activity.

In Loyang, Shao knew many high and, at times, powerful officials, as well as the prominent philosophers and intellectuals of his time. Among his acquaintances were the officials Fu Pi and Wang Kung-ch'en, both of whom recommended Shao for office, and Wen Yen-po, Ssu-ma Kuang, and Lü Kung-chu.[76] These men opposed Wang An-shih and his "new" party. Shao thus was aligned with the "old" party. Its associates were his friends, and he shared their political views.

Two men often mentioned as close to Shao were Fu Pi, an official, and Ssu-ma Kuang, an official and the famous historian. Shao sustained a friendship with these men over many years on both the personal and the intellectual level based on common interests in history, political philosophy, and political action. The historical records suggest that these and other officials often visited Shao and discussed current affairs with him.[77] Shao's interest in history and political philosophy was no doubt linked to his interest in the *Ch'un-ch'iu*, which was widely seen as embodying basic principles for political action. In Shao's thought, this classic was second in importance only to the *Yi-ching*.

One incident reflects Shao's close relationship with Ssu-ma Kuang and Fu Pi. Shao's grandson Shao Po wrote that when Ssu-ma Kuang began writing historical essays, Fu Pi had some doubts about what Ssu-ma Kuang would say about Ts'ao Ts'ao and wrote to Shao to ask his opinion. Shao Po noted that his family still had a copy of Shao Yung's reply.[78] Unfortunately, Shao Po did not transcribe the letter.

Shao Yung was on friendly terms with many scholar-officials of high rank and was greatly respected by them. The fact that they recommended him for office several times is certainly significant. Moreover, they looked to him for advice. One important instance of such behavior occurred after Wang An-shih's reform policies were implemented in 1070–71. At that time, several officials who were friends of Shao Yung asked his advice on resigning from office. In writing about this, Shao Po-wen said:

Shao [Yung] replied, "This is precisely the time when wise men ought to exhaust their efforts. The reforms are indeed severe, but if one can ease them one bit, then the people will receive a favor of one bit. What gain is there to give up one's official position?"

Alas! Master K'ang-chieh [Shao Yung] deeply understood the affairs of the world, but he did not therefore attract attention only to gain a hollow reputation such as this. It is wrong for the world to regard Master K'ang-chieh as a recluse.[79]

From the various data available, Shao Yung emerges as a person with strong political views and interests, interests he shared with other scholars and with officials. Shao's philosophical writings include his political theories, and his poetry reveals his opinions about particular political events and participants. Several poems specifically refer to politically active friends.[80] Thus, Shao Po-wen was certainly not in error in vigorously refuting the contention that his father had no interest in political affairs.

Shao's reclusive style of life was not inconsistent with his political interests, and his life of "retirement" certainly did not entail a physical retreat to the woods or mountains. The mere fact that Shao was recommended for office indicates political involvement. He claimed that his main reason for not accepting office was his aim of following the life of a retired scholar. Here, we see the influence of his father and grandfather. Among the other reasons Shao offered for not serving in office were illness, the idea that his destiny was ordained by heaven, and his view that his services were not needed when government was good.[81] Although perhaps questionable, these reasons were not in conflict with his primary motivation. At age 60, however, Shao began to lead a decidedly withdrawn style of life, and there was a pronounced shift in his behavior away from concern for the affairs of society.[82]

The political division that pitted Wang An-shih's "new" party against the conservatives' "old" party was accompanied by an intellectual opposition. Wang An-shih's "new learning" (*hsin-hsüeh*) was opposed by the followers of the *tao* learning (*tao-hsüeh*) in Lo-yang. Ch'eng Yi, for example, was a leader in both the old party and in the *tao-hsüeh* movement. A situation in which philosophical developments were associated with specific political alignments was not uncommon. Still, because members of both groups were part of the ruling class and shared the same discourse, they were more like each other than they were like other (non-elite) groups. Although they had different ideas about what to do, both groups were concerned with the same set of problems and made many of the same fundamental assumptions. They agreed on what the questions were, but they disagreed on the answers.

As an intellectual movement, *tao-hsüeh*, which had origins in the T'ang dynasty with Han Yü, was concerned with recovering the "true teachings," the *tao*, of Confucius. An orthodox line of transmission of the *tao*, called the *tao-t'ung*, was believed to exist. Han Yü brought increased attention to this belief by asserting that, until his own recovery of it, the *tao* had been lost since Mencius. Although Shao Yung's contemporaries were concerned with the recovery and perpetuation of Confucian teachings, not until the Southern Sung period would the question of orthodoxy begin to have overwhelming importance. In the twelfth century, this intellectual movement gained the name of *tao-hsüeh*, and the term *tao-t'ung* was used for the first time.[83]

Although later thinkers had serious doubts about Shao Yung's orthodoxy, in his own time there was no question about the appropriateness of his concerns and intellectual activities. He obviously shared philosophical, historical, and political interests with members of the Loyang community. Like others, Shao was interested in the *Yi* learning, as well as the other classics, most notably the *Ch'un-ch'iu*. This classic, along with the *Shu-ching*, stimulated the historical interests widespread among Northern Sung intellectuals.

A brief look at the emphases of the other "six masters" reveals that the characteristics Shao shared with his contemporaries and peers were far more important than the differences. The Ch'eng brothers and Shao Yung were interested in different aspects of the *Yi* learning. The Ch'eng brothers focused on moral philosophy and based much of their thought on the *Yi-ching* and the *Li-chi*. Two chapters in the *Li-chi*, the *Ta-hsüeh* and the *Chung-yung*, were important to the moral thought developing in the Northern Sung. Shao was clearly familiar with moral philosophy and held strong views in that area, but he was not drawn to it for special study. Of the five classics, the one that received the least attention from Shao Yung was the *Li-chi*. Nonetheless, Shao used many terms and concepts found in that classical text.

With Ssu-ma Kuang, Shao shared an interest both in history and in the images and numbers branch of the *Yi* learning. In addition to his historical writing, Ssu-ma Kuang wrote several essays on the *Yi* learning. His philosophical thought closely followed that of the Han philosopher Yang Hsiung. Although Ssu-ma was a historian and Shao was not, for both men the *Ch'un-ch'iu* was an important text for historical knowledge. Ssu-ma, however, was oriented toward practical political affairs and historical particulars, whereas Shao turned toward theoretical reality and the attainment of knowledge.

The philosophical interests of Chang Tsai and Chou Tun-yi, the two remaining "six masters," also centered on the *Yi* learning. They wrote on both morality and the images and numbers. Chou's *T'ai-chi t'u shuo* (On the diagram of the Supreme Ultimate) and *T'ung shu* (Explanatory text) and Chang's *Cheng meng* (Correct discipline for beginners), for example, have much in common with Shao Yung's thought. In addition, many other Northern Sung philosophers based their thought on the *Yi* learning. None, however, gained the fame of the so-called five founders: Chou, Chang, Shao, and the two Ch'eng brothers.[84] Shao Yung had differences with others of his time, and his ideas were considered difficult to understand. However, Shao's characteristics were sufficiently similar to those of the intellectual leaders of his period that he was recognized without question as one of them.

Shao Yung's social and intellectual context thus was, in broadest terms, that of the scholar-official class. He was associated politically with a group of conservative officials. His philosophical thought was part of a movement that sought, in the name of the *tao*, to preserve what was regarded as the essential features of the Chinese cultural past. Although the aim of this movement was avowedly conservative, the results were hardly so. In part because *tao-hsüeh* possessed such highly synthetic tendencies, its positions were not simply restatements of ideas dredged up from the past. This movement broke new philosophical ground. As one of the founders of *tao-hsüeh*, Shao Yung thought and lived in the mainstream of Northern Sung culture.

3

Beginning a Theory

At the beginning of the Sung, when the generation of great Confucians emerged, there were none who did not regard explaining the tao of change as their responsibility. Therefore, Ch'en T'uan of Hua-shan founded the line of succession, and Chou Tun-yi of Lien-hsi and Shao Yung of the western capital [Loyang] searched out from afar the accomplishments of Fu Hsi, King Wen, the Duke of Chou, and Confucius.
—Hao Ling-ch'uan[1]

In his explanation of change, Shao Yung was concerned with most kinds of change in the phenomenal world, the world that human beings experience. His vision encompassed the activities of individual things, the processes of nature, developments in human society, the temporal periods of the universe, and human awareness and knowledge of the various forms of change. He focused on no less a task than explaining the nature of the universe and the human experience of knowing it. He described the patterns that make up the structure of the universe and the methods by which human beings attain knowledge, as well as the fundamental universal processes, their operations, and their interrelationships. He also discussed the system of symbols—the hexagrams of the *Yi-ching*—that were the major traditional explanation of change. By representing situations and alterations in situations, the hexagrams emphasized the link between human behavior and nature.

Shao did not address the question of the ultimate constituents of reality. This fundamental question in early Greek philosophy was not a primary problem in Chinese philosophy. In contrast to Greek ontology with its questions on being and reality, Chinese ontological thought was dominated by an interest in cosmology. For Shao Yung, as for many other Neo-Confucian philosophers, questions about reality tended to center on how the universe developed and on processes of change and activity. Shao accepted the fundamental belief of his culture that the universe was made of *ch'i* (see below) and focused on the question of how the universe, or reality, was ordered. He believed that knowledge of that ordering would lead to an understanding of the processes of change. Because of their emphasis on processes and activity rather than matter and basic substance, the Chinese philosophers conceptualized the world in a different way from the early Greeks and often asked different questions.

The aim of my analysis in the following chapters is to reconstruct the explanatory structure of Shao Yung's thought on the universe. By this I mean that I shall make explicit the assumptions and concepts that Shao Yung accepted implicitly but seldom, if ever, discussed explicitly. However, I do not claim that Shao Yung consciously thought about this theoretical aspect of his philosophy. I treat his thought as an explanatory theory because that seems to be the most useful way for bringing order to his thought and combining its diverse elements into a single, comprehensible system.

By emphasizing the implicit theoretical structure of his thought, I hope to make explicit the theoretical context of his ideas. The theoretical context is important because it provides ideas with their meaning. It is the theory (as a form of context) that makes possible the meaning of concepts. This interrelationship is particularly apparent in cases like that of Shao Yung, whose thought existed in a philosophical and cultural milieu that is no longer extant or viable. Shao's concepts of number, the images, and the fixed positions of heaven and earth are just a few examples of ideas whose meaning is obscure without a knowledge of their theoretical context.

This analysis of Shao Yung's thought is not concerned with questions of historical development. Although of great interest and importance, the history of these ideas is simply beyond the scope of this discussion. However, where relevant, the relationship of Shao's ideas to those of others is pointed out. Still, the central question of this study pertains to the internal structure of Shao's thought and not to a delineation of its historical relationships.

A Theory of Explanation

One major feature of Shao's thought is that its epistemological aspects are equivalent in importance to, or rather are part of, its ontological aspects. In many respects, certainly in general terms, Shao Yung's views about the nature of reality coincided with the basic views of his culture. He took for granted various conceptual ways of dividing up the universe—between heaven and earth, for example, or the triad of heaven, earth, and humans. Another division, and one that was particularly important in Shao's thought, assumed three major domains: the ineffable Absolute, the world of nature, and the world of humans. Whatever division Shao used in any particular discussion, in his conception of the universe, the realm of human experience was on a par with the "stuff" of the universe. ("Stuff" is conceived in both dynamic and static terms, as both forces and things.) In other words, the phenomena of human experience, human consciousness, and human knowing were just as much a necessary part of reality as the "things" that were experienced.

The two primary aspects of Shao Yung's thought, his ontological and epistemological theories, are explanatory in nature; their aim is to make intelligible certain phenomena, "to reduce the seemingly unrelated richness of experiential data to certain principles or categories in terms of which any and all given phenomena might be understood."[2] His ideas are explanatory, rather than merely descriptive, because they close issues and do not leave them open for further investigation. His thought as expressed in the *Huang-chi ching-shih* serves as a demonstration of what he believed was so. Shao's ideas are all-encompassing. All "things" are at least potentially accounted for in his system.

A comment about the nature of theory should help to clarify certain potentially puzzling aspects of Shao's thought. Theories consist of propositions or statements composed of words or symbols. What is known is the set of propositions, not the objects or events to which the propositions refer or about which the propositions are made.[3] Shao Yung's ontological and epistemological theories are propositions or statements about the structure and processes of reality and about knowledge.

In light of the highly symbolic nature of much of Shao's thought, this distinction is crucial. Shao's concepts, including his charts and diagrams, were no more isomorphic with eleventh-century reality than twentieth-century physics is with the natural world today.[4] A theory is like a map. A map is not isomorphic with the territory; it is an abstraction of certain aspects of it, a statement about the territory. The two—the map and the territory—are not the same. This distinction applies to Shao's thought as well; that is, discourse about an event or an experience is different from that event or experience itself.

An explanatory theory has two different kinds of reference: those phenomena or entities that are being explained and those entities or phenomena in terms of which explanations are being offered. The difference is again comparable to that between the territory and the map or a thing and its name. Although related, the two are not the same.[5] As the discussion in the following chapters indicates, Shao was aware of this distinction.

The explanatory aspect of Shao's discourse is knowledge in the form of propositions, or conceptual knowledge. The propositions, as noted above, are claims about the nature of reality and about knowledge and methods of knowing. In Shao's thought, these propositions appear in two different forms: diagrams or charts, and prose.[6] Both, however, are propositions. Both the charts and the prose are statements about reality, or the universe, but they are not that reality itself.

In Shao Yung's thought, as in all thought based on the *Yi-ching*, the system of reference is complicated by the existence of at least two possible referents for each of Shao's statements. What Shao says may apply not only to the phenomenal world, but also to the charts and the diagrams, which include the trigrams and hexagrams of the *Yi-ching*. The phenomena to be explained exist on two levels of reality: immediate human experience and a theoretical level symbolized by the system of the charts and diagrams. Abstracted from experience, the theoretical level was traditionally conceived as an explanation of the phenomenal world. Thus, when Shao Yung discusses an event, he may be referring either to a situation in human experience or to the hexagrams (or other symbols) that symbolize that situation, or to both.

Although both the ontological and epistemological aspects of Shao's thought may be considered explanatory theory, the two have different goals. These two aspects of Shao's thought are tied together by the implicit assumption, similar to that found in Buddhism, that one must understand the nature of reality before one can "know" it. Intellectual knowing—knowing the nature or characteristics of existence—is a prerequisite for the ultimate mystical experience of knowing. The two goals clearly involve different conceptions of knowing.

Shao's ontological ideas have as their object an intellectual or conceptual knowledge of the universe. The goal of his epistemological ideas is also an intellectual kind of knowledge—of knowledge itself. However, his epistemological ideas ultimately aim at surpassing conceptual knowledge to attain another kind of knowledge: sagely knowledge. The highest kind of knowledge, it is a mystical, spiritual, or experiential knowledge that cannot be put into words. A "how-to" kind of knowledge, it cannot be verbalized because it does not occur at the level of words, in contrast to conceptual knowledge or understanding, which employs words and propositions. Just as the experience of seeing a red scarf differs from the description of that experience, so experiential knowledge differs from conceptual knowledge.

The two aspects of Shao Yung's thought are reflected in the arrangement of the *Huang-chi ching-shih*. As Shao Po-wen explained:

The *Huang-chi ching-shih shu* has twelve chapters [*chüan*] altogether. Chapters 1 and 2 summarize the numbers of the [cosmic periods, which consist of] cycles [*yüan*], epochs [*hui*], revolutions [*yün*], and generations [*shih*]. These [numbers] are what the *Yi* calls the numbers of heaven and earth.

Chapters 3 and 4 show the regulating of revolutions by epochs, and they set forth the numbers associated with revolutions.* Under the yearly [system of ten heavenly] stems and [twelve earthly] branches, these chapters record a table of the successive years from Emperor Yao [2357–2256 B.C.] to the Five Dynasties [A.D. 907–60], in order to make manifest the

---

*The text has *generations*, but here *revolutions* makes better sense.

traces of division and unity, and order and disorder, of the world. Moreover, they verify [the regularity of] human affairs with the seasons of heaven.

Chapters 5 and 6 show the regulating of generations by revolutions and they set forth the numbers associated with generations. Under the stem and branches system for dating years, they record, from Emperor Yao to the Five Dynasties, the traces of flourishing and decline, order and disorder, gain and loss, and depravity and uprightness, which the *Shu* and the [*Tso*] *Chuan* record. Moreover, they verify the [regularity of the] seasons of heaven with human affairs.

Chapters 7 through 10 exhaust the numbers of the pitchpipe notes and tones with the numbers of *yin* and *yang*, and *kang* and *jou*, and they exhaust the numbers of the categories of moving, growing, flying, and walking things with the numbers of the notes and tones. These numbers are what the *Yi* calls the numbers of the myriad things.

Chapters 11 and 12 discuss the reason that the *Huang-chi ching-shih* was written. These chapters exhaust the numbers of the [categories of] sun, moon, stars, and zodiacal space and [the numbers of the categories] of flying, walking, moving, and growing things in order to complete the patterns [*li*] of heaven and earth and the myriad things. They record the affairs of [the categories of] sages, emperors, kings, and hegemons in order to make clear the *tao* of the great mean and extreme uprightness. The increases and decreases of *yin* and *yang*, and the order and disorder of past and present, can be seen in comparison. Therefore he [Shao Yung] called the book *Supreme Principles That Rule the World*, and he called the chapters *Perceiving Things*.[7]

The comments of others (see Chapter 9) indicate that these dual aspects of Shao Yung's thought were not as clear to everyone as they were to Shao Po-wen. The ambiguousness of some scholars' statements suggests that the ontological and epistemological, as well as the conceptual and experiential, aspects of Shao's thought were not always separated. Since these kinds of knowledge are not mutually exclusive, it may have been thought not necessary to separate them explicitly.

For example, Chu Hsi described Shao's thought as being concerned with the comprehension of pattern (*ming-li*).[8] Both *ming* (to comprehend) and *li* (pattern or principle) could be used in several senses. *Ming* could refer to understanding in a conceptual and verbal sense or to comprehension in a mystical, experiential sense. Or, both meanings could apply. *Li* could refer to the pattern of particular things and to the pattern of the various types of movements of heaven and earth, or it could be used as an alternative term for the Absolute. Because of the nature of the vocabulary, the ideas, and the conception of reality, it was thus possible that, as a description of Shao's thought, *ming-li* could be used in several senses simultaneously.

What elements are necessary to make an explanatory theory? As Stephen Gaukroger has noted, in order for a theoretical discourse to be an explanation, several elements that, in effect, provide the structure of the explanation must be present. Although explanations vary in terms of how they explain, all are designed to make something clear or intelligible.[9]

Two questions must be considered. What was it that Shao wanted to explain? As indicated by the preceding discussion, Shao wanted to explain change (in nature and in human history) and knowledge. Second, because what counts as an explanation in one system does not necessarily count as one in another, what does and what does not count as an explanation? In order to answer this second question, we need to discover the theoretical structure, or how it is constructed, because the theoretical structure determines what counts as an explanation in a particular discourse. The following analysis of Shao's thought is basically an attempt to answer this second question.

An explanatory structure can be broken down into four major aspects, beginning with the set of entities (things, events, forces) that are used in the explanations. Explanations are given in terms of these entities, and these entities make up what may be called the ontology of the discourse or the conceptual tools. They are primary in themselves and cannot be reduced to any other entity. They have specific relations with each other, and they often are, or can be, of more than one species (for example, events as well as forces). In Shao Yung's thought, most, but not all, of these entities appear in the charts and diagrams.

Second, there must be a domain of evidence, which is tied to the ontology. The evidential domain consists of the phenomena that can confirm, establish, or refute explanations offered in a particular discourse. The domain of evidence, like the ontology, differs from discourse to discourse. It determines what counts and what does not count as evidence, and it is drawn from a wider field of investigation. In Shao's thought, the evidential domain consists of the natural and human worlds as abstracted into patterns and categories. These patterns and categories were well established in Chinese thought as part of the *Yi* learning, and some date as far back as the Shang dynasty.[10] The domain of evidence consists of the symbolic and theoretical realm of the images and numbers.

Third, a set of concepts must link the ontology with the domain of evidence. These concepts are peculiar to a particular discourse. Shao's thought relies on six major concepts. Some of these (or versions of them) are unique to Shao's thought; others are not. However, Shao combined them all in a system that was original with him.

Finally, there must be a proof structure, which is the logic of the system. The proof structure basically determines the way in which problems can be posed, but it does not determine their resolution. It also places constraints on the relations between concepts in the discourse; that is, it determines what relations between the concepts in the system are valid. It includes concepts not peculiar to that discourse. In Shao's thought, the proof structure derives from the *Yi* learning and consists of assumptions fundamental to correlative thinking.

In sum, then, an explanatory theory comprises a set of statements whose aim is to make something understandable. Its theoretical structure, which may or may not be entirely explicit, is composed of four aspects: the conceptual tools or ontology of the discourse, the domain of evidence, a set of concepts that links these two aspects, and a logical system or proof structure. The proof structure determines the kinds of problems that can be posed because it specifies the valid relations possible between concepts in the system.

The following analysis of Shao Yung's thought is based on this view of an explanatory theory. Although Shao obviously was aware of the various kinds of change that he wanted to explain, I do not assume (or deny) that he was aware of any part of this theoretical structure. He was, however, interested in and knowledgeable about theory, and he understood that his ideas concerning natural and historical change and development from the one to the many were the foundation for his epistemological ideas about the sage's ability to return to the one.

Conceptual Tools

Shao employed a number of axiomatic concepts, or "conceptual tools" to explain change. In theoretical terms, they are the ontology of his explanatory discourse. In this section, I examine these primary concepts and some related assumptions and briefly discuss the implicit logical framework surrounding Shao's thought. For his part, Shao did not discuss the logical principles on which his thought was based; he assumed them without question.

Shao Yung began with a set of fundamental cultural assumptions about the nature of reality, or the universe. These beliefs included ideas about the "substance" of reality, ideas about the shaping of primal substance (*ch'i*) into particular things, along with the ordering and classification of things, and ideas about the phenomena of motion and change. Three assumptions are particularly relevant to Shao's thought. The first is that Shao, like others, assumed an inherent order to the universe. From the seasons to social relations, he believed that set patterns were built into the structure of things. These patterns could be symbolized variously by the numbers, by the images, and by the hexagrams and trigrams. (For example, the trigrams represented, among other ideas, both the directions of the compass and relationships within the family.)

A second assumption, and an important one, is that there are both perceived and unperceived levels of physical reality.[11] Although some scholars conceive of these levels as visual and nonvisual, the distinction involves all the senses. I refer to these levels as *sensorial* and *subsensorial*. The terms reflect the common Chinese conception of reality as analogous to the root and branches of a plant.[12] The visual image of root and branches suggests not only that there is a source from which things come, but also that the source is not accessible to the senses and is below that which is perceived. The ancient Chinese idea of mother earth as the one, the source of all things, further contributes to the Chinese conceptualization of reality in terms of above and below. To refer to this unseen level of reality as supra-sensorial, above the senses, or metaphysical would be to suggest a misleading framework and imply inappropriate ideas from Western philosophy.

Related to this assumption is a third distinction concerning ontological entities. Shao assumed that reality held two kinds of entities: finite things or events and that which is amorphous and infinite, or the ultimate One. Finite things are particular objects, events, and ideas, and they are known to us through sense experience. They are entities to which one can apply names or "fixed terms," to borrow a phrase from Han Yü's *Yüan tao lun* (An inquiry on the Way).[13] In contrast, that which is infinite cannot be known through ordinary sense experience. This assumption relates to the conception of reality as a whole and parts.[14] The whole is infinite, whereas its parts are the particular things of everyday experience.

Shao's fundamental assumptions and concepts were associated with different social groupings. A rough breakdown from the most general to the most narrow consists of three levels: Chinese culture in general, the elite literati culture, and the *Yi* learning, a particular philosophical tradition. The concepts Shao used to explain change can be divided into several kinds of entities that reflect these distinctions. Some concepts, the most general ones, belonged to the epistemological imperatives of the culture. Others tended to be more characteristic of the literati culture, and still others—the most specialized of all—were identified with the images and numbers branch of the *Yi* learning.

Acceptance of the epistemological imperatives of the culture is not restricted to any social group. Although different groups at different times may understand them differently, the assumption of their existence is so basic that they themselves are never questioned. Many of these concepts may have originated with a particular school of thought, but at some point they become accepted by the culture as a whole. Moreover, as society develops, new epistemological imperatives appear. *Yin* and *yang*, *wu-hsing* (the five phases), and *ch'i* are examples of epistemological imperatives of Chinese culture in Shao Yung's time. The twentieth century has witnessed the appearance of others, derived in particular from Marxist thought.

Less widely accepted were certain beliefs and concepts of the literati culture. One became acquainted with them through education in a textual tradition. More sophisticated and complex than the cultural imperatives, these beliefs included, for example, ideas about historical development, methods of governmental rule, analyses of human nature, and many ideas based on the *Yi-ching*, as well as certain Buddhist concepts and views.[15]

The specialized concepts that Shao used in his explanations, especially the concepts of the images and numbers (*hsiang-shu*), helped to make much of his philosophy virtually unintelligible to nonspecialists. The concepts derive from several Han texts: the *Hsi-tz'u chuan* (also called the *Ta-chuan*, the "Great commentary"), one of the commentaries attached to the *Chou Yi*; the *Li-chi* (Book of rites); the *Huai-nan Tzu*; and the *Lü-shih ch'un-ch'iu* (Chronicles of Mr. Lü).[16] The vocabulary in these texts resembles that which Shao Yung used, and these works often group entities by fours or twos. The concepts themselves, however, date from a much earlier period. In Shao's thought, these entities—the images and numbers—appear in a series of charts that are related to two ancient diagrams, the *Ho T'u* (the River chart) and the *Lo Shu* (the Lo writing; see Fig. B7).

Knowledge of these different sources of Shao's thought helps sort out some of the complexity of his thought. Some concepts used by Shao had both general and specialized meanings. *Yin* and *yang*, for example, were both epistemological imperatives of the culture and particular entities, with specific meanings, in the charts. Ambiguities and multiple meanings are common in Shao's thought, but knowing that he employed different kinds of concepts helps one avoid confusion. Moreover, all the entities in his explanations were related in well-defined ways. There was a definite structure to their relationships. In this section, I examine the various entities, both those not in the charts and in the charts, and I consider their interrelationships. Again, these entities or concepts were not the objects Shao was trying to explain; they were his conceptual tools.

The epistemological imperatives and literati concepts in Shao's thought were *t'ien-ti* (heaven and earth), *wan-wu* (the myriad things), *ch'i*, *tao*, *shen* (spirit), and *hsin* (heart/mind).[17] Since their existence was assumed without question and they were the foundation of other concepts, Shao Yung did not discuss them in detail. However, Shao's frequent references to these entities leave no doubt about their fundamental importance. These entities do not appear explicitly in the charts. Some of these entities exist on the sensorial level of reality (heaven and earth) and others on the subsensorial level (*ch'i*). In the following discussion, I first consider those concepts that are parts of the whole and then those concepts that represent the whole.

T'ien-ti, heaven and earth, was a term for the universe or all of nature.[18] Dating from the earliest period in Chinese history, this concept asserted the division of the universe into two basic realms, the sky and the earth. These realms existed on the sensorial level of reality, the level of appearances and human experience. Although heaven and earth suggested at times the notion of two powers or forces, Shao Yung thought of them primarily as actual, phenomenal things (*wu*). They were vast in size, but they still had limits. "As for the size of things, there is nothing larger than heaven and earth; and yet even they are finite." [19] In this sense, heaven and earth were part of the realm of the myriad things (*wan-wu*), or all the particular things in existence.

The myriad things were all the things and events in the phenomenal world, the world of human experience. Although the term *wan-wu* usually referred only to living things, the meaning of *wu* (things) ranged from physical objects to ideas and abstractions. However concrete or abstract, whether animate or inanimate, *wu* were regarded as specific and finite, as particular things with definite limits, and they existed on the sensorial level of reality.

The characteristic of finiteness was, moreover, not limited to the physical body of things. Shao also applied this characteristic to time and space.

There are one-day things, one-month things, one-hour things, one-year things, ten-year things, and there even are 100-, 1,000-, and 10,000 [-year things]. Heaven and earth are also things, and there also are numbers for them. Sparrows are three-year things, and horses are 30-year things. [The lives of] all flying and walking things can be inferred with numbers. Humans are 120-year things.[20]

In contrast, the second kind of entity represented the whole of reality. Of this second type, *ch'i, tao, shen,* and *hsin* are the primary cultural givens, and they do not appear in the charts.

Ch'i, a term with many meanings and therefore virtually impossible to translate, is the basic substance of everything.[21] It ranges in form from a totally undifferentiated gaseous-like state, as the ultimate One, in which reality is a unity, to the many particular things of the phenomenal world. Moreover, all states of it exist simultaneously. Depending on the context, the word *ch'i* has been translated as air, ether, fluid, lifebreath, material substrate, matter, material force, and vital force. Like other philosophers, Shao Yung sometimes employed alternative terms, such as *chih* (matter) or *ch'i* (vessel, utensil) to indicate different states of *ch'i*. Except for the specific instances when it was used in the sense of wind or atmospheric air, *ch'i* existed at the subsensorial level of reality. In terms of the metaphor of root and the branches, *ch'i* is the root. As such, it is the source of all sensorial things.

The few remarks Shao made on the concept of *ch'i* concerned primarily the question of change and activity. For instance,

Unitary *ch'i* divides and becomes *yin* and *yang*. Mostly *yang* is heaven. Mostly *yin* is earth.

The dragon* is able to be large and is able to be small, and yet it also has that which controls it. It is controlled by the *ch'i* of *yin* and *yang*. If it obtains the [appropriate] circumstances, then it can change and transform [itself]. If it loses the opportunity, then it cannot.[22]

Here, *yin* and *yang* are entities in the charts and the two basic forces in the phenomenal world. Like Chang Tsai, Shao assumed that everything was *ch'i* and that *ch'i* was one. To account for the differences in phenomena, Shao pointed to the division of *ch'i* into *yin ch'i* (for earth) and *yang ch'i* (for heaven). Elsewhere, Shao postulated a further division of *ch'i*.

Yin and *yang* exhaust the great size of heaven, whereas *kang* and *jou* exhaust the great size of earth.

When humans obtain the *ch'i* of centrality and harmony, then *kang* and *jou* are in balance. If *yang* is greater, then *ch'i* is biased toward *kang*. If *yin* is greater, then *ch'i* is biased toward *jou*.[23]

These statements about *ch'i* are not contradictory but simply

---

*The dragon symbolized various celestial phenomena, often the sun or related to the sun.

more or less specific. In a two-part division, heaven is *yang* and earth is *yin*. In the next division, the *ch'i* of heaven divides into *yin* and *yang*, and the *ch'i* of earth into *kang* and *jou*. This dualistic pattern was fundamental to Shao's thought.

Shen (spirit) was an alternative concept for conveying the idea of the One and suggested a different perspective. In representing the idea of the whole, *ch'i* and *shen* are united in one ontological state that is inaccessible to the senses. When *ch'i* coalesces, it takes on form and becomes perceivable. As a sense object, *ch'i* has to have form or an appearance. Shao used the term *t'i* for the phenomenal forms or appearances of *ch'i*. *T'i* is thus an ontological state in which *ch'i* has condensed to the point that particular things are distinguishable. "*Ch'i* is the dwelling place of spirit [*shen*]. Forms [*t'i*] are the dwelling place of *ch'i*."[24] The idea suggested here is that spirit (*shen*) is contained within *ch'i* on the subsensorial level of reality and analogously *ch'i* is contained within *t'i* (forms or appearances) on the sensorial level.[25] Shao did not mean, however, that spirit and *ch'i*, on the one hand, and forms and *ch'i*, on the other hand, are different things ontologically. Rather, spirit and *ch'i*, and *ch'i* and forms, are different aspects—motion and stillness—of the same entity.

One important difference between the sensorial and subsensorial levels is that distinct things exist at the sensorial level. Things are distinguishable. However, as *ch'i* or *shen*, the subsensorial level always exists in a state of wholeness. Substituting *hsing* (forms) for *t'i*, Shao said: "Forms can be split, but spirit cannot be split."[26]

In addition to these entities not explicitly in the charts, Shao employed a specialized set of entities in the charts and elsewhere. These constituted the more restricted ontology of the images and numbers learning. In a sense, the relationship of these entities to the ones explored above is analogous to a map of a map. Basic cultural concepts are maps of reality in that they provide a particular way of experiencing the world; specialized entities are further abstractions of the basic concepts. Here, the entities of the images and numbers learning are abstractions of certain features of the world as perceived by Chinese culture. Even these features, however, are abstractions.

The specialized entities of the images and numbers learning used by Shao to explain change and activity in the world of human experience were *t'ai-chi* (the Supreme Ultimate), *liang-yi* (the two forces), *ssu-hsiang* (the four images), *pa-kua* (the eight trigrams), *liu-shih-ssu kua* (the 64 hexagrams), *tung-ching* (movement and stillness, or motion and rest), *yin-yang*, and *kang-jou* (hard and soft, or strong and weak). Much of the explanation took the form of charts and diagrams rather than prose. As is common in symbolic thought, in certain contexts sets of paired terms were used interchangeably. Also, on occasion, the concepts of *tao*, *shen* (spirit), *hsin* (mind), and *li* (pattern, principle) were used as alternative terms for *t'ai-chi*. These terms had other meanings in different contexts, and they did not appear in the charts.

The ideas in the following statement by Ts'ai Yüan-ting are central to Shao's thought. In his commentary to the chart "Fu Hsi shih hua pa-kua t'u" (see Fig. B1) in Shao's *Huang-chi ching-shih*, Ts'ai quoted an important passage from the "Great Commentary," the third appendix to the *Yi-ching*.

The Great Commentary says, "The *Yi* has *t'ai-chi*, which gives rise to *liang-yi* [the two forces]. The two forces give rise to *ssu-hsiang* [the four images]. The four images give rise to *pa-kua* [the eight trigrams]. The eight trigrams decide auspiciousness and inauspiciousness. Auspiciousness and inauspiciousness give rise to great accomplishments."

Its method is two from one, four from two, eight from four. In reality, then, *t'ai-chi* divides and becomes *yin* and *yang*. Within [both] *yin* and *yang* there also is *yin* and *yang*. They come forth spontaneously. They do not depend on an intelligent [outside] source. Their order begins with *ch'ien* [the first trigram] and ends with *k'un* [the last trigram], and [the resulting entities] take *yin* and *yang* in alternation as their numbers.[27]

T'ai-chi, translated here as Supreme Ultimate, refers to the Absolute. It is the one reality from which, it was believed, everything derives and to which everything eventually returns. It is the whole. Depending on the context, the Absolute was conceptualized as a power, a spirit, a process or way, or "stuff." To use Western terms, it is matter, the vitalizing force that gives rise to life, and the patterns of life combined. No dualism in the Cartesian sense of mind and body is involved here.[28] *T'ai-chi* is not just mind or just matter; *t'ai-chi* is infinite and is all.

T'ai-chi exists at the subsensorial level of reality. Not a thing (*wu*), it does not have boundaries or limits, either in space or in time, as things do. Actually, it makes no sense to speak of limits in relation to *ta'i-chi*, because even if it had limits, they could not be known. For Shao, only particular, discrete things can be objects of knowledge based on the senses. *T'ai-chi* is not accessible to, or known through, the senses.

However, in order to talk about the Absolute, one has to resort to specific terms, such as *t'ai-chi*, *tao*, *shen*, or *yi* (the one). Since the referent of these terms differs from the referent of an appropriate name or term, Shao believed that such terms are fundamentally different. Just as there are two kinds of entities, there are also two kinds of names: appropriate names and "forced" names (*ch'iang-ming*). Forced names are not true names, because they are not names in the ordinary sense. In ordinary usage, a name refers to a particular, finite thing or to general classes of such things.

Names or terms applied to finite things and applied appropriately are "appropriate names." Inappropriate use severs the proper connection between name and thing. Such a situation is then an occasion for *cheng-ming*, or the rectification of names. This view of names and entities assumes that names have a strict isomorphic correspondence to the "reality" to which they refer. This correspondence between names (words) and their referents is necessary for morally correct social usage. The inappropriate or indiscriminate application of words to things was disparaged and even regarded as immoral.[29] Since Shao was concerned with understanding and clarifying the structure of reality, names were an important problem closely related to one's conceptualization of reality.

Shao believed that terms such as *t'ai-chi* when applied to the One are "forced names." "Can one [really] name *t'ai-chi*, and can one [really] know it? Therefore one forces a name on it and calls it *t'ai-chi*. *T'ai-chi* is what has no name."[30]

From the perspective of the One, ultimate reality, or *t'ai-chi*, names are the "guest of reality."[31] Names come and go, and none is attached permanently to *t'ai-chi*. Since reality in its state of wholeness has no phenomenal appearance and is not knowable in sense experience, no term applied to it can be an appropriate name. A name can be an appropriate name only if it fully reflects or captures the reality to which it refers. Otherwise it is a forced name and thus really no name at all.

Since *t'ai-chi* could not be adequately represented by a single term, alternative terms were used to refer to ultimate reality. A particular term was selected according to the emphasis of the discussion. For example, *tao* might be used when the emphasis was on the process of regular movement. As Shao Po-wen commented, "The seasons of heaven trace out increase and decrease; the classics of the sages record failure and success; their *tao* is like this. One can comprehend it in ideas but cannot seek it in words."[32]

Or, as Shao Yung said, through the mouth of his woodcutter: "The *tao* of heaven and earth is complete in humans. The *tao* of the myriad things is complete in one's body. The *tao* of the myriad mysteries is complete in one's spirit. [Thus] the world's ability to act is complete. What is there further to think and to ponder?"[33]

Shao Yung also used the term *hsin* (heart/mind) to refer to ultimate reality.

The learning of *hsien-t'ien* [discussed below] is a method of the mind [*hsin-fa*]. Therefore, the charts all start from the center, and the myriad transformations and myriad events are produced by the mind.

The mind of heaven and earth is the source of the myriad living things.

One can say that the [*Tai-*]*hsüan* [*ching*; Classic of the great mystery] that Yang Hsiung wrote makes manifest the mind of heaven and earth.[34]

In numerous passages in the *Huang-chi ching-shih*, Shao refers to the One as spirit or as mind. In asserting the identity of *shen* (spirit) and the ultimate One, Shao said: "There is no place *shen* is and no place *shen* is not. The reason the perfect man penetrates the minds of others is that he is based in the One. *Tao* and One are forced names of *shen*. 'Regarding *shen* as *shen*' are perfect words."[35] The commentary adds: "*Shen* is *li* (pattern; principle).... [The One] is the *li* of heaven and earth and the myriad things. Therefore [Shao] said, 'Mind is *t'ai-chi*.' He also said, '*Tao* is *t'ai-chi*.'"[36] In speaking about the One in regard to activity, Shao Yung said: "*Shen* is the ruler of change and therefore has no place. Change is the activity of *shen* and therefore has no bodily form."[37] (Shao's ideas on the topic of *shen* culminate in his ideas concerning the mind of the sage; see Chapters 7–8).

Although they had different meanings, *ch'i*, *tao*, *shen*, and *hsin* were ultimately equivalent to *t'ai-chi*, the Supreme Ultimate, in

Shao Yung's explanatory ontology. However, since *t'ai-chi* was the only one to appear in the *hsien-t'ien* charts, it alone was part of the specific ontology of the images and numbers learning. Each of these terms and concepts, including *t'ai-chi*, involved different questions and contexts and thus offered a different point of view for considering the ultimate One. *Tao* suggested ideas of process and movement; *ch'i* the idea of primal substance; *t'ai-chi* cosmological structure; *shen* and *hsin* notions of life force, vitality, and human consciousness.

Shao started with the fundamental, cultural concept of a triadic division of the universe (heaven, earth, and humans). Although divided into three realms, the universe was still conceived of as ultimately a whole. Shao Yung altered the meaning of the triad by making *shen* and *hsin*, which carried connotations of human consciousness, equal in necessity and significance to such concepts as *ch'i* and *tao* that referred to substance and structure. That is, in Shao's thought, the human element of the triad signified (in addition to human society) human consciousness and knowledge. The human realm was not simply a third kind of thing, in addition to heaven and earth, in the phenomenal universe.[38] Reality was not only matter and structure, but also consciousness of it. This idea undoubtedly derived from Buddhism.

In addition to *t'ai-chi*, the *hsiang-shu hsüeh* ontology included the *liang-yi*. The two forces, which exist on the subsensorial level of reality, are not two different kinds of entity, but rather two complementary and contrasting aspects of the whole (*t'ai-chi*). Representing a whole and dependent on each other, the two forces in one sense stand for actuality and potentiality, the basis for activity and change. They epitomize the element of interdependence inherent in all relationships that makes change possible. Another way of viewing them is to see them as the necessary result of the maximal state of *t'ai-chi*. As Nathan Sivin has pointed out, in Chinese physics, any maximal state was seen as inherently unstable; it would eventually break down, first into the polarities of *yin* and *yang* and then eventually into the myriad objects of the world.[39]

The concept of *liang-yi*, like the other pairs of concepts, is an example of a *hemilog*.[40] I have coined this term to avoid the cumbersome ways that have been used to refer to the pairs of polarized, complementary concepts. A hemilog has certain characteristics. It is a two-part concept, and the meaning of each part is determined by their mutual relationship. A balance between the parts is often the ideal state. Each hemilog forms a whole, and one of the parts cannot form a pair with a member from another hemilog. Other hemilogs are *yin-yang, kang-jou, t'ien-ti,* and *tung-ching. Tung-yin, kang-yang,* or *ching-kang* cannot be hemilogs.

The two forces are *tung*, movement or motion, and *ching*, stillness or rest. As Ts'ai Yüan-ting noted, "Motion and rest are what the *Yi* calls the two forces."[41] *Tung* and *ching* correlated with other hemilogs, some of which belonged to slightly different, but related, symbolic systems, such as the lines and numbers. Thus, *tung* correlated with the unbroken (*yang*) line and *ching* with the broken (*yin*) line in the *Yi-ching*.* (These lines are combined in groups of three and six lines to form the eight trigrams and 64 hexagrams of the *Yi-ching*.) *Tung* and *ching* also correlated with *yang* and *yin* and *kang* and *jou*,[42] as well as with heaven and earth and *ch'ien* and *k'un*, the first and last of the 64 hexagrams and eight trigrams. As David Nivison has noted, the use of one normally calls forth the others through the association of ideas.[43] Thus, *yang* and *yin, kang* and *jou, tung* and *ching, t'ien* and *ti*, and the lines from the *Yi-ching* were alternative terms and symbols for the two forces. These correlations are significant because they provided ways of expressing slightly different emphases and ideas in conjunction with the two forces.

Another entity in the *hsiang-shu* ontology was the four images (*ssu-hsiang*). According to Ts'ai, "*Yin, yang, kang,* and *jou* were what the *Yi* called the four images."[44] In the charts, two sets of symbols were used to represent the four images: (1) *yang* and *yin, kang* and *jou*; and (2) the four combinations of the broken and unbroken lines;† the numbers 1, 2, 3, 4; and the classifications (of greater and lesser) *t'ai-yang, shao-yin, shao-yang,* and *t'ai-yin*.[45]

The parts of these sets bore different relationships with each other. The lines associated with the first group of images—*yang, yin, kang,* and *jou*—differed from those associated with the second

---

*Respectively, ▬, ▬ ▬.
† ☰, ☷, ☲, ☵.

group. In the first group, *yang* and *yin* and *kang* and *jou* were treated as two pairs.* Thus, the first set was a dualism or two pairs, whereas the elements in the second set were in a quaternary relationship. Both of these relationships were important, but different, patterns of reality in Shao's explanations.

The eight trigrams, *pa-kua*, were another entity in the *hsiang-shu* ontology. The eight trigrams are *ch'ien, tui, li, chen, sun, k'an, ken,* and *k'un*.† Discussed below, this order of enumeration was called the order of Fu Hsi and the *hsien-t'ien* charts. The numbers one through eight were associated with the eight trigrams, as were the directions of the compass and the series *t'ai-yang, t'ai-yin, shao-yang, shao-yin, shao-kang, shao-jou, t'ai-kang,* and *t'ai-jou*.⁴⁶‡ In contrast to the other series, this series was organized numerically in a binary alternation of the unbroken and broken lines or the numbers one and two.⁴⁷ Again, the significance of these differences is that these sets are different theoretical models for explaining characteristics of the world of human experience.

As the discussion below will indicate, Shao Yung spoke about these entities in many ways. In the following passage, for example, he emphasized a relationship of production.

When *yin* and *yang* are produced, they split into the two forces. The two forces mix and produce the four images. The four images mix and complete the eight trigrams. The eight trigrams mix and produce the myriad things.

Therefore the two forces produce the categories of heaven and earth. The four images fix the forms of heaven and earth, and the four images produce the categories of the eight trigrams. The eight trigrams fix the forms of sun and moon, and the eight trigrams produce the categories of the myriad things.⁴⁸

The final item in Shao's explanatory ontology is the 64 hexagrams. The hexagrams are closely related to the eight trigrams. Although recent scholarship has raised doubts about the traditional view that the trigrams predated the hexagrams, the hexagrams are

---

*And thus the correlated lines were ▬, ▬▬, ▬, ▬▬, or simply the two sets of the lines associated with *tung* (▬) and *ching* (▬▬).
†Respectively, ☰, ☱, ☲, ☳, ☴, ☵, ☶, ☷.
‡The lines for this series are, respectively, ▬, ▬▬, ▬, ▬▬, ▬, ▬▬, ▬, ▬▬.

graphically the equivalent of two trigrams each.⁴⁹ In addition to having a name and a unique configuration of six lines, each hexagram is associated with a two-digit number and a direction.⁵⁰ Each digit ranges from one to eight. The first hexagram, for example, is associated with the number 1-1, the second 1-2, the ninth 2-1, the tenth 2-2, the sixty-third 8-7, and the sixty-fourth 8-8.⁵¹ The names of these hexagrams are *ch'ien, kuai, lü, tui, po,* and *k'un.**

Shao Yung further correlated the 64 hexagrams with the cosmic periods (*yüan* cycles, *hui* epochs, *yün* revolutions, and *shih* generations); the calendrical periods (*sui* years, *yüeh* months, *jih* days, and *ch'en* hours); the eight trigrams; and numbers based on multiples of 1, 12, and 30.⁵² These series are discussed further below. However, to give a brief illustration of the correlations of the hexagrams with numbers, *ch'ien* was correlated with the number 1, *kuai* with 12, *lü* with 12, *tui* with 144, *po* with 26,121,388,032,000,000, and *kun* with 313,456,656,384,000,000.⁵³† The hexagrams and their correlations symbolized various aspects and situations of phenomenal reality and so served in different kinds of explanations.

These concepts, then, are the entities that Shao Yung used in his explanatory discourse. They were the givens in the *hsiang-shu* branch of the *Yi* learning, and they did not originate with Shao Yung. Although some scholars have credited Shao with constructing the so-called *hsien-t'ien* charts of Fu Hsi, it is more likely that he simply introduced these to the Confucian literati. Shao lived at a time when knowledge from the esoteric traditions was being revealed.⁵⁴

This explanatory ontology, in effect, served as a map of the phenomenal world experienced by Shao's contemporaries. Shao used aspects of this map to discuss and clarify the phenomena of change. His subtle and sophisticated remarks often had two or three referents simultaneously—phenomenal reality, the *hsien-t'ien* charts and diagrams, and the hexagrams. He wanted to explain not only the various kinds of change in the universe, but also the conceptions of the *Yi* learning regarding change. These conceptions consisted of the hexagrams of the *Yi-ching* and the entities in the charts and dia-

---
*Respectively, ☰, ☱, ☲, ☳, ☴, ☷.
†The numbers are obtained by alternately multiplying by 12 and 30, and with the same process simultaneously applying to the first, ninth, seventeenth, etc., hexagrams.

grams. All these givens had specific relationships to each other, and these relationships were graphically laid out in the various charts. However, although many charts are associated with the thought of Shao Yung, the extent to which he constructed new charts or reconstructed older ones remains unclear (see Appendix A). The various works on the *Yi* learning written by scholars from the Sung to the Ch'ing contain additional charts that are not closely related to Shao Yung's thought. Still, all the charts were based on the fundamental concepts of the *Yi* learning, and all were in some sense symbolic maps of the universe.

In addition to these explicit concepts, one further aspect of Shao's explanatory theory concerning change must be briefly considered: the logic of the system, or the implicit logical principles on which his thought is based. As noted earlier, this refers to the system of concepts that specify not only the relations that can hold between the elements of the discourse but also the way in which questions can be asked.[55] The logic of Shao Yung's philosophical system of thought was based on concepts and assumptions that were not unique to Shao's thought but were characteristic of thought in general in eleventh-century China.

In terms of the discussion here, the most fundamental assumption was the validity of correlative, or associational, thinking.[56] In this type of logic, all things in the universe are associated with other things on the basis of established categories or classes. The categories form a "natural" classification scheme into which all things fit. Joseph Needham has quite aptly called it an immense "filing system."[57] The classification scheme of *yin* and *yang* and the five phases was the most common one in Chinese thought. Shao Yung used the four images in place of the five phases, thus differing in certain structural details, but not in his acceptance of correlative thinking.

In a system based on correlative logic, the significance or explanation of any event is based on the correlations. Meaning is thought of as something that indicates the category of correspondence. Understanding and explaining, therefore, involve knowing the classes and knowing to what other entities the thing or event in question is correlated. Relationships between things are a matter of the categories. In the Chinese system, the context is important also in terms of assigning the relative weight of *yin* and *yang*—type characteristics so that the system balances. That is, in a context involving a pair, more *yang* associated with one aspect entails less *yin* with the other. The sum of *yin* and *yang* is always 1.

Furthermore, the kinds of questions that can be asked are determined by the logical system or proof structure. For example, with correlative thinking, one does not explain an animal's behavior by asking whether the behavior is learned or inherited. That kind of question simply does not belong to the system. One asks, instead, whether the animal belongs to a *yin* or *yang* category, or to which of the four images the animal corresponds. Many of Shao's questions thus ultimately concern the categories of correlation. Indeed, the point of most of his questions regarding behavior was to determine the classification of an event or thing. The answers were explanations because they helped clarify the functioning of movement and response.

The system of categories and correlations is a closed one. There is a set number of categories, and there are fixed rules for making correlations between the images (the symbols that represent categories) and the things of the world. There are no potential unknowns awaiting discovery, nor can there be. Since the entire universe is mapped, the logic of the system allows for definitive explanations and eliminates the need for further investigation.

Correlative thinking is based on concepts and assumptions associated with the *Yi-ching*. Some of the categories, including *yin* and *yang* and *kang* and *jou*, originally derived from other intellectual traditions, such as the naturalists' school and the thought of the *Lao Tzu*. During the Han dynasty, however, the various aspects of correlative thinking became part of the *Yi* learning and were to continue to be widely accepted and used in philosophical discourse until the Ch'ing dynasty. Thus, the logic of correlation and the validity of specific categories and concepts were by no means unique to Shao Yung's thought. Although he used the less-common system of the four images, the proof structure of his thought belonged to the centuries-old tradition of *Yi* learning.

To summarize, Shao Yung's philosophical thought may be analyzed as a theory of explanation of change and activity in the universe. Shao utilized a series of given concepts, or conceptual tools.

Those entities, which were widely accepted by Chinese philosophers, were heaven and earth, the myriad things, *ch'i, tao, hsin,* and *shen,* as well as such specialized concepts drawn from the images and numbers learning as *t'ai-chi,* the two forces (*tung* and *ching*), the four images (*yin, yang, kang, jou*), the eight trigrams, and the 64 hexagrams. The implicit logic of his system of thought was correlative thinking. This type of thinking determined the types of questions that could be asked and the types of relationships possible between the concepts. Both the entities that Shao used to explain change and the logical principles that he accepted were givens and were not questioned.

4

The Theoretical Structure of Reality

> *The descriptive task of epistemology concerns the internal structure of knowledge and not the external features which appear to an observer.... The internal structure of knowledge is the system of connections.*
> —Hans Reichenbach[1]

Another order of conceptualization crucial to Shao Yung's theory of the structure of the world involves further elaboration of the concepts of the images and number. The images and numbers symbolize categories that describe the structure of the universe and that are a means by which the particulars of experience can be ordered systematically. The categories do not, in ontological terms, have an existence prior to experience itself. Rather, the categories and their symbols (the images and numbers) are based on the world of human experience.[2] The purpose of this chapter is to consider in further detail this theoretical level of reality and its relationship to the world of experience.

The realm of the images and numbers is a theoretical order that systematizes the world of human experience. This theoretical realm constitutes a level of abstraction that differs from, and yet is clearly derived from, everyday experience. These two kinds of reality, that of theory and that of experience, were referred to as *hsien-t'ien* and *hou-t'ien*, respectively. Since Shao was concerned primarily with the theoretical aspects of reality, his thought was commonly called *hsien-t'ien hsüeh*, or the learning of *hsien-t'ien*. The questions of how to translate these terms and how these terms came to be applied to the phenomenal world and its theoretical structure are discussed below. First, however, I examine the images and numbers and their relationship to the phenomenal world.

The Images

The categories of this symbolic, *hsien-t'ien* realm consist of the four images of the realm of heaven and the four images of the realm of earth (see Fig. B5). The four images of heaven are sun (*jih*), moon (*yüeh*), stars (*hsing*), and zodiacal space (*ch'en*), and the four images of earth are water (*shui*), fire (*huo*), earth (*t'u*), and stone (*shih*). Zodiacal space and earth were seen as the space in which the other entities are located.

The eight images of heaven and earth are visual symbols of the fundamental categories of *ch'i* after *ch'i* has broken down from its original state of unity. From the unified One (*t'ai-chi*), *ch'i* first split into the two forces of *tung* and *ching*, then into the four images of *yin*, *yang*, *kang*, and *jou*, and then again into a greater and lesser subdivision of *yin*, *yang*, *kang*, and *jou* (see Fig. B4). The images of heaven and earth correlate with various other sets of symbols, including the eight trigrams. As Wang Chih noted in his commentary, sun, moon, stars, and zodiacal space, and water, fire, earth, and stone are alternative names (*pieh-ming*) for the eight trigrams.[3] This comprehensive system of categories is thus a theoretical ordering system for the phenomenal world and allows seemingly unrelated events to be connected.

All things and events belong to a category. Each of the eight images represents a different pattern of behavior or activity in the phenomenal world, and the particulars of experiences are classed on the basis of their perceivable behavior. The *hsien-t'ien* realm thus is a realm, or level of reality, of classes. Shao Yung assumed that the categories in this realm "naturally" fall into two (correlated) sets of four entities each.[4]

Although the names of the images, or categories, are terms for concrete or visible things, the images of heaven and earth clearly do not exist on the same level, or in the same way, as particular things and events. However, the relationship between these theoretical categories and concrete human experience is very close. The names of the images themselves provide an obvious link to phenomenal experience. Moreover, in conceptual terms, the nature of the Chinese language helps to reinforce the tie.

An important factor that enables these symbols to remain close to, and part of, ordinary experience is the nature of Chinese nouns. Most nouns are "mass" nouns.[5] That is, they emphasize the "stuff" of things, such as horseness, treeness, birdness. Chinese nouns intrinsically tend to possess a class-like characteristic, and to a greater degree than many, but not all, nouns in English. Consequently, the Chinese did not view the distinction between a mass noun and a class as critical. The use of the same term for the class and for the particular instances of the thing or event within the class was not necessarily a point of confusion or concern. In Shao's *hsien-t'ien* discourse, even though the names of the images could be used both for the particular thing and for the class, the images were classes. (This phenomenon was not unique to China or to Shao. In the Talmud, for example, concrete nouns are also used to represent abstract ideas.)

Shao was aware of the potential confusion that could arise from using the same term for a particular thing as for its class. Judging from his comments on this topic, he considered this concern part of the long-standing philosophical problem of *ming* (names). Shao recognized that the problem of names involves the problem of referent as well as that of point of view. He accepted the position that all statements are made from a particular viewpoint. He realized, however, that the referent of a specific name (or term) can be either a particular thing or an abstract class. Although the same terms are used for entities in the *hsien-t'ien* realm and in the phenomenal, or *hou-t'ien*, realm, names or terms do not function in the *hsien-t'ien* realm in the same way as they do in the *hou-t'ien* realm. In the world of human activity and experience, names can refer to particular things and events or to general concepts and ideas. In the *hsien-t'ien* realm, names and terms refer only to categories, that is, to the images.

In expressing his ideas about the relationship between names and reality, Shao was particularly concerned with the categorizing function of names. That is, reality or *ch'i* is ultimately a whole, an undifferentiated unity. Any experience in the ordinary sense, however, is an experience of a particular thing. The whole must be chopped up, and selected aspects singled out. For Shao, a name thus represented a piece of the whole of reality from the viewpoint of a particular person at a particular time.

When an event became recognized as such and distinguished from the whole and from other events, a name became attached to it. The name represented a specific experience.

The past and present are like morning and evening in [the movements of] heaven and earth. If one observes the present from the viewpoint of the present, then one calls it the present. If one observes the present from the viewpoint of the future, then the present is also called the past. If one observes the past from the viewpoint of the present, then one calls it the past. If one observes the past from the viewpoint of the past, then the past is also called the present. From this one knows that the past is indeed not necessarily the past, and the present is not necessarily the present. They both are [called what they are] from the viewpoint of the self's observing them.[6]

A name could even outlast the reality: "From this one knows that the situation in which the name exists while the reality is lost is still better than one in which both the name and the reality are lost."[7]

Shao recognized that words function as terms both for particular things and for abstract classes. That a name or a term has different referents is not necessarily indicative of error. It may be a matter of perspective. Shao was saying, in effect, that once an event occurs and a name is given to it, then a category is recognized. The particular event may or may not continue, but the category does continue. The continued use of the term as a category does not depend on the continued existence of the corresponding "reality."

A name that still exists even though the reality is lost becomes a different kind of name. When we continue to understand and use a name after its particular referent is gone, we use it as a general term or category. The name of the category derives from the name of the particular thing possessing certain characteristics. This category or class includes all objects or events with those characteristics. Thus, a particular word can function either as a name of a particular thing or as the name of a class. If it is the name of a class, the particular thing may or may not still exist. The thing does not have to be gone, however, for its name to be a general term.

In Shao's view, words that refer to the particulars of reality as experienced by specific persons function in the *hou-t'ien* realm. The same words used in the *hsien-t'ien* realm are used as categories, or what Shao called the images. Thus the level of conceptualization on which terms in the *hsien-t'ien* realm are used differs from the level in the phenomenal world. Moreover, although not all names for the images are mass nouns, they function as if they were. "Sun" and "moon," for example, are not mass nouns, but as the names of images they function like the mass nouns "fire" and "water."

The formation of each category as a category was not idiosyncratic to Shao. The images encapsulated general cultural ideas of long standing on how things fit together.[8] The link between an image and a particular experience was reinforced by the explicit recognition and general agreement that a particular experience occurred according to the patterns of the *hsien-t'ien* relationships. Thus Shao Yung's claim that animals behave in certain ways because they belong to certain categories was readily accepted.[9]

As mentioned above, the images in effect categorize patterns of behavior. Here, behavior refers to what a thing does in the world of the senses—what can be seen and heard or otherwise perceived—and to the kind and amount of *ch'i* that a thing is, or has, on the subsensorial level of reality. Shao assumed that the behavior perceived by the senses is as it is because of the nature of a thing's *ch'i*. Thus, Shao Po-wen's comment that "things have *ch'i* classes [*lei*]" refers to the basic assumption that all things are composed of *ch'i* and hence belong to some category of *ch'i*; that is, they are associated with a particular image.[10] Things and their behavior are classified in the system of the images according to their category of *ch'i*. The commentator Huang Chi was referring to this idea when he said: "*Ch'i* has *yin* and *yang*. Forms [*t'i*] have *kang* and *jou*."[11] Here Huang was distinguishing between the realms of heaven and earth. Heaven is characterized by *ch'i*, which has *yin* and *yang* "forms" or forces. In contrast, earth is characterized by hard and soft (*kang* and *jou*) forms, such as mountains and rivers.

For Shao Yung, perceivable change can be understood by knowing the *ch'i* categories, which are symbolized by the images. For heaven, these are greater *yang* and *yin* and lesser *yang* and *yin*, or sun, moon, stars, and zodiacal space. For earth, these are greater *jou* and *kang* and lesser *jou* and *kang*, or water, fire, earth, and stone. In order to explain the phenomenon of change in the world of particular things, Shao Yung focused on the images of heaven and earth. He looked to the *hsien-t'ien* realm, the categories of which were givens, to provide understanding of the world of experience. For Shao, change in the phenomenal world was explicable by the images, their relationships, and their correlations.

The Numbers

Shao also employed certain numerical groups as conceptual categories to explain activity and change in the phenomenal world. These numerical groups, commonly referred to as the numbers (*shu*) consisted specifically of sets of 2, 4, 8, 12, and 30 entities. Like the images, the numbers were seen as deriving from phenomenal experience. Unlike the Platonic Forms, they were not considered to be categories that exist before or separate from phenomenal reality. Shao's ideas on numbers were based on a tradition as ancient as the beliefs about the images.

In Shao's thought, the numbers are significant because they indicate the regularity and structure of the universe. The divisibility of phenomenal reality into countable parts is "proof" that reality has a specific order, and the applicability of numerical patterns to universal processes of change makes it clear that such processes are structured. Here, again, in Shao's view, to understand change on the phenomenal level one needs to understand the theoretical structure of reality. The regularity of the structure is such, moreover, that its elements can be represented not only by the images, but also by the numbers.[12]

Numbers are units of measure and are used over a field of similar entities; that is, they are used for things on the same level of experience. They are a measure of homogeneity.[13] If, for example, a room contained only a table, one would not say that there were seven things in the room—a table, four legs, one tabletop, and a coat of paint. These entities are not equivalent types of things. In the *hsiang-shu* ontology, numbers can be used because they refer to entities that are categories of a whole (the universe). Providing the phenomenal world with structure and organization, all the categories are on the same level of experience. These entities in Shao's explanatory discourse function as symbols that reflect how sensorial or phenomenal reality is perceived (see Figs. B1, B4, B5, and B6).

Shao more often focused on number understood in a pronominal sense, rather than in a descriptive sense. His interest was in the idea that there is a two-part or a four-part entity, rather than that there are two things or four things of a certain kind. He was concerned with the relationships of classes and expressed the relationships in numerical terms. However, he did not generally pursue the question of how many entities there are in any particular class.

If one considers all of Shao Yung's thought, as reflected in his own and others' writings, the evidence indicates that numbers were, for Shao, an important way to convey the idea of "knowable order." Although he did not reject special consideration of some numbers, such as two and four, the meaning of numbers for Shao Yung ultimately did not lie in their possession of some magical power. Particular numbers themselves apart from their context were not what was important. It was what numbers signified—order, regularity, pattern—that was important. Even though numbers were not magical for Shao, however, they often were so for others who looked to Shao as their authority. Moreover, despite his interest in assigning numbers to things, Shao was very selective and highly unusual in his use of numbers to take measurements.

Shao Yung did not believe that numbers control reality. Rather, he repeatedly suggested that phenomenal reality is patterned and that one pattern is numerical. Phenomenal reality consists of patterned relationships, whose structure can be known. Besides a numerical relationship, he acknowledged other patterned relationships of movement and response or correlation by category. Numbers are simply a way (to Shao an extremely important way) of characterizing certain aspects of reality.

One example of a numerical relationship important in Shao's thought is the double geometrical progression (see Chapter 6 for further discussion of numerical relationships).[14] In a geometrical relationship the same ratio exists between each number in a series; in this case, 2. Thus, *t'ai-chi* is associated with 1, the two forces with 2, the four images with 4, and the eight trigrams with 8, and, with the insertion in the series of the intermediary numbers of 16 and 32, the 64 hexagrams with 64.

In explaining Shao Yung's ideas about numbers, Shao Po-wen commented:

> What are the numbers? They are the periodic revolutions [*yün*] of *tao*, the moments [*hui*] of principle [*li*], the degrees [*tu*] of *yin* and *yang*, and the temporal regulators [*chi*] of the myriad things. They are fixed in the dark mystery and verified in the light. They are hidden in the subtle mystery and made manifest in the brightness. They are that by which the changes are completed and the spirits are moved.[15]

Influenced by Lao Tzu in respect to the hidden and the manifest, this passage claims that numbers represent the regularity of the various dynamic aspects of the universe. Numerical sets, for example, the four seasons, are known through the "light," or phenomenal experience. Why they are what they are is a separate question. According to Shao Po-wen here and Shao Yung in other passages, that question is not answerable. The processes and order of the universe can, however, be seen in numerical terms. Everything, no matter how large, has a numerical aspect.[16]

Shao Yung believed in a "natural" tendency in the activities of nature and human beings for events and things to clump together, especially in groups of two and four. Shao based this belief on observations of nature and society. Certainly no sane person in Northern Sung China denied the reality of *yin* and *yang* or the four seasons. Of course, Shao's observations were not systematic, and they were shaped by the inherent ideas and expectations of his culture. Such ideas formed his conceptual framework, and he observed what he was prepared to observe. He believed, moreover, that the relational patterns were available for anyone to observe.[17]

For Shao, calendrical time was among those things and activities of nature and society that had numerical features. The most important divisions were the units of 2, 4, 12, and 30. Shao (and others) regarded these numbers as being known from actual experience. The myriad things of the world and the cosmic periods of the universe were also examples of things representable by numbers. One *yüan* (cycle), for instance, was 129,600 ($12^2 \times 30^2$) years, and the number of the myriad things, which represented the ultimate extension of the double geometric progression, was 289,816,576 ($17,024^2$; see discussion in Chapters 5 and 6).[18]

In particular, Shao was interested in correlating the basic numbers of 2, 4, 12, and 30 with various classes of things. Making correlations was one way of presenting his ideas on the interrelatedness of things and the regularity of the structure of things. He used numbers to expose the relational order or structure of phenomena.

Through the use of numbers, he seems to have been suggesting that the number of things and the amount of time is finite. Numbers like those mentioned above certainly suggest extremely long periods of time and an overwhelming multiplicity of things. However, since the *Yi* learning often associated particular entities with certain numbers without any presumption that the number indicated actual quantities (for example, the "Great Commentary" says that one, three, five, seven, and nine belong to heaven, and two, four, six, and eight to earth), it would be difficult to claim that for Shao these numbers indicated exact quantities of phenomenal things.[19]

The use of numbers to symbolize characteristics of the world was of course not unique to Shao Yung; it was a fundamental aspect of the *hsiang-shu* learning. Some texts and philosophers emphasized different sets of numbers; others used the same ones Shao did. Shao Po-wen, for example, defended Shao Yung's use of the numbers ten and twelve against nine and six,[20] arguing that since ten minus one is nine and twelve divided by two is six, ten and twelve are ultimate numbers (*chi-shu*). He also pointed out that "both the *Great Expansion* and the [*Huang-chi*] *ching-shih* are based on four, and four is the number of the four images," and that the *T'ai-hsüan* of Yang Hsiung used the number three as its base. However, "although the methods of the sages were not the same, that whereby they made the numbers is identical [*yi*]."[21] That is, they derived the numbers from the phenomena of the universe.

Shao Yung, along with others of this branch of the *Yi* learning, such as Yang Hsiung of the Han, correlated numbers with the images. Both the images and numbers are symbols, but they represent the universe in different ways. Numbers represent a grade of theoreticity more abstract than the images. The arithmetic manipulation of numbers was used to represent the processes of change and the resulting variety of things. The kinds of manipulations (such as multiplication and division) possible with numbers reflect some of the kinds of changes possible in the universe.

Shao Yung also applied the concept of number to non-numerical entities in the *hsiang-shu* ontology through the relationship of association. *Tao, shen* (spirit), and *hsin* (mind), for example, though emphasizing different aspects or kinds of reality, also represent the unity or wholeness of reality. Since they are each in some sense equivalent to *t'ai-chi*, the number one is associated with them.[22]

One further example of Shao's use of number to reflect order, structure, and relationships is his particular arrangement of the 64 hexagrams in a circle and in a square starting with *ch'ien* and ending with *k'un* (see Fig. B3).[23] This arrangement results in many interesting relationships among the hexagrams. For example, all the hexagrams or numbers in the same row have the same lower half. That is, all the hexagrams have the same trigram on the bottom, and all the numbers have the same digit. Similarly, the upper half of each hexagram or number in each column is the same.

This arrangement became known in the West in the late seventeenth century through the Jesuit missionary Joachim Bouvet (1656–1730). Bouvet introduced these ideas to the philosopher and mathematician Gottfried Leibniz (1646–1716), who subsequently developed a binary system of notation that paralleled Shao's arrangement of the hexagrams. The broken (*yin*) lines were represented by 0 and the unbroken (*yang*) lines by 1, and the sequence went from 0 to 63. The order of Leibniz's sequence, however, is the reverse of Shao Yung's. Leibniz started with 0 or the hexagram *k'un*, at the upper left-hand corner of the square, whereas Shao started with the hexagram *ch'ien*, at the lower right-hand corner.[24] Shao may or may not have been aware that his arrangement of the hexagrams could be used in a system of binary notation.

For Shao Yung and others, investigating numbers and their operations was one possible way, but certainly not the only way, of understanding the world. Shao believed that every event and thing has a numerical aspect. Working from the numerical principles of those things that are immediately accessible to ordinary sense experience, one extends numerical principles to include all things and processes. Given the belief that the universe is regular and predictable, Shao assumed that a knowledge of the world's numerical structure would lead to further understanding of the universe and its processes of change.

The Symbolic Realm and the Phenomenal World

In order for the realm of images and numbers to be acceptable as a way to explain change in the phenomenal world, the relationship between these two realms of reality needed to be both clear and believable. This matter was of concern to others before Shao, including the writers of the "Great Commentary" and Wang Pi (226–49), whose commentaries on the *Yi-ching* and the *Tao te ching* apparently influenced Shao Yung.[25] In several passages, Shao expressed his ideas about the relationship between this symbolic realm and the world of experience. His comments on the relationship between ideas (*yi*), words (*yen*), images (*hsiang*) and numbers (*shu*) can be understood in more than one sense. On the one hand, ideas and words represent the world of experience, and images and numbers the symbolic or theoretical realm. On the other hand, these four elements are simultaneously aspects of both the *Yi-ching* (and its theoretical position) and the world of experience.

The superior man, in relation to the *Yi*, examines the images, the numbers, the statements [*tz'u*], and the ideas.*

If there are ideas, there must be words. If there are words, there must be images. If there are images, there must be numbers. After the numbers were established, then the images were produced. After the images were produced, then the words were clear. After the words were clear, then the ideas were manifest.

The images and numbers are [like] the net and the trap. Words and ideas are [like] the fish and the hare. When one catches a fish or a hare, and one says that it must have been due to the net and trap, that is permissible. If one discards the net and trap and seeks for the fish and the hare, then I have not yet seen one be successful.[26]

---

*In the *Yi-ching*, numbers are represented by the lines of the hexagrams. The undivided (*yang*) lines symbolize odd numbers and the divided (*yin*) lines even numbers. The "images" are the hexagrams and other symbols mentioned in their interpretations, and "statements" (or "words") and "ideas" refer to the trigrams and the interpretations of the lines individually and to the hexagrams as a whole.

Shao's point is that certain kinds of structure (represented by numbers and images) are necessary for human experience in, and comprehension of, the phenomenal world (represented by words and ideas). Just as there are things in the phenomenal world, there are things in theoretical realm. With an allusion to a passage in the *Chuang Tzu*, Shao compared the images and numbers to nets and traps, and words and ideas to fish and hares. Just as one cannot capture a fish or a hare without a net or a trap, one cannot have words and ideas without images and numbers.[27]

Shao was undoubtedly aware of a similar passage in which Wang Pi spoke of ideas, images, and words.

The images emerge from ideas, and words clarify the images. To exhaust ideas, nothing is as good as the images. To exhaust the images, nothing is as good as words. Words are controlled by the images. Therefore one can examine words in order to understand the images....

This is like [the fact that] the purpose of the trap is to catch the hare. When one catches the hare, one forgets the trap. The purpose of the net is to catch the fish. When one catches the fish, one forgets the trap. Thus words are the hare's trap. Images are the fish's net.[28]

According to Wang Pi, when an idea begins to form, an image is developed to express it and then a word is proposed to represent it. An image helps express an idea, and a word helps express an image. Once the idea is thoroughly understood, the image can be discarded, and once the image is understood, the word can be discarded. Wang Pi wanted to pay attention "not to the symbol but to the underlying meaning of the symbol,"[29] and thus he emphasized the primacy of ideas over images and words.

Shao's point differs from Wang Pi's. Shao proceeded from numbers to images to words to ideas, whereas Wang Pi proceeded from ideas to images to words. Wang Pi was reacting against the learning of images and numbers and was trying to establish the importance of meaning and the moral emphasis of the *yi-li* learning.[30] In contrast, Shao was suggesting that numbers and images exist on a higher level of theoreticity than do words and ideas. The numbers and images reflect a theoretical reality abstracted from phenomenal reality. Although Shao did not often use the term *li* (pattern, principle), which came to be extremely important in the Ch'eng-Chu school of Neo-Confucianism, the numbers and images are functionally equivalent to the concept of *li* as pattern. (Shao tended to use *li* to contrast the *li* of earth with the *tao* of heaven.) In Shao's view, an idea has to be made known through words, and the meanings of words can be made clear through the images.

Numbers are even more abstract, because they arise as soon as reality ceases to be a unity. The images imply the numbers, since numbers are the most abstract way to symbolize the divisions of phenomenal reality, such as day and night or the four seasons. Shao emphasized the structure of reality. In his view, reality has a definite shape, and its divisions can be represented by numbers. He used numbers to indicate the abstract structure inherent in phenomenal reality. In contrast, Wang Pi was presenting the Taoist view (with which Shao agreed) that part of human experience precedes verbalization; that is, the process of forming an idea does not entirely occur consciously in words.[31]

In terms of discussing the relationship between the realm of the images and numbers and that of words and ideas, Shao Yung and Wang Pi had different concerns. Shao was not emphasizing, as Wang Pi was, that one uses words to understand the images and images to understand ideas. Shao was claiming that although reality is ultimately a whole ontologically, we can look at experienced reality (with all its multiple aspects) in different ways, or according to different levels of abstraction. Numbers, or numerical divisions, represent the most abstract level because they represent regularity or the idea of pure structure without specific referents. Many things can be divided into two parts or four parts. The things are different, but the numerical division is the same.[32]

Shao also made the point that without the numbers and images ordinary sense experience is impossible. Words and ideas cannot exist without regularity and the system of categories—the images—that reflects the regularity. (Shao's reasons for holding this position, particularly his idea of consciousness, are discussed below.)

In speaking about the relationship between the world of experience and the theoretical realm of the numbers and images, Shao Yung said: "*T'ai-chi* is one. It does not move. It gives rise [*sheng*] to two. When there is two, then there is spirit [*shen*].... Spirit gives rise to the numbers. The numbers give rise to the images. The

The Theoretical Structure of Reality · 79

images give rise to things [*ch'i*]."[33] Quoting Huang Chi, Wang Chih elaborated on Shao's view: *t'ai-chi* is originally one, but when it moves, it produces two (stillness and movement). The two are *t'ai-chi* and *shen* (spirit). Here, *shen* represents the dynamic aspect of reality, but it is not ontologically separate from that which is still (*t'ai-chi*). Numbers, as an aspect of reality, are thus produced with this first step from stillness to movement.[34] Shao also said: "Not moving is *t'ai-chi*'s nature [*hsing*]. When it is aroused [*fa*], then [there is] spirit. [After there is] spirit, then [there is] number. After [there are] numbers, then [there are] the images. After [there are] the images, then [there are] things. The changes of things return to spirit."[35]

From this passage, it is apparent that "one" is not a number in the same sense as the other numbers are.[36] "One" represents the whole and not a part of the whole. Since numbers arise only when the whole is divided, numbers represent divisions. Shao is saying that the nature of *t'ai-chi* is absolute stillness or rest (*ching*). With the first movement of *t'ai-chi*, spirit is born. Once there is spirit, there is division and thus number arises. Once reality, or *ch'i*, can be split, it can be split into numerical divisions. Once these divisions are possible, then there can be the images to symbolize the divisions of *ch'i*. The images allow one to understand the behavior of physical phenomena. In this context, spirit is the activity or movement (*tung*) of *t'ai-chi* or *ch'i*.[37]

Further commenting on the relationship between the phenomenal world and the symbolic realm of the images, Shao said:

The images arise from [*ch'i*] forms [*hsing*], numbers arise from disposition [*chih*], names arise from words [*yen*], ideas [*yi*] arise from activity [*yung*]. The numbers of the world emerge from its pattern [*li*]. If [the numbers] are far from the pattern, then the [numbers] become artificial [*shu*]. When people of the world become artificial with numbers, they thereby are lost from the pattern.[38]

According to Huang Chi, "forms" refers to the physical features of the world, such as heaven and earth, water and fire, thunder and wind, and mountains and marshes. "Disposition" refers to the characteristics of things, such as highness and lowness, brightness and darkness, drumming and dancing, and penetration and blockage. "Words" refers to the names of the eight trigrams, and "activity" to different kinds of movement, for example, riding and supporting, advancing and retreating, dividing and uniting, and taking from and giving to.[39] Each of these series of eight items consists of four pairs and is modeled on the pattern of the hemilog.

In addition to emphasizing that concrete experience is the basis of such abstractions as the images and numbers, Shao was saying that numbers are based on the inherent patterns of the universe. Thought that strays too far from the natural divisions becomes artificial, with no true foundation in the world. In this passage, Shao clearly linked the phenomenal world and its abstract structure. These two aspects of reality, called the *hou-t'ien* and *hsien-t'ien* realms, occur together and, from an ontological viewpoint, cannot be separated.

Some people use numbers for devious purposes. However, from Shao's view, when they do so, they misuse numbers. Moreover, such people are not pursuing an understanding of the universe. They are not concerned with truth, but are simply interested in manipulating numbers for such popular purposes as fortune-telling.

These passages from Shao Yung and that from Wang Pi have several precedents. A passage in the *Tso Chuan* reads: "Tortoises are the images. Stalks are the numbers. After things were produced, there were the images. After images, there were words. After words, there were numbers."[40] This passage clearly emphasizes the link between the phenomenal world and the images. People derived the images, words, and numbers from the myriad things of the world. Theoretical constructs come from the world of experience.

In a similar vein, the "Great Commentary" emphasizes that the images and numbers derived from the phenomenal universe.

The Master [Confucius] said: "Written characters do not completely express words. Words do not completely express ideas. And yet can the ideas of the sages not be manifest?"

The Master said: "The sages established the images in order to completely express ideas. They set up the trigrams and hexagrams in order to completely express the true and the false. They attached their explanations to completely express their words. They changed [the lines] and completed the process in order to completely express what is advantageous. They [thus] stimulated [the people] as with drums and dances to completely express spirit.

The sages were able to observe all the phenomena under the sky. The sages considered how to describe the phenomena, and so represented their forms and character with symbols. Therefore these representations are called the images.[41]

Shao Yung further distinguished between the inner images and numbers and the outer images and numbers.

That which is naturally so and does not change is the inner images and inner numbers. Other [things] all are outer images and outer numbers.

The *Yi* has inner images. These are the numbers of *li* [pattern]. The *Yi* also has outer images. They point to things and do not change.[42]

Shao is saying that there are two kinds of symbols: abstract ones, such as numbers and lines, and concrete ones, such as the images of heaven and earth (sun, moon, water, fire). Whereas the concrete symbols represent things that appear as different particular examples (all horses vary somewhat), the abstract symbols are already abstracted from the level of particulars to the level of classes. Shao's view here reflects that of Wang Pi, who said that there is no need for a horse if one already has the idea of firmness or a cow if one has the idea of compliance.[43]

Shao categorized the images or symbols in the *Yi-ching* into word images, appearance images, and number images.[44] In contrast to appearance images, which refer to things that can be seen, word images or word symbols represent things that do not have a visual aspect. Word images are those images that stand for ideas. For example, under the first hexagram, *ch'ien* are the word images *yüan*, *heng*, *li*, and *cheng*, which have been translated as originating growth, prosperous development, advantageous gain, and correct firmness.[45] An example of an appearance image is the mare, which is associated with *k'un*, the second hexagram.[46] Number images are numbers. Nine and six are particularly important in the *Yi-ching*, because they represent *yang* and *yin* lines, respectively.

The realm of the images and numbers is thus a conceptual level of reality, which in Shao's thought functioned as a theoretical statement about the phenomenal world. In this context, the theoretical level is the *hsien-t'ien* realm, and the world of experience the *hou-t'ien* realm. Although *hsien-t'ien* and *hou-t'ien* have other meanings as well, here the two terms contrast the experience of particulars with theoretical reflection on that kind of reality.⁴⁷

In the following passage, Shao Po-wen attempted to clarify *hsien-t'ien* and *hou-t'ien*.

> Someone asked: "The *Huang-chi ching-shih* discards [the five phases of] metal, wood, water, fire, and earth, and uses [the four images of] water, fire, earth, and stone. Why is this so?"
>
> [Shao] replied: "Sun, moon, stars, and zodiacal space are the four images of heaven. Water, fire, earth, and stone are the four forms [*t'i*] of earth. Metal, wood, water, fire, and earth are the five phases.
>
> "The four images and the four forms are *hsien-t'ien*. The five phases are *hou-t'ien*. *Hsien-t'ien* is what *hou-t'ien* emerges from.*
>
> "Water, fire, earth, and stone are what the five phases emerge from. Water, fire, earth, and stone are the basic forms [*pen-t'i*]. Metal, wood, water, fire, and earth are the final activities [*chih-yung*]. . . .
>
> "Metal comes from stone and wood arises in the earth. When there is stone, afterward there is metal. When there is earth, afterward there is wood. Metal accordingly changes and afterward completes wood. It is one category of growing things. How do I discard the five phases and not use them?"
>
> The *Huang-chi ching-shih* emphasizes the basic forms, whereas the "Hung Fan" emphasizes the final activity. They both have what they view as primary, but they return to the same point.⁴⁸

The "Hung Fan" (Great plan) chapter in the *Shu-ching* is the textual source of the term *Huang-chi*. The discussion in the "Hung Fan" emphasizes the five phases and the activities of the ruler that would enable him to unify the empire.⁴⁹ The "Hung Fan" was concerned with activities, whereas the *Huang-chi ching-shih* was concerned with theoretical patterns of activities. In contrasting these two works, Shao Po-wen was indicating the relationship between the *hou-t'ien* and *hsien-t'ien* realms. They are two different aspects of the universe: *hou-t'ien* refers to the realm of particular experience, and *hsien-t'ien* to the realm of the abstract patterns of structure,

---

*This is true only in an epistemological sense; that is, our categories of thought help determine what we experience.

which particular experience follows. Shao focused on the *hsien-t'ien* realm.

Although this passage from Shao Po-wen's commentary seems to indicate a temporal sequence by stating that *hou-t'ien* emerges from *hsien-t'ien* (that is, the phenomenal world comes from the abstract symbolic world, almost in a Platonic sense), Shao himself did not see the relationship strictly in temporal or cosmological terms. This passage is not an accurate statement of Shao's view. As noted above, for Shao Yung the distinction between *hsien-t'ien* and *hou-t'ien* was one of different levels or realms of reality. One level may be called the "stuff" of experience and the other the patterns of that "stuff." They exist simultaneously.[50]

Shao Yung held the view, quoted earlier from the "Great Commentary," that *t'ai-chi* gives rise to the two forces, the four images, the eight trigrams, and also heaven and earth and the myriad things. Although, as a concept, *sheng* (to give rise to, give birth to, produce) referred to cosmological development, it also concerned the active nature of reality and denoted the idea of constant change. As the "Great Commentary" says, "Production and reproduction is what is called [the process of] change."[51] Shao Yung did not conceive of the relationship of these entities, from *t'ai-chi* to the myriad things, as one in which the birth of a new entity entails the demise of the previous entity. As Shao Po-wen explained, *t'ai-chi* does not exist before or after the phenomenal things that it gives rise to, nor does it have a beginning or end. *T'ai-chi* exists simultaneously with everything else, including the two forces, the four images, and the eight trigrams, as well as the phenomenal world of heaven and earth and the myriad things. Or, to paraphrase Donald Munro, the unity remains a whole even while there are discrete things.[52] Shao Po-wen said:

T'ai-chi is before heaven and earth and yet is not before. It is after heaven and earth and yet is not after. It ends heaven and earth and yet does not end them. It begins heaven and earth and yet does not begin them. It permeates and thoroughly blends with heaven and earth and the myriad things, and it does not have a before and after, or a beginning and end.

When there is *t'ai-chi*, then the two forces, four images, eight trigrams, and even heaven and earth and the myriad things already are complete. One cannot say that today there is *t'ai-chi* and then only tomorrow there are the two forces and then only on the following day there are the four images and the eight trigrams.

Although it is said that *t'ai-chi* produces the two forces, the two forces produce the four images, and the four images produce the eight trigrams, in fact they are all complete at one time.[53]

To say that the whole and the parts exist at the same time is another way of referring to Shao's view of the two levels of reality, the subsensorial level (called by various terms, such as *t'ai-chi* and *ch'i*) and the phenomenal level of the senses. From the point of view of human consciousness, both levels exist at the same time. The subsensorial level does not exist prior to or independently of the phenomenal world.

To clarify these relationships, Shao Po-wen offered two analogies: "This is like the case that when there is a form, there is a shadow. When there is one, there is two and three and numbers without limit."[54] Unfortunately, these analogies miss the mark. Although there can be no numbers two and three (in a series) without a number one, the reverse is not true. These analogies are also defective in that their parts exist only on the level of the senses. In Shao's thought, however, the temporal coexistence of *t'ai-chi* and the particular things of the phenomenal world is possible because of the two different levels of reality in the universe, the sensorial and the subsensorial. This division does not imply, however, that phenomenal reality is but an illusion, a "front" for an unperceived true reality, as does the concept of Brahman in Hinduism.[55]

We can now consider the problem of the meaning and perhaps translation of the term *hsien-t'ien*, which has been the subject of a certain amount of disagreement among scholars. The *Yi-ching* says of the great man: "He may precede [*hsien*] Heaven [*t'ien*], and Heaven will not act in opposition to him; he may follow Heaven, but will act [only] as Heaven at the time would do."[56]

Hsien-t'ien, which has no equivalent in English, has been translated and explained in a variety of ways—former heaven, prior heaven, pre-creation, *a priori*, what antedates Heaven, Prior to Heaven, and the former sky or celestial [plan].[57] The source of much of the disagreement appears to arise from our ignorance of the development of the uses of this term and the great number of different meanings it has. Even Shao Yung (and others) used it in different ways.

Depending on the context, *hsien-t'ien* had three primary meanings in Shao Yung's thought. One meaning, philosophically the most important one, appears in the preceding discussion. In this sense, *hsien-t'ien* refers to the abstract structure whose pattern the phenomenal world, called *hou-t'ien*, follows. This level was represented by an elaborate system of symbols, the numbers and the images. Since the concepts of this theoretical realm were seen as deriving from human experience, the idea of *hsien-t'ien* is not equivalent to that of the *a priori* in Western philosophy. In Shao's thought, *hsien-t'ien* in this context was a level of conceptualization abstracted from the level of particular human experiences. As Shao Yung said, "The learning of *hsien-t'ien* is [a matter of the] mind. The learning of *hou-t'ien* is [a matter of the] traces [*chi*]. Coming out and departing [*ch'u-ju*], having phenomenal existence and not having it [*yu-wu*], dying and being born [*ssu-sheng*] are the *tao*."[58]

The image here is coming out from the One, the unity of existence, or undifferentiated *ch'i*, into this phenomenal world of living things. At death, an object does not become nonexistent, but departs from this world and returns to the original One. This kind of movement is called the *tao*, and such patterns are the subject of the learning of *hsien-t'ien*. The commentary that follows Shao Yung's remarks reads: "The learning of *hsien-t'ien* is not something that can be transmitted in words but is comprehended with ideas in the mind. The learning of *hou-t'ien* can be examined with words and writing. Thus there are forms and traces."[59] In this meaning, *hsien-t'ien* refers to the theoretical realm (or level) of symbols, in contrast to the realm of phenomenal reality, or *hou-t'ien*.

Hsien-t'ien also refers to a particular historical stage. The period before Yao, the first of the three legendary sage emperors, was *hsien-t'ien*, and the period after him *hou-t'ien*. Shao Yung said: "[The time] before Yao is [called] *hsien-t'ien*. After Yao it is [called] *hou-t'ien*. *Hou-t'en* is the time of following laws."[60]

Although the terms *hsien-t'ien* and *hou-t'ien* are not explicitly used, this idea is reflected in the chart entitled "Ching-shih yi-yüan hsiao-chang chih shu t'u" (Chart of the numbers of the waxing and waning of one cycle that rule the world).[61] This chart divides cal-

86 · *The Theoretical Structure of Reality*

endrical time into two long historical periods, from the beginning to Yao, and from the Hsia dynasty to the Sung. The reference to "following laws" is a continuation of an earlier passage: "Laws began with Fu Hsi, were completed with Yao, and were changed with the three kings."[62] This use of *hsien-t'ien* and *hou-t'ien* as historical terms influenced some historical writing, particularly that of the twelfth-century scholar Hu Hung.[63]

The apparent but indirect source of both these meanings of *hsien-t'ien* was still another meaning that appears in Shao's thought. The images and numbers in Shao's thought were symbols in a series of charts and diagrams, related to the ancient *Ho T'u* (River chart) and the *Lo Shu* (Lo writing). Although not all the details are known, these two ancient diagrams, like the charts and diagrams used by Shao (see Fig. B7), went through many versions before they reached the form known to the Sung philosophers.[64] The charts and diagrams were in one sense cosmic maps, symbolizing the two major divisions of the universe, the sky and the earth. Through use of the images and numbers, the charts visually represented the celestial and earthly patterns of order, change, and transformation in the phenomenal world. The charts and diagrams were special maps, far more abstract than the maps of the stars and planets of the astronomers.

In early cosmological thought, earth was conceived of as square and heaven as round. Thus, charts in the form of a square symbolized earth, and those with a round plan symbolized heaven.[65] As Ts'ai Yüan-ting commented, "What is round moves and is heaven. What is square is still and is earth."[66] Esoteric cults built up traditions around these charts and paired specific sky (round) plans with specific earth (square) plans. The round diagrams were forms of what Schuyler Cammann has called celestial or sky plans.

The Chinese traditionally associated one of these sky plans with the mythological ruler Fu Hsi and another with (the historically later) King Wen of the Chou dynasty. Since the chart of Fu Hsi was regarded as having developed earlier, it was called the Former Chart of Heaven (*Hsien t'ien t'u*), and that of King Wen the Later Chart of Heaven (*Hou t'ien t'u*). In addition to the one particular *hsien t'ien t'u*, many other charts that Shao discussed and used in his thought were associated with Fu Hsi (see Figs. B1–B3) and were also called *hsien-t'ien* charts or the charts of Fu Hsi. Moreover, as mentioned earlier, Shao became so associated with these charts that his thought was called *hsien-tien hsüeh*, the learning of *hsien-t'ien*.

The two charts most commonly called the *hsien-t'ien t'u* and the *hou-t'ien t'u* consist of the eight trigrams arranged in a circle so that their positions are correlated with the cardinal directions (see Figs. B2 and B8).[67] The most obvious difference between these two charts is the placement of particular trigrams and the trigrams' association with different directions of the compass. In alluding to the arrangements of the charts, Shao Po-wen quoted Shao Yung:

> The orderly sequence of the eight trigrams of the *hsien-t'ien* chart begins with *ch'ien* and ends with *k'un*. This is *hsien-t'ien*, the eight trigrams of Fu Hsi. The natural ruler of the *Chou Yi* emerges from *chen*, and when it reaches completeness, it is called *ken*. This is [*hou-t'ien*,] the eight trigrams of King Wen.
>
> Not only is [the sequence of] the eight trigrams [different] like this, but also the [sequence of the] 64 hexagrams is not the same. The *Yi* of Fu Hsi has no writing and only has charts of the trigrams, [which symbolize] the waxing and waning of *yin* and *yang*. The methods of the sages [Fu Hsi and King Wen] were not the same.[68]

In the chart of Fu Hsi (Fig. B2), the trigram *ch'ien* is due south, *k'un* due north, *li* due east, and *k'an* due west. *Tui* is southeast, *chen* is northeast, *sun* is southwest, and *ken* is northwest.[69] In the chart of King Wen (Fig. B8) or the *Chou Yi* chart, *li* is due south, *k'an* is due north, *chen* is due east, and *tui* is due west. *Sun* is southeast, *ken* is northeast, *k'un* is southwest, and *ch'ien* is northwest.

Shao Yung said that the chart of King Wen symbolized the activity (*yung*) of heaven and earth and that the arrangement of the trigrams symbolized the responses of things to the seasons of heaven and to the directions of earth.[70] In contrast, the chart of Fu Hsi symbolized the forms (*t'i*) or the images of heaven and earth.[71] Thus, although both charts consisted of the eight trigrams in a particular arrangement, to Shao they symbolized different aspects of reality.

The Ch'ing scholar Ch'iao Ts'ai commented that the directional positions in Shao Yung's *hsien-t'ien* chart were concerned with opposing forms (*tui-tai chih t'i*) whereas those in his *hou-t'ien* chart represented constantly circulating activity (*liu-hsing chih yung*). Ch'iao was referring to such opposing (and correlated) forms as heaven above and earth below, and the sun in the east and the moon in the west. As Ch'iao noted, these were the fixed positions of heaven and earth in the "Great Commentary." His comments on the *hou-t'ien* chart referred to the course of the seasons—the recurring cycle of spring, summer, autumn, and winter.[72]

As with many events in Chinese history, the earlier something is purported to be, the later the account of it appears in the written records. Although the Chinese traditionally believed that the chart of Fu Hsi preceded the chart of King Wen (hence the names), until recently modern scholars have tended to be skeptical of this ordering. However, recent evidence indicates that the traditional order may have been correct.[73]

A fairly literal translation of *hsien-t'ien* and *hou-t'ien* is clearly meaningless in the senses of abstract structures and historical stages. It would, however, be appropriate in reference to the charts. Thus, no single translation can do justice to these terms. In Shao's thought, the terms *hsien-t'ien* and *hou-t'ien* used in reference to abstract structures can be translated as "theoretical" and "phenomenal" (or "experiential"); in reference to historical stages as "before civilization" and "after civilization"; and in reference to the charts as "former sky" and "later sky." These suggested translations apply, however, only to Shao Yung's thought.

To sum up briefly, although *hsien-t'ien* had several meanings, the one of concern here is the theoretical level or symbolic realm of experience. The *hsien-t'ien* realm consisted of the four images *yin*, *yang*, *kang*, and *jou*, as well as the four images of heaven and the four images (or forms) of earth. These were correlated with the eight trigrams in the order of enumeration associated with Fu Hsi, *ch'ien*, *tui*, *li*, *chen*, *sun*, *k'an*, *ken*, and *k'un*. The entities (images) in this realm symbolized categories of *ch'i* and were not the concrete particulars of human experience. The same terms were used, however, for both the theoretical and the concrete aspects of reality. The *hsien-t'ien* realm was a level of reality in which the categories of subsensorial *ch'i* were symbolized by forms that were drawn from the phenomenal world of human experience and that were regarded as the ultimate manifestations of those categories. The *hsien-t'ien* realm was an abstraction of the way the universe was conceptualized in the *Yi* learning.

Numbers for Comparisons

For Shao, since numbers were a way of representing abstract structure without necessarily implying any specific content, they could be used to make comparisons. In particular, he compared qualities that were not numerical, thus applying his view that numbers could be used to express non-numerical ideas. With a set of numbers based on multiples of ten and starting with one (one, ten, one hundred . . . one million), he compared things in terms of their size and people in terms of their wisdom, using his customary method of correlations and permutations of classes of things.[74]

Shao began with the important, but unstated, assumption that classes are homogeneous in size, no matter how many parts they have.[75] A class, moreover, is equal to the number one, or to the whole of the quality under consideration. Therefore, the only member of a class of one entity is large in comparison to a member of a class of one thousand entities. One out of one is larger than one out of one thousand. For Shao, one object is larger than another object if it belongs to a class with fewer items.

Shao was, in effect, talking about fractions. One thousand out of one thousand is equal to one out of one, or one (the whole). However, one out of a class of one thousand is a small thing, whereas the one out of a class of one is the largest of things. What Shao has done is to provide a numerical method, using fractions, for comparing things. Although Shao Po-wen commented that Shao Yung was talking about size (*chü-hsi*), it is clear that Shao had several points of comparison in mind. Size did not refer just to physical size.

With this use of number, Shao Yung was addressing in yet another way the long-standing philosophical problem of the relativity of human judgment. This idea, first discussed by Hsün Tzu and Chuang Tzu, was of great interest to Shao Yung.[76] Chuang Tzu stressed that a thing is judged to have a certain quality only in comparison with something else with that quality. What is large, or long, or old in one situation may be small, or short, or young in another. (This view is another version of the idea of the relativity of *yin* and *yang*. That is, what is *yin* or *yang* in one context may be the reverse in another context.) Thus, as Chuang Tzu said:

There is nothing in the world bigger than the tip of an autumn hair, and Mount Tai is tiny.

Men claim that Mao-ch'iang and Lady Li were beautiful, but if fish saw them they would dive to the bottom of the stream, if birds saw them they would fly away, and if deer saw them they would break into a run. Of these four, which knows how to fix the standard of beauty for the world?[77]

Hsün Tzu was concerned more with the problem of how one's state of mind could interfere with one what saw, heard, understood, or knew. He recognized that one's emotional and mental states could prevent one from observing things correctly or from knowing the truth.

If one fails to use his mind, then black and white may be right before his eyes and he will not see them; thunder or drums may be sounding in his ear and he will not hear them. How much more so with a man whose mind is obsessed!...

One may be obsessed by desires or by hates, by the beginning of an affair or by the end, by those far away or those close by, by breadth of knowledge or by shallowness, by the past or by the present.[78]

Shao Yung was offering another way to judge things and to make comparisons. Although he agreed with Chuang Tzu on the importance of perspective and with Hsün Tzu on the importance of an unclouded or clear mind, Shao was saying that under certain conditions numbers can be used to express comparisons.[79] There can be an objectivity based on a method of numerical description that is explicit and available to all.[80] Shao recognized that attitude alone was not sufficient for objectivity, and he offered a method that was independent of an individual's point of view or state of mind.

That Shao Yung was thinking of using numbers to compare more than the sizes of things is evident as he turned from a discussion of things (*wu*) to a discussion of humans (*jen*).[81] With things, size (of the form or the object) is the important characteristic. With humans, however, the quality of wisdom, on a scale ranging from wise (*hsien*) to stupid (*yü*), is the essential characteristic. In the context of Shao's thought, moreover, this characteristic was important because he was ultimately concerned with the knowledge of the sage.

In developing his idea, Shao used numbers (based on ten) and correlated them with classes of things beginning with the four social classes.[82] Instead of greater or lesser in terms of size, he talked about greater or lesser in terms of wisdom. Wisdom in humans is analogous to size in things. Thus, given the assumption of the identity of the classes, the one out of one is much wiser than the one out of one thousand. The one of one has all the wisdom, whereas the one of one thousand has wisdom equal to only one one-thousandth part of the whole.

Shao's method of quantifying wisdom was flawed in that he did not propose an objective way to assign numbers to particular people. What he did was simply draw an analogy. A sage appears only rarely. Less intelligent people appear frequently. One hundred one-hundredths are equivalent to one, ten one-tenths are equivalent to one, and one one is equivalent to one. In the first case there are many parts and so each part is small; in the third case there is only one part and so it is big. Just as there are more of the smaller things and fewer of the larger things, so there are more less-intelligent people and fewer more-intelligent people.[83] Huang Chi commented that "The sizes of things are divided according to large and small, and it is simply a matter of the physical body. The sizes of people are divided according to wisdom and stupidity, and it is a matter of one's character."[84]

In both cases, one is comparing size, but the characteristic under consideration differs. With things it is a matter of large and small bodily form. With humans, however, it is a matter of wisdom and stupidity. Unlike many today who are obsessed with numerical forms of comparison, Shao Yung realized that numbers can represent different kinds of things and that the meaning of numbers does not lie in the numbers themselves.

In the context of Chinese philosophy, Shao's conception of making numerical comparisons was highly unusual. However, it fit well into his own thought, because it reflected his view that the structure of the universe is regular. Since numbers represent patterns of regularity, one can apply them to human wisdom. Even though wisdom was ordinarily thought of in qualitative terms, Shao showed that wisdom, much like *ch'i*, could also be discussed in quantitative terms.

This use of the idea of quantity had historical precedents. In some theories of human nature (*hsing*), the quality of *ch'i*—good or bad, pure or muddy—was thought of in terms of amount, which one received from Heaven.[85] Shao Po-wen, for example, said: "Things have size, and people have intelligence. Both are so because of what they have received [from heaven]."[86] Shao Yung himself believed that the balance of the kind of *ch'i* that one has determines one's nature. Moreover, he assumed that if there can be more or less of something, then one can talk about that something in numerical terms.[87] Although statistics and numerical comparisons are widespread in the twentieth century, it was not common in eleventh-century China for a philosopher to pursue, as Shao Yung did, the implications of making comparisons in terms of number and amount.

Shao employed numbers in connection with his concept of the sage and the sage's unique role. Elaborating on his father's ideas, Shao Po-wen said:

The sage then unites [*chien*] a million things into one and is also able to unite a million people into one. It is not that he unites only humans and things into one, he also is able to unite heaven and earth into one.

Since he is able to unite heaven and earth into one, he therefore can restore heaven and earth. Since he is able to unite a million things into one, he therefore can complete the myriad things. Since he is able to unite a million people into one, he therefore can understand thoroughly the aims of the world.

This [method] is that whereby he can produce a million things and nourish a million people. One human self truly completes heaven and earth and the myriad things. Only the sage can then reflect on himself [*fan-shen*] and so achieve wholeness [*ch'eng*]. If he acts repeatedly like this, then he is not burdened by heaven and earth.[88]

For Shao, even the activity of the sage could be placed in a numerical framework. Shao conceived of the sage (see Chapters 7–8) as one who can unite the universe through a mystical experience in which all subject-object distinctions are obliterated. In the passage quoted above, the statement that the sage unifies all things refers to this. Reflecting Buddhist ideas, Shao's view was that the sage reverses the cosmological process, in which the myriad things proceed from original unity to the many.[89] Through an epistemological experience, the sage reunites the myriad things into the One.

By uniting all things into one, Shao meant experiencing or "perceiving" reality as a whole by obliterating all distinctions. Only the sage is capable of this kind of experience because he alone has complete wisdom. The sage is the wisest of all. He "is" one out of one, or the fraction $1/1$, which equals one, the whole. People of lesser wisdom share the fund of knowledge with others; they may "be" one out of ten or one of one hundred. These less-wise people have only a portion of the whole of wisdom.

To summarize, Shao Yung's conceptions of the images and numbers were based on the *Yi* learning. Shao, however, extended the use of numbers and the images to represent order and regularity. He began with the basic cultural assumption that events in the realms of heaven, earth, and human society could be classified into fundamental groups of two or four entities. The abstracted classes constituted a theoretical level of reality, the *hsien-t'ien* realm, and they were represented by a set of symbols, the images and numbers. All aspects of human experience, from moral concepts to the social classes to the calendrical seasons, act as they do because of the fit of things. That fit was characterized primarily, but not exclusively, by binary and quaternary structures. The symbolic realm was a conceptualization of the theoretical patterns of the activity of phenomena.

In Shao's thought, the numerical divisions 2, 4, 10, 12, and 30 were treated as known entities. Indeed they were widely accepted in Chinese culture as fundamental to the universal structure. Shao was not trying to investigate empirical instances, and there is no evidence that he performed any observations under controlled conditions. Rather, he was using numerical entities and the images to describe and explain phenomena of change. The division of things into two, four, or other numbers of parts was natural to him because these divisions were based on unquestioned assumptions in the epistemology of the culture.

Shao was not engaged, moreover, in practical work, such as

correcting the calendar. The discrepancies between his symbols and experience was not an intellectual concern for him. He was not dealing with the kinds of problems that led to questions about the discrepancies between calendrical or astronomical theory and the universe. As a philosopher, his aims were not those of a modern mathematical astronomer.[90] For his purposes, the numbers that he used served their symbolic functions sufficiently well because they formed a coherent system. Even though it was well known that a year has more than 360 days, the use of the circle with 360 degrees as an analogy for the year was still common in his culture. Clearly, if taken literally, the circle provided a defective map for the number of days in the year.

Shao used numbers both literally and figuratively. The four images were literally four and the eight trigrams were literally eight, but the phrase "ten thousand things" did not literally mean only ten thousand. It symbolically represented the myriad things of the world. Shao possibly intended the number 289,816,576 to represent the number of things or classes of things in the world, but considering the long history of numerical ideas, I think this unlikely. This large number and other, even larger, numbers were more likely intended to convey the idea of a definite, though perhaps uncountable, number of things in the world.

Probably Shao's most unusual use of number, certainly so for philosophers, occurred in relation to the problem of comparing and judging things. For Shao, the number one symbolized the whole, the extreme, the best of anything. Anything less was a proportion of the whole and could be expressed in numerical terms as a fraction. For all quantitative comparisons, one out of one was greater than one out of ten. This is not to say, however, that a quantitative comparison could not also be put into another, nonnumerical or qualitative, framework as well. This way of using numbers reflects the Chinese cultural pattern of thinking in terms of wholes and parts rather than in terms of the one versus many dichotomy more common in Western culture.[91]

5

Concepts of Change: A Focus on Cosmology

> *People say that it is unfortunate that Confucius had no territory. I alone think that this was not so. A single fellow regarded a hundred mou as his territory. A great minister regarded a hundred li as his territory. A feudal lord regarded four provinces as his territory. The emperor regarded the nine regions as his territory. But Confucius regarded ten thousand generations as his territory.*
>
> —Shao Yung[1]

Establishing the Concepts

The core of Shao's explanatory theory is a set of six interrelated concepts, which Shao discussed in sequence in the *Huang-chi ching-shih*. These concepts focus on phenomena of change and on those structures of the universe that are the foundations for change. They are concerned with major characteristics of the universe and connect human consciousness and the world of experience, on the one hand, and the realm of theory, on the other hand. In the theoretical realm, the *hsien-t'ien* realm, the images were of particular importance. The six concepts had their origin in the *Yi* learning and were:

1. The forms and activities (*t'i-yung*) of heaven and earth (*t'ien-ti*);
2. The changes and transformations (*pien-hua*) of heaven and earth;
3. The movements and responses (*kan-ying*) of the myriad things (*wan-wu*);

4. The consciousness (*ling*) of humans and other living things;
5. The ends and beginnings (*chung-shih*) of heaven and earth; and
6. The duties and accomplishments (*shih-yeh*) of the sages and worthies (*sheng-hsien*).

By employing this system of concepts to address the problem of change, Shao Yung implicitly presented the idea of a moving observational point. The cumulative effect of Shao's presentation is a demonstration that no single perspective can enable one to observe all facets of the universe adequately. In addition, Shao Yung advanced the idea that all events or elements of behavior can be understood in terms of a larger whole, in space or in time. No act or event is an isolated incident. Everything is part of a larger network. An event in its entirety consists of the interaction of two complementary, opposing forces or aspects. In Shao's view, change involves a constant process of initiation and completion.

Regardless of how they are translated, the six concepts have strong connotations of activity. Behind these concepts is the assumption of a correspondence among all levels, kinds, and aspects of reality, a fundamental idea in Shao's system. Correspondence is possible because of the regularity of the universe, and this regularity can be described in numerical terms.

The following passage by Ts'ai Yüan-ting indicates the phenomena that to Shao need to be explained and that account for the different kinds of change. In effect, Ts'ai briefly outlines Shao's *hsien-t'ien* thought, that is, Shao's thinking on fundamental universal patterns.

Master K'ang-chieh regarded the book *Huang-chi ching-shih* as the learning of *hsien-t'ien*. His *tao* is wholly based on Fu Hsi's charts of the trigrams. However, the words that he employs and the passages that he writes are his own. Moreover, the classics that he cites and the meanings that he draws out form a separate theory of their own.

Therefore, what the scholars mostly feared and had doubts about were his essentials. Moreover, they regarded K'ang-chieh's book as aimless and floundering around, thereby causing the moral categories to be thoroughly involved in confusion.

After one thoroughly understands it, however, one sees its accomplishments. Its fundamental principle is what Master [Ch'eng] Ming-tao called the method of doubling. Therefore, if one goes to form [*t'i*] from activity [*yung*], then [it is] 2 from 1, 4 from 2, 8 from 4, 16 from 8, 32 from 16, 64 from 32. If one goes to activity from form, then [it is] 32 from 64, 16 from 32, 8 from 16, 4 from 8, 2 from 4, 1 from 2.*

One is *t'ai-chi* and is the so-called "between one movement and one stillness" [entity].† Thus it should be said that that which embodies the principles of heaven and earth is change, and that is all. There cannot be anything in addition to it.

Mr. Yang [Hsiung]'s *T'ai-hsüan* has 81 headings. Mr. Kuan [Lang]'s *Tung-chi* has 27 images. Mr. Ssu-ma [Kuang]'s *Ch'ien-hsü* has 55 sections. All these were what they wrote without understanding. Although the application of K'ang-chieh's learning differs [from theirs], in actuality [his learning] consists of the [arrangement of the] *kua* that Fu Hsi drew.

Therefore [Shao's] book illustrates the forms and activities of heaven and earth with [the images of] sun, moon, stars, and zodiacal space, and water, fire, earth, and stone.‡

It illustrates the changes and transformations of heaven and earth with [the images of] cold, hot, day, and night, and rain, wind, dew, and thunder.

It illustrates the movements and responses of the myriad things with [the images of] nature, feelings, form, and body, and walking, flying, grassy, and woody things.

It illustrates the ends and beginnings of heaven and earth with [the images of] cycles, epochs, revolutions, and generations, and years, months, days, and hours.

It illustrates the duties and accomplishments of the sages and worthies with [the images of] sages, emperors, kings, and hegemons, and the *Yi, Shu, Shih,* and *Ch'un-ch'iu.* Since the Ch'in and the Han, there has only been one person like this.[2]

Ts'ai mentioned only five of the six concepts, but the reason for his omission of the concept of *ling* will become apparent in the following discussion. According to Ts'ai, Shao's book concerns the realm of *hsien-t'ien,* the theoretical realm of the symbols, which represent the patterns of activity in the universe. Although Shao followed the principles contained in Fu Hsi's chart of the trigrams, (*kua*), rather than those in King Wen's chart, Shao's writings and his theories were his own. Shao's originality, his deviance from stan-

---

*These series are the reverse of Shao's ideas; the misstatement may be a copyist's error.
†See Fig. B1.
‡See Fig. B5.

dard interpretations, was the source of scholars' fears and doubts concerning his thought. Ts'ai pointed out that in Shao's thought the phenomenon of change embodied all the principles of nature, and this phenomenon was based on doubling. With his system of concepts, Shao showed how each level or aspect of phenomenal reality was represented by a corresponding pattern in the *hsien-t'ien* realm.

Each of Shao's six concepts is represented by a set of eight images. These images are presented in the chart entitled "Ching-shih t'ien-ti ssu-hsiang t'u" (Chart of the four images of heaven and earth that rule the world; see Fig. B5). In this chart, the images are arranged on three levels in six separate series. Each series represents a different aspect of the universe. Each series contains eight images, four each for the realms of heaven and earth.

The images are arranged systematically by kind of *ch'i*. For the realm of heaven, the order of enumeration is greater *yang*, greater *yin*, lesser *yang*, lesser *yin*; for the realm of earth, greater *jou* (soft), greater *kang* (hard), lesser *jou*, lesser *kang*.[3]* The relationship among different entities is thus clearly laid out. All images with greater *yin* *ch'i*, for example, are related because of their similar *ch'i*. In their categorizing function, the images correlate all things possessing the *ch'i* that a particular image signifies.

In the "Ching-shih t'ien-ti ssu-hsiang" chart, the order in which each series of images and its related concept is to be considered follows the sequence presented in Shao's text. Each concept builds on, or presupposes, the preceding concepts. For example, the first series (sun, moon, stars, zodiacal space, and water, fire, earth, stone) consists of the most fundamental images. These images are the source of some of the images on the other levels, and they are the models on which analogies are based. The concept that Shao applied to this first series is the forms and activities (*t'i* and *yung*) of heaven and earth.

The images in the next series (heat, cold, day, night, and rain, wind, dew, thunder) are associated with Shao's second concept,

---

*Shao is inconsistent in the enumeration orders for earth. Three series (water, fire, etc.; rain, wind, etc.; walking, flying, etc.) follow the order beginning with greater *jou*. The other three series reverse the order. The chart itself does not indicate the order, which is an issue only when these ideas are restated in prose form.

the changes and transformations of heaven and earth. Each entity (image) in the second series is related to a corresponding image in the first series on the basis of its category (*lei*) or kind of *ch'i*. The categories are named either in terms of *yin, yang, kang,* and *jou* or in terms of the first series of images. Thus heat, in the second series, is in the greater *yang* or sun category, and day is in the lesser *yang* or stars category. This reasoning applies to the remaining four series associated with the other four concepts.

Yin and *yang* and *kang* and *jou ch'i* thus constitute the basis on which relationships between (and among) things are formed. Shao called a state in which *ch'i* is balanced *chung-ho chih ch'i* (*ch'i* of centrality and harmony).[4] Through their fund of *ch'i* (often abbreviated to *yin* and *yang, kang* and *jou*), various things in different areas of experience are related. From the images themselves, however, these relationships may not be apparent without a knowledge of the kind of *ch'i*. For example, the categories rain and walking things are related because both are greater *jou ch'i*.

Moreover, the kind and amount of *ch'i* ascribed to something depends on context and is therefore constantly open to change. As mentioned earlier, what is *yang* in one context may be *yin* in another. *Yin* and *yang* do not exist alone or independently of each other.[5] For example,

The horse and ox are both in the *yin* category, but if one were to distinguish closely between them, then the horse is *yang* and the ox is *yin*.

Animals of the water are not different from animals of the land. Each [kind] has [those with] cold and hot natures. But if we compare them in general, then the land [animals] are *yin* in the midst of *yang* and the water [animals] are *yang* in the midst of *yin*.[6]

Multiple interdependent relationships exist because changes in one thing bring changes in related things. A thing may be *yang* in one context and *yin* in another because of the amount of *yin* or *yang ch'i* it possesses in comparison to something else and not because of the kind of *ch'i* within the object itself. These relationships are important in explaining change.

In Shao's view, the structure of the universe is orderly. Like other philosophers, Shao assumed that the universe can be divided into three major realms or powers (*san-ts'ai*), heaven, earth, and humans. He then incorporated this belief into his own binary system, emphasizing duality in structure, rather than triadic divisions, at each subsequent level of reality.

In Shao's thought, the most fundamental division of phenomenal reality is the two realms of heaven and earth. Here, the realm of earth includes all phenomena usually attributed to the two separate realms of earth and humans in the triadic division. At the next level of conceptualization, the realm of earth is split into the sphere of human beings and their activities and the sphere of all other kinds of living things, both plant and animal. A further division of the human world results in two more realms: political rulers and the classics. Although Shao did not explicitly discuss this conceptualization of reality, these levels are implicit in his six concepts and in Shao's discussion in the *Huang-chi ching-shih*, which takes up these levels in this order.

This view of reality stresses a binary structure. What is one entity on one level becomes a pair of entities on the next level. Each new entity splits further as the process continues on succeeding levels. The reverse is also true; a pair of entities on one level can become unified on the next level. That new entity can then join with another entity to form a single entity. In one direction, the process begins with *t'ai-chi*, which represents the whole of reality, or reality as one without distinctions. Distinctions are formed on the basis of this dialectical process. In the other direction, the process begins with the myriad things of the world. The structure of the dualities, moreover, is that of the hemilog, a duality with dependent and complementary parts.

Moreover, as noted earlier, all elements in the entire structure exist simultaneously. That is, *t'ai-chi*, as undifferentiated reality, exists at the same time as the myriad, distinct things of reality.[7] Thus, it is possible to focus on any level of the structure in order to examine the entities on that particular level. Since there is no implication that each level or each producer is destroyed as the next one is produced, there is no single temporal or spatial standpoint from which one must view the many aspects and levels of reality. Moreover, one can proceed either way in the process, toward synthesis or toward division.

To summarize, Shao Yung's six concepts explaining change assume an orderly and regular structure to the universe. Multiple levels or aspects of reality exist, and perceivable forms can be correlated on the basis of the subsensorial categories of *ch'i*. These categories are symbolized by the images of heaven and earth in the "Ching-shih t'ien-ti ssu-hsiang" chart. Since all events are part of numerous contexts, no single perspective is sufficient for understanding the phenomena of change. There are, however, certain principles embodied in the phenomena of change.

The Forms and Activities of Heaven and Earth

The first of Shao's six concepts is the forms and activities of heaven and earth (*t'ien-ti chih t'i-yung*). It is represented in the "Ching-shih t'ien-ti ssu-hsiang" chart (Fig. B5) by a set of eight images on the first row of the chart (sun, moon, stars, and zodiacal space, and water, fire, earth, and stone). This concept lays the foundation for the other concepts and addresses such basic concerns as identifying the most fundamental things in the universe, explaining the activities and change associated with these entities, and describing, in terms of pattern, the processes of change.

Shao's concept of the forms and activities of heaven and earth operates on two levels: the sensorial level of phenomena and the senses, and the subsensorial level of *ch'i*. That is, there are the forms and activities of phenomena, and there are the forms and activities of imperceivable *ch'i*. In order to explain change and movement in the phenomenal universe, Shao Yung used the categories and actions of *ch'i*.

Like other philosophers of the *Yi* learning, Shao Yung considered the phenomenal universe to have two primary realms: the realm of heaven or the sky and the realm of earth. "Unitary *ch'i* divides and becomes *yin* and *yang*. That half in which *yang* is more becomes heaven. That half in which *yin* is more becomes earth."[8] Shao viewed heaven and earth as the largest of all things. Moreover, as noted earlier, the characteristic of finiteness determined whether something was a thing. An infinite "object" was not a thing in the sense of *wu*.

Each of the two realms, heaven and earth, has its own particular entities and characteristics. These parallel each other; whatever pertains to heaven has its equivalent on earth, and vice versa. The closeness of the relationships between the entities of heaven and of earth is like "the mutual response between a thing and its shadow, or a sound and its echo."[9] Moreover, the dominant activities and things of these two great realms occur in patterns with two or four parts.

Among large things, there are none larger than heaven and earth, and yet they also are limited. *Yin* and *yang* exhaust the greatness of heaven. *Kang* and *jou* exhaust the greatness of earth.

When *yin* and *yang* are exhausted, the four seasons are completed. When *kang* and *jou* are exhausted, the four directions are completed. The four seasons and the four directions are called the greatest [things] of heaven and earth.[10]

Shao Po-wen's comment on this passage reads:

The *tao* that established heaven is called *yin* and *yang*. The *tao* that established earth is called *jou* and *kang*. The *tao* of heaven and earth is nothing more than [the activity of] *yin* and *yang*, and of *kang* and *jou*.

Yin and *yang* increase and decrease and thereby make the cold and the hot. With [one cycle of] one cold and one hot, the four seasons are completed.

Kang and *jou* alternate in succession and thereby there are levels and hills. With one level and one hill, the four directions are completed.

The four seasons are the *tao* of heaven. The four directions are the *li* of earth.[11]

According to Shao Po-wen, Shao Yung's view was that the interaction of *yin* and *yang* constitutes the *tao* or way of heaven and that their interaction is responsible for all activity in the realm of heaven. *Tao* is not a thing (*wu*) but a term for the interaction between *yin* and *yang*. The completion of one cycle of interaction results in the completion of the course of the four seasons, or one year. Thus the "*tao* of heaven" refers to the activity of *yin* and *yang* that results in the cyclical progression of the four seasons.

Tao in this sense differs from Shao's use of *tao* as an alternative term for *t'ai-chi*. Here its meaning is similar to the early Taoist use of the term as "way of the universe." This usage also has similarities to one modern use of the term "mind." Stressing that there is not an invisible essence called mind, Gilbert Ryle, for instance, argues that the concept of mind refers to the totality of all activities that are called mental. Mind is not a thing in addition to these activities.[12]

Parallel to the *yin* and *yang* of heaven are the *kang* and *jou* of earth. Like *yin* and *yang*, *kang* and *jou* constantly interact with one another. Their interaction is termed either *tao* or *li*. The activity of *kang* and *jou* results in the completion of the four directions, which together form earth. Thus, the activity of earth is the production of the four directions. This activity is analogous to the activity of heaven, which is the production of the year.[13]

The four directions and the four seasons were aspects of the world of phenomena. Shao explained them, however, by reference to the activity of subsensorial *ch'i* (in the forms of *yin* and *yang*, *kang* and *jou*):

Heaven emerges from movement [*tung*]. Earth emerges from stillness [*ching*]. When one movement and one stillness interact, the *tao* of heaven and earth is completed.

At the beginning of movement, *yang* arises. At the apogee of movement, *yin* arises. When one *yin* and one *yang* interact, the activity [*yung*] of heaven is completed.

At the beginning of stillness, *jou* arises. At the apogee of stillness, *kang* arises. When one *kang* and one *jou* interact, the activity of earth is completed.[14]

For Shao, *tung* (movement or motion) is the source of *yin* and *yang*, and *ching* (stillness or rest) the source of *kang* and *jou*. Movement is the origin of heaven and its primary activity, the four seasons, and stillness the origin of earth and its primary activity, the four directions.

In elaborating on these ideas, Shao Po-wen commented that the forms (*t'i*) of heaven and earth consist of the movement of heaven (*t'ien tung*) and the stillness of earth (*ti ching*).[15] In other words, *tung* and *ching*, the two great forces of *ch'i*, are the respective forms of heaven and earth. Their interaction is called *tao*. Thus, like *tao*, *t'i* and *yung* are not "things" that exist in addition to the six fundamental entities of *tung, ching, yin, yang, kang, jou*. Rather, *t'i* and *yung* describe these fundamental entities and their functioning. Shao Yung also drew a parallel between the basic forces and *wu*, things. That is, just as heaven and earth are the greatest of things, *yin* and *yang*, *kang* and *jou*, and *tung* and *ching* are the greatest forces.[16]

Shao then relates the concept of the forms and activities of heaven and earth to the world of phenomena.

> The greatness of *tung* is called greater *yang*. The smallness of *tung* is called lesser *yang*. The greatness of *ching* is called greater *yin*. The smallness of *ching* is called lesser *yin*.
>
> Greater *yang* is sun. Greater *yin* is moon. Lesser *yang* is stars. Lesser *yin* is zodiacal space. When sun, moon, stars, and zodiacal space intermingle, the forms of heaven are completed.
>
> Greater *jou* is water. Greater *kang* is fire. Lesser *jou* is earth. Lesser *kang* is stone. When water, fire, earth, and stone intermingle, the forms of earth are completed.[17]

Here, Shao Yung connected the phenomenal level of reality with the subsensorial level of *ch'i*. Up to this point, he was primarily considering entities on the level *ch'i*. As indicated above, these entities are important because they explain what happens on the phenomenal level. Now, in the world of experience, the primary entities or forms of heaven and earth—the sun, moon, stars, and zodiacal space, and water, fire, earth, and stone—and the changes and movements of these entities become the object of Shao's explanations. These forms or entities, moreover, are the perceivable representations of the eight forms of *ch'i*.

Shao's idea of the forms of heaven and earth thus has several referents.[18] On the subsensorial level, the forms of heaven and earth are forms of *ch'i*—*tung* and *ching*, *yin* and *yang*, and *kang* and *jou*, as well as the eight entities of greater and lesser *yin*, *yang*, *kang*, and *jou*. These entities, or "images," are categories of *ch'i*. On the sensorial level, the forms of heaven and earth are perceivable entities: the sun, moon, stars, and zodiacal space, and water, fire, earth, and stone. These entities are also called images. The images of heaven and earth correlate with the eight trigrams. The eight trigrams and the eight images are also the forms (*t'i*) of heaven and earth.[19]

The eight fundamental categories of things result from a process of movement called *sheng* (production). The emergence of *tung* and *ching* from *t'ai-chi* is the model for further production. Thus, one becomes two, and then each one of the two becomes a new "one," which further divides into two (see Fig. B4). This pattern is the doubling mentioned by Ts'ai Yüan-ting. In the realm of heaven *yin* is *ching* and *yang* is *tung*; in the realm of earth *jou* is *ching* and *kang* is *tung*. Yin, yang, kang, and *jou* then further divide to produce eight entities. Two charts in the *Huang-chi ching-shih* indicate this process of production (see Figs. B1 and B4). With eight entities, moreover, different sets of relationships become possible. For instance, one set consists of four pairs, or four hemilogs; another is composed of a set of eight entities.

The eight images were regarded as falling "naturally" into two groups of four: the four images of heaven—sun, moon, stars, and zodiacal space—and the four images (or "forms") of earth—water, fire, earth, and stone.[20] As illustrated in the "Ching-shih t'ien-ti ssu-hsiang" chart (Fig. B5), the four images of heaven and the four forms of earth are further associated with several other groups of four entities. Two such groupings are, for example, eyes, ears, nose, and mouth, and appearances, sounds, odors, and flavors (these eight entities form the series associated with Shao's concept of *ling*, the fourth of his six concepts.)

The relationship between the four images of heaven and the four forms of earth is based on the principle of correspondence between categories. Moreover, this correspondence is characterized by spontaneity (*tzu-jan*). As Shao Po-wen said, the fundamental assumption is that "when the images are complete above, the forms must respond below. This always is the pattern [*li*] of spontaneity."[21]

A particularly important consequence of Shao Yung's theoretical structure of the universe is the constancy and regularity achieved by the repetition of two and four. In emphasizing that heaven and earth are corresponding realms, Shao accepted the widespread beliefs that the categories within these realms also correspond with each other and that this relationship of correspondence serves as the model for analogous associations within the realm of earth alone.

As noted above, various terms were used to refer to the eight images, or the forms of heaven and earth. To emphasize the parallelism of the two realms, the four images of heaven were called *hsiang* (images), and the four images of earth were called *t'i* (forms) or *hsing* (forms). The four forms of earth (water, fire, earth, and stone) were viewed as the earthly counterparts of the four images of heaven (sun, moon, stars, and zodiacal space). Furthermore, the existence of the *hsiang* was considered necessarily to entail the existence of the *hsing* or *t'i*.[22]

The translation of *t'i* as forms may seem somewhat unusual. In Shao's thought, however, when the term refers to the images, either of earth alone or of both heaven and earth, it has the sense of forms (*hsing*). *T'i* does not have the meaning of essence or substance, or that out of which things are made. *Ch'i* has that role and forms the material substrate of the universe. *T'i* also does not mean spirit or vital force; no such entity distinct from *ch'i* exists. In other words, *t'i* does not refer to an invisible reality, such as an inner essence, in contrast to an outer application or external function.

T'i refers to entities that either have or can develop an appearance of some kind. That is, *t'i* refers to forms accessible or potentially accessible to at least one of the human senses. In general, a visual model of reality predominated. Thus, the eight images—the sun, moon, and so forth—are visible forms. Moreover, since *tung* and *ching*, and *yin*, *yang*, *kang*, and *jou* (which are also *t'i*) are divisions of *ch'i*, they have the potential to become perceptible "things."

T'i represents the static aspect of things, or the outer form. Shao Po-wen, for example, compared *t'i* to the physical aspects of humans and *yung* to the human spirit (*ching-shen*). Shao Po-wen's point was that the spirit "rules" the physical body and so is responsible for all actions.[23] Thus, in Shao's thought, *yung* represents the active and dynamic aspect of all things in the phenomenal world, and *t'i* the aspect of form, shape, or appearance. This view reverses that of many others, who compared *t'i* and *yung* to inner and outer, respectively, and so regarded the spirit as *t'i* and the body as *yung*.

The images of heaven and earth and their correlative entities appear in various *hsien-t'ien* charts. For example, the eight images correlate with the eight trigrams, which are arranged in the *hsien-t'ien* chart of Fu Hsi so that specific cardinal directions are assigned to each trigrams (see Fig. B2). Thus, in terms of its correlations, greater *yang* is sun in heaven and fire on earth, occupies the direction of due south in the chart, and is *ch'ien* of the eight trigrams. Sun and fire are two of the forms of heaven and earth. When the correlations are made with *kang* and *jou* of earth instead of *yin* and *yang* of heaven, then although the pairings of the four images of heaven and of earth remain the same (sun-fire, moon-water, stars-stone, zodiacal space—earth), different trigrams and directions are associated with them. For example, greater *jou* is moon in heaven and water on earth, occupies the direction of due north in the chart, and is *k'un* of the eight trigrams. In contrast, although greater *yin* is also moon in heaven and water on earth, it is *tui* of the eight trigrams, and its directional position is southeast (see Figs. B1, B2, and B5). The significance of these correlations is addressed below.

Shao's concept of the forms and activities (*t'i-yung*) of heaven and earth provided the foundation for explaining change in the world of human experience. This concept referred to the realms of both phenomenal experience and *ch'i*, and most of Shao's ideas were symbolized in the *hsien-t'ien* charts. The eight fundamental categories of *ch'i* are represented by the eight basic phenomenal forms of heaven and earth: the sun, moon, stars, and zodiacal space, and water, fire, earth, and stone. The change and activity associated with these eight entities result from the interactions of the corresponding kinds of *ch'i* at the subsensorial level of reality.

The eight images correspond in the realm of heaven to the categories of greater and lesser *yang* and *yin ch'i*, and in the realm of earth to greater and lesser *kang* and *jou ch'i*. The interactions of the eight categories are called the *yung* (activity) of heaven and earth. This mixing of *ch'i*, which occurs at the subsensorial level of reality, causes the activity and movements of things in the phenomenal world.

An essential part of Shao's concept of the forms and activities of heaven and earth is the notion of *sheng*, which involves several ideas about change. In one sense, *sheng* means to give birth to or to produce. This meaning of *sheng* emphasizes continuing linear development within a particular process.[24] From the viewpoint of whole cycles or processes, *sheng* refers to an oscillating or cyclical movement. Not only are these two meanings of *sheng* found in the *Lao Tzu* and the "Great Commentary," but the second meaning is associated with the ancient ideas concerning the opening and closing of the Sky Door and the actions of T'ai-yi (Supreme One, the chief diety), who came through this supposed pivot of the heavens.[25] Shao used the terms "opening" and "closing" to represent the idea of alternation.[26] In Shao's thinking, one can thus recognize the kind of thought structure and conceptual framework found in the *Lao Tzu* and the "Great Commentary."

Finally, the concept of change as *sheng* involves the development of different levels of organization of reality. The interaction of two aspects, such as *yin* and *yang*, or perhaps four aspects results in a new entity. That new entity exists on a different level from its parts. Change involves processes with a beginning and a completion. One aspect emerges to begin the process. A second aspect completes the process. Consequently, a new whole or entity is formed. For example, the four directions combine to make space and the four seasons combine to produce time.

The Changes and Transformations of Heaven and Earth

The concept of the changes and transformations (*pien-hua*) of heaven and earth is the second of Shao's six interrelated concepts. It is represented in the "Ching-shih t'ien-ti ssu-hsiang" chart (Fig. B5) by a set of eight images on the second row (heat, cold, day, night, and rain, wind, dew, thunder). This concept concerns calendrical and meteorological changes and emphasizes the distinction between the two realms of heaven and earth. Although the words *pien* (change) and *hua* (transform) can in some contexts be used interchangeably, Shao made a functional distinction between them. He applied these terms to different realms of the universe, to different forms of *ch'i*, and to different kinds of activities. He associated *pien* with the realm of heaven and *hua* with the realm of earth.[27]

With this concept as well as with the others, Shao addressed the important theoretical question, which was part of his idea of a moving observation point, of defining an event. In observing events in the phenomenal world, one can focus on different levels of reality, both in time and in space. The shape of events is different at each level. For example, on a social level, the seasons may be complete events. However, in terms of the solar cycle, they are aspects of a whole, the year. Thus there is no fixed reference point for making all determinations. As Shao said, "After the extreme of winter, there is the breathing out. After the extreme of summer, there is the breathing in. This is the breathing of one year of heaven and earth."[28] In speaking of processes within an event, Shao was saying that summer and winter follow each other to complete the whole event. Here, he was not speaking of summer and winter as whole events in themselves. Shao used this kind of perspective to explain many other events.

Shao discussed several kinds of change with his concept of the changes and transformations of heaven and earth, including the development of new entities and change in external form. The set of images corresponding to this concept was regarded as developing from the images that are the forms (*t'i*) of heaven and earth. In the realm of heaven, the interaction of the entities symbolizing change results in the production of a new level of organization of reality. In the realm of earth, the transformations are of another kind.

The images that symbolize the concept of the changes and transformations of heaven and earth represent *ch'i* categories. These categories are heat, cold, day, and night (*pien*) in the realm of heaven and rain, wind, dew, and thunder (*hua*) in the realm of earth. The alternation of heat and cold represent the passage of the four seasons, or one full year. Thus the entities of heat and cold also mean the year. Whereas heat and cold symbolize the passage of time in terms of temperature, day and night symbolize the passage of time in terms of lightness and darkness. To quote Shao Yung:

Sun becomes heat, moon becomes cold, stars become day, and zodiacal space becomes night. Heat, cold, day, and night intermingle, and the changes of heaven are completed.

Water becomes rain, fire becomes wind, earth becomes dew, and stone becomes thunder. Rain, wind, dew, and thunder intermingle, and the transformations of earth are completed.[29]

One category of things develops into another and two categories can correlate with each other because of *ch'i*. For example, in the realm of heaven, sun correlates with heat because both have/are the *ch'i* of greater *yang*, and moon correlates with cold because both have/are the *ch'i* of greater *yin*. In the realm of earth, water correlates with rain because both have/are the *ch'i* of greater *jou*, and fire correlates with wind because both have/are the *ch'i* of greater *kang*. As Shao Po-wen said: "Greater *yang* becomes sun, and heat also is the *ch'i* of utmost *yang*. Greater *yin* becomes moon, and cold also is the *ch'i* of utmost *yin*."[30] Shao Po-wen similarly elaborated the entire series, emphasizing that all these images are categories of *ch'i* and that this is the basis of the relationship of things and events. He also pointed out that the changes of heat, cold, day, and night result in the completion of a year. Thus he stressed Shao Yung's view that the changes of heaven are concerned with concepts of time, in particular the year as an event.[31]

In commenting on the meaning of Shao's ideas, Huang Chi said:

The essence [*ching*] of sun and fire becomes the heat of summer. The essence of moon and water becomes the cold of winter. The brilliance of the star bodies becomes the brightness of day. The darkness of the zodiacal space body becomes the darkness of night. *Ch'i* has no form and so changes.

When water-*ch'i* moistens and flows downward, it becomes rain. When fire-*ch'i* flares up and expands, it becomes wind. When earth-*ch'i* rises and moistens, it becomes dew. When stone-*ch'i* strikes within and attacks, it becomes thunder. Matter [*chih*] has form [*hsing*] and so is transformed.[32]

Although, as discussed previously, Shao conceived of *ch'i* as the material substrate of the universe, he spoke of the differences in the forms of *ch'i* of heaven and earth. That is, both heaven and earth are made of *ch'i*, but *ch'i* assumes different forms and is called by different names. However, since *ch'i* constantly rises and falls between these two realms, the differences are only in the forms, not in basic substance. The different forms are the phenomenal things of the universe.

In distinguishing between the two realms of heaven and earth, Shao described earth as having forms (*hsing*) or things (*wu*), whereas heaven simply has *ch'i*. In the realm of earth, the state of *ch'i* is often called *chih* (matter). *Ch'i* as matter has definite shapes and forms (*hsing*).[33] Shao's view thus was that, in the context of the concept of the changes of heaven and the transformations of earth, the *ch'i* of heaven is comparable to matter (*chih*) of earth.

Heaven takes *ch'i* as matter [*chih*], and it takes spirit as spirit. Earth takes matter as matter, and it takes *ch'i* as spirit.

Heaven can be fully exhausted with principle [*li*]. It cannot be fully exhausted with forms [*hsing*]. The methods of the *hun-t'ien* [spherical heavens cosmological school] can be fully exhausted with forms, but can heaven?[34]

Since the realms of heaven and earth are characterized by different forms or states of *ch'i*, different terms indicate the different kinds of activities in these realms. To distinguish between the two kinds of changes, Shao said, "*Ch'i* changes [*pien*], and forms [*hsing*] are transformed [*hua*]. Forms can be split, but spirit cannot be split."[35]

Clearly the meanings of *pien* and *hua* differ slightly. *Pien* was applied to the meteorological and calendrical changes characteristic of the year, whereas *hua* was applied to atmospheric phenomena. The former concerns concepts of time; the latter does not. Another important difference is that the change (*pien*) images of heaven (heat, cold, day, and night) have no tangible form, whereas the transformation (*hua*) images of earth (rain, wind, dew, and thunder) do, although not necessarily a visual form. However, the earth images do not have the same order of predictability as the heavenly images. The pattern of *hua* is not as regular as the pattern of *pien*.

As a result of the activities of the forms (or images) of heaven, the changes of heaven lead to the development of two new entities, the year and the cycle of day and night. The year and the diurnal cycle exist on a level of reality more abstract than that of the forms of heaven (sun, moon, stars, and zodiacal space) and in a different way from various *ch'i* of heaven (greater *yang* and *yin* and lesser *yang* and *yin*). The changes of heaven exist on the level of time. As Shao said, "Heaven moves and so makes day and night. The sun moves and so makes heat and cold [i.e., a year]."[36]

In contrast, the transformations of the realm of earth involve physical alterations. Rain, wind, dew, and thunder are not completely new kinds of entities that exist in a different way from the forms of earth from which they develop. The transformations of earth, like the forms of earth, are concepts of space, not time.

In saying that the *ch'i* of heaven changes and the forms of earth are transformed, Shao was reiterating the idea that the constant intertwining of *yin* and *yang* and *kang* and *jou ch'i* on the subsensorial level is manifested as sensorial phenomena. On the phenomenal level, the visible actions of the entities of the sky—the sun, moon,

112 · *A Focus on Cosmology*

stars, and zodiacal space—were understood as the result of the mixing of *ch'i* on the subsensorial level. The cycle of day and night and the year (symbolized by heat and cold) emerge from the celestial cycle. Thus the activities of the celestial bodies give rise to temporal phenomena symbolized by the images of heat, cold, day, and night. Similarly, in the realm of earth, the mixing of water, fire, earth, and stone *ch'i* results in the transformations of earth—the atmospheric phenomena of rain, wind, dew, and thunder.

Shao Yung used the arithmetic processes of multiplication, addition, and subtraction to symbolize the mixing and intertwining of *yin* and *yang ch'i* and *jou* (soft) and *kang* (hard) forms (*hsing*). He distinguished between form numbers and activity numbers and assigned the former to the realm of earth and the latter to the realm of heaven. "What are the form numbers? They are [those of] living things. What are the activity numbers? They are [those of the] cyclical movements. Cyclical movements belong to heaven. Living things belong to earth." [37]

He correlated the number ten with the four images of greater and lesser *yang* and *kang*, and twelve with the four images of greater and lesser *yin* and *jou*. Ten and twelve were the form numbers (*t'i-shu*) of the eight images.

The form number of greater *yang* is ten. The form number of greater *yin* is twelve.

The form number of lesser *yang* is ten. The form number of lesser *yin* is twelve.

The form number of lesser *kang* is ten. The form number of lesser *jou* is twelve.

The form number of greater *kang* is ten. The form number of greater *jou* is twelve.[38]

In further discussion, Shao said that the form number of the set of *yang* and *kang* images is 160 (10 + 10 + 10 + 10 = 40; 40 × 4 = 160), and the form number of the set of *yin* and *jou* images is 192 (12 + 12 + 12 + 12 = 48; 48 × 4 = 192). These two sets of images also have activity numbers (*yung-shu*), respectively 112 (160 − 48 = 112) and 152 (192 − 40 = 152).[39]

When the activity number of the *yang* and *kang* set of images mixes with the activity number of the *yin* and *jou* set of images, the result or product is the change number (*pien-shu*) of sun, moon, stars, and zodiacal space. Moreover, when the activity number of the *yin* and *jou* set of images mixes with the activity number of the *yang* and *kang* set of images, the result is the transformation number (*hua-shu*) of water, fire, earth, and stone. In other words, the product of the activity numbers, 17,024 (112 × 152), is both the change number of the four images of heaven and the transformation number of the four images of earth.[40]

The change number is also the *tung-shu* (the moving things number; i.e., the number for animals); the transformation number is also the *chih-shu* (the stationary things number; i.e., the number for plants). The categories moving things and stationary things correlate respectively with greater *kang* and *jou* and with lesser *kang* and *jou*. They are categories of the myriad things (discussed in the next section). Their product is 289,816,576 (17,024^2), which, according to Shao Yung, is the total number of moving and stationary things. Shao Po-wen further pointed out that this number is what the *Yi-ching* calls the number of the myriad things.[41]

For Shao Yung, numbers provided a way of expressing the idea of the constant processes of change that produce the myriad things of the world. Numbers are symbols that represent aspects of the universe in certain ways. Arithmetic manipulation, in particular, symbolizes the interaction of the different kinds of *ch'i* that results in various things in the universe. The kinds of manipulation possible with numbers reflect the various kinds of change possible in reality. Thus, numbers are an alternative to other, non-numerical concepts that are used to explain change, such as the rising and falling or expanding and contracting of *yin* and *yang ch'i*.[42] The lines and hexagrams of the *Yi-ching* are, moreover, graphic symbols of the numbers.

Shao realized, however, that numbers cannot answer the question why things are as they are. "The images and numbers of heaven can be obtained and extrapolated. But if it's a matter of understanding the spirit of heaven, then it cannot be estimated."[43]

To summarize, the concept of the changes and transformations of heaven and earth was intended to explain meterological and calendrical changes. The changes of heaven (heat, cold, day, and night) and the transformations of earth (rain, wind, dew, and thunder) are the phenomenal result of the subsensorial intermingling of the eight basic kinds of *ch'i*. The changes of heaven lead to the development of new entities related to time, namely, the year and the cycle of day and night. The transformations of earth, however, involve changes only in form.

Phenomenal experience results from the activity of *ch'i*. *Ch'i* is perceivable only in its coalesced states, which are divided into eight basic categories. The forms (*t'i*) of heaven and earth—sun, moon, stars, zodiacal space, and water, fire, earth, stone—and the changes and transformations (*pien-hua*) of heaven and earth are symbols of the eight categories of imperceivable *ch'i*. Their interactions can be represented by numbers and by the lines of the hexagrams. In addition to the various charts, the hexagrams and the numbers associated with them are graphic symbols that represent the patterns of change and transformation in the universe.[44]

The Movements and Responses of the Myriad Things

The third of Shao's interrelated concepts is concerned with explaining the behavior of the myriad things in this world. Basing his ideas in great part on views of resonance that had developed in the Han dynasty with the *Yi* learning, Shao called this concept the "movements and responses of the myriad things" (*wan-wu chih kan-ying*).[45] Scholars have traditionally referred to the pattern of activity with which Shao was concerned here as "resonance." However, for reasons that will become apparent in the following discussion, this term does not express Shao's idea fully.

This concept is symbolized by eight images in the third row in the "Ching-shih t'ien-ti ssu-hsiang" chart (see Fig. B5). The images on this level belong to the realm of earth alone and refer specifically to the myriad things (*wan-wu*) of the world. Shao was concerned here with explaining change in the behavior or activities of things. Although humans are usually included as one of the myriad things, this concept does not emphasize human interaction with the world. To a great extent, but not exclusively, this concept deals with other kinds of living things. Shao employed the concept of *ling*, or consciousness, to treat human epistemological activity (see Chapter 6).

With this third concept, the pattern of Shao Yung's thinking—

his idea of a moving observation point and his constant use of both analytic and synthetic approaches, with the latter used almost as a form of proof of the former—becomes more apparent. The parallelism between the realms of heaven and earth that is so evident with the first two concepts is not an element here. Rather, the distinction is between a set of four aspects of human beings and other living things—nature, feelings, form, and body—and a set of four characteristics that can be used to categorize living things—walking, flying, being grassy, and being woody.[46]

These eight images are categories of *ch'i* and so correlate with the images on the first two levels of the chart. The first set of images is associated with those of the realm of heaven and the second with those of the realm of earth. Thus, for example, nature (*hsing*) is in the same category as heat and sun, and walking things are in the same category as rain and water. In all cases, the reason for the particular correlation of categories is that things in those categories have/are the same kind of *ch'i*. The category of walking things, for example, is greater *jou ch'i*, and that of nature is greater *yang ch'i*.

In Shao's view, with one cycle of the intermingling of the eight *ch'i* categories of change and transformation, the realms of heaven and earth mix and myriad things are produced.[47] Shao Yung presented a series of correlations utilizing the terms "response" (*ying*) and "transformation" (*hua*). These terms derive, respectively, from the concepts of the movements and responses of the myriad things and the changes and transformations of heaven and earth.[48] The correlated entities consist of the four aspects of living things (nature, feelings, form, and body), the four categories of living things (walking, flying, grassy, and woody things), and the four transformations of earth (rain, wind, dew, and thunder). Since these terms and many of their relationships were an accepted part of the *Yi* learning, neither here nor in any other place did Shao explain what he meant by these terms. In commenting on the significance of this series of correlations, Shao Po-wen said, "That whereby the living things of heaven and earth have ten thousand variations and differences lies in the intertwining and alternation of movements and responses. The intertwining and alternation of movements and responses are called changes and transformations."[49]

In this indirect way Shao Po-wen stated the question that Shao

Yung was addressing. That is, given all the variations among things in the world, how does one account for their formation? Shao Yung answered that the variation results from the workings of movement and response. Moreover, this activity is virtually equivalent in pattern to the activity of change and transformation. A significant difference is that the concept of movement and response applies to the things on this earth, whereas the concept of change and transformation applies to the spheres of heaven and earth. Both, however, are based on the assumption of the activity of *ch'i* structured by the categories of the eight images.

One important implication of this position is that the separation of reality as a whole (*ch'i*) into a multitude of separate things does not depend on perception. The different categories (represented by the images) are there regardless of whether anyone experiences them. The categories by which humans perceive things are part of the reality that is being perceived and are not a product of the perceiver. In the very process of perception, the perceiver does not shape the reality perceived.[50] Thus, change and transformation occur, and movement and response occur, and differences among things are produced—all in a somewhat predictable fashion. This was not Shao's entire position, however, and he had more to say about the role of human consciousness and perception in shaping reality (see chapter 6).

In using the concept of the movements and responses of the myriad things to explain their behavior, Shao was implicitly dealing with both ontology and understanding or epistemology. Shao began with the assumption that all things move, change, and behave in various ways; the question was how to account for this phenomenon.

His answer was that a thing acts as it does because it is completing an event or entity—with other things of the same kind of *ch'i*. A particular thing is associated with other things in the same *ch'i* category. To understand the activities of a particular thing, one must see that thing as an aspect of a larger whole and its behavior in terms of that whole. Shao expressed this idea in the following statements.

When *yang* obtains *yin*, there is birth. When *yin* obtains *yang*, there is completion.

Yang cannot stand alone. It must obtain *yin* and only then can it stand. Therefore *yang* regards *yin* as the basis. *Yin* cannot be seen by itself. It must wait for *yang* and only then can it be seen. Therefore *yin* regards *yang* as the leader. *Yang* controls the beginning of a thing and enjoys its completion. *Yin* fulfills its pattern and ends its labors.

The original unity is *ch'i*. When something emerges, then it becomes *yang*. When it disperses, it becomes *yin*. Thus two are one and that is all. Six are three and that is all. Eight are four and that is all. Thus, one may speak of heaven and not speak of earth. One may speak of the ruler and not speak of the minister. One may speak of the father and not speak of the son. One may speak of the husband and not speak of the wife.

And yet, when heaven obtains earth, the myriad things are born. When the ruler obtains the minister, the myriad transformations are carried out. When the father obtains the son and the husband obtains the wife, the way of the family is completed. Therefore, when there is one, then there are two. When there are two, then there are four. When there are three, then there are six. When there are four, then there are eight.

When one is born, one's nature is of heaven. When one is completed, one's form is of earth. Birth and completion, completion and birth—this is the *tao* of change.[51]

Shao thus understood the behavior of two things in terms of the new entity that emerges from the interaction of the two things. The new entity exists on a different level of reality from the two things. What Shao calls movement and response does not mean action and reaction, or stimulus and response, in the sense of twentieth-century psychology. Rather, it means movement and completion. Shao's concept of movement and response refers to behavior with an emerging aspect and a completing aspect, that which begins and that which completes. A completed entity or event exists in a different way from those things that began and completed it. It becomes the whole, and they are the aspects. In this view, all events are part of some pattern, and in effect the end and beginning are produced together.[52]

This conception of behavior is applicable in many contexts. To use an example of Shao's, a husband and wife and a father and son interact—literally, move and respond—and so form a family. The family is a new whole, which exists on a different level from its members. Its members are aspects of the whole. Before their interaction, no such entity as the family existed, and the individual people were the whole entities. Another example is a ritual ceremony. The leader moves or acts, and the followers then respond. Their behavior is not a reaction to that of the leader, but rather a completion of his; both together constitute the ceremony. The ceremony is a different entity from the behavioral acts of the participants. It is a whole, and their acts are aspects of it. Further examples of this pattern of birth and completion, or the idea that the end is produced with the beginning, appear in Shao Yung's poetry.[53]

This conception of behavior is what Shao means when he says two, then one, or one, then two. A husband and a wife, then a family. A family, then a husband and a wife. The two and the one exist in different senses, or on different levels of reality, simultaneously, just as *yin* and *yang*, the four images, and the eight trigrams exist at the same time as *ta'i-chi*.

Not only did Shao understand the concept of the movements and responses of the myriad things as the completion of other things, but he also made it clear that things "respond according to the category." As he said, "Mucus from the nose—the eye sees it. Words from the mouth—the ears hear them. Things respond according to the category."[54] Each thing is/has a particular type of *ch'i* that makes it what it is. The eight kinds of *ch'i* are organized into categories (*lei*) symbolized by the images. On the basis of their *ch'i*, all things belong to a category. All things in the universe are associated with a particular image. Movement and response is possible because the images on all levels of reality correlate with each other. For this reason, the eye cannot see words, nor can the ear hear mucus.

Moreover, in order for a thing in one category in the realm of earth to respond to a thing in another category in the realm of heaven, the categories have to correlate appropriately. Examples of appropriate correlations are greater *kang* with greater *yang*, and lesser *jou* with lesser *yin*. Thus Shao Po-wen commented, "*Ch'i* that moves is like this. Everything can be inferred according to the category."[55] Shao Yung said:

Yang obtains *yin* and so makes rain. *Yin* obtains *yang* and so makes wind. *Kang* obtains *jou* and so makes clouds. *Jou* obtains *kang* and so makes thunder. If there is no *yin*, then there cannot be rain. If there is no *yang*, then there cannot be thunder.

Rain is *jou* and belongs to *yin*. *Yin* cannot stand alone. Therefore it obtains *yang* and only then arises. Thunder is *kang* and belongs to forms [*t'i*]. Forms cannot function by themselves. They must wait for *yang*, and only then can they act.[56]

Shao Yung next set forth his concept of the changes and responses of the myriad things.

Heat changes the nature of things, cold changes the feelings of things, day changes the forms of things, and night changes the bodies of things. Nature, feelings, forms, and bodies intermingle, and the movements of moving and stationary things are exhausted.

Rain transforms the walking types of things, wind transforms the flying types of things, dew transforms the grassy types of things, and thunder transforms the woody types of things. Walking, flying, grassy, and woody types intermingle, and the responses of moving and stationary things are exhausted.[57]

Shao is saying here that the natures of things consist of *yang ch'i*, and so they are what heat (also *yang ch'i*) changes. The feelings of things consist of *yin ch'i*, and so they are what cold (also *yin ch'i*) changes, and so forth.[58] Heat and cold, and all the other images, are symbolic terms for *yang* and *yin* and *kang* and *jou*. Thus Shao's statement that things "respond according to the category" is an explanation (of behavior) on the level of *ch'i*. This view is based on the belief, explicitly stated by Huang Chi, that the activity of *ch'i* on the subsensorial level is responsible for experiences on the phenomenal level.[59] Moreover, this activity occurs according to the particular patterns of interaction of the eight images of the realms of heaven and earth.

To elaborate further, Shao's view is that things subsumed in the categories (images) on the second row of the chart change (or transform) things in the categories on the third row. Such activity is possible because of their responses at the level of *ch'i*. Although the term used for the behavior of things categorized under the third-row images is literally "response," their behavior is actually a completion of an event or entity started by things belonging to the second-row images. This phenomenon is possible because things on both levels belong to the same *ch'i* category. Thus it is not that the images change or transform other images, but that the kind of *ch'i* symbolized by one image interacts with an appropriate kind of *ch'i* symbolized by another image. As Shao Po-wen explained, "The nature of a thing belongs to *yang*. Therefore it is what heat changes. The feelings of a thing belong to *yin*. Therefore they are what cold changes." [60] Heat and natures both belong to the *yang* category, and cold and feelings to the *yin* category.

Shao implicitly assumed that correspondence between categories is impossible unless the same number of categories exists in each realm. The division of the universe into numerically equal segments made correspondence possible. That the world possesses a regularity that can be represented by numbers was thus extremely important. Shao emphasized the particular division two and four, but other philosophers in the *Yi* tradition emphasized different numerical divisions. Yang Hsiung of the Han dynasty, for instance, based his thought on a ternary division.

Shao Yung gave numerous examples of the behavior of specific types of plants and animals based on the categories to which they belonged. For Shao, the actions of a thing can be explained by indicating its *ch'i* category.

Trees are the children of stars. Therefore the fruits of trees resemble stars.

Leaves are *yin*. Blossoms and fruits are *yang*. Branches and leaves are soft and yielding, whereas the roots and trunk are hard and firm.

The fur of the tiger and leopard is like grass. The feathers of the eagle and sparrow hawk are like wood.

The branches and trunk of a tree are what earth and stone have completed. Therefore they do not change. The leaves and blossoms are what water and fire have completed. Therefore they change.

Fish are the family of water, and insects are the family of wind.

The tides of the sea are the breathing of the earth. The reason that they respond to the moon is that they follow their category.[61]

From these few passages, it is apparent that Shao used the images as categories of *ch'i*, that is, *yin*, *yang*, *kang*, and *jou*. Moreover, these categories in turn often implied the characteristics of movement and stillness (*tung* and *ching*). As Shao said, "That which obtains the *ch'i* of heaven is movement. That which obtains the *ch'i* of earth is stillness."⁶² Shao's frequent use of metaphor should not obscure the highly systematic nature of his thought. Instead of lesser *yang*, Shao said stars, and instead of lesser *kang*, trees. Whatever his terminology, however, on the ontological level explaining behavior was a matter of knowing the categories.

Shao also explained the movements and responses of the myriad things in terms of understanding the behavior of a thing as an aspect of a larger whole. From the viewpoint of the new entity (or whole), when something changes (*pien*), something else responds (*ying*). Again, this explanation does not entail the idea of a simple action and reaction or stimulus and response sequence. Instead, the idea was one of fulfilling a whole or completing a cycle. "Heaven changes [*pien*] the seasons, and earth fulfills [*ying*] things. When it is a matter of the seasons, then *yin* changes and *yang* fulfills. When it is a matter of things, then *yang* changes and *yin* fulfills. Therefore the seasons can be known beforehand, and things must follow and be completed. Thus when *yang* welcomes, *yin* follows, and when *yin* meets, *yang* follows."⁶³

The idea is that just as the four seasons succeed each other, living things follow a four-stage course of development from birth to death. Thus there are different levels of "wholes." The four seasons complete the whole that is the year, and the four stages of the growth cycle complete the whole that is an organism. There is also the whole of heaven and earth, which is completed by the interaction between the course of a year and the activity of living things. The action of one aspect is called change (*pien*) and that of the other is called response (*ying*), but from a broader viewpoint what actually happens is the completion of an event or entity. Thus Shao went on to say:

When there is change, then there must be response. Thus that which changes on the inside responds on the outside. That which changes on the outside responds on the inside. That which changes below responds above. That which changes above responds below. Heaven changes and the sun responds. Therefore that which changes follows heaven and that which responds imitates the sun.

Therefore the sun is regulated by the stars. [The phases of] the moon are calculated according to the zodiacal space. Water emerges from earth. Fire is hidden away in stone. Those things that fly perch in trees. Those things that walk stay close to the grass. The mutual association between the heart and lungs and the mutual connection between the liver and gall do not have any other *tao* of change and response.[64]

Here Shao was talking about behavior based on the mutual association between things. From a limited viewpoint, one may believe that the sun gives off more heat in the summer than in the winter. However, from a broader viewpoint, as heaven changes the seasons from one to the next, the sun accordingly gives off more or less heat. Thus that which initiates change is comparable to heaven, and that which completes it is comparable to the sun.

Commenting further on the relationship between change (or movement) and response, Shao Yung said, "That which is based in heaven loves the higher. That which is based in earth loves the lower. Therefore, the relation between change and response is constant oppositions."[65]

Shao Po-wen elaborated on this concept in the following comments:

To move [*kan*] means to sing [*ch'ang*]. *Yang* sings with *yin*.... To respond [*ying*] means to harmonize with [*ho*]. *Yin* harmonizes with *yang*....

Nature, feelings, form, and body have their basis in heaven. Walking, flying, grassy, and woody things have their basis in earth. What is based in heaven has [the potential for] movement in itself. What is based in earth has [the potential for] response in itself. One movement [*kan*] and one response [*ying*] is the *tao* of heaven and earth and the *li* [*pattern*] of the myriad things.[66]

"To sing" and "to harmonize with" may also be translated "to lead" and "to follow". Regardless of which translation is used, Shao Po-wen was emphasizing the idea that in behavior a movement or a change is followed by an appropriate response. Moreover, these two aspects are analogous to a cycle of *yin* and *yang*. As stated in the "Great Commentary," the cycle of one *yin* and one *yang* is called the *tao*.[67] Here *tao* and *li* are virtually equivalent concepts, except that *tao* is applied to heaven and earth and *li* to the myriad things.

To sum up, Shao's concept of the movements and responses of the myriad things is intended to explain the behavior of things according to two different approaches. From the level of reality of *ch'i*, the changes and responses of things on the phenomenal level result from the activity of *ch'i* on the subsensorial level. Things interact with other things according to their category of *ch'i*, and these categories are represented by the images.

From the viewpoint of things as aspects of larger wholes, the concept of movement and response is not a matter of action and reaction, but of the beginning and completion of an event. What moves and what completes exist on one level of reality, whereas the larger entity of which they are aspects exists on another level of reality (for example, the four seasons and the year).

Thus, Shao's concept of movement and response involves the idea of the completion of a cycle or of some larger entity. Moreover, what is known in phenomenal experience has an ontological basis in *ch'i*. The idea of movement and response is comparable to the pattern of the increasing and decreasing of *yin* and *yang*, and *kang* and *jou*. It is symbolized by the images in the charts as well as by the trigrams and hexagrams. Indeed, this concept has as its referent not only the world of immediate experience, but also the system of the hexagrams, themselves symbols of situations in the phenomenal world.

6

Concepts of Change: Human Beings and the Universe

> *People all know that Chung-ni [Confucius] is Chung-ni but they do not know why Chung-ni is Chung-ni. If they do not wish to know why Chung-ni is Chung-ni, then the matter is finished. If they must know why Chung-ni is Chung-ni, then aside from heaven and earth, what else is to be said?*
> —Shao Yung[1]

Human Consciousness

The fourth concept in Shao Yung's system of interrelated concepts is *ling*, or, *ling yü wan-wu*. In general terms, *ling* suggests the notion of consciousness in the sense of awareness and recognition of the surrounding world. *Ling yü wan-wu* is a more explicit term and may be translated as "consciousness" or "awareness of the myriad things." The concept of *ling yü wan-wu* is comparable to the concept of the movements and responses (*kan-ying*) of the myriad things. The concept of *ling*, however, applies primarily to human epistemological activity, whereas *kan-ying* applies to all living things and to all kinds of behavior. The fact that in the *Huang-chi ching-shih* Shao discusses the concept of *ling* immediately after *kan-ying* makes their closeness apparent. Considering the development of Shao's thought, one might even argue that *ling* is a subdivision of *kan-ying*. That question, however, is not one that needs to be settled here.

The concept of *ling* is represented by eight images located on the first row of the "Ching-shih t'ien-ti ssu-hsiang" chart and interspersed between the primary images of heaven and earth (see Fig. B5). Four images are associated with heaven (eyes, ears, nose, and mouth) and four with earth (appearance, sound, odor, and flavor).² This concept has much in common with certain ideas of Chih Yi of the T'ien-t'ai school of Buddhism on *chih-kuan* (cessation and contemplation).³

The concept of *ling* represents a different aspect of Shao's thought from those discussed above, which concern chiefly ontological and cosmological questions. Although embracing similar questions, the concept of *ling* introduces the area of epistemological problems. In terms of the structure of Shao's discussion in the *Huang-chi ching-shih*, the concept of *ling* apparently represents the point at which Shao said, in effect, This is what we know, but how do we know it? The problem of explaining human consciousness of and knowledge of the world thus became a critical issue for Shao. As the following discussion indicates, by linking this epistemological problem with problems concerning the structure of reality, Shao raised new questions about the ontological structure of the universe.

Of critical importance in this aspect of Shao's thought is the duality not of heaven and earth but of human beings and the phenomenal world. In terms of the system of correlations, what pertains to human beings is associated with heaven and what pertains to the phenomenal world with earth. Moreover, although Shao's ideas on consciousness went beyond his numerical thought, these ideas did require the assumptions about numerical relationships that Shao made, because of the importance of the idea that things correlate with each other according to their categories.

Shao Yung began the presentation of his concept of consciousness with two series of correlations involving the new set of images. The first series matches the four aspects of living things (nature, feelings, form, and body) and the four kinds of living things (walking, flying, grassy, and woody things) with the four sensory characteristics (appearance, sound, odor, and flavor). In the second series, the sense organs (ears, eyes, mouth, and nose) are substituted for the four sensory characteristics.

Walking things of nature complete appearances. Walking things of feelings complete sounds. Walking things of forms complete odors. Walking things of body complete flavors.

Flying things of nature complete appearances. Flying things of feelings complete sounds. Flying things of forms complete odors. Flying things of body complete flavors.

Grassy things of nature complete appearances. Grassy things of feelings complete sounds. Grassy things of forms complete odors. Grassy things of body complete flavors.

Woody things of nature complete appearances. Woody things of feelings complete sounds. Woody things of forms complete odors. Woody things of body complete flavors.

The nature of walking things completes ears. The nature of flying things completes eyes. The nature of grassy things completes mouths. The nature of woody things completes noses.

The feelings of walking things complete ears. The feelings of flying things complete eyes. The feelings of grassy things complete mouths. The feelings of woody things complete noses.

The forms of walking things complete ears. The forms of flying things complete eyes. The forms of grassy things complete mouths. The forms of woody things complete noses.

The body of walking things completes ears. The body of flying things completes eyes. The body of grassy things completes mouths. The body of woody things completes noses.[4]

Shao Po-wen offered the following explanation for these correlations. "Things have sound, appearance, odor, and flavor. Humans have ears, eyes, mouths, and noses. This [passage] further says that humans and things have that which fit [*ho*]. The living things of heaven and earth all have that which fit according to their category [*lei*]."[5]*

Introduced here is the important concept of harmonious fit (*ho*). Although a basic assumption in Shao's thought, Shao seldom used this term. In Shao's view, there is a harmonious fit between the ways that humans (and animals) experience the world and that which they experience. Phenomenal things potentially have four kinds of characteristics—sound, appearance, odor, and flavor. In humans, each sense has its own sensory channel. Through that channel one perceives objects with the characteristic appropriate for that

---

*The order of these eight images varies slightly in different passages, but no new pairings are implied. Eyes, ears, nose, and mouth correlate with appearance, sounds, odors, and flavors, respectively.

channel. Thus, the eye has the capability of seeing and some things have a visual aspect to them. The ear has the capability of hearing and other things have an auditory aspect to them. Moreover, since all these images are categories of *ch'i*, the fit of things is ultimately based on the categories that structure the world.

In Shao's thought, the concept of *ho* is applicable both to reality as perceived through the senses, such as odors and sounds, and to reality on a level of organization not accessible to the unaided human senses. In eleventh-century China, this second kind of reality was undifferentiated *ch'i*. In the twentieth-century, however, it would be something like atoms, molecules, or sound waves. Thus, when Huang Chi said that "*ch'i* has no form [*hsing*]," he was not claiming that *ch'i* is not real.[6] Rather, form is a characteristic that applies to things of the perceived world. In the view of Shao Yung and his contemporaries, *ch'i* has a material reality and exists independently of any perceiver. In contrast to the application of *ho* to the level of odors, sights, sounds, and flavors (phenomena that require human involvement), the concept of *ho* applied to *ch'i* does not involve human awareness or consciousness.

Shao expressed his ideas about harmonious fit, on the level of *ch'i*, in the charts by the arrangements of the images and the eight trigrams. As discussed above, each of the eight trigrams represents a different kind of *ch'i*. Thus, *ch'ien* stands for greater *yang*, *tui* for greater *yin*, *li* for lesser *yang*, *chen* for lesser *yin*, *sun* for lesser *kang*, *k'an* for lesser *jou*, *ken* for greater *kang*, and *k'un* for greater *jou*. The images of eye, ear, nose, mouth, appearance, sound, odor, and flavor also are specific kinds of *ch'i* (respectively, those of the trigrams given in the above order; see Fig. B5). Thus, for example, eyes are greater *yang* or *ch'ien*, ears are greater *yin* or *tui*, and so on. As a result of the movement of *ch'i* and the response of things according to their *ch'i* categories, there was a "natural" fit between the eye and appearances, the ear and sounds, the nose and odors, and the mouth and flavors. Thus, Wang Chih explained:

The ear belongs to [the category of the trigram] *tui* [greater *yin ch'i*], *tui* and *k'an* [lesser *jou ch'i*] intermingle, and *k'an* rules sound [*jou ch'i*].

The eye belongs to *ch'ien*. *Ch'ien* and *sun* intermingle, and *sun* rules appearances.

The mouth belongs to *chen*. *Chen* and *k'un* intermingle, and *k'un* rules flavors.

The nose belongs to *li*. *Li* and *ken* intermingle, and *ken* rules odors.[7]

Thus, the intermingling of kinds of *ch'i* results in distinct things. As discussed in Chapter 5, Shao expressed this intermingling by the concepts of the changes and transformations of heaven and earth and of the movements and responses of the myriad things. The eight kinds of *ch'i* are symbolized by the eight trigrams and by the images that constitute the "Ching-shih t'ien-ti ssu-hsiang" chart. At the level of *ch'i*, the subphenomenal level, there is no human or animal involvement. There is no need for a perceiver. Indeed, there is nothing that sense perception can perceive. The characteristics and activities of *ch'i* are knowable because human consciousness can abstract the patterns. These patterns are then symbolized by the trigrams and the images, along with the rules for their interactions. Thus, the trigrams and the images symbolize that which is not accessible to the senses. They are symbols for a kind of reality outside human sense experience, but still an aspect of that experienced reality.

Not only does the concept of harmonious fit apply to material reality (*ch'i*), which exists independently of human experience, it also applies to that social reality or conceptual reality that is dependent on human beings or that human beings make. In order to discuss the role of human consciousness in the formation of phenomenal reality, Shao introduced the crucial idea of *shan*. In the passages by Shao Yung quoted above, *shan* has the unusual meaning of to complete, to perfect, or to finish. In similar contexts in other passages, both Shao Yung and Shao Po-wen substituted the world *pei* (to complete).[8]

With the concept of *shan*, originally derived from Buddhism, Shao added a significant dimension to his theory of reality.[9] To Shao, the activity of the eye completes the appearance of an object, the activity of the ear completes the sound, and so on. In other words, nothing has an appearance unless someone sees it, and nothing makes a sound unless someone hears it. This is not to say, however, that the object is not there or that sound waves are not produced. Rather, Shao was saying that the concept of sound implies the concept of hearing, and the concept of flavor necessitates the concept of tasting. Moreover, sound and hearing, flavor and tasting, and so on exist in a different way from *ch'i*. It is a question of the kind of reality. This view bears a remarkable resemblance to certain Buddhist ideas and to certain strains in modern thought, such as the views of William James and the position of idealism.[10]

If seeing completes the appearance of something and hearing completes the sound, then the existence of appearance, sound, flavor, and odor depends on humans (and other living things perhaps). This kind of reality is not independent of someone's experience; it absolutely requires a perceiver. This kind of reality entails, and is part of, a relationship between the perceiving subject and itself, the perceived object. Thus, those things that are called appearance, sound, flavor, or odor are concepts on the level of human experience. They have a social and conceptual reality, which is different from a material or physical reality.

Moreover, human (and perhaps animal) consciousness functions on the phenomenal and social level of reality, not on the level of *ch'i*. There are distinct things because someone perceives them; there must be a perceiver if there is to be something perceived. The consciousness of sentient beings determines and shapes this kind of reality.

[In the experience of] human beings, [within the categories of] heat, cold, day, and night, there are no things that do not change.

[Within the categories of] rain, wind, dew, and thunder, there are no things are not transformed.

[Within the categories of] nature, feelings, form, and body, there are no things that do no move.

[Within the categories of] walking, flying, grassy, and woody things, there are no things that do not respond.

Therefore the eye completes the appearances of all things, the ear completes the sounds of all things, the nose completes the odors of all things, and the mouth completes the flavors of all things. Is not human consciousness [*ling*] of all things also not fitting?

Nature, emotions, form, and body have their basis in what belongs to heaven. Walking, flying, grassy, and woody things have their basis in what belongs to earth. What is based in heaven is said to divide *yin* and to divide *yang*. What is based in earth is said to divide *jou* and to divide *kang*.

That which divides *yin*, divides *yang*, divides *jou*, and divides *kang* is called heaven and earth and the myriad things.

That which completes heaven and earth and the myriad things is called a human being.[11]

Ling is not equivalent to any single English concept. Moreover, the English word "consciousness" has meanings that do not apply to *ling*. The particular word chosen to translate *ling* thus must vary with the context and, even then, may not be entirely satisfactory. In the phrase *ling yü wan-wu* (human consciousness of all things), the meaning of *ling* suggests the ideas of action on the myriad things with one's spirit, having an effect on them, or having a special spiritual relation with them. The concept of *ling* assumes the functioning of a human spirit in the sense of a motivating force (not spirit as some kind of absolute entity). *Ling* also suggests the idea of intelligence. As Shao Yung said:

Since heaven and earth are produced from this *tao*, how much more so are humans and things? Humans are the most intelligent [*chih ling*] of things, and the intelligence of things does not match the intelligence of humans. Since humans and things are produced from this *tao*, is it any wonder that humans are more intelligent than things? From this one knows that humans also are things, but as for the most intelligent, then it is the human.[12]

The concept of *ling yü wan-wu* not only implies that humans are aware of, or conscious of, the myriad things, but also that this relationship of consciousness has a specific effect on the myriad things—namely, the completion of a thing as that particular thing by virtue of a perceiver's conscious experience. This conception of *ling* implies a relationship between perceiver and perceived in which the act of perception "makes" reality. Shao is saying that a thing is not a thing—that is, it is not completed—until someone senses it. A sound, for example, is not a sound until someone hears it, not because the sound waves are not there, but because the concept of sound involves a relationship between the perceiver and the perceived. This relationship is required for there to be that entity called sound. Unheard sound waves are not sound; the concept of sound implies human experience. For Shao, human beings are necessary in this process because "that which completes heaven and earth and the myriad things is called a human being."[13]

Moreover, the fixed correspondences of the categories of *ch'i* make the relationship of completing possible. Thus, the eye correlates with the category of appearances, not with that of sounds, and so on. In Shao's view, the categories naturally fit together into groups of four, for which the four images are the model. The significance of the number four (and two) is that it reflects the absolute regularity of the universe and so makes possible the world of human experience. Although for Shao there was a definite number of categories (four each for heaven and for earth), the importance of that specific number was secondary to the idea that there was a constant number.

In elaborating on Shao Yung's thought, Shao Po-wen added that the mind enables humans to complete phenomena through their senses. That is, the mind (literally, the organ of the mind, *hsin chih kuan*) is able to complete the pattern (*li*) of all things. Therefore, the ability of humans to be conscious of all things depends ultimately on the functioning of the mind and not simply on the functioning of the other (four) sense organs. Moreover, Shao Po-wen said that since heaven and earth produce all things, everything embodies the one principle (*yi tuan*) of heaven and earth. Since humans, specifically the sages, are able to complete heaven and earth and unite all things, humans form a triad with the two realms of heaven and earth.[14] Thus, all three—heaven, earth, and humans—are "producers" of phenomenal reality, or reality as it is known to humans.

Shao Yung's position is reminiscent of Mencius' statement that "all things are complete within me."[15] Shao would agree that all things in the universe, including oneself, are made up of the same "stuff" (*ch'i*), which "behaves" according to a single *tao*. *Ch'i*, moreover, embodies both the active and the still aspects of things (the activities and the forms of things) and the principles of change. What Shao Yung added to this was the idea that human consciousness plays a critical role in the formation of some kinds of reality. That is, not all kinds or levels of reality are independent of the functioning of the human mind.

In another passage, Shao Yung explained how consciousness of the phenomenal world was possible.

The reason that humans are able to be conscious of the myriad things is that their eyes can receive [*shou*] the appearances of the myriad things, their ears can receive the sounds of the myriad things, their noses can receive the odors of the myriad things, and their mouths can receive the flavors of the myriad things.

Sounds, appearances, odors, and flavors are the forms of the myriad things. [The functioning of the] eyes, ears, nose, and mouth is the activity of the myriad people.

Forms have no definite activity. They only change this activity. Activity has no definite form. It only transforms this form. Form and activity intermingle, and the *tao* of humans and things is thereby completed.[16]

This passage, which reflects the influence of Buddhism (and particularly Chih Yi's thought) in its use of the term *shou* (to receive), is concerned with Shao's idea of harmonious fit, which makes human consciousness possible.[17] In fitting the perceiving channel with what is perceived, Shao emphasizes that humans have the capability for these kinds of sense perception. Moreover, human consciousness depends on sense perception. Without seeing, hearing, smelling, and tasting, human beings would have no consciousness. Without the senses, humans would have no means by which to be aware of the phenomenal world. Even though the mind is a sense organ, its functioning depends on the other senses. (The general cultural view was that there were five senses. Shao Yung's omission of the sense of touch was unusual but understandable in light of his quaternary structure.)

Shao also related these ideas to the concepts of *t'i* (form) and *yung* (activity). Sounds, appearances, odors, and flavors are the *t'i* of things because they have form (*hsing*). The functioning of the senses is the *yung* of humans.[18] Each sense has no specific object with which it must interact, but it can only have a relationship with objects of the appropriate kind; that is, the eye cannot hear sounds, nor can the ear see appearances. The intertwining of *t'i* and *yung* results in the completion of the *tao* of humans and things, since only then are there such things as the sounds, appearances, odors, and flavors of the world.

The concept of *ling* is thus similar to the concept of *kan-ying* (movement and response). Both are concerned with the completion of a new whole or new entity by the interaction of two entities, which become two aspects of the whole. *Ling* differs, however, in certain crucial respects. It involves the "principles of change and response between humans and things," rather than only between things.[19] Moreover, through the functioning of the human sense organs, which include the mind, the concept of *ling* embraces the making of the phenomenal world as it is known by humans.

With the concept of *ling*, consciousness, Shao Yung introduced an epistemological element strongly influenced by Buddhism into his views about the nature of reality. Previously he had established two levels of reality, perceived and unperceived. Human consciousness functions on the perceived level, and what people know or are aware of has a social and conceptual reality. This kind of reality differs from that on the subsensorial level, since the shape and characteristics of perceived reality depend on a perceiver. In contrast, the structure or categories of *ch'i* exist independently as part of *ch'i*. In other words, human consciousness is an essential aspect of the phenomena that constitute perceived reality. Experience on the phenomenal level results from the fit between the patterns of *ch'i* on the subsensorial level and the sense organs of humans. These patterns, symbolized by the images, enable the sense organs of the perceiver to fit the perceived objects appropriately.

The Ends and Beginnings of Heaven and Earth

Literally "the ends and beginnings of heaven and earth," the concept of *t'ien-ti chih chung-shih* concerns cyclical patterns of time. This concept is represented by two sets of four images located on the second row of the "Ching-shih t'ien-ti ssu-hsiang" chart and interspersed between the images symbolizing the concept of the changes and transformations of heaven and earth (see Fig. B5). Like the other concepts and their eight images, four of the images for this concept are associated with heaven (cycle, epoch, revolution, generation) and four with earth (year, month, day, hour).

The concept of the ends and beginnings of heaven and earth is closely related to the concept discussed next, the duties and accomplishments of the sages and worthies. Both are based on similar ideas. Shao assumed that certain kinds of activities of humans and of nature are cyclical, that change is inevitable, and that change exhibits regularities. To the concept of ends and beginnings, or cycles, Shao linked such aspects of his thought as his ideas about numbers, about history, and about the problem of knowledge and point of view. In terms of the idea of completing a whole, this concept is similar in structure to that of the movements and responses of the myriad things. The ends are not conceived as reactions to the beginnings. Rather, the ends complete that which the beginnings started, and new entities are thereby formed. The *Ta-hsüeh* (Great learning) expressed this idea in the simple statement, "Affairs have their ends and beginnings."[20]

Basic to this concept, as to all six concepts, is the quaternary division. All things, in the broadest sense of the word "thing," including events and classifications of all kinds, can be subdivided into four parts or aspects. For Shao, this "natural" division is based on the phenomena of the universe. The four seasons, the four cardinal directions, and the four limbs of human beings, for example, are "evidence" of the naturalness of the four-part division. "Heaven has four seasons, earth has four directions, and humans have four limbs. These are marked off with one's fingers. One can observe heaven to grasp the patterns and one can examine earth. The patterns [*li*] of heaven and earth are complete in pointing to the palm of one's hand."[21]

In this reference to the hand, Shao understood the thumb as representing the center, or earth, and the four fingers as representing the four directions.[22] Shao's point was that, whatever realm of reality one examines, there is a basic quaternary division to things. Time is divided into the four seasons, space into the four directions, and human activities into the four classics.[23] Moreover, the four parts of each whole are arranged in a definite system. The four seasons occur in a predictable sequence with a beginning and an end. Likewise, the four directions have specific relationships with each other. The four classics also have a definite set of relationships, not only temporal, but also political and ethical. In these various areas of experience, the four parts combine to make one, a whole, which can be repeated any number of times.

With the concept of the beginnings and ends of heaven and earth, Shao emphasized that change occurs within a definite universal structure. Change is not random but has distinguishable and predictable segments. The segments can be represented either by numbers or by what Shao called the "four treasuries" (*ssu fu*).

The numbers of the *Yi* exhaust the ends and beginnings of heaven and earth. Someone asked [me] whether heaven and earth also had ends and beginnings, and I said, "Since they have waxing and waning, how can they not have ends and beginnings?" Although heaven and earth are large, they also are matter with form, and they are two things.[24]

The four treasuries, which are the model for many four-part entities, derive from the *Yi-ching*. Shao Yung said:

The capability of heaven to complete things is called august heaven. The capability of humans to complete the people is called the sage. If one says that august heaven is able to be different from the myriad things, then it is not what is called august heaven. If one says that the sage is able to be different from the myriad people, then he is not what is called the sage.

When the myriad people and the myriad things are the same, then the sage is of course not different from august heaven. When it is thus, then the sage and august heaven follow the one *tao*.

When the sage and august heaven follow the one *tao*, then the myriad people and the myriad things also can follow the one *tao*. When the myriad people of one generation and the myriad things of one generation can follow the one *tao*, then the myriad people of ten thousand generations and the myriad things of ten thousand generations can follow the one *tao*. This is clear.

In august heaven's completion of things and in the sage's completion of the people, they both have the four treasuries. The four treasuries of august heaven are spring, summer, autumn, and winter. *Yin* and *yang* ascend and descend in their midst.

The four treasuries of the sages are the *Yi*, *Shu*, *Shih*, and *Ch'un-ch'iu*. Etiquette and music succeed and fail in their midst.[25]

Thus, the four treasuries are the seasons and the classics, and their pattern is the one *tao* that the realms of heaven, earth, and humans alike follow. To maintain the parallelism between the natural and human realms, Shao poised august heaven against the sages, the founders of Chinese culture. There is no indication, however, here or elsewhere, that Shao anthropomorphized heaven. Although not well defined by Shao Yung, august heaven represents the forces of nature. To Shao, the changing states of etiquette and music, traditionally seen as a reflection of political order and chaos, were analogous to the changes of *yin* and *yang ch'i*, whose rising and falling is behind the changing of the seasons.

The four seasons and the four classics correlate not only with each other but with another series of four entities based on the biological life cycle that suggests the idea of the development of an organism. This series consists of four stages: birth (*sheng*), growth (*chang*), maturity or harvest (*shou*), and death or being hidden away (*ts'ang*).[26] This cycle was used to represent the patterns of things that are not biological organisms, such as the year, classics, or human history. Like the seasonal cycle, change within this cycle exhibits features of development and decline. The idea of regularity in change through fixed segments remains important here. Change has no amorphous qualities. In speaking of the four treasuries, Shao Yung said:

Spring is the treasury of things being born. Summer is the treasury of things growing. Autumn is the treasury of things maturing. Winter is the treasury of things dying.

The multitude of the named things are called the ten thousand. Although they are said to be ten thousand, they are double that. And this multitude is able to emerge from these four treasuries of august heaven.

The *Yi* is the treasury of the people being born. The *Shu* is the treasury of the people growing. The *Shih* is the treasury of the people maturing. The *Ch'un-ch'iu* is the treasury of the people dying.

The multitude of the named people are called the ten thousand. Although they are said to be ten thousand, they are double that. And this multitude is able to emerge from these four treasuries of the sages.

The four treasuries of august heaven are the seasons. The four treasuries of the sages are the classics. August heaven teaches human beings with the seasons. The sages copy heaven with the classics. How fitting are the affairs of heaven and humans![27]

Shao's pattern of birth, growth, maturity (or harvest), and death (or hiding away) is modeled after the explanations of the first and second hexagrams, *ch'ien* and *k'un*, attributed to King Wen. Both of these hexagrams, which symbolize the principles of male and female, and heaven and earth, explain the four characteristics of originating growth (*yüan*), prosperous development (*heng*), advantageous gain (*li*), and correct firmness (*cheng*) in the same way. These were regarded as the four stages of growth and were called the four "virtues" of nature.[28]

Shao discussed these four virtues in connection with the hexagrams and his concept of change and response.²⁹ He further correlated them with the four seasons and with the four virtues of benevolence (*jen*), etiquette (*li*), righteousness (*yi*), and wisdom (*chih*).³⁰ Not only was Shao's version of the four-stage growth pattern firmly rooted in the *Yi-ching* through its relationship to *ch'ien* and *k'un*, his four treasuries also were closely associated with the principles of male and female, *yang* and *yin*, and *tung* and *ching*. As with these hemilogs, the interaction of the four stages of the four treasuries resulted in the formation of new entities or wholes. Not only was a year not a whole without all four seasons following and developing in the correct order, the Chinese people and culture also were not a whole without the four classics. Moreover, the quaternary pattern of the four treasuries was the means by which the sage and august heaven became one, or from another point of view, followed the same *tao* and so behaved alike.

The phenomenal aspect of the ends and beginnings (or cycles) of heaven and earth, which are experienced by humans as seasonal change, have a subsensorial basis in the patterns of *ch'i*. Shao's comment, quoted above, on the ascending and descending of *yin* and *yang* in relation to the four seasons alludes to this fact. The activity of *yin* and *yang ch'i* is responsible for the passage of the seasons, and such activity is symbolized by the four correlated stages of *sheng*, *chang*, *shou*, and *ts'ang*. Thus, spring is the beginning of *yang*, summer the extreme of *yang*, autumn the beginning of *yin*, and winter the extreme of *yin*. Not knowable through ordinary sense experience, these changes of *yin* and *yang ch'i* are manifested in the corresponding temperatures, warm, hot, cool, and cold, which are accessible to the senses. These temperatures in turn correspond to the times of things being born (*sheng*), things growing (*chang*), things being harvested (*shou*), and things being hidden away (*ts'ang*).³¹

Thus, the idea of the four treasuries was one way by which Shao expressed his concept of the ends and beginnings of heaven and earth. With this concept, Shao claimed that the universe exhibited temporal cycles, most of which have a quaternary structure. The four treasuries of heaven (the seasons) correlate with the four treasuries of the sages (the classics, discussed in the next section). Shao observed things from the perspective of a larger whole, and he recognized the pervasiveness of cyclical patterns in the universe.

He regarded all cycles based on the developmental pattern of living things as possessing similar internal patterns with stages of development and decline.

The fact that the internal structure of the four treasuries is based on the four sequential stages of living things indicates the close relationship between those cycles that belong to the realm of heaven and those that belong to the realm of earth. Although the seasons are part of the cyclical pattern of the heavens, as they progress to form a year they follow the pattern of the growth cycle, a characteristic of the realm of earth. Thus, a year has stages analogous to birth, development, maturity, and decline.

In addition to cycles patterned after the growth of living things, Shao Yung discussed other cycles based on phenomena associated with the realm of heaven. Although their internal structures follow numerical patterns, in contrast to the pattern of development and decline associated with the growth cycle, all cycles are ultimately interrelated through their association with the quaternary structure.

Besides the four treasuries, Shao's cycles of heaven and earth include one set of four cosmic cycles and another set of four calendrical cycles. The set of cosmic cycles consists of what Shao called cycle (*yüan*), epoch (*hui*), revolution (*yün*), and generation (*shih*), and the set of calendrical cycles of year (*sui*), month (*yüeh*), day (*jih*), hour (*ch'en*). These cycles are related numerically, based on the numbers 12 and 30. Moreover, with various combinations and permutations, these two sets of four cycles correlate with the four images of heaven (sun, moon, stars, and zodiacal space) and with the 64 hexagrams and their correlated numbers. All these relationships are expressed in the "Ching-shih t'ien-ti shih-chung chih shu t'u" (Chart of the numbers of the beginnings and ends of heaven and earth that rule the world).[32]

In Shao's view, one cycle (*yüan*) equals twelve epochs (*hui*), one epoch equals 30 revolutions (*yün*), and one revolution equals twelve generations (*shih*).[33] Or, one cycle has twelve epochs, 360 revolutions, and 4,320 (1 × 12 × 30 × 12) generations. In comparable fashion, one year (*sui*) has twelve months (*yüeh*), 360 days (*jih*), and 4,320 hours (*ch'en*; a day had twelve hours in traditional Chinese timekeeping). Or, twelve hours equal one day, 30 days equal one month, and twelve months equal one year.

Since one generation (the last entity of the first set) is equal to 30 years (the first entity of the second set), one cycle is equivalent to 129,600 (1 × 12 × 30 × 12 × 30) years.[34] Shao also figured out various other numbers. For example, he noted that an epoch's epoch (an epoch squared) is 144 (12^2) (12 × 12) and a generation's generation is 18,662,400 ($4,320^2$).[35]

Shao often used these two sets of cycles in a metaphorical sense. As with other elements of the *Yi-ching*, such as the hexagrams, these cycles became models used to understand other things. Shao Po-wen, for example, compared one cycle (*yüan*) in the great transformation (*ta-hua*) of the universe to one year in a human being's life.[36] He also commented that, although one could extrapolate Shao Yung's numbers further, the significance of the numbers of a cycle was to clarify change in the universe. When an extreme (end) is reached, then there is a new beginning. Shao Po-wen's point was that numbers are one way to represent cycles, and the segmentation symbolized by numbers is more important than the calculations possible with numbers.

The cycles and the numbers associated with them were regarded as having a basis in reality. Shao Po-wen, for instance, commented that these numbers, which begin with 1 and alternate 12 and 30, are based in the universe itself. They are not simply derived from human imagination.

> These numbers are manifest before us and do not need further investigation. This theory of waxing and waning, filling and emptying, is not recorded in books, which men search in order to obtain these [numbers]. But it is stored in the functioning [of the world]. These are what the *Yi* calls the numbers of heaven and earth.[37]

Shao Yung did not originate the ideas of either the cosmic or the calendrical cycles. By the Han dynasty, elaborate systems of the cycles of the cosmos had already been developed. The Triple Concordance system, for example, consisted of a set of eclipse cycles called the Concordance Cycle, Epoch Cycle, Phase Coincidence Cycle, Coincidence Month, and Rule Cycle. The numbers involved were large. For example, a Concordance Cycle equaled 1,539 years, an Epoch Cycle three Concordance Cycles, and a Rule Cycle nineteen years of 365.25 days. Also, within this system, the

140 · *Human Beings and the Universe*

Great Planetary Conjunction Cycle equaled 138,240 years, and the Grand Polarity Superior Epoch 23,639,040 years. This last number was the period of the Great Year. Moreover, the Quarter Day system, which developed in the Later Han, had a Great Year of 227,936,324,009,998,800 years.[38]

Based on the culture's calendrical divisions of year, month, day, and hour, the numbers 12 and 30 were regarded only as rough approximations of the structural divisions of time.[39] These numbers were thought to be knowable directly from human experience and not something that had to be learned from books. Since time was viewed as cyclical, with cycles within cycles, Shao indicated the regularity of the passage of time by breaking the cycles into separate, numerically equal segments. Since *yin* and *yang* (*ch'i*) are that which wax and wane, the segments of time were also seen as segments of *ch'i*.[40]

Shao Yung also correlated the four cosmic cycles of cycle, epoch, revolution, and generation with the four seasons, which he then correlated with human political affairs.[41] Through these associations, Shao connected time in the universe to the cyclical pattern of human society. Although time in the universe and time in human society were different aspects of reality, both followed the same *tao* of a ceaseless ending and beginning, beginning and ending, or waxing and waning, filling and emptying. It was believed that understanding one kind of time would aid in understanding the other. As Shao Po-wen stated, the changes of the seasons were "nothing more than the increasing and decreasing of *yin* and *yang*."[42] And as Shao Yung said, "The seasons have waxing and waning. Affairs have following and changing."[43] Shao believed that the numbers representing the cycles of heaven and earth could be used to help people understand not only the principle (*li*) of the rising and falling of *yin* and *yang*, which give rise to the passage of the seasons, but also the traces of flourishing and decline in human society.[44]

In the attempt to understand the unknown, much explanation was, and still is, done by the use of analogies that compare the unknown to the known. The Chinese often applied the idea of roundness and the visual image of a circle to temporal and spatial aspects of the natural world. Heaven, for instance, was regarded as round and earth as square, and time, as an aspect of the movements of heaven, was compared to a circle. Thus, the cosmic and calendrical cycles were regarded as the cycles of heaven. Moreover, a circle has 360 degrees, just as, in Shao's thought, a year has 360 days and a cycle has 360 revolutions.[45] Since it had long been known that 360 was not the exact number of days in a year, it would be a mistake to interpret Shao as ignoring the reality of experience in favor of constructing a perfect astronomical system. That was not Shao's aim.

Here the unknown to be explained was the structure of temporal change in the phenomenal world of human experience. The known was a realm of theoretical structure, the symbolic world called the *hsien-t'ien* realm. The model for this realm was the circle, and the year and other recurrent time periods were understood as analogous to it. Shao's purpose in discussing the relationships of the symbols, or images, was to exhibit the patterns of phenomenal experience. Indeed much of Shao's thought was about the model, or the analogy, used to explain change. He seldom addressed the separate question of the application of the model to experience. He simply assumed that his model applied. Moreover, since he did mention Yang Hsiung's ternary system and he did respect Yang Hsiung, Shao may have believed that different mathematical models could be applied to the phenomenal world, as nineteenth-century mathematicians learned was possible.[46]

Shao's assumptions about the regularity of the universe and the length of time cycles did not agree with the most advanced knowledge of contemporary mathematical astronomers. Shao's knowledge of astronomy was probably closer to that of a thousand years earlier.[47] In traditional China, astronomy included such areas as astrology and fate prediction that are not part of that field today.[48] The background and social standing of those engaged in these branches of astronomy varied widely, and they could easily have had no contact with each other. Shao and most other philosophers of the eleventh century did in fact live in an intellectual and social world separate from that of the mathematical astronomers. Thus, many philosophers, as well as some astronomers, had little opportunity to keep up with the latest discoveries and theories in that field of knowledge.

This lack of exchange of knowledge between philosophers and

mathematical astronomers was not unique to the Sung. It had been the situation for centuries. During the Han dynasty, however, astronomers and philosophers had in part shared the same world. Two men often considered among Shao Yung's forerunners, the Han scholar Cheng Hsüan and the Han philosopher Yang Hsiung, for example, had some knowledge of astronomy through the *Yi* learning.[49] But after the Han, these two groups for the most part ceased to share knowledge. Shao's knowledge of astronomy most likely included Han knowledge, because it was part of the philosophical tradition he had inherited. The extent of any further knowledge he had, however, is not known.

Many post-Han developments in astronomy were not incorporated into the philosophers' world. For example, because events had not always occurred as theory had predicted, by Sung times astronomers had gradually come to accept the view that the universe was irregular and that unpredictable events did occur.[50] Moreover, after the Han, astronomers discarded the concept of cosmic cycles, because the data did not support this assumption, but this concept remained a part of the *Yi* philosophical tradition.[51]

Shao Yung certainly knew that developments in the field of the *Yi* learning and cosmology diverged greatly from those in the field of calendrical science and astronomy. For example, in a passage concerning the calendar, Shao said:

The calendar cannot not have remainders [*ch'a*]. Today those who study the calendar know only calendrical methods and do not know calendrical principles. One who was able to make calculations was Lo-hsia Hung. Those who were able to make interpolations were Kan Kung and Shih Kung. Lo-hsia Hung knew only calendrical methods. Yang Hsiung knew calendrical methods and also knew calendrical principles.[52]

This reference to remainders makes it clear Shao knew that the number of days in a year or in a month is not a round number. Thus in discussing the regularity of the universe, Shao was not speaking in terms of mathematical astronomy and calendrical science, but rather in the philosophical context of the *Yi* learning. He recognized, too, that in Yang Hsiung's time, these areas of knowledge had not been so separate.

The aims, focus, and methodology of the field of astronomy and calendrical science differed from those of the superficially similar field of the images and numbers branch of the *Yi* learning. Shao Yung was a philosopher and not an astronomer. He was concerned primarily with clarifying the *hsien-t'ien* realm and not with further investigation of the phenomenal world. He was trying to explain patterns that were already known, patterns that for the most part were stated in the *Yi-ching*.

Moreover, his few correct statements on astronomy were common beliefs in Chinese culture. For example, Shao said that the moon has no light of its own and merely reflects the light of the sun.[53] Others of his time, including Chang Tsai, the Ch'eng brothers, and the scientist Shen Kua, also expressed this idea.[54] The idea dates to the Han period, and Wei Po-yang's *Ts'an-t'ung-ch'i* even contains a diagram entitled "Chart of the Moon Receiving the Light of the Sun."[55] But even this apparently straightforward idea had different meanings in different areas of knowledge. Yü Yen, a Han student of the *Yi* learning, explained this idea as symbolizing man's spirit (*shen*) entering into *ch'i*.[56] Since *yang* is bright and *yin* is dark, *yang* confers on *yin* its brightness, which *yin* then receives. The sun is greater *yang* and the moon is greater *yin*. The sun and moon also symbolize heaven and earth and male and female.

In the Sung and later periods, the meaning of many symbols was no longer completely understood. Nor was the intellectual background of the symbols generally known. This situation often contributed to misinterpretations of certain passages or aspects of Shao's thought. Just as the yellow and the white or the dragon and the tiger were symbols in the alchemical tradition, the sun and the moon were important symbols, with a long history, in the *Yi* tradition. Someone ignorant of this branch of learning would not know that the sun and moon were major symbols for *yang* and *yin* and for heaven and earth. Such a person would not realize that Shao's statement about the sun and moon was more than a statement about nature, that it was an implicit reference to other ideas for which the sun and moon were symbols and a non-explicit reference to other discussions of these ideas.[57]

To summarize, Shao's concept of the cycles of heaven and earth was concerned with change in the sense of cyclical time periods. Shao believed that the passage of time could be symbolized by its division into numerous interrelated cycles, ranging from the very large to the very small. The cosmic cycles of cycle, epoch, revolution, and generation and the calendrical cycles of year, month, day, and hour were based on numerical relationships involving the numbers 1, 12, and 30. The cycles of the four treasuries were based on the biological model of a four-stage life cycle of birth, growth, maturity (or harvest), and death (or hiding away). The four treasuries of heaven were the four seasons, and those of earth were the four classics. With these various kinds of cycles, Shao Yung showed that the idea of waxing and waning, or the idea of the movement of *yin* and *yang*, could be expressed in both numerical and biological terms. Moreover, he assumed an interdependent relationship between time and *ch'i*—a remarkably modern view.

But Shao was a philosopher, not an astronomer. His thought, his assumptions, and his goals were those of the images and numbers branch of the *Yi* learning. He was concerned with explaining a theoretical world of symbols, particularly those related to the *Yi-ching*, not with investigating the physical world. Since for Shao, as for others, the symbols represented the patterns of the phenomenal world, they were an attempt to explain change in the universe. The validity of the connection between the physical world of experience and the world of theory was not a belief Shao challenged.

The Duties and Accomplishments of the Sages and Worthies

The concept of the duties and accomplishments of the sages and worthies (*sheng-hsien chih shih-yeh*), the sixth of Shao Yung's interrelated concepts, focuses on historical patterns of human behavior. Like the preceding concept, this idea predicates cycles as a fundamental pattern of the universe. The four classics are the focal point, but their significance lies more in their symbolic role than in their textual details. Along with the four seasons, the four classics are one set of the four treasuries. Shao used these two series to link together in a highly structured way the affairs of humans and nature.

In the "Ching-shih t'ien-ti ssu-hsiang" chart, this concept is represented by eight images located on the third row of the chart and interspersed between the images for the concept of the movements and responses of the myriad things (see Fig. B5). The four images correlated with the realm of heaven are sage (*huang*), emperor (*ti*), king (*wang*), and hegemon (*pa*). Those correlated with the realm of earth are the four classics: the *Yi*, *Shu*, *Shih*, and *Ch'un-ch'iu*.

The structure of this concept is similar to that of the other concepts in that it involves two aspects combining to form a larger whole or entity. Here, the two aspects consist of the duties of the sages, or what they ought to do, and the accomplishments of the sages, or what they actually did do. The relationship between duties and accomplishments is not seen as one of stimulus and response, or action and reaction, but rather as the completion of a new entity that exists on a different level—the ideal society of perfect virtue and perfect government. Because of the ideas suggested by this concept, I have translated *shih* as "duties" rather than as "affairs," the common meaning of the term.

As with his other concepts, Shao Yung expressed his ideas here in a way typical for him but unusual for most other philosophers. Rather than an extended discussion, he offered numerous sets of correlations. As elsewhere, his method of presentation was primarily one of demonstration, and only rarely was his argument self-explanatory. To his "verbal charts," however, other writers added commentaries that rephrased Shao's correlations in prose form and that made the assumptions behind the correlations explicit.

Shao Yung based his concept of the duties and accomplishments of the sages and worthies on several ideas. First, he assumed that the four seasons and human history follow an identical pattern of development and decline. Human history can be, and is, symbolized by the four classics. The seasons and classics are comparable entities in their respective realms of heaven and earth. They are the four treasuries. In addition, the classics are both historical records and symbols of the historical patterns contained in them.[58]

To Shao, human history follows the same four-stage pattern of birth, growth, maturity, and death as the seasons of the year. The development and decline, or the waxing and waning, of nature and of human affairs is the inevitable way of the universe. This cyclical pattern is repeated after the completion of every cycle. Each classic represents a particular stage in history and can be correlated with a specific season. "If one contemplates spring, then one will know what the *Yi* preserves. If one contemplates summer, then one will know what the *Shu* preserves. If one contemplates autumn, then one will know what the *Shih* preserves. If one contemplates winter, then one will know what the *Ch'un-ch'iu* preserves."[59]

Each classic and its related season represent the same stage in the four-stage growth cycle. Both the *Yi* and spring, for example, contain the principles associated with the stage of birth. Moreover, since Shao viewed each classic as the historical record of a particular era in the development of society, he assumed not only that the principles of development could be derived from historical particulars, but also that they could be verified by them. One can contemplate the principles or patterns of a particular season and thereby know what patterns and what kind of historical events are preserved in the classic correlated with that season.

Shao's idea that the four classics symbolize the four-stage growth cycle was inseparable from his view of the historicity of the events contained in the classics. Since the *Yi, Shu, Shih,* and *Ch'un-ch'iu* consist respectively of the duties and accomplishments of the three sages (*san-huang*), the five emperors (*wu-ti*), the three kings (*san-wang*), and the five hegemons (*wu-pa*), the four classics therefore resemble spring, summer, autumn, and winter.[60] To Shao, these categories delineated the early rulers of China, from the founders of Chinese civilization to the usurpers of the late Chou period.

Not only did the classics record actual historical events, they also represented political and social history. Thus, Shao was saying that political and social history follow the same cycle of birth, growth, maturity, and death, as the seasons do. Moreover, an element of "ought" is associated with each season and with each classic or historical period. Each stage has a particular duty to fulfill, and no stage can fulfill the duty of another stage. Shao does not say, however, where that duty comes from. It is simply a phenomenon of the universe. "In regard to the *tao* of ruling, one must understand its changes. One cannot act in error, just as the season of spring cannot carry out the commands of winter."[61]

To emphasize his belief that the classics are history, Shao associated each classic with a particular period and with the rulers of that period. He symbolized the social and political characteristics of each period and its rulers by the particular term used to designate the rulers. The terms *huang*, *ti*, *wang*, and *pa* implied different methods of governing, which in turn depended on the morality of the age. Although Shao considered the method of the sage ruler (*huang*) the ideal, he recognized that the method of rule had to fit the characteristics of the period. "The *Yi* began with the three sages, the *Shu* began with the two emperors, the *Shih* began with the three kings, and the *Ch'un-ch'iu* began with the five hegemons."[62]

The three sages are Fu Hsi, Yao, and Shun; the two emperors Yü and T'ang; the three kings Wen, Wu, and the Duke of Chou; the five hegemons Duke Huan of Ch'i, Duke Mu of Ch'in, Duke Hsiang of Sung, Duke Wen of Chin, and King Chuang of Ch'u.[63] In most passages, however, Shao speaks of five, not two, emperors. In Shao's view, the four kinds of rulers—sages, emperors, kings, and hegemons—followed each other in succession, in a fixed order. The necessity of the order derived from past experience, just as did the order of the seasons.

A certain type of rule was associated with each kind of ruler. These varied from a rule that transformed the people with the *tao* to one that led them by force, or from one that used the method of non-action to one that used the method of cunning and strength.[64] The method of governing reflected the conditions of the times and changed according to the stages of the cycle. Since the people changed with the times, what was required to maintain order and virtue in society changed too. What was appropriate for one age did not work in another. The different kinds of governing reflected human adaptation to fit the universal cycles of change and to bring about the best society possible. Shao said:

The so-called sages, emperors, kings, and hegemons are not only those called the three sages, five emperors, three kings, and five hegemons.

But if one uses [the method of] non-action, then one is a sage. If one uses [the method of] kindness and good faith, then one is an emperor. If one uses [the method of] impartiality and correctness, then one is a king. If one uses the method of cunning and strength, then one is a hegemon.

After the hegemons, then [the rulers] were usurpers [*chien-ch'ieh*].[65]

Although these four terms for different kinds of rulers referred to historical figures, in this passage Shao is quite clear that they also symbolize general types. The three kings, for example, were specific historical people, King Wen, King Wu, and the Duke of Chou, but the term *king* also represented a particular type of rule. It symbolized the third stage of the cycle of the four treasuries, a stage represented by the *Shih* (Book of poetry). In particular, the term symbolized the time when virtue was still present, but declining. In other words, the rulers, their historical periods of rule, and the classics with which they were associated all served as symbols for aspects of the four-part universal pattern.

In using specific historical figures to symbolize the various stages in the cycle, Shao focused on the cycle, not on the examples. Shao's point was that the three sages represented the stage of birth, the five emperors the stage of growth, the three kings the stage of maturity, and the five hegemons the stage of death. Through both specific comments and further sets of correlations, Shao emphasized that he was talking about a pattern and was using historical events to validate it. For example, "The laws began with Fu Hsi, were completed with Yao, were changed with the three kings, reached an extreme with the five hegemons, and were cut off with Ch'in. As for the traces of order and disorder of ten thousand generations, there are none that escape this [pattern]." [66]

In other words, human events occurred according to a cyclical pattern. In (Chinese) history, the first cycle began with the sage ruler Fu Hsi and reached its final stage with the five tyrants at the end of the Chou dynasty. The Ch'in dynasty marked the end of the last stage of the first cycle. The historical events of this time became symbols of the stages in the cyclical pattern that characterized human history, just as seasonal events symbolized the pattern in nature.[67] Shao does not indicate the beginning of the second cycle, nor does he account for the period from the Han dynasty through the T'ang dynasty, but he does note that the Sung period is the beginning of a new cycle. His lack of attention to the Han–T'ang period undoubtedly reflects his interest in theory, rather than in data.[68]

To Shao, events throughout history reflect the patterns of the universe. Historical events, in effect, visibly mark particular stages in the pattern, which Shao called *tao* or *li*. Shao's point was that historical change did not occur in an unstructured way, but followed a four-stage course.

Shao Po-wen commented that "the seasons of heaven wax and wane in progression. The classics of the sages treat failure and success in succession. Their *tao* is like this. One can comprehend it in ideas but cannot seek it in words."[69] Here, Shao Po-wen emphasized the parallels between the activities of nature and those of human society. Both nature and society follow the same *tao*. The classics recorded, by means of specific examples that serve as symbols, the principles of the development and decline of human society. The seasons reflect the same principles as they operate in *ch'i* in the realm of nature. The *tao* or pattern is not written down. It is not a matter of words, but it can be understood by observing the functioning of the universe. The four-part cycle of development and decline was neither an arbitrary construction of the human imagination nor something imposed on otherwise unstructured activities of nature and humans.

Not all modern scholars interpret Shao's view of history as cyclical, however. Hou Wai-lu claimed that Shao had a regressive theory of history and that his four kinds of rulers present a picture of decline, not progress or cyclical activity.[70] However, Hou's opinion was not absolutely fixed; he also recognized that to Shao the Sung could be a new beginning.[71] Lo Kuang, a modern (but not Marxist) scholar, countered that, for Shao, the trend of history is downward, with occasional periods of flourishing. Subsequent good periods never reach the previous high. Thus, for Lo, Shao viewed history as cyclical, with larger and smaller cycles.[72]

In my view, these interpretations misrepresent Shao's position. Shao was saying that history follows a cyclical pattern similar to that of the four-stage life cycle. Thus, the three sages represent the beginning of social development; the five emperors the period of vigorous growth; the three kings the height of growth, when things are fully mature; and the five hegemons decline and eventual death. Instead of a continuous descent downward, there is birth, growth, maturation, and finally decline. As Shao Yung said: "The age of the three sages is like spring. The age of the five emperors is like summer. The age of the three kings is like autumn. The age of the five hegemons is like winter."⁷³ Shao assumed that there would always be another spring. Moreover, to Shao, the Sung period marked the beginning of a new cycle.

This universal *tao* of historical development is based in subsensorial reality. The movement of *ch'i* is manifested in the pattern of the "successive ages."

> When the *ch'i* of heaven and earth revolves from north to south, then there is order. [When it revolves] from south to north, then there is disorder. If disorder lasts long, then [*ch'i*] returns [to the course of] from north to south. The *tao* of heaven and the affairs of humans are like this. If one lays out the successive ages, one can see the pattern [*li*] of waxing and waning.⁷⁴

As Huang Chi noted, this pattern is symbolized in the *hsien-t'ien* charts of the eight trigrams and 64 hexagrams by means of their arrangement. From the 360 lines, which symbolize the *ch'i* of the *kua* (here, the hexagrams), one can extrapolate the successive periods of order and disorder. Moreover, the cyclical pattern of historical development can be confirmed by observing its realization in historical particulars. For example, Yao, Shun, Yü, T'ang, Wen, and Wu represent the transformations from the northwest to the southeast in the charts, and they ruled during periods of order. The states of Wu, Chin, Sung, Ch'i, Liang, and Ch'en (the Six Dynasties, 222–588) represent activity in the southeast, and their rule was a time of disorder.⁷⁵ Thus, there is a mutual fit between the *kua ch'i* and the events of history.⁷⁶ The pattern occurs on the subsensorial level of *ch'i*, it is recorded in the classics as historical development, and it is symbolized by the charts and diagrams.

The pattern is repeated in successive cycles, but particular events and people are not duplicated. There is certainly no indication that Shao Yung saw the historical process as literally repeating itself. Shao was talking about the structure of change, the *tao*, not the particulars involved. Utilizing the nature of Chinese nouns as mass nouns, Shao used particular names to refer to general categories.

A focus on nature, rather than on human history, makes Shao's point clear. Thus, for example, spring (along with the *Yi* and the three sages) symbolizes the first stage of the cycle, when *yin* was decreasing and *yang* was increasing. Every year when the cycle repeats, spring reappears, but the spring of a particular year does not reoccur. Each separate spring, however, exhibits the same principle of birth. The pattern of the cycle repeats itself, but the particulars do not. Similarly, in the cycles of human history, particular historical figures do not reappear, although the stages they represent do. This kind of thinking was common in Chinese culture. A typical way of expressing the idea that anyone can become morally perfect, for example, was to say that anyone can become a Yao or a Shun.

Through correlations, Shao Yung indicated the many activities to which his concept of the duties and accomplishments of the sages and worthies referred. Thus, after correlating the four classics with the four stages, with various permutations, he proceeded to add further correlations that made clear not only the numerous dimensions of this concept but also the layers of interrelationships among things.

The *Yi* of the *Yi* is called birth-birth. The *Shu* of the *Yi* is called birth-growth. The *Shih* of the *Yi* is called birth-maturity. The *Ch'un-ch'iu* of the *Yi* is called birth-death.

The *Yi* of the *Shu* is called growth-birth. The *Shu* of the *Shu* is called growth-growth. The *Shih* of the *Shu* is called growth-maturity. The *Ch'un-ch'iu* of the *Shu* is called growth-death.

The *Yi* of the *Shih* is called maturity-birth. The *Shu* of the *Shih* is called maturity-growth. The *Shih* of the *Shih* is called maturity-maturity. The *Ch'un-ch'iu* of the *Shih* is called maturity-death.

The *Yi* of the *Ch'un-ch'iu* is called death-birth. The *Shu* of the *Ch'un-ch'iu* is called death-growth. The *Shih* of the *Ch'un-ch'iu* of called death-maturity. The *Ch'un-ch'iu* of the *Ch'un-chiu* is called death-death.[77]

This set of correlations and permutations is followed by similar sets that incorporate various, deliberately selected groups of four entities:[78]

1. The four stages: birth (*sheng*), growth (*chang*), maturity (*shou*), and death (*ts'ang*);

2. The four political symbols: ideas (*yi*), words (*yen*), images (*hsiang*), and numbers (*shu*);

3. The four virtues: benevolence (*jen*), etiquette (*li*), righteousness (*yi*), and wisdom (*chih*);

4. The four aspects of humans: nature (*hsing*), feelings (*ch'ing*), form (*hsing*), and body (*t'i*);

5. The four types of wise men: sages (*sheng*), worthies (*hsien*), talents (*ts'ai*), and adepts (*shu*);

6. The four types of rulers: three sages (*san-huang*), five emperors (*wu-ti*), three kings (*san-wang*), and five hegemons (*wu-pa*); or simply, sages, emperors, kings, and hegemons;

7. The four types of dynasties: Yü (the period of rule of sage-emperor Shun), Hsia, Shang, and Chou;

8. The four types of rulers in the third stage: King Wen, King Wu, Duke of Chou, Duke Shao;

9. The four types of rulers of states: Mu of Ch'in, Wen of Chin, Hsüan of Ch'i, and Chuang of Ch'u;

10. The four methods of rule: transform the people (*hua*), teach the people (*chiao*), persuade the people (*ch'üan*), and lead the people (*shuai*);

11. The four political tools: the way (*tao*), virtue (*te*), accomplishments (*kung*), force (*li*);

12. The four values of the rulers: spontaneity (*tzu-jan*), yielding (*jang*), correctness (*cheng*), and struggle (*cheng*).

By using numerous sets of correlations, Shao demonstrated how his concept of the duties and accomplishments of the sages and worthies functioned in history. For example, a sage (*huang*) rules with the method of non-action (*wu-wei*), an emperor (*ti*) with kindness and good faith (*en hsin*), a king (*wang*) with impartiality and correctness (*kung cheng*), and a hegemon (*pa*) with cunning and strength (*chih li*). These methods respectively involve the actions of transforming the people with the *tao*, teaching the people with virtue, persuading the people with accomplishments, and leading the people with force.[79] Moreover, the four kinds of rulers respectively value spontaneity, yielding, correctness, and struggle.[80] The duties of the rulers depend on the age, and their accomplishments must be judged in the context of their times. One result of these correlations was to affirm a view of reality with multiple, interrelated aspects.

Shao reinforced the link between the four-stage pattern and human experience by setting up correlations using particular dynasties and rulers, both of which represented types. Thus, he correlated the four virtues and the four dynasties, the four aspects of humans and the four [types of] rulers in the third stage of the cycle, and the four types of wise men and the four [types of] rulers of states. Shao selectively used historical data from the *Ch'un-ch'iu* and several other works, including the *Tso Chuan*.[81]

These correlations allowed Shao to use historical data as evidence to show that these cycles operated in the world. Although others would justifiably argue with him, in Shao's view there is a four-part structure to human history as well as to the processes of nature. Shao used these series to show that change occurs cyclically not merely in his theory but in actual experience. He used particulars from the past to provide evidence for his theory of change in the universe. The truth of his theory he did not doubt. Since the universe included human history, historical data provided the evidence for the human world just as "observations" of nature did for the natural world. As Hou Wai-lu said, the point of the correlations was to show that everything obeyed the *tao* of *hsiang-shu*, or the *tao* of the images and numbers.[82]

By adding the entities of the hemilog *t'i* and *yung* (form and activity) to the correlations with the classics, Shao introduced a further aspect to his vision of reality.

The sages, emperors, kings, and hegemon are the form [*t'i*] of the *Yi*. The [dynasties] Yü, Hsia, Shang, and Chou are the form of the *Shu*. [The rulers] Wen, Wu, Chou, and Shao are the form of the *Shih*. [The states] Ch'in, Chin, Ch'i, and Ch'u are the form of the *Ch'un-ch'iu*.

[The symbols] ideas, words, images, and numbers are the activity [*yung*] of the *Yi*. [The virtues] benevolence, righteousness, etiquette, and wisdom are the activity of the *Shu*. [The human characteristics] nature, feelings, form, and body are the activity of the *Shih*. [The types of wise men] the sage, worthy, talent, and adept are the activity of the *Ch'un-ch'iu*.[83]

In Shao's thought, as noted above, *t'i* refers to something that has an appearance perceivable through the senses, whereas *yung* is the activity that a thing exhibits. Historical phenomena, which are symbolized by the classics, exhibit both characteristics. As the following passages indicate, the concept of *t'i* and *yung* was closely related to Shao's concept of the duties and accomplishments of the sages and worthies.

Activity [*yung*] is [the functioning of] the mind, and forms [*t'i*] are the traces.

In the midst of mind and traces, there are those things that adaptive behavior [*ch'üan*] preserves, and those things are the duties of the sage.

In the midst of forms and activity, there are those things that change [*pien*] preserves, and those things are the accomplishments of the sages.

Change is august heaven's giving birth to the myriad things. Adaptive behavior is the sage's giving birth to the myriad people. If one were to succeed without the living things and the living people, would one call it change and adaptation?[84]

Here Shao introduced the ideas of change (*pien*) and adaptive behavior (*ch'üan*) to explain his concept of the duties and accomplishments.[85] In his view, when activity or change occurs in the realm of heaven, corresponding behavior occurs in the realm of earth. The behavior in the realm of earth balances out the activities of heaven. Earthly behavior adapts or adjusts itself to heavenly events. Shao correlated the activity of change (*pien*) of august heaven with the adaptive behavior (*ch'üan*) of the sage. "Heaven and earth give birth to the myriad things. The sage gives birth to the myriad people. The changes of the *tao* of heaven are [equivalent to] the adaptive activities of the *tao* of kings."[86]

Wang Chih commented as follows on these ideas.

Heaven has no mind, and so the activities of the *tao* of heaven are manifest in the seasons. The sage has no actions, and so the forms of the mind of the sage are apparent in the classics. The classics are the traces of the sage.

Therefore, the age of the three sages is like spring.... The age of the five emperors is like summer.... The age of the three kings is like autumn.... The age of the five hegemons is like winter.[87]

Thus Shao's concept of the duties and accomplishments of the sages and worthies is based on the mutual relationship between heaven and earth. Seasonal change in heaven initiates activity. In order for activity to be completed, humans must act in a corresponding and adjustive way. Their activities balance, or bring to full cycle, that which was inaugurated by the changes in the realm of heaven. It is the duty of the sage to complete the actions of heaven, and the accomplishments of the sages are recorded in the classics.

Their accomplishments reflect the various methods of governing and the extent to which these methods have enabled rulers to bring about the ideal society. Like the seasons, these duties and accomplishments exhibit a cyclical pattern. Both follow the four stages of birth, growth, maturity, and death.

Shao did not describe the different methods of governing associated with the four kinds of rulers simply to demonstrate the cyclical pattern of history, nor did he present his sets of correlations simply to establish the interrelatedness of all aspects of reality. Rather, he wanted to make the further point that the aim of each method of governing is to return the people (*kuei chih*) to unity. In the first stage, the rulers use *tao*, and in the following stages, they respectively use virtue (*te*), accomplishments (*kung*), and force (*li*).[88]

Each ruler uses a method that reflects the people's capabilities and needs at that stage in history. Like the Buddhists, Shao saw a decline in the level of morality across the people in the four stages. That is, at first the people spontaneously or naturally behaved in a moral way. Then they needed an ethical code to help them behave morally, a development represented by the rulers' valuing the virtue of yielding. In the third stage, the people were even less moral and so needed government, an idea that implied *cheng*, rectification or correctness. By the fourth stage, morality had declined so much that the rulers had to adopt the method of struggle. Small struggles were conducted with words and large ones with troops.[89]

Shao made the point that although the five hegemons were not true kings (*wang*), they were still better than barbarians. Barbarian rule was not even part of the four-stage cycle. The struggle characteristic of the fourth stage still involved morality, an important aspect of Chinese culture but not of barbarian culture. As Shao said, "The five hegemons were those who borrowed an empty name in order to struggle for real benefits."[90] Although the hegemons used the title "king," they were not true kings (*chen-wang*), and thus their titles did not correspond to any reality. They were "empty" names (*hsü ming*). The benefits for which they struggled—a well-ordered and moral society—were, however, quite real.

For Shao, Chinese culture began with a state of unity, harmony, or oneness during the period of the three sages (*san-huang*). As time passed, changes occurred, and moral unity was lost. As morality became increasingly elusive and difficult to re-establish, the methods needed to govern became more and more severe. The aim (and duty) of rulers in all periods was to restore the original harmony. Since circumstances had changed, however, this aim could not be realized with the same methods. Thus each kind of ruler used the method appropriate to the times.

By correlating the kinds of rulers and their governments with the four classics, Shao emphasized that this process of change follows the cyclical, four-stage pattern. The four classics represent the four stages. This pattern is part of the universe and cannot be altered. "When heaven and earth began, these four [classics] began with it. When heaven and earth end, [the classics] will end with it. Their beginnings and ends follow [those of] heaven and earth."[91]

This pattern is also that of the seasons, and just as the seasons wax and wane, so rulers and dynasties rise and fall. "Since it is so, then the sages, emperors, kings, and hegemons are the seasons of the sages. The *Yi*, *Shu*, *Shih*, and *Ch'un-ch'iu* are the classics of the sages. Seasons have waxing and waning. Classics have following and changing."[92] The concept of *yin-ke* (follow and change) in human affairs parallels that of *hsiao-chang* (waxing and waning) of the four seasons. *Yin-ke* refers to the successive changes of rule. In both human affairs and nature, however, action involves adaptive or adjustive behavior, not behavior independent of other things. The succession of dynasties, for example, reflects adaptive behavior that is part of the four-stage pattern.[93]

The idea that, although their methods were different, all rulers had the aim of returning to a unity is another version of the problem of names and reality. This problem was, in turn, associated with the *Ch'un-ch'iu*, as Shao was well aware.[94] Shao was addressing the question of how to reconcile the differences in past rulers' behavior with the claim that each had benefited society or intended to do so. His answer was that they shared the same aim, the same mind, or the same *tao*. In terms of actual behavior, Shao readily admitted that "the former sages and the later sages did not embark on the same path," and he gave examples of some differences.[95] As Shao Po-wen commented, "That in which the sages are similar is their minds. That in which they differ is their traces."[96]

Shao's position was that one cannot simply imitate the sages' actions and thereby attain the *tao* they were following, because the times do not remain the same. The past and present differ, and different actions are needed. Even the hegemons contributed to society, but if kings or emperors acted as the hegemons had, then their actions would not be considered contributions.[97]

Shao thus discussed the relationship between the general category and the particular event in the context of the relationship between name and reality, or term and referent. In his view, when one is looking at a pattern, the names of particulars can function as general terms or names of categories, rather than as proper names. The behavior of those who are called sages, emperors, kings, and hegemons differed considerably. All, however, made contributions (*kung*) to the world. The same name (*kung*) was given to different acts, and this was justified by the fact that the conditions were not the same.[98] *Kung* is a category, or a general term, and not a specific act in a historical context. Shao applied similar reasoning to the kinds of rulers themselves; even though based on actual persons, their titles referred to categories.

Shao argued that the four seasons and the four classics functioned in the same way. "If the seasons of heaven are not deficient, then the year will be successfully completed. If the classics of the sages are not in error, then the virtue of the people will be completed. Heaven has its constant seasons, and the sages have their constant classics."[99] One experiences a particular season or a particular classic, but from the viewpoint of pattern, from the viewpoint of the *tao*, the seasons and the classic are general terms. The pattern, or *tao*, cannot be seen; one knows it only from the particulars.

Heaven is produced from the *tao*. Earth is completed from the *tao*. Things take on form from the *tao*. Humans take on behavior from the *tao*. Heaven, earth, humans, and things then are different. In that they come from the *tao*, however, they are alike. The *tao* is a way. The *tao* has no form. When one implements it, then it is seen in affairs.[100]

Shao's thinking was based on the distinction between a correct (*cheng*) *tao* and a faulty (*yeh*) *tao*. Since one's duties (or *tao*) depend on one's position, the correct *tao* for one person may be a faulty *tao* for another. Those who carry out their proper duties are following the correct *tao*. Those who carry out inappropriate duties—the duties of another—are following a faulty *tao*. What is appropriate depends on the times and one's position. A father's duties are those of a father and not those of a son.[101] In a state, order and prosperity arise from following the correct *tao* and chaos and decline from following a faulty *tao*. Restoring harmony requires different means in different ages, and therefore an act that is a contribution when performed by one ruler may not be a contribution when performed by another ruler. There can be a single name for different realities as long as that name is a general term or category.[102]

Shao also addressed the problem of preserving the *tao* when there are no particular things or events to implement it.

Although King P'ing's name was king, the reality [of his rule] did not fit [even] [that of] the feudal lords of a small state. Although [the rulers of] Ch'i and Chin were feudal lords, the reality [of their rule] assumed [that of] a king. This is [the problem of] name and reality in the *Ch'un-ch'iu*.

Tzu-kung wished to do away with the sacrificial lamb at the new moon ceremony. Lamb was the name. Etiquette was the reality. The name being preserved while the reality is lost is better than the name and reality both being lost. If one preserves its [a reality's] name, how does one [not] know that a later generation, without a king, will on account of this [preservation of the name be able to] have what has been awaited?[103]*

In other words, preserving a name may allow a future generation to reproduce the lost reality, which may be those activities characteristic of a true king, of a feudal lord, or of certain kinds of etiquette. Shao implied that loss of the name as well as the activities it represented would make it more difficult to regain the original reality. Shao was not suggesting, however, that a future generation would necessarily reproduce the past; he was merely indicating that historical names can be viewed as categories that refer to kinds of events with certain characteristics. Indeed, names did function this way in Chinese historiography, particularly in regard to the stereotypes of virtuous and wicked rulers.[104] Names were a place to store knowledge in society.

---

*King P'ing (770–720 B.C.) was the reigning Chou monarch when the capital (near modern Sian) of the Western Chou was sacked and subsequently moved to Lo-yang, the capital of the Eastern Chou. Tzu-kung was a disciple of Confucius. The passage refers to an exchange between Tzu-kung, who cared more about the sacrificial lamb, and Confucius, who cared more about the ceremony.

The recognition that Shao Yung was thinking about cyclical concepts in a context that included the problem of names and reality is an important key to understanding Shao's ideas on observation and on patterns and structure. Shao was implicitly asking the question What is it, in a context that correlates the human and the natural realms, that one observes and contemplates? Shao's answer was that one observes particular things and events, but contemplates the repeating category or role of these things and events.

Shao clearly recognized that names can stand for particular things and events or for abstractions of them. Moreover, the application of names can be appropriate or not, and the very act of applying a name does not make it appropriate. Its appropriateness depends on whether the reality possesses the characteristics suggested by the name.[105] That is, if the events normally named winter were misnamed spring, the name would not be appropriate. But the acts of teaching the people with virtue and of leading them by force could both be called meritorious as long as the circumstances were appropriate.

For Shao, there was nothing inherently necessary in any particular name. His view was the Taoist one that names are a convention of society. Once a name is decided on, however, then there is a standard for judging the appropriateness of future applications of that term. Moreover, a name or a term can be applied both to a specific object or to a general class. This distinction was the source of much misunderstanding of Shao. He applied to categories names that were usually used to refer to particular objects.

These ideas were related to Shao's discussion and clarification of the concept of the four treasuries, the seasons of heaven and the classics of the sages. Both the seasons and the classics were symbols of the same *tao* or pattern, which was known through the particulars of experience. Shao argued his position by showing that the terms *past* and *present* can refer to different things and yet still be used correctly, because a word (a name) is always used from a particular point of view.[106] Moreover, a word can be used as the name of a particular thing or as a category. The fact that different terms (names) can be applied appropriately to the same reality and the same terms to different realities was a matter of perspective. When different things are called by the same word, that word is being used as a category rather than as a particular name. This was how Shao used the "seasons of heaven" and the "classics of the sages."

In Shao's view, the waxing and waning of the seasons of heaven is a correlate to the successive changes of rule (*yin-ke*) represented by the four classics of the sages.[107] The pattern, but not the particulars, is repeated endlessly. However, unlike the Buddhist view, there is no destruction of the universe at the end of each cycle. There is simply a "great transformation" (*ta-hua*), and the cycle starts over.[108]

Another important question that Shao was addressing here was the locus of meaning—Is it in the word, in the referent, or in the context?[109] To Shao, the appropriate assigning of names or terms to reality depends on context. Since different realities can be called by the same term, the meaning is not completely in the word. But since the same reality can be called by different terms, the meaning is not completely in the referent. For instance, the term *today* has many referents, and a particular person may be a ruler, a father, a husband, a son, and a brother. Shao's emphasis on perspective was another way of talking about the idea of context.

Shao was not saying that words or names have no meaning. A ruler who carries out the duties of a minister and a minister who carries out the duties of a ruler are following a faulty *tao*, not a correct *tao*.[110] To judge the correctness of the usage of a term, one needs to know how the term is being used. Moreover, it can be difficult to distinguish between the use of a term as a general category or as a particular name.

To summarize, Shao's concept of the duties and accomplishments of the sages and worthies was related to his belief in the cyclical course of human history. For Shao, human history follows the same pattern as the four seasons, the four-stage life cycle. The four classics are both records of the past and symbols of the pattern of human affairs. The names of the classics are both names of particular things (texts) and names of general categories for certain types of government and political conditions. The classics of the sages are comparable in the realm of earth to the seasons in the realm of heaven. Both are phenomenal manifestations of an unseen *tao* inherent in *ch'i*, and they represent the pattern of the universe. Shao's development of the concept of the duties and accomplishments of the sages and worthies indicates the importance of the *Ch'un-ch'iu* in his thought and its concern with the problem of names and reality.[111] In the context of this problem, Shao raised several theoretical issues, including the problem of observing particulars but seeing patterns and the location of the meaning of names (terms).

The six concepts discussed in these two chapters constitute Shao's explanatory theory of change and the nature of reality. Shao saw the universe as highly structured (both in space and time), and he regarded certain patterns as fundamental. Two important ones are the two-part pattern of *tung* and *ching* (or *yin* and *yang*, or *kang* and *jou*), and the four-part pattern of the four treasuries. With these six concepts, Shao explained change and activity in the universe. Shao dealt with two levels of reality: the sensorial or phenomenal level, and the subsensorial or subphenomenal level. Structure on the phenomenal level reflects that on the subsensorial level, the level of *ch'i*. This latter reality is a unity, from which all things are produced in an ontological sense and to which all things return, in an epistemological sense, in the mind of the sage.

7

To Recognize a Sage

> *Learning that consists of memorization is not sufficient to be considered an accomplishment.*
> —Shao Yung[1]

The implicit goal of Shao Yung and most Chinese philosophers was to restore a lost unity and harmony, a goal that applied to most fields of activity—politics, society, morality, knowledge. The expression of this goal, however, varied considerably. Political unification, social harmony, moral agreement, and the ultimate consciousness of having no mind are some examples of conceptions of the idea of unity in the Chinese philosophical tradition.

For Shao Yung, the goal of unity was embedded in ideas pertaining to the sage.[2] His focus was on unity in an epistemological sense. Given the dynamics of Shao's philosophy, his ideas about the sage were needed to complete his system of thought. The explanatory aspects of his thought dealt with the multiplicity of things in the world, the production of things from the original One, and the phenomena of change. Depending on the context, the One was variously called *t'ai-chi*, *tao*, *hsin*, or *ch'i*. Moreover, the production of the many things from the One was understood both ontologically and epistemologically. To attain the goal of unity, Shao needed a way to return to the One. It could not be done in an ontological sense because the process of cosmological development cannot be reversed. However, it could be done epistemologically and, in theory, politically, socially, and morally. Shao's ideas about the sage and his kind of knowledge serve to achieve this goal.

This chapter and the next one concern the sage. After a brief consideration of Shao Yung's conceptualization of knowledge, I discuss Shao's views on the characteristics of a sage and the knowledge a sage had. In the following chapter, I treat the topic of consciousness and Shao's concept of reflective perception (*fan-kuan*) and compare Shao Yung's concept of the sage with those of others.

Knowledge and Non-knowledge

Chinese philosophers have long been aware that there are different kinds of knowledge. The conflicts between the early Confucians and Taoists over book knowledge versus practical knowledge and the controversial views of the late Mohists on the problem of names and terms testify to this awareness. Regardless of their orientation, however, philosophers tended to be interested more in knowledge related to action than in other kinds of knowledge. Except for certain Buddhists, Chinese philosophers have had little interest in such theoretical areas as logic or formal reasoning.

The epistemological problems of interest to Chinese philosophers more often dealt with "knowing how" rather than "knowing that."[3] Shao Yung was no exception. He was no more interested than most other Chinese philosophers in discussing the validity of claims about the world. Rather, he emphasized knowledge that determined the appropriateness of certain terms and knowledge that would result in a desired action. This second kind of knowledge was recognized as so closely related to action that the two were often considered indistinguishable. Although Wang Yang-ming's "knowledge and action are one" is perhaps the most famous statement of this view, knowledge and action were regarded as inseparable from earliest times.[4] The goal of the knower, the highest form of whom was the sage, was not to possess knowledge in the form of statements but to be able to do something.

Although language was sometimes seen as a form of action, more often, as numerous passages in the Confucian *Analects* reveal, the conceptualization consisted of a dichotomy between rhetoric and action. The bias against rhetoric in favor of action was not regarded simply as an attitude without significant consequences for society. Rather, this attitude was seen as representing a set of values. These values in turn reflected patterns of behavior associated either with a well-ordered and harmonious society or with a conflictual and chaotic society. The preference for "how to" knowledge paralleled the preference for action over rhetoric. Moreover, knowledge in the form of statements was seen at best as mere talk, a reflection of social disorder or a cause of it. Although this was the early Taoists' view of Confucian knowledge, the Confucians, too, valued action-oriented knowledge, though of a different kind from the Taoists'.

Shao Yung distinguished three types of knowledge: that contained in words, that exhibited in actions (or service), and that existing in one's consciousness. He assigned the highest value to the last type. Shao Yung's view was close to the historical views of literati culture, with one significant exception. A common saying held that the highest goal was to establish oneself through virtue, the next highest through service, and the lowest through words. For virtue, Shao substituted the consciousness of the sage, a deviation that reflects a Buddhist influence.

> When the world is about to be well ordered, then people certainly value actions. When the world is about to become chaotic, then people certainly value words. When they value actions, then the winds of sincerity blow. When they value words, then the winds of treachery blow.[5]

Substituting righteousness and profit for actions and words, Shao developed this idea further.

> When the world is about to be well ordered, then the people certainly value righteousness. When the world is about to become chaotic, then the people certainly value profit. When they value righteousness, then the winds of courtesy blow. When they value profit, then the winds of thievery blow.[6]

In turn, Shao linked the ideas of righteousness and profit with social harmony and conflict. Shao backed up these claims with a reference to history: "The three kings were ones who valued actions. The five hegemons were ones who valued words. Those who value actions must enter into righteousness. These who value words must enter into profit. When righteousness and profit are separate, how far away is unity!"[7]

Huang Chi pointed out that Shao was discussing the ebb and

flow of change in human society by using specific historical examples, from Yao and Shun to King Hsüan of Ch'i. Huang suggested that historically words came to be valued only after actions were no longer sufficient by themselves.[8] The rise of the importance of words reflected a fall in morality or a disruption of social harmony. Shao expressed this view with his ideas on the different kinds of government associated with the four kinds of rulers (see Chapter 6). The passage quoted above reflects Shao Yung's view, widely accepted in the culture, that among the types of knowledge mere statements about reality are not what is valued. Moreover, this passage contains the unstated epistemological assumption that knowledge leading to action is better than knowledge leading only to words.

Shao further delineated the three kinds of knowledge, of which the highest was that of the sage.

Therefore, one knows that saying it with the mouth is not as good as performing it with the body, and performing it with the body is not as good as completely understanding it in the mind.

When one says it, people hear it. When one performs it, people see it. When one completely understands it in the mind, one's spirit knows it. The perception and acuity of other people still cannot be tricked. How much less the perception and acuity of one's own spirit?

Therefore, one knows that having no shame because of one's words is not as good as having no shame because of one's performance, and having no shame because of one's performance is not as good as having no shame because of one's mind.*

Having no verbal faults is easy compared to having no physical faults. Having no physical faults is easy compared to having no mental faults. How difficult it is to have no mental faults. How can I find a no-mental-faults person and talk about the mind with him?†

From this, one knows that the way in which the sage establishes himself in a faultless place is that he perfects his affairs in his mind.[9]

The three kinds of knowledge—knowledge that lies in words, in actions, and in one's consciousness—are arranged in a hierarchy,

---

* A restatement of Confucius' idea in *Lun-yü* 2:18; see Chan, *Source Book*, 24.
† An allusion to a statement in chap. 26 of the *Chuang Tzu*, also intended partly as humor; see Watson, *Chuang Tzu*, 302.

with the last as the highest. What makes one a sage is the state of mental perfection. Only the sage achieves that state. This substitution of the consciousness of the sage for the Confucian notion of virtue as the third and highest level shows the influence of Buddhism. For instance, Chi-tsang (549–623) of the San-lun (Three Treatise) school wrote in similar terms of his concept of *kuan-pien* (observation and discrimination). Chi-tsang said that the Buddha understands in the mind, announces from the mouth, and proclaims his knowledge as truth. The Boddhisattvas understand in the mind, announce from the mouth, and see their knowledge as theory.[10]

When speaking of the vast understanding and knowledge of the sage, Shao pointed out that by "knowledge" he did not refer to everything usually called "knowledge." Shao contrasted genuine knowledge, which he simply called knowledge, with "reckless knowledge." Others, including Chuang Tzu, also made this distinction.[11] Shao emphasized that reckless knowledge did not apply to the sage.

If someone were to say to me, "Beyond heaven and earth there are other worlds different from this world," then I do not know that. Not only do I not know that, but a sage also does not know that.

Whenever we talk about knowing, we mean that one's mind knows. When we talk about speaking, we mean that one's mouth speaks. But if one's mind does not know, then how can one's mouth speak?

If one knows when the mind is not able to know, one's knowledge is called reckless knowledge [*wang chih*]. If one speaks when one's mouth is not able to speak, one's words are called reckless words [*wang yen*]. How can I follow a reckless man and pursue reckless knowledge and reckless words?[12]

Shao was saying that unless one's knowledge is based on specific and real experience, it is not knowledge. Real knowledge corresponds to something in the physical universe. What is in the mind must be based on something in the world outside the mind. What is called knowledge is something that the mind, as a sense organ, attains after the perceptual activity of the other sense organs. Since speculation is not based on any actual, phenomenal experience of which one is consciously aware, speculation is unfounded and is therefore not knowledge. (In making this point, Shao used language similar to that of Chuang Tzu in his discussion of words, names, and knowledge.)[13]

In comparing speaking and knowing, Shao was trying to clarify what knowledge is. The mouth must say something for speech to be acquired. Similarly, there must be an experience for knowledge to be acquired. In distinguishing unfounded or reckless knowledge and real knowledge, Shao treated knowledge as analogous to language. He conceptualized the problem of knowledge as resembling the problem of names and realities. Words or names should not be applied indiscriminately or chaotically. There are proper and improper uses of words. A word applied improperly is a reckless word. For example, if a tyrant insists on being called a king, the term *king* in this instance is a reckless word.

A similar situation exists with reckless or unfounded knowledge, which is expressed with reckless words. Just as there is no true referent in this instance for the term *king*, so with reckless knowledge no actual things are experienced by the senses and subsequently attained by the mind. One can have no knowledge of a reality insensible or inaccessible to the senses ("empty" in Chinese terms) because there is no phenomenal basis for obtaining it in the mind. This is not to say, however, that at some later time, the means may not be found by which such a reality can become sensible.

Although reckless words and forced names similarly involved inappropriate uses of words, Shao did distinguish between them. In Shao's view, forced names were used intentionally to refer to the absolute or to what was not within the realm of perception. In the case of the referents of forced names, no names were appropriate. Reckless words, however, expressed unfounded opinions, and hence they involved irresponsible behavior.

In his commentary, Huang Chi adduced Tsou Yen's theory of the nine continents beyond the sea and the Buddha's idea of four great continents as examples of reckless words and reckless knowledge. Huang implied that a similar judgment of Shao Yung's *hsien-t'ien* learning would not be accurate. Shao's learning differed from these wild claims; it was based on observations of this world and on conclusions drawn from these observations. For example, by understanding the characteristics of one day, one could know or understand one cycle (*yüan*); by understanding day and night, one could know the "openings and closings" of the universe.[14] From the Chinese perspective, this was possible because everything followed the same *tao*. Analogical thinking was acceptable, and its conclusions were not reckless knowledge.

Huang was talking about the recognition of pattern. For Shao too, what can be inferred is pattern, not the existence of particulars. By repeated observation, one can understand the pattern of a thing. However, one sees not the pattern but the events that constitute the pattern. Moreover, from the pattern of one year, one can understand all years, as well as other comparable (and related) four-part cycles. The sage thus avoids speculation about the possible (but unknown) existence of particular things. Such speculation is simply reckless knowledge and not real knowledge at all. For Shao, the sage studies the patterns of the behavior of things and events already known to exist. Using slightly different terminology, Wang Chih characterized the attainment of such knowledge as completing the *li* of all things.[15] In Shao's view, although one cannot see the *li*, or pattern of things, one can come to know it by observing and understanding repeated occurrences. For Shao, knowledge of *li* depends on experience and is not *a priori* knowledge in the Western sense.

Characteristics of the Sage

To Shao, the concept of the sage was not vague or fuzzy. The sage is located in this world, the world of phenomenal experience. "And yet, humans are also things, and a sage is also a human."[16] The sage does not possess any unique existence that excludes him from the class of humans. He is not a deity or a spirit.

But the sage is no ordinary person. "From this, one knows that humans are the epitome of things, and the sage is the epitome of humans."[17] A sage is the perfection of a human being. The sage ranks higher than the superior man (*chün-tzu*) or a worthy, who in turn far outranks ordinary people. The sage does not differ in nature from other people; what makes a person a sage is his accomplishments. The distinction between a sage and others is based on actions, not on endowment at birth.

As a result of his efforts, a sage is capable of things a lesser person is not. "[A sage] can with one mind perceive ten thousand minds, with one self perceive ten thousand selves, with one thing perceive ten thousand things, and with one generation perceive ten thousand generations."[18] Shao's point is that a sage can use one thing to know all similar things because he understands the principles or patterns (*li*) of things. The sage knows that the patterns of all similar things are the same. As Shao Po-wen noted, all minds, selves, things, and generations are the same in that each has the same *li*.[19] Thus by observing and contemplating the characteristics of one spring, the sage can understand the characteristics of all springs (and all things correlated with spring).

The term Shao Yung used in this passage to express the idea of perceive is *kuan*. A crucial term in Shao's thought, this term has a variety of meanings. Shao used it here, as he did elsewhere, in several senses simultaneously. *Kuan* can mean to observe, to contemplate, to understand, and to perceive (both in the sense of to see and to understand). Here Shao was using it primarily in the sense of understanding, but an understanding based ultimately on sense experience. By using such a term as *kuan*, Shao reinforced the link between what we see and what we understand. In other words, Shao was emphasizing, in an indirect and nonexplicit way, the idea that although they are not seen in the same way as physical objects are, the patterns (*li*) of things are part of the phenomenal world. They are not objects perceived by the senses, but ideas abstracted from sense experience.

Shao went on to say that "[a sage] is one who can substitute for heaven's ideas [the ideas of] his mind, substitute for heaven's words [the words of] his mouth, substitute for heaven's work [the work of] his hands, and substitute for heaven's affairs [the affairs of] his self."[20] Shao thus emphasized the sage's ability to identify with heaven and nature.[21] The sage can go beyond the ordinary, limited perspective of human beings. He is not confined to the particular viewpoint of a specific person; he can view all things from the standpoint of the whole, from the viewpoint of *tao* or *t'ai-chi*. The sage can become confluent with the whole, and when he does so, he no longer is a thing within it. Rather, he becomes a substitute for heaven, a substitute for the forces that constitute the patterns of change in the universe.

Another of the sage's characteristics is that he "can understand the seasons of heaven above, know completely the patterns of earth below, and, in the middle, penetrate the feelings of things and thoroughly reflect human affairs."[22] Since the sage understands the "*tao* of *yin* and *yang* and waxing and waning," he therefore understands the seasons in the realm of heaven above. Moreover, since he understands the "principles of the hard and soft and the level and the hilly," he understands activities in the realm of earth below. In the realm of humans and other living creatures, the sage knows the distinctions of greatness and fineness and the classes and categories. Thus he understands the occasions of benefit and harm and of success and failure.[23] In this way, the sage understands the patterns of the universe.

The final characteristic of the sage is that he "is one who can restore the order of heaven and earth, insure the departure and arrival of the transformations, make possible the advance and retreat of the past and the present, and display and hide humans and things."[24] The sage forms a triad with heaven and earth and so becomes one with the universe. The sage has the power to regulate the activities of nature, to control time, and to influence human affairs.[25]

In his commentary, Wang Chih summarized the four main characteristics of the sage as the superiority of the sage's understanding (*shih*), the greatness of the *tao* of the sage, the fineness of the *li* of the sage, and the abundance of the power of the sage.[26] In other words, the sage understands all things and has the power of the universe; hence he can carry out the functions of the universe from the greatest to the smallest. These characteristics entail the attainment of cosmic powers (in a metaphorical sense).

The characteristics of the sage according to Shao Yung parallel those traditionally ascribed to the Buddha as he attained enlightenment. The Buddha was able to remember his former existences and the cycles of dissolution and evolution of the universe, he gained the power of superhuman vision, and he understood the workings of karma and the process of cause and effect that led to existence.[27] However, Shao's conception of the universe and its forces clearly differed from the ideas of Buddhism.

Shao admitted that a sage did not appear every generation and that he himself had never seen one. However, he had examined the sage's mind and had studied the sage's traces and activities. Therefore, he could recognize one by means of *li*. He knew the qualities that made one a sage—that is, he knew the pattern of the sage—and he would be able to recognize one:

> Alas, the sage! It is not that every generation yields a sage. I have not seen one with my eyes. Although I have not seen one with my eyes, I have examined into his mind and observed his traces, and I have searched out his forms and investigated his activities. Although it be 111,000 years, I still would know one by means of the pattern.[28]

From the discussion above, it is clear that the concept of the sage implied certain kinds of action as well as knowledge. Knowledge and action were tied together. Shao compared the sage to august heaven.[29] Whereas the sage acted in the realm of human society, august heaven acted in the realm of nature. By commenting on the relationship between the different aspects of reality, Shao laid the groundwork for the next step in his discussion:

> The *tao* of *tao* is completed [*chin*] by heaven. The *tao* of heaven is completed by earth. The *tao* of heaven and earth is completed by things. The *tao* of heaven and earth and the myriad things is completed by humans. If a person can know the method whereby the *tao* of heaven and earth and the myriad things is completed by humans, then he can complete the people.[30]

Such a person is the sage. As Shao Po-wen commented, since the sage knows that the *tao* of all things is complete (*pei*) within the self, the sage can complete the pattern of all things. Once he has done that, he can complete the people and then rule them.[31]

As noted above, Shao only partially explained the concept of august heaven. The context in which he used this term suggests, however, that "august heaven" refers to the natural forces of the realm of the sky, not to a god or a directing consciousness. Shao briefly described and compared august heaven and the sage.

> The capability of heaven to complete things is called august heaven. The capability of humans to complete the people is called the sage. If one says that august heaven is able to be different from the myriad things, then it is not what is called august heaven. If one says that the sage is able to be different from the myriad people, then he is not what is called the sage.

When the myriad people and myriad things are the same, then the sage is of course not different from august heaven. When it is thus, the sage and august heaven follow the one *tao*.

When the sage and august heaven follow the one *tao*, then the myriad people and the myriad things also can follow the one *tao*. When the myriad people of one generation and the myriad things of one generation can follow the one *tao*, then the myriad people of ten thousand generations and the myriad things of ten thousand generations can follow the one *tao*.[32]

Shao's conception of august heaven was perhaps a personification of the realm of heaven. If so, however, he conceived of august heaven for heuristic purposes, to complete a comparison between the realm of nature and the realm of human society. Shao's point was that the sage's actions and those of august heaven or the forces of nature are comparable, for both follow the same *tao*. Just as august heaven completes all things by giving them life, so the sage completes the people by giving them benevolence and virtue. Both august heaven and the sage are able to carry out their activities because "in august heaven's completion of things and in the sage's completion of the people, both have the four treasuries."[33]

As discussed above, the four treasuries of the sage and of august heaven are one manifestation of the *tao*. Since the *tao* is the pattern of the activities of things, it is not a (physical) thing and cannot be experienced through the senses. The classics serve to reveal the sage's work, however, just as the seasons exhibit the functioning of heaven.

Shao described as spontaneous or natural (*tzu-jan*) the rule of the sage and of the universe. The concept of spontaneity was based on the assumptions that there is no outside directing intelligence and that things occur without force or artificiality. In a passage reminiscent of the *Lao Tzu*, Shao gave his view of the concept of *tzu-jan*, an important characteristic of the sage's behavior. To Shao, the sage accomplishes everything without forced actions and with ease.

The natural is called having no action [*wu-wei*] and having no being [*wu-yu*]. Having no action is not not acting. It is not deliberately acting. Therefore, [the sages] could be vast.

Having no being is not not existing. It is not deliberately existing. Therefore [the sages] could be great. Those whose vastness and greatness were both complete and who did not deliberately act and deliberately exist—were they not the three sages?

From this one knows that they were able to transform the world with the *tao*, and the world also returned to the one with the *tao*.

Therefore the sage had the words, saying, "When one does not act purposively, then the people will be naturally transformed. When one does not have duties, then the people will be naturally enriched. When one loves stillness, then the people will be naturally upright. When one has no desires, then the people will be naturally simple." This is what these ideas mean.[34]

The three sages were sages because they were able to rule with spontaneity. They transformed the people with the *tao*, and they were able to keep their ideas stored in their minds, with no outer traces, or actual vocalization. This ideal way did not last, for the next group of rulers, the five emperors, had to use words and teaching. Because the people were in need of moral teaching, the ideas of the five emperors and the following rulers could not remain unspoken.[35]

The hidden and the manifest as contrasting aspects of reality resemble the model of thought found in the *Lao Tzu*. Shao spoke of *piao* and *li*, the manifest and hidden, in various places. He envisioned a progression from what is inside, silent, and still to what is outside, full of sound, and active. Ideas originally exist in the mind with no outward traces or manifestations.[36] When words come out of the mind, they have sound and so acquire traces. The traces of the images and numbers are even more manifest than the traces of words, because the images and numbers have a visual aspect. The ideal action of the sage is to maintain or to restore the initial stillness or oneness through non-action (*wu-wei*) and non-being (*wu-yu*).

According to Shao, historical development, just as cosmological development, exhibits a progression from the initial state of unity and stillness to one of myriad variations and activity. As discussed above, each of the four kinds of rulers had to use different methods to return the people to the initial unity. The sages used the *tao*, with *wu-wei* and *wu-yu*. The emperors used virtue, with the method of yielding. The kings used accomplishments, with the method of rectification. And, the hegemons used force, with the method of struggle for benefits.[37]

The times changed. Although in the beginning people behaved well naturally, they soon needed a moral code and had to be taught virtue. Then the efforts of government were needed to rectify names and restore order. In the last stage they struggled over benefits and profits. This struggle was greater if it involved troops and less if it involved only words. Wang Chih emphasized, moreover, that these ideas were based on historical rulers and periods.[38]

Shao's thought here has some similarities to the Buddhist notion that once the universal time period (kalpa) reaches the halfway point, there is a decline in human morality. Although Shao Yung did not greatly emphasize ideas of morality, he did make them an essential part of his theory about cycles and their stages, for virtue was one of the qualities of the sage. What is not present in Shao's thought is an analogue to the idea of karma (actions and the effects of one's actions on one's existences). In Buddhism, karma accounts for development and decline and all universal processes. In Shao's thought, there is no human-based source of the processes of universal change. Instead, change is inevitable, and its processes are external to and independent of human motivation. Change occurs naturally.

In summary, the characteristics of the sage involve both action and knowledge. Through his understanding, the sage becomes one with the universe in an epistemological sense. Through his behavior, the sage as ruler unites the universe in the political, moral, and social realms. The sage's actions in the human realm are, moreover, comparable to august heaven's actions in the realm of nature. Both the sage and august heaven carry out the one *tao* through their respective four treasuries. The *tao* remains the same for all people, all things, and all times.

The Knowledge of the Sage

For Shao, the goal of the sage is to know reality in its totality as an undifferentiated whole. Both the object of this kind of knowledge and the knowing experience itself are not the same as in ordinary knowledge gained from the senses. Shao's concept of the sage's knowledge refers to a particular state of consciousness or a particular kind of comprehension. Shao classified this state of consciousness as the highest form of knowledge. He tried to make it comprehensible by comparing it to states of consciousness derived from everyday experience.

Shao used no single term to refer to the absolute, the object of the sage's knowledge. In light of his ideas concerning appropriate and forced names, moreover, there were no terms he thought totally appropriate. *Shen* (spirit), *tao*, *t'ai-chi*, *hsin* (heart/mind), *yi* (one), *chung* (the center, in the middle), and *li* (pattern, principle) were his designations for the absolute. In addition, there were terms used by other philosophers, such as *t'ai-hsüan* and *t'ai-ch'u*, that he acknowledged but did not regularly use.[39]

None of these terms are truly appropriate because appropriate names have to "fit" the reality to which they refer. With absolute reality, this fit is not possible because, unlike phenomenal things, it has no boundaries, limitations, or form. Absolute reality has no specificity. Names or terms, however, apply to distinct, specific things—things whose limits can be delineated. Applying a name to absolute reality is thus using a name inappropriately. Nonetheless, it has to be done if one is to talk about the concept of the absolute. Shao's view here recalls that of Lao Tzu: "The way that can be told is not the constant way; the name that can be named is not the constant name."[40]

Shao's uses of some of these "non-constant" names are illustrated in the following statements.

Hsin is *t'ai-chi*. I also say that *tao* is *t'ai-chi*.

There is no place where *shen* is. There is no place where *shen* is not. The reason that the perfect man penetrates the minds of others is that they are based in the One. "*Tao*" and "One" are forced names of *shen*. "To regard *shen* as *shen*"—these are perfect words.

Shen is the ruler of change. Therefore it has no location. Change is the activity of *shen*. Therefore it has no form.

One *yin* and one *yang* is called *tao*. *Tao* has no sound and no form, and it cannot be seen. Therefore one borrows the [word] *tao* of *tao-lu* [road] and gives it that name. When people make a journey, they certainly follow a road. One *yin* and one *yang* are the road [*tao*] of heaven. Things are produced from it and are completed by it.

T'ai-chi is the ultimate of *tao*. *T'ai-hsüan* [Great Mystery] is the origin of *tao*. *T'ai-su* [Great Simplicity] is the root of appearances. *T'ai-yi* [Great

One] is the beginning of numbers. *T'ai-ch'u* [Great Beginning] is the beginning of duties. When they are successfully completed, then they are one.

Ch'i is one and that is all. What rules it is *ch'ien*. *Shen* also is one and that is all. When *shen* rides *ch'i*, the changes and transformations are able to enter and leave in the midst of being and non-being, life and death. [*Shen*] has no location and cannot be measured.

The learning of *hsien-t'ien* is a method of the mind. Therefore, the charts all arise from within.* The myriad transformations and the myriad affairs are produced in the mind.

The origin of heaven and earth arises from within.[41]

In summarizing Shao's ideas, Shao Po-wen also referred to the absolute or the One as "the mind of heaven and earth, the origin of changes."[42] As Shao Yung himself said, "The mind of heaven and earth gives birth to the origin of the myriad things."[43] From these remarks, one can see that Shao Yung attempted to convey the idea of absolute reality in a variety of ways. He used different terms to suggest its various aspects, because no one term could embody all its characteristics.

Since absolute reality, whatever it is called, is the goal of the sage's knowledge and since it is not a thing (*wu*) as known in ordinary experience, for the sage the process of knowing clearly differs from that of everyday knowledge. At some stage, ordinary knowledge involves sense perceptions. In knowing absolute reality, however, the senses cannot be used, at least not in the same way, because there are no things, no objects. The distinction between subject and object cannot be made. Nonetheless, this kind of knowledge does involve experience.

In talking about the sage's experience of knowing, Shao Yung was in a position equivalent to someone trying to describe sound to a deaf person. Just as he employed different designations for absolute reality, Shao used different terms and analogies to describe the sage's experience of knowing. Like the terms applied to absolute reality, however, the analogies Shao offered to elucidate the sage's

---

* *Chung*, translated here and in the next quotation as *within*, could also be translated as *emptiness*.

experience of knowing are not truly appropriate, for no analogy can represent all aspects of this process of knowing.

Like the various terms for the absolute, the analogies represent different models to help people understand an unknown process of knowing. They attempt to present such equivalent notions as penetrating the One, confluence with the whole, or becoming one with all. A particular type of epistemological activity allows the sage to return to the ontological wholeness of reality, in which there are no "things," and no distinctions.[44] The fundamental concept is to reverse the movement of cosmological development, which proceeds from the One to the many. The sage's kind of knowing goes from the many to the One; it merges back into the one reality preceding particular things. The processes of change, by which the cosmological development of phenomenal things occurs, are reversed in the epistemological experience of the sage.

The most common analogies used by Shao are expressed in the ideas of penetrating (*t'ung*), clarifying (*ming*), and attaining (*te*) the *tao* or *li*. Each of these concepts presents a different image of behavior, but they share the central idea of having no awareness of self apart from other things. That is, in the process of knowing, the self merges with the whole, dissolving the subject-object distinction. Indeed, this is Shao's idea of knowing reality.

The following passages are representative samples of Shao's presentation of these ideas.

Hsien-t'ien learning resides in wholeness [*ch'eng*]. If one is whole to the utmost, one can penetrate [*t'ung*] spirit-brightness [*shen-ming*]. If one is not whole, then one cannot attain the *tao*.

This one who completes his own nature can complete the nature of other things. Not only is it so with fish, but it is so with all the things of the universe. Like Chuang Tzu, he can be said to be good at penetrating things.

Lao Tzu was one who understood [*chih*] the forms of change. Lao Tzu's five thousand words on the whole all were concerned with clarifying [*ming*] the patterns of things.

The learning of the superior man regards soaking the self [*jun shen*] as basic. His ruling of others and responding to things are both additional matters.

One who attains the patterns of heaven not only soaks the self, but also can soak the mind. He not only soaks the mind, but even nature and destiny he also soaks.

If the mind is one and not divided, then one can respond to the myriad changes. This is the reason that the superior man empties his mind and does not move.

When one engages in learning and nourishes the mind, the fear is that one will not follow the straight *tao*. If one gets rid of benefit and desire, follows the straight *tao*, and rests in wholeness to the utmost, then there is nothing one does not penetrate.[45]

In sum, the "object" of the sage's knowledge is not an ordinary phenomenal thing (*wu*), nor for the sage is the process of knowing similar to ordinary knowing. Rather, the "object" is reality as a whole, and the process of knowing involves merging with the whole. The goal of this epistemological experience suggests the original ontological state. Shao was acutely aware of the fact that ordinary language is inadequate to describe the sage's kind of knowing, and he used a variety of analogies to convey his ideas about the process. This process of knowing clearly differs from that which functions through *ling* (consciousness) and the sense organs.

8

To Become a Sage

> *Learning consists in not stopping. Therefore Wang T'ung said that it is simply [a matter of continuing to study] to the end of one's life.*
> —Shao Yung[1]

As discussed in Chapter 7, Shao Yung ascribed certain characteristics to the sage. In his external behavior, the sage is identified by particular kinds of actions and words. Although the *tao* the sages follow is constant for all time, their actions and words vary according to the age. The sage also pursues a particular type of knowledge, the object of which is reality as a whole. The goal is a type of consciousness or state of mind, which is not attained through ordinary sense perception. It is not consciousness in the common sense of awareness, for it is not concerned with the world of the senses and there is no subject-object distinction. In this chapter, I discuss the characteristics of this state of mind and the method to be used to obtain it.

Consciousness and Reflective Perception

In Shao Yung's view, the ultimate state of mind is one in which one perceives, or completely comprehends, a thing from the viewpoint of the thing and not from the viewpoint of oneself. Shao called the method used to achieve this particular kind of consciousness *fan-kuan* (reflective perception). In elaborating on the meaning of this concept, Shao used several other terms and concepts, the most important of which are *ling*, consciousness, and *kuan-wu*, to observe, to contemplate, to comprehend things. In developing his thought on *fan-kuan*, particularly on *kuan*, Shao Yung conceived of knowledge in terms of, and as analogous to, sense perception. This approach was not unusual, and we see in it the influence of such philosophers as Chuang Tzu and Hsün Tzu and of some schools of Buddhism.

Although Shao set a goal of attaining a state of consciousness that somehow overcomes the senses, consciousness in the sense of *ling* uses the senses and operates on the perceptual level of reality. Things exist whether observed or not, but they are not "completed" until seen or otherwise perceived by someone. The idea of completion entails perception and awareness by a perceiver.[2] For instance, ears receive sounds and eyes receive colors, but the acts of hearing and seeing do not occur unless one is aware of or conscious of the sounds and colors. In this sense, humans complete sounds and colors. For Shao Yung, *ling* referred to this active relationship between the perceiver and perceived and to the human ability to have such a relationship.

The concept of *ling* thus applies to the interaction between the human mind and the phenomenal world. Shao believed that most living beings have consciousness, but that humans have the highest kind of consciousness, and hence only they are able to "complete" things. Thus, "humans are the most *ling* of things," and "the consciousness of things does not equal the consciousness of humans."[3] The sage, as the epitome of human beings, has the ability to achieve another kind of consciousness, one that surpasses *ling*. In this state, the sage goes beyond ordinary sense experience.[4] The sage uses *fan-kuan*, reflective perception, to achieve this extraordinary state.[5] The term *fan-kuan* was used in Ch'an Buddhism to describe a method of meditation and contemplation, often in conjunction with the concept of *kuan-hsin* (contemplating the mind). Hui Ssu, a Northern Ch'an teacher and a forerunner of the T'ien-t'ai school of Buddhism, is said to have used the method of *fan-kuan tzu-hsin* (reflective perception of one's mind), and Shen Hsiu of the Northern school of Ch'an Buddhism wrote a piece called *Kuan-hsin lun* (On contemplating the mind).[6]

In order to explain what he meant by *fan-kuan*, Shao first discussed the meanings of *kuan-wu*. He conceived of consciousness as a continuum with ordinary sense perception at one end and a state of mystical unity at the other. In the following passage, Shao used *kuan* in three distinct senses, each of which built on the previous sense.

That which is called *kuan-wu* is not observing [*kuan*] things with one's eyes. It is not that one observes things with one's eyes but that one contemplates [*kuan*] them with one's mind. It is not that one contemplates them with one's mind but that one understands [*kuan*] them by means of pattern [*li*].*

Of the things of the world, none do not have pattern in them. None do not have nature [*hsing*] in them. None do not have destiny [*ming*] in them.* As for that which is called *li*, one thoroughly penetrates it and then it can be known. As for that which is called nature, one completely fulfills it and then it can be known. As for that which is called destiny, one completely extends it and then it can be known.

These three [kinds of] knowledge are true knowledge [*chen-chih*]. Even a sage has nothing with which to surpass these. And one who does surpass these [kinds of knowledge] is not one who is called a sage.[7]

Shao thus equates comprehension with total and perfect perception. In a three-step process, one proceeds from ordinary sense experience, to thought, and finally to the third stage of "knowing" reality by having the *li* reflect directly in one's mind. In the third state, there is no longer any distinction between the perceiving subject and the perceived object. Each step in these three stages involves a further blurring of that distinction.

In the stage of sense experience, the subject and object are clearly distinct before contact. The eye belongs to the perceiver, and the characteristics of appearance belong to the phenomenal object to be perceived. The act of seeing begins a relationship between the two. Seeing, however, is not a physical process on the level of *ch'i*. It is

---

*This is a comparison. Each succeeding level is better, or more valued, than the preceding level. Compare Shao's use of *yi* (easy) and *nan* (hard) in the passage on verbal, physical, and mental faults in Chapter 7. For a similar passage in the *Chuang Tzu*, see Watson, *Chuang Tzu*, 57–58. There the term used is *t'ing* (listen) instead of *kuan*.

*These three concepts, found in the *Yi-ching* (see Chan, *Source Book*, 269), are of central importance in Neo-Confucianism. The concepts of nature and destiny are also important in the *Mencius* and in various Han texts.

not equivalent, for example, to a camera lens's receiving the refraction of light waves. The relationship of seeing exists on a different level of reality from light waves, because it involves *ling*, or human awareness. Although the subject and object are distinct entities, in the process of observation the distinction between subject and object begins to be blurred because of the phenomenon of consciousness.

The next stage, that of thinking about or contemplating something, links subject and object more closely. One idealist position in Buddhism suggests that things do not exist outside of the mind, that reality depends on, or is, our consciousness of it.[8] Shao's view was not quite so extreme, for he did recognize that some kinds of reality, such as *ch'i*, do not depend on human consciousness. However, once they become an object of thought, even those things that exist independently of oneself also exist in some sense "in" the mind, as ideas. Ideas are things that belong to or "exist" in the mind. The mind is the habitat of ideas, just as the earth is the habitat of metal and water. Since ideas are part of the perceiving subject, the distinction between subject and object is further blurred at this second stage. At this point, however, it is still possible to distinguish between the perceiving self and the perceived not-self, the object. One is aware that one is thinking about something.

At the third stage of total reflection, however, any subject-object distinction is invalid and impossible to make. The two entities merge into, or return to, the One, like the reflection in a mirror. Shao called this ultimate kind of knowledge *chen-chih*, true knowledge.[9] Shao imagined a state of mind in which unwanted thoughts and individual feelings are eliminated because there is no awareness of self and other. Like *t'ai-chi*, this state has no movement and no distinctions. A sage's mind becomes confluent with absolute reality, much as the reflection in a mirror becomes confluent with the images reflected in it. In contrast to ordinary knowledge and observation of things in the phenomenal world, the sage's experience of knowing involves perfect reflection attained through introspection (*fan-shen*).[10]

Shao was saying that ordinarily we see a thing with our eyes, and we contemplate and think about a thing with our minds. On the highest level of experience—that of the sage—however, the patterns (*li*) of things are reflected without impediment in his absolutely still and clear mind. He is able to perceive, to understand or know completely, absolute reality as it is in a thing. A sage thus "sees" the reality, the *li*, of a thing through its "reflection."

In describing the sage's state of mind, Shao was trying to explain in words a phenomenon that did not occur in words. In order to do this, he employed concepts from all of China's intellectual traditions, and he used various sense images. For example, Shao utilized the Confucian concept of wholeness or sincerity (*ch'eng*), as well as the Taoist and Buddhist image of a pure, clear, empty, and reflecting mirror.[11] Drawing from the *Yi-ching*, he also spoke of the sage's mind as the ability to investigate the pattern thoroughly, to exhaust the nature (*hsing*) fully, and to fulfill destiny.[12] These ideas were merely alternative ways of talking about perfect knowledge, however, and did not refer to separate kinds of knowledge.

In regard to these concepts and the highest kind of knowledge, Shao said:

What heaven confers on me is called destiny [*ming*]. When destiny is in me, it is called nature [*hsing*]. When nature is in things, it is called pattern [*li*].

After the pattern is investigated to the utmost, one knows the nature. After the nature is fully developed, one knows the destiny. After the destiny is known, knowledge has reached its limit.[13]

Like many other philosophers, Shao conceived of the sage's knowledge in terms of perception, particularly visual acuity.

That whereby a mirror is able to be bright and clear is that it is able not to obscure the forms of the myriad things. Even so, a mirror's ability not to obscure the forms of the myriad things is not as good as the ability of water to unite with* the forms of things. Even so, water's ability to unite with the forms of the myriad things is, further, not as good as the sage's ability to unite with the sentiments of the myriad things.

That whereby a sage is able to unite with the sentiments of the myriad things is the sage's ability to perceive reflectively [*fan-kuan*]. That which is called reflective perception is not perceiving things [*kuan wu*] from

---

*The term *unite with* suggests the idea of bringing into a unity, so that one does not know which is the reflection and which the thing. Thus, it means to form a whole.

the viewpoint of the self. Not perceiving things from the viewpoint of the self is perceiving things from the viewpoint of things. If one can perceive things from the viewpoint of things, how can there be a self in between?[14]

Comprehension is thus a perfect form of reflection, which is, in turn, the perfect form of perception. The visual image is that of a perfect reflection of something in a mirror or in absolutely still water. *Kuan* is best understood as having three primary meanings, one for each level of experience. One sees or observes things external to oneself. One contemplates and intellectually understands things with one's mind, through one's mental processes. And, one has complete insight into, or total knowledge of, things by means of their perfect reflection in one's absolutely still, clear mind.

This changing meaning of *kuan* in Shao's concept of *fan-kuan* did not go unnoticed by Chinese commentators from the Sung to the Ch'ing. Shao Po-wen, for example, noted that *kuan* is used differently at each step. At the first step, one sees (*kuan*) the forms of things. At the second step, one "sees" the sentiments of things (here "sees" is used metaphorically in the sense of understand). At the third step, one "exhausts" or completes the natures of things and totally comprehends the absolute reality of things.[15] Huang Chi emphasized that at the third stage the mind is empty of all conscious thought. It does not calculate. The pattern or nature in things can be "grasped" by such a mind by being reflected in the mind.[16] Wang Chih also emphasized that this true knowledge (*chen-chih*) refers to "perceiving" the reality (*shih*), or pattern (*li*), of things.[17]

Only at the third level of *kuan* is complete unity reached. The three levels can be compared, but they are not equivalent. Thus, still water reflects better than a mirror. Water can reflect so well that it can be difficult to distinguish between the reflected image and the thing. However, the mind of the sage can reflect even better. The sage's mind can reflect perfectly. To do so, the mind must be absolutely still, void, and clear.

Since Shao used the term *kuan* in several different senses, no single translation of *kuan* is completely satisfactory. It was not unusual that Shao did this, for a number of the philosophical terms commonly used by him and by others had several distinct uses.[18] The context, of course, allowed one to know the relevant meaning.

Kuan thus meant not only to see and observe things but also to contemplate them and to understand them. Shao believed that the further removed one is from the level of experience of sense perception and its emphasis on the single viewpoint of the self, the more unbiased one can become. For Shao, the self is the impediment to perfect perception or reflection. But what did he mean by the self?

The Self and Reflective Perception

The self was an important element in Shao's concepts of *fan-kuan* and *kuan-wu*, and Shao discussed it in several passages. Part of the meaning of *fan-kuan*, as seen in the passages quoted above, is that there can be no intrusion of the self, no awareness of the distinction between self and other. Perfect reflection is not like the process of observing or seeing, for in these processes there is a perceiver. It is also not like the process of thinking, for that process seems (at least) to have a thinker. Thus there are subject and object, thinker and thoughts. *Fan-kuan* suggests the idea of an almost physical merging. An image and its reflection in a mirror do literally merge, although they do so only in a limited way.

Different conceptions of the self existed in Shao's intellectual milieu.[19] The usual Confucian term used was *chi*, which normally had social implications. Shao instead used the Buddhist term *wo*, again in several different senses.[20] Shao's two basic conceptions were ontological and what may perhaps be called psychological. The first addressed the question of whether the self consisted of a permanent nature of some sort, such as *li, shen*, or *hsü* (emptiness). The second referred to the view of the self as a particular person in contrast to all others and included an awareness of "this" versus "that" or subject versus object.

Shao Yung utilized both these concepts of self as he developed his concept of *fan-kuan*. Indeed, his intent seems to have been to enable people to discard the more common meaning of self as a particular person and to have them realize, both intellectually and experientially, the other, more "spiritual" meaning of self. (Shao's other concepts of the self are not immediately relevant in this context and so will not be discussed.)[21]

With his concept of *fan-kuan*, Shao Yung was proposing to eliminate the individual self as a perceiver, as a particular person distinct from others. Shao's goal was to observe, contemplate, and understand (perceive) a thing in terms of itself and not in terms of the separate perceiver.²² There should be no awareness of separation between subject and object; they are to form a whole. This is possible for the sage because he completely empties his mind and the object perfectly fills it, like a reflection in a mirror. The sage's mind and the object are identical, and there is no question or possibility of distinguishing between subject and object. In Shao's concept of *fan-kuan*, one gains perfect "insight" through total identification with the other.

Shao expressed these ideas in the following statements.

If one perceives things from the viewpoint of things, it is their nature [that one perceives]. If one perceives things from the viewpoint of one's self, it is a matter of one's feelings.* The nature is public and clear. The feelings are private and obscured.

If one does not perceive a thing from the viewpoint of the self, then one can perceive a thing from the viewpoint of the thing.

The sage benefits things and has no self.

If one relies on the self, then it is a matter of one's feelings. If it is a matter of one's feelings, then there are obscurations. If there are obscurations, then things are murky.

If, however, one depends on the thing, then it is a matter of its nature. If it is a matter of its nature, then it is a matter of spirit [*shen*]. If it is spirit, then it is clear and bright.

Have no preconceptions, no dogmatism, no obstinacy, and no self.† If you unite these things and speak of them, then they are one. If you divide them and speak of them, then they are two. If you unite them [again] and speak of them, then they are two. If you divide them [again] and speak of them, then they are four.

It begins with having preconceptions and is completed with having a self. If there are preconceptions, afterward there is dogmatism. Dogmatism is produced from preconceptions. If there is obstinacy, afterward there is a self. The self is produced from obstinacy.

---

* *Ch'ing* (feelings) could also be translated as "circumstances."
† An allusion to *Lun-yü* 9.4; see Chan, *Source Book*, 35.

In the learning of the principles [*li*] of things, sometimes there is that which one does not understand [*t'ung*]. One cannot force understanding. If one forces understanding, then there is a self. If there is a self, then one loses the *li* and enters into techniques [*shu*].*

If the mind is whole and not split, then it can respond to the myriad changes. This is how the superior man empties his mind and does not let it move.[23]

In these and other passages, Shao stated both how people normally think—they make a distinction between themselves and others—and how, with the sage as the model, they can overcome this way of thinking. Anyone who tries to perceive a thing from a particular viewpoint, or to force understanding, will end up with a partial and biased understanding. Some aspects of the thing will be obscured because the whole cannot be seen or understood from one angle only. Moreover, one's mental state will contribute to mistakes or inaccuracies in perception. Anyone, however, who tries to perceive a thing from the viewpoint of total identification can understand it completely. The reality of a thing is its nature (*hsing*), which is equivalent to *li* (pattern, principle). These terms referred to a thing's pattern of activity or behavior. To Shao one cannot totally understand a thing without complete identification with it; one has to forgo distinguishing between oneself and the thing.

For Shao, self-awareness clearly is a necessary part of the formation of a self. The self appears with conscious thoughts, preconceptions, and obstinacy. These things separate the self from the surrounding world, cloud the mind, and prevent one from reaching a state of perfect understanding. They act like specks of dust on a mirror, because they interfere with the process of reflection.

Understanding involves getting past the outer, obscuring aspects of a thing and penetrating to its core. This had to be done with total ease and without force, however, for otherwise one's deliberateness would break up the unity and separate the self and the other. Here again we see the use of the inner-outer distinction and the concept of *wu-wei* of the *Lao Tzu*.

In explaining Shao's ideas, Huang Chi distinguished a *yu-wo chih hsin* (a mind that possesses a self) from a *wu-wo chih hsin* (a mind

---

* *Shu* (techniques) were considered an inferior type of knowledge.

that does not possess a self). At the level of conscious thinking, the sage's mind, like the minds of others, is aware of self and other. When one perceives with one's mind, and not merely with one's eyes, one's mind is a *yu-wo chih hsin*.[24] Such a mind thinks and contemplates and differentiates between thinker and thoughts.

At the level of perfect reflection, there is no awareness of self. Huang Chi called this kind of sage's mind a *wu-wo chih hsin*. This "no-self" mind does not perceive with the mind but with *li* and so is identical with *li* through the process of reflection. There is no consciousness or awareness on the part of the perceiver. If there were, then there would be a relationship between the self and the other, rather than unity. Total awareness leads to, and indeed means, the state of no awareness. The self in these two concepts mentioned by Huang Chi was the individual self of a particular person, not *li* or a universal self.

This concept of *wu-wo chih hsin* is not the Buddhist concept of no-self. In Buddhism the concept of no-self refers to the view that there is no essential nature, no self-causing nature, or no eternal nature in things. In the Buddhist view, all things depend on other things for their existence and hence are ultimately void.[25]

Shao's idea of a no-self mind was equivalent to his idea of no-mind, or having no deliberate intentions. Some have erroneously associated his idea of no-mind with his ability to foresee. Shao did not use the concept of no-mind in the context of foreknowledge, an ability that he explained in natural terms.[26] Shao is reported to have told a story about an adept (a *tao-jen*) who, when asked about foreknowledge, replied that it was "having no mind." When asked if "having no mind" could be studied, the *tao-jen* answered that if desire leads one to study "having no mind," then on the contrary it would be a case of "having a mind."[27] Allowing the *tao-jen* to speak for him, Shao thus said that anyone who deliberately tried to cultivate a state of no-mind in order to do something with it, such as knowing the future, would not succeed. The reason is that no-mind is not a method (*shu*) for dealing with the phenomenal world. Rather, it is a state of consciousness. In Shao's thought, this concept is applied to the kind of knowing that a sage has, in which he merges with the *tao*, or with all of reality, and consequently has no (individual) self.

After establishing this idea of the individual and limited self, which was overcome successfully only by the sage, Shao presented his other view of the self as equivalent to the principles of reality or the whole of reality itself. Shao Po-wen noted the similarity between Shao Yung's concept of *fan-kuan* and the idea that "all things are complete within me." [28] Although Shao Po-wen did not mention it, this idea was basic, in slightly different senses, both to Mencius and to the T'ien-t'ai school of Buddhism.[29] This idea means that one has within oneself the principles of all things because reality is ultimately one. All things have a single principle or pattern. The Marxist scholar Yang Jung-kuo has pointed out that Shao Yung did express this idea in several of his poems.[30]

Huang Chi noted that the idea of the unity of things, based on their having a single pattern (*li*), was the point of an earlier statement by Shao that with one mind the sage can perceive (*kuan*) all minds, with one self he can perceive all selves, with one thing he can perceive all things, and with one generation he can perceive all generations.[31] Shao's concept of the self as the *li* of the universe applies, however, only to the sage.

The conception of the self as all, or as equivalent to the universe, is an ontological conception. Everything is *ch'i*, or *li* if one looks at it from a different viewpoint, and the patterns in one are the patterns in all. For Shao, the ultimate wholeness can be described both in ontological and in epistemological terms. One can view the ultimate in terms of a state of reality, for example, *ch'i*, or one can understand it from the viewpoint of knowing. This understanding is *chen-chih* (true knowledge). The ontological state of unity corresponds to the highest state of knowing, and the epistemological experience of wholeness coincides with the ontological state of oneness.

For example, on the subsensorial level (that stratum which exists but cannot be known through normal sense experience), the idea of wholeness is represented by such concepts as *t'ai-chi*, absolute stillness, *ch'i*, or what one chart calls "between one movement and one stillness" (see Fig. B4). In this state, movement has not yet arisen (*wei-fa*), and there is only the stillness of *t'ai-chi*. Shao also expressed this idea as a balance between *yin/yang* and *kang/jou*.[32] In other words, the true knowledge of the sage is epistemologically equivalent to attaining the ontological state of the *ch'i* of centrality and harmony.

In Buddhist thought, that which in ontological terms is called nirvana, suchness, or void is, in epistemological terms, called enlightenment. Although Shao's concepts and terms differed from those of Buddhism, the structure of his thought was similar. However, his concept of reality differed from that in Buddhism; *ch'i*, *tao*, or *t'ai-chi* is not identical to nirvana or shunyata (the void). Both Buddhism and Shao Yung conceived of returning to the state of absolute reality, the One. In Buddhism this idea is expressed in Chi-tsang's theory of the double truth and Chih Yi's theory of *chih-kuan* (cessation and contemplation).[33] This dual approach, or use of two viewpoints often simultaneously, was a further aspect of Shao's attempt to convey his ideas about ultimate reality and the process of knowing of the sage through a variety of terms and analogies.

Shao concluded his discussion of the concept of reflective perception and the sage's ability to use this method to achieve a unity with the universe with the following statement.

From this one knows that the self is also the other, and the other is also the self. The self and the other both are things.

This is that whereby [the sage] can use the eyes of the world as his own eyes. There is nothing its eyes do not see. This is why he can use the ears of the world as his own ears. There is nothing its ears do not hear. This is why he can use the mouths of the world as his own mouth. There is nothing its mouths do not say. This is why he can use the minds of the world as his own mind. There is nothing its minds do not think.

The observations of the world—in terms of seeing, are they not vast? The listenings of the world—in terms of hearing, are they not far? The words of the world—in terms of discussions, are they not lofty? The thoughts of the world—in terms of joy, are they not grand?

[The sage's] seeing is the most vast, his hearing is the most distant, his discussing is the most lofty, and his joy is the most grand. He is able to engage in activities that are vast to the utmost, distant to the utmost, lofty to the utmost, and grand to the utmost, and yet in the midst of it all there is no one doing it. How can one say that he is not one who is most spiritual and most sagely?

It is not only I who say that he is the utmost spiritual and utmost sagely one, but the whole world says that he is the utmost spiritual and utmost sagely one. It is not only the whole world of one time that says that he is the utmost spiritual and utmost sagely one, but the whole world of ten million generations says that he is the utmost spiritual and utmost sagely one. After this, no one really knows.[34]

The sage attains the state of no-self when he can combine all the world's events of seeing, hearing, and the like into one such great event. With that achievement, he merges himself with, or identifies himself with, the world. The sage then does not have a separate viewpoint. Consequently, he does everything. But, as Shao says, there is no "one" doing it. There is no self in opposition to the other. The sage is thus equivalent to *tao*.

Shao Po-wen commented that when we perceive things with our eyes, we see the phenomenal aspects. When we perceive things in our mind, we rarely achieve a full understanding because our minds are occupied by other things. These preoccupations prevent us from paying total attention. When, however, we perceive things according to their *li*, then we have a perfect understanding because we are "seeing" from the standpoint of *tao*, or the whole. There is a perfect reflection of the thing in the mind. We are not using a private or particular viewpoint, and there is no self intervening in this process of perception.[35]

There is a method for attaining this knowledge. One first views selves from the viewpoint of selves, families from the viewpoint of families, states from the viewpoint of states, and finally the world from the viewpoint of the world. The method is to begin with the small, the nearby, the familiar, those things that are easier to identify with. Gradually, one expands one's consciousness to the point of total identification with the universe, a state that is paradoxically one of no consciousness.[36]

In this ordering, we see the influence of an idea prominent in such texts as the *Ta-hsüeh*, the *Chung-yung*, and the *Analects*. Order results from first ordering oneself, then the family, then the state, and finally the whole world. The cultivation of order, if it is to be successful, must proceed in proper sequence, starting with the smallest part and finishing with the whole. Shao in effect utilized this idea when he talked about the understanding of the sage, who started with the self, and then proceeded to the family, the state, and finally to the world.³⁷ In Buddhism, too, learning to meditate utilized methods that began with concentration on something small, nearby, and familiar.

In summary, in his concept of reflective perception, which was equivalent to true knowledge, the knowledge of the sage, Shao Yung utilized two conceptions of self. One concept emphasized the idea of one person as distinct from another. Used in an epistemological sense, this meaning of self involved an awareness on the part of the perceiver between subject and object. The other conceived the self ontologically as one with the universe. Its patterns were those of the universe, and its *ch'i* was that of the universe.

Kuan-wu and *Fan-kuan* in the Philosophical Context

Through use of the terms *kuan-wu* and *fan-kuan*, Shao implicitly evoked several distinct intellectual contexts. With the formation of these concepts, Shao Yung was responding to philosophical questions already posed in his culture and was adding to what others had said before him. In particular, certain Buddhist ideas, as well as ideas of Chuang Tzu and Hsün Tzu, were an important part of the background of Shao's concepts. In these other contexts, the term *kuan* was used in several different ways, whose multiple meanings and associations were carried over into Shao's thought.

Shao Yung's thought had close ties to that of Chuang Tzu. Shao's concepts of *fan-kuan* and *kuan-wu* owed much to Chuang Tzu's ideas about observation and knowledge. Chuang Tzu contrasted the observation of things from the point of view of particular things and from the point of view of *tao*, or the universe, and pointed out that one's claims and judgments about things were relative to particular viewpoints in space and time. Words and one's use of them were clearly social conventions. To overcome the biases of particular points of view, one should view things from the point of view of the whole. Too often people merely know the appearances of things from their limited points of view. However, to borrow a Kantian contrast, the sage can know a thing-in-itself because he can view it from the point of view of *tao* or the whole. Passages like the following from the *Chuang Tzu* express these views.

From the point of view of the Way, things have no nobility or meanness. From the point of view of things themselves, each regards itself as noble and other things as mean.

There is nothing in the world bigger than the tip of an autumn hair, and Mount T'ai is tiny.[38]

Two other ideas of Chuang Tzu are relevant to Shao Yung's thought. If, in judging things, we use ourselves as the standard, we end up with unsupportable claims. If, however, we use the object itself as the standard, then we may end up with a more reliable kind of knowledge. The famous conversation between Hui Tzu and Chuang Tzu (which is quoted by Shao Yung) concerning what the fish enjoy reflects this idea.[39] Another of Chuang Tzu's ideas is that of "listening" on different levels; one progresses from listening on the level of the senses to listening on the conceptual level and finally to listening on the level of spirit.[40] Shao Yung clearly used a similar framework for his idea of *kuan*.

The influence of Buddhism is also apparent in Shao Yung's thought. Shao made no direct references to specific Buddhist texts, but he did use terms derived from, or similar to those used in, Buddhism. The concepts of *chih-kuan* (cessation and contemplation), *wu* (enlightenment), *wo* (self), *shou* (to receive), and *shan* (to complete), in the context of perception and consciousness, all contributed to the formation of Shao's concept of *fan-kuan*. For instance, the following statement by Shao Yung paraphrases Chih Yi's words on his theory of cessation and contemplation. "If one perceives things from the viewpoint of things, it is a matter of their nature [which one perceives]. If one perceives things from the viewpoint of one's self, it is a matter of one's feelings."[41]

Shao's concepts of perception and consciousness exhibit certain similarities to the ideas not only of the T'ien-t'ai school of Chih Yi and the Hua Yen school of Fa Tsang but also to the ideas of the Consciousness-Only school, which analyzed the processes of perception and postulated eight divisions of consciousness.[42] The first six divisions consist of the five senses and the mind. These correspond to Shao's first and second levels of "seeing with the eyes" and "perceiving with the mind." The seventh, the *manas* consciousness, or consciousness of intellection, is an awareness of self as subject and in this sense is comparable to Shao's second level of "perceiving (or, contemplating) with the mind." The *alaya*, or eighth consciousness, the storehouse consciousness, as the level of absolute reality, corresponds to Shao's highest level. On this level there is no self, and things are perceived according to *li*. Like the adherents of these idealistic schools, Shao used the terms *shou* (receive) and *shan* (complete), as in the eye receives the colors, the ear receives the sounds, and the eye completes the colors, the ear completes the sounds.[43]

A further influence on Shao's concept of *fan-kuan* are the ideas of Hsün Tzu on perception and knowledge, the obstacles to knowledge, and the ability to have unbiased perception. The passage by Shao Yung quoted immediately above continues with these words, which echo Hsün Tzu: "The nature is public and clear. The feelings are private and obscured."[44]

Like Hsün Tzu in the past and like many of his own contemporaries, Shao Yung conceived of knowledge as analogous to perception. In developing his ideas on the sage, Shao Yung not only used many elements from the Chinese intellectual tradition, but even the textual sources of many of his ideas are identifiable. To help elucidate the significance of Shao's particular concepts concerning the knowledge of the sage, a brief comparison with the philosophical position of a contemporary, Chang Tsai, may be useful. The contrast between Shao and Chang indicates two of the ways in which philosophers used the same assumptions and ideas from the tradition.[45]

Shao's concepts of reflective perception (*fan-kuan*) and seeing things as things (*yi wu kuan wu*) contain similarities to the concept of expanding the mind (*ta-hsin*) of Chang Tsai. Shao and Chang used different words, but their positions were extremely close. Both Shao and Chang argued for merging the self with the whole, so that there is no consciousness of self and other.

Chang Tsai's concept of *ta-hsin* implies expanding one's consciousness until it encompasses all things in the universe. When this state is achieved, there is no distinction between oneself and the world.

If one expands one's mind, then one can embody all the things of the world. If some things are not yet embodied, then one's mind still has things outside of it. The minds of ordinary people stop with the narrowness of hearing and seeing. The sage, however, completely develops his nature and so does not restrict his mind to seeing and hearing. He sees the world as not having a single thing that is not himself. This is why Mencius said that if one completely develops one's mind, then one will know nature and heaven. Heaven is so vast that there is nothing outside of it. A mind that has things outside of it cannot unite itself with the mind of heaven. Knowledge from seeing and hearing is knowledge derived from contact with things. It is not what one's virtuous nature knows. What one's virtuous nature knows does not sprout from seeing and hearing.[46]

Rather than speak of no-self, however, as Shao Yung did, Chang Tsai said that everything becomes one's own self. Whether stated in a positive or a negative way, the idea in both cases is that there is no subject-object distinction. Chang distinguished the sensorial knowledge of ordinary people, which he called *wen-chien chih chih* (knowledge from hearing and seeing), and the qualitatively different knowledge of the sage, or *te-hsing chih chih* (knowledge from one's virtuous or moral nature).[47] For Chang, it was this second kind of knowledge that enabled the sage to merge with universe. His allusion to Mencius makes it clear that he was thinking of a Mencian type of moral and spiritual cultivation.

Thus, Chang and Shao attached different meanings to the view that the sage becomes one with the universe. Whereas Chang Tsai was speaking more in moral terms and in the sense of moral cultivation, Shao Yung was speaking in epistemological terms and dealing with states of consciousness. Moreover, for Shao Yung, the epistemological experience of achieving unity with the universe was, in an ontological sense, equivalent to reversing the cosmological process, which went from the one to the many.

The difference in the terms used by Shao and Chang reflects the problem that arises when language developed in one epistemological context is used in another. The result is that some terms are not adequate to express new ideas because they are based on different metaphysical assumptions. Words have to be used metaphorically, analogies have to be made that are obviously just analogies, words have to be used in new and unusual ways, and new phrases have to be coined. To solve the problem, Shao used such phrases as *fan-kuan* (reflective perception), *pu yi wo kuan wu* (perceiving things not from the viewpoint of the self), and *yi wu kuan wu* (perceiving things from the viewpoint of things), and Chang Tsai used the phrase *ta-hsin* (expanding the mind).

The problem was to find appropriate words to convey ideas whose significance did not lay in words. This was a concern not only to those Neo-Confucian philosophers who developed aspects of the thought of Lao Tzu and Chuang Tzu but also to the Madhyamika school of Buddhism. There it found expression in Chi-tsang's theory of the double truth.[48] In this theory, one proceeds from affirmation of either being or non-being, to affirmation of both or denial of both, to either affirmation or denial of both, or neither affirmation nor denial of both. Rather than follow the Buddhists in applying logic to the problem of the inappropriateness of certain words, Chinese philosophers generally chose to offer analogies, many of which appealed to the visual sense.

Chang Tsai and Shao Yung also differed in conceptualizing the idea of achieving a mystical universal unity. Their choice of words to express this idea reflects their differences, and indicates how, in certain contexts, an affirmative and a negative statement can be used to convey structurally similar ideas. To say that all is self and to say that there is no-self are alternative methods of trying to convey the idea that when consciousness is expanded to the point that it includes everything (and there is nothing outside of it), then, paradoxically, there is no consciousness, in the usual sense of subject-object awareness.

In discussing the knowledge of the sage, Shao was talking about a kind of comprehension that was in effect a particular state of consciousness. He organized his thought on this subject around his concept of *kuan-wu*, perceiving things. Shao believed that human beings have a higher kind of consciousness than other living things and that the sage has the highest kind of all. The three levels of consciousness are sense perception, conscious thinking, and a merging of the self with the whole. At this highest level, the sage no longer has any awareness of self in contrast to other. The sage achieves this ultimate state by means of reflective perception (*fan-kuan*), which Shao explained as perceiving things not from the viewpoint of the self but from the viewpoint of things. For Shao, the sage's knowledge was not a matter of knowledge in the form of statements, nor was it a matter of moral knowledge and its cultivation. However, his concept of sagehood did entail moral action, primarily in the political realm.

9

Within the Intellectual Traditions

> *Han Hsin was surely never a true credit to his country,*
> *While Shao Yung was truly a hero among men.*
>   —*Wang Yang-ming*[1]

In a description, just as the relationship between subject and object helps to determine what is seen and described, so the background against which an object is placed influences one's experience of it. The interdependency between figure and ground becomes particularly apparent as one tries to describe Shao Yung's thought and determine its position within the intellectual traditions of China. Beyond a gross classification within the *Yi* learning, it is by no means simple to categorize Shao's thought. What others said and thought about his philosophy changed significantly over time.

Since a philosopher is essentially engaged in a dialogue with others, both of his own and of other times, the meaning of his ideas is determined within a context of relationships. By themselves a philosopher's writings can lead to only a partial understanding of his ideas. To learn how Shao Yung's thought was understood, we need to place his thought within its intellectual context, to establish its antecedents and its ties to specific traditions and to ongoing developments in Chinese thought.

The views of others help to point out characteristics of Shao's thought that may or may not be obvious from his writings alone. At the same time, they comment indirectly on the observer. Those who lived closest in time to Shao shared a similar intellectual milieu and responded to many of the same concerns. His successors, however, lived in different contexts with changed tensions. In contrast to Shao's contemporaries, their remarks often exhibit less awareness of the subtle interconnections among the elements in Shao's thought. In general, the integrity of Shao Yung's philosophical system was obscured over time as people failed to see how its elements functioned together. Later scholars tended to see a narrower focus to Shao's thought, and so the question of authorship and the data of a commentary is extremely important.

To say, however, that earlier writers were right about Shao Yung and later ones were wrong is to ignore the essential, contextual aspect of ideas and philosophical thought. The meaning of ideas is profoundly affected by their relationships. All assessments of Shao, mistaken or not, contribute to the meaning of his philosophy within the context of Chinese culture. For modern scholars especially, both positive and negative judgments reveal the cultural expectations that Shao and others faced and to which they implicitly responded.

The antecedents of Shao's thought and its links with the various Chinese traditions of knowledge are crucial aspects of his philosophy. On the one hand, the antecedents provided his primary concepts, assumptions, and particular problems of concern. Although essential in shaping his philosophical system, the antecedents did not prevent it from further development. On the other hand, the links with different systems of thought help to reveal the context of his philosophy. Some of these intellectual ties were openly recognized, such as those with the Confucian classics; others, such as those with Buddhism, were ignored or minimized.[2] Both types of ties, however, contribute to the effort of establishing why his thought was interpreted as it was. The purpose of this chapter is to examine the views of others to determine the meaning and significance of Shao's ideas.

Contemporary Sung Opinion

The eleventh century witnessed a remarkable fluidity and diversity in intellectual activity. Although the separations between different intellectual traditions were not always clear and by no means absolute, specific traditions were recognized. Philosophers pursued many interests, but some more than others. From their comments about Shao Yung, it is apparent that eleventh-century Confucian intellectuals regarded four topics as particularly important: the personal, moral, and intellectual qualities of a thinker; the practicality of an idea, that is, whether an idea could be implemented both on a personal level and on a social and political level; the question of Buddhist and Taoist influences; and the sources and transmission of one's ideas. (All those quoted below were prominent intellectuals; those contemporary with Shao knew him personally.)

Of his philosopher-friends, Shao Yung (K'ang-chieh) was most partial to Ch'eng Hao (Ming-tao). One account says: "K'ang-chieh particularly liked Ming-tao. He praised him as equal to Fu Pi, Ssuma Wen-kung [Kuang], and Lü Shen-kung [Kung-chu]."[3]* Moreover, because of Ch'eng and Shao's especially close relationship and Ch'eng's great respect for Shao, Shao Po-wen asked Ch'eng Hao to write his father's epitaph.[4] Thus, what Ch'eng Hao had to say about Shao Yung is important. Ch'eng knew Shao well and had a good relationship with him. They were familiar with each other's ideas and shared many fundamental beliefs, particularly in the area of Confucian moral thought. Although Ch'eng did not share Shao's more specialized philosophical interests, he was favorably disposed toward Shao and respected Shao both as a person and as a philosopher.

Ch'eng went beyond the usual stereotypes in commenting on Shao's moral, intellectual, and personal qualities. Ch'eng remarked that Shao was filial and virtuous, intelligent and energetic, as well as informal, congenial, and possessed of a sense of humor.

When the master was young, he was naturally high-spirited and talented, energetic and full of lofty ambitions. In his studies he respected the high and the far. It is said that the achievements of the former kings can certainly be extended to his learning.

The older he became, the more admirable was his virtue. He pondered the lofty and obvious. He reflected on the transformations of heaven and earth and the increases and decreases of *yin* and *yang*. He thereby fully understood the changes of the myriad things. Afterward, when withdrawing, he adapted [himself] to [them], and when spreading out, he returned [to them].

---

*All three were prominent officials in the conservative clique and close friends of Shao Yung.

After he had been in Loyang for almost thirty years, he began living in a thatched hut, the walls of which did not shield him from the wind and rain.* He had prepared the food himself in caring for his father and mother, and he held to this even after things became abundant.

If he discussed learning with others, he never was forceful in talking to them, and yet those who came to ask questions formed a crowd every day. The village was transformed by him; the far and the near venerated the teachings of this master. In Loyang there were those who would not go to the prefectural offices, and yet insisted on going to the master's cottage.

The master's virtue was exquisite. By looking at him, one could know that he was a wise man. Yet, clear and bright, comfortable and easy, he did not engage in externals and did not establish boundaries. He was upright and not obstinate, understanding and not corrupt. When he met people, he made no distinction between the high and low, the near and far. He was pleasant and congenial all day long and did not wish to be greatly different from other men.[5]

Elsewhere, the Ch'eng brothers described Shao as "benevolent and not deceitful," "relaxed and indulgent," and "heroic... and not submissive."[6] Another long passage by the Ch'eng brothers touches on both Shao's thought and his personal characteristics.

Yao-fu's [Shao Yung's] learning first, from pattern [*li*], infers ideas, words, images, and numbers. He said that the patterns of the world must emerge from these four things. After extending [things] to pattern, he said that when the self attains this great pattern, then the myriad affairs come from the self. There are none that are not fixed. And yet it is not necessary to have a teaching to summarize it. Also it is hard with [his thought] to rule the world's states.

As a person, he was upright. He approved of not having [excessive] etiquette and not being [overly] respectful. He certainly approved of poking fun. And even if [the subject] were heaven and earth, he also would poke fun at it. As in his "Biography of Mr. No Name," he asked questions of heaven and earth. Heaven and earth did not respond, but amused themselves as the seasons came and went.[7]

This passage indicates several important characteristics of Shao's learning. The Ch'engs recognized that the concept of pattern (*li*) was central to Shao's learning and took his connection with the

---

* A reference to Shao Yung's decision to become more reclusive at the age of sixty.

Yi learning and the charts for granted. The Ch'engs saw Shao's thought, however, as unrealistic for political application.

Although the Ch'engs knew that Shao's many topics of discussion might be confusing, they also realized that his thought had a unifying thread. Once, when a student asked Ch'eng Hao what Shao was talking about, Ch'eng simply said, "The way of the inner sage and outer king." [8] This famous phrase reflects two primary Confucian concerns—governing society and cultivating one's virtue—as well as the contemporary concern for the practicality of ideas.[9]

In Ch'eng Hao's view, Shao's learning was not empty words. "Those who achieve virtue with their words have in the past made trouble for people. But with the master's teaching, one arrives at one's goals. Thus if I were to describe it, I would call it peacefulness [*an*] and fulfillment [*ch'eng*]." [10] Here Ch'eng is saying that trouble results when ideas are not put into practice. One cannot become virtuous merely through words. Ideas must be put into action. The results of practicing Shao's ideas are contentment and a sense of wholeness.

Ch'eng Hao clearly saw that one goal of Shao Yung's learning was to effect a change in one's actions, to engage in moral cultivation or to transform oneself spiritually. Although Ch'eng recognized that Shao's thought seemed to encompass the ways and principles of the entire universe, he was also aware that Shao's aim was not simply to describe, or even explain, the universal patterns. The aim was, ultimately, for the individual to have an experience of "peacefulness" and "fulfillment." Ch'eng also said about Shao Yung, "Although Yao-fu's *tao* is biased and mixed, still when his writings are unrolled,* their applications are extremely thorough and furthermore can be carefully carried out." [11] Although there is an inconsistency between this comment about Shao's mixed teachings (or *tao*) and other comments by Ch'eng about Shao's pure *tao*, Ch'eng's emphasis here is on the applicability of Shao's teachings. Ch'eng regarded Shao's teachings as practical, but only on the personal level. Ch'eng obviously recognized that the many varied elements in Shao Yung's thought made it impossible to describe it

---

*That is, unrolled and spread out in order to be read.

consistently in only one way. No single description could be accurate. Thus, he also likened Shao's thought to "castles in the air."[12]

Ch'eng Hao was critical of what he regarded as the lack of political and social content in Shao's thought. Thus he said that although Shao understood the pattern or principles of the *tao* (*tao-li*), it was unclear to him whether Shao had achieved anything in Confucian activities (*ju-shu*).[13] Speaking from a Confucian perspective, Ch'eng liked the broad and penetrating qualities of Shao's learning, but he was concerned about its applicability, a crucial aspect of Confucianism. Ch'eng seems to be suggesting that Shao's version of Confucianism was questionable and useless politically.

In the eleventh century, an orthodoxy had yet to be established, but intellectuals were becoming increasingly interested in seeking out the historical origins of systems of thought, an activity that led to the formulation of the concept of the *tao-t'ung* in the twelfth century. The fact that they gave only scant and insufficient attention to Buddhism as a source of ideas testifies to the Confucian bias of this notion. It was not just a matter of finding the sources and transmission line; one had to have the correct line to the truth, which was conceived to be the original *tao* of Confucius according to Mencius.[14]

The purity of one's ideas—the inclusion of the right ideas and the exclusion of questionable ones—was important to the Ch'engs. Their assessment of Shao varied. Ch'eng Hao said that he had met many people, but only three whose *tao* was not mixed: Chang Tsai, Shao Yung, and Ssu-ma Kuang.[15] However, the Ch'engs also wrote:

> The learning of men of today is [learning] that broadly inquires and strives to understand. How seldom in the end there are none with aspects that have not entered into Ch'an learning. Among those who are especially established, without doubt, there are none like Tzu-hou [Chang Tsai] and Yao-fu [Shao Yung]. And yet I fear that the flow of their theories has not yet avoided this defect.[16]

Here then there is acknowledgment of Ch'an elements in Shao's learning, the broadness of which is nonetheless admired. The Ch'eng brothers objected to Ch'an Buddhism because it "attains only 'resting' places and has no practical places or morality."[17] The spiritual aspect to Shao's thought did not compensate for its perceived lack of practical political and moral emphases.

Other Sung figures commented on the purity of Shao's thought. Ch'ao Yi-tao (1059–1129) claimed, for instance, that Shao "alone understood the *tao* of the former sages. He was not a Taoist or a Buddhist."[18] Although there was some disagreement concerning the extent of Buddhist and Taoist elements in Shao's thought, the consensus was that he was certainly a Confucian.

Another aspect of Shao's thought that was troublesome for its violation of Confucian standards was his interest in prediction and divination. The comments of others reveal their ambivalence toward this area of knowledge. Once, when asked by Ch'ao Yi-tao about Shao's ideas on numbers (divination, fate calculation, prediction of destiny), Ch'eng Yi replied that although they had lived near each other for over thirty years and had talked about everything in politics, they had not said one word about numbers.[19] The Ch'eng brothers knew that some aspects of Shao's thought, particularly those connected to numerology, were judged to be nonclassical, but they regarded his thought in these areas as different from popular conceptions. They recognized Shao's ultimate Confucian basis. "Shao Yao-fu's method of numbers [*shu-fa*]* comes from Li Yen-chih [Chih-ts'ai]. But when Yao-fu extended his numerological recipes, he attained pattern [*li*]."[20]

In terms of the eleventh-century concern about the line of transmission of the *tao*, Shao Yung's thought was widely recognized as part of the images and numbers (*hsiang-shu*) branch of the *Yi* learning. In comparison, the systems of his contemporaries Chou Tun-yi and Chang Tsai were seen as tied to both the *yi-li* (morality) and the *hsiang-shu* branches of the *Yi* learning. The antecedents accorded Shao's thought thus were not unique to Shao. Being recognized as part of an ongoing tradition was important, and although there were suggestions later regarding the originality of certain aspects of Shao Yung's thought (see below), during his own time no one suggested seriously that Shao's thought, or most of it, was not based on previous learning.[21]

---

* *Shu-fa* can refer to calculations of fate and methods of prediction as well as more theoretical ideas of numerology.

Ch'eng Hao's opinion was that, of Confucius' seventy disciples, only Tseng Tzu clearly carried on Confucius' tradition and that from Tseng Tzu the tradition went to Tzu Ssu and Mencius. The remainder of Confucius' disciples studied what their talents allowed them, and although they all venerated Confucius, they went in many different directions. The result was that the way of Confucius was not transmitted for a thousand years, and scholars now did not know their origins.[22] Ch'eng believed that Shao Yung, however, was different.

Only the learning of the master [Shao Yung] is regarded as having a tradition. The master obtained it from Li Yen-chih, and Yen-chih obtained it from Mu Po-chang [Hsiu]. If one pushes further back into its stream of development, one will find far back a transmission of doctrines.

Today the words of Mu and Li and their accomplishments can indeed be seen. Moreover, the master is pure and unmixed, vast and great. And that which he himself has attained is much indeed.[23]

Ch'eng Hao was no doubt overstating the situation. He could not have believed that other scholars were not identified with particular traditions. He himself, for example, was quite conscious of being an heir to the *yi-li*, or moral philosophy, branch of the *Yi* learning. Here, however, he was merely praising Shao and emphasizing the line of transmission associated with Shao's thought. Despite the esoteric background of Shao's ideas, people knew who taught whom. Although Ch'eng's remarks clearly indicate a familiarity with Shao Yung's thought, they also suggest that among Shao's contemporaries there was little recognition of the role and influence of the *Ch'un-ch'iu* in Shao's philosophy.

Later Sung Opinion

After the Ch'engs, the focus of remarks about Shao Yung changed somewhat. Philosophers tended not to comment so much on his personal characteristics or the question of the practicality of his ideas. Instead, their primary interests lay in describing his ideas and placing him in a historical context. Often, they recorded their personal reactions to Shao's ideas.

Yang Shih (Kuei-shan; 1053–1135), an important disciple of the

Ch'eng brothers, had high praise for Shao's thought. However, he claimed that he did not understand its finer aspects.

> The *Huang-chi* is everything that Confucius had not yet said. And yet it discusses the changes of past and present, order and chaos, success and failure, as if it were fitting together the two halves of a seal. Therefore I do not dare summarize it. I regret that I have not yet entered his [Shao's] gateway....
> The *hsien-t'ien* learning of K'ang-chieh is not transmitted in the world. Without a mind that can mysteriously penetrate heaven and earth, one is not sufficient to understand it. I have often amused myself with it, and yet my vulgar knowledge and shallow experience are not yet sufficient to provide a key to unlock its secrets.[24]

While modestly admitting his own lack of a complete understanding of Shao's thought, Yang Shih, in contrast to a few others, had no doubts that Shao's thought fit into the Confucian tradition.

Yang went on to describe some of Shao's ideas, particularly the positions of the eight trigrams in the *hsien-t'ien* charts.

> The eight trigrams have fixed positions. The *hsien-t'ien* [chart] places *ch'ien* and *sun* in the south, *k'un* and *chen* in the north, *li* and *tui* in the east, *k'an* and *ken* in the west. [Shao] also matched the eight trigrams with the ten numbers, and only *ken* and *k'an* together became three numbers. This certainly has a theory [behind it].
> He matched periods with the lines [of the trigrams and hexagrams] and the origin of this is the "Great Commentary." And he divided them into [the categories of] stars, sun, and solar periods [*ch'i-hou*]. The *Yi* did not have the lines displayed [in this way].
> His current [of thought] is clear in the apocryphal books. The charts that have been handed down for generations and studied affirm this. Master Yang's [Yang Hsiung's] *T'ai-hsüan* indeed uses these [ideas].[25]

Yang Shih then described the *T'ai-hsüan* and added:

> Today's calendrical books are also like this. Thus from the Han to today, they have similarly used this theory.... [Yang] also said that the trigrams are different from those of King Wen. If this were so, none of the categories could be understood.
> K'ang-chieh's learning investigates to the extreme the hidden forces [governing] heaven and humans, and seems to be forever playing. Since I have not yet been able to penetrate its principles, how much less do I dare discuss its truth or falsity?[26]

Yang Shih's view of Shao was shared by many Confucian intellectuals in the latter half of the eleventh and first half of the twelfth centuries. Yang lacked a thorough knowledge of the more subtle aspects of Shao's thought. He recognized the non-classical or apocryphal elements in Shao's thought, and he knew that these same elements were the bases of other systems of thought, such as those of Yang Hsiung and of calendrical books and almanacs (which included predictions and calculations of fate). Although willing to consider the subject to some extent, Yang thought that it was ultimately understandable only through some esoteric process. Yang recognized that Shao's thought was concerned with an understanding of universal forces, but, beyond that, Yang humbly claimed to have little knowledge.

Hsieh Liang-tso (Shang-ts'ai; 1050–1103), another disciple of the Ch'eng brothers, also thought highly of Shao Yung, but his comments again emphasize the difficulty of understanding Shao's thought and scholars' ambivalence toward it.

[Shao] Yao-fu's *Yi* numbers are extremely penetrating. Up until now, those who have made predictions have certainly been deficient. Only Yao-fu is not so. By pointing to one or two recent incidents I can immediately verify this now.

[Ch'eng] Ming-tao said that he would like to transmit things from [Shao] as a younger brother would. But where can one find the effort for an older-younger brother relationship! If one wanted to study with [Shao], it would require twenty years of work! What Ming-tao said is extremely apt.

One day, because he had no duties, the Examiner [Ch'eng Hao?] cast his horoscope with [Shao's] theories, and everything came out fitting together. He went out and said to Yao-fu, "Yao-fu's numbers simply are the method of doubling. From this one knows that the Great Mystery does not always equalize matters." Yao-fu, startled, clapped him on the back and said, "Big brother, you are so bright!"

Another day Yi-ch'uan asked Ming-tao, "What about the numbers that are doubled?" Ming-tao said, "I've forgotten everything." He thereupon lamented that his mind did not have biased attachments like this.[27]

The twelfth-century commentator Chang Hsing-ch'eng offered a concise analysis of Shao Yung's *Yi* learning (see Chapter 2). Chang admired Shao and praised him extravagantly for the breadth, thoroughness, and subtlety of his thought. He pointed out, moreover, that Shao's thought was concerned both with the ways of the natural and of the human world, and he addressed the question of placing Shao in a historical context. Thus he said that Shao had learned from Li Chih-ts'ai, who in turn had heard the *tao* from Mu Hsiu, but that he had not examined who transmitted these teachings before Mu Hsiu.[28]

Chang, however, neglected one major aspect of Shao's thought: Shao's epistemological ideas on the processes of ordinary knowing and sagely knowing. Chang's oversight began a trend, far more obvious in later centuries, not to recognize the role of the individual perceiver and knower in Shao's philosophy.

As seen from the above remarks, Shao Yung's contemporaries recognized that his thought descended from a branch of Han dynasty *Yi* learning. Ch'ao Yi-tao readily associated Shao Yung with such Han dynasty thinkers as the philosopher Yang Hsiung, the astronomer and mathematician Chang Heng (78–139), and the alchemists Kuan Lang (Tzu-ming) and Wei Po-yang.[29] Cheng Shao-mei of the Sung classified Shao Yung's *Huang-chi ching-shih* with the *T'ai-hsüan ching* of Yang Hsiung, the *Tung-chi chen-ching* of Kuan Tzu-ming, and the *Chou Yi ts'an-t'ung-ch'i* of Wei Po-yang. Shao's work, moreover, received the most favorable judgment from Cheng.[30] The works of Kuan and Wei are particularly noted for their association with traditions of Taoism and alchemy.

The role of Ch'en T'uan's thought as a forerunner to Shao's philosophy was increasingly recognized in the twelfth century. Shao was certainly aware of his debt to Ch'en T'uan (Hsi-yi), and several of his poems contain flattering references to Ch'en.[31] The references to Ch'en T'uan's thought throughout informal Sung historical accounts of Shao Yung attest to his importance. Shao Po-wen links Shao Yung directly to Ch'en T'uan, and, by mentioning others such as the recluse Chung Fang (Ming-yi), who had also studied with Ch'en T'uan, he indirectly (but clearly) associates Shao Yung with specific aspects of Ch'en's thought. He even cites, for example, Ch'en's belief that one's destiny or fate determined whether one became a high-ranking or low-ranking official and that one's destiny was a matter of one's physiognomy.[32] The linking of fate and physiognomy (based on one's *ch'i*) belonged to the same complex of Han ideas that were fundamental to the *Yi* learning (which were a source of Shao's ideas). Shao Po-wen also wrote that Shao Yung frequently recited certain phrases of Ch'en T'uan.[33]

In the century after Shao Yung, Chu Hsi and others credited first Ch'en T'uan and then Shao Yung with reviving the charts and making public that esoteric knowledge passed down in a tradition linked to the alchemists.[34] These twelfth-century scholars said that before Ch'en this knowledge had been transmitted so secretly that even the line of teachers was not publicly known. Their comments reflect both their interest in establishing historical precedents and their recognition that fields of knowledge formerly held in secret were coming into the public domain.

Li Chih-ts'ai's biography in the *Sung History* says that Li's teacher in the *Yi* learning was Mu Hsiu, who studied under Chung Fang, a student of Ch'en T'uan.[35] Li Chih-ts'ai's biography also mentions that this current of learning dates to the Ch'in and Han periods. However, knowledge of the direct line of teacher–student relationships breaks down with Ch'en T'uan, for nothing is known about his teachers.[36] The biographies of other Sung philosophers interested in the *Yi* learning, such as Chu Chen, also record the lines of transmission of these teachings, but the list of known teachers always begins with Ch'en.[37] Thus Ch'en T'uan was a particularly important link in the transmission of these teachings, a link that Shao Yung recognized. Ch'en T'uan began the process of revealing an esoteric tradition to the public, and Shao Yung continued his efforts.

Ch'en T'uan, a *chin-shih* who never took office, is known as a Taoist recluse. He followed the learning of the images and numbers, with its charts, diagrams, and numbers. He composed a work entitled the *Lung T'u* (Dragon chart), but it is no longer extant.[38] Like all the charts, however, it is thought to have been a variant or offshoot of the *Ho T'u* or *Lo Shu*, two early charts associated with the *Yi-ching* (see Fig. B7).[39] Ch'en himself denied any connection with the alchemists' tradition and according to one account even identified as a Confucian.[40] However, others associated Ch'en's thought with various kinds of knowledge that are often grouped under the rubric "the techniques of the adepts" (*fang-shih*).[41] This kind of knowledge, which included such areas as physiognomy, alchemy, and prognostication, is sometimes loosely described as Taoist. It was also closely associated with the *Yi-ching*.

In describing Ch'en's thought, a Ch'ing dynasty account mentioned that Ch'en T'uan's knowledge involved both the learning of *yang-sheng*, nourishing life, and the techniques (*shu*) of knowing the future. The former was associated with alchemy and the thought of Wei Po-yang of the Later Han and the latter with Kuan Lu (208–55) and Kuo P'u (276–324).[42] At least since the Han dynasty, these two elements have been regarded as part of the *fang-shih* and Taoist tradition. Although Ch'en T'uan was perhaps one of the most well known adepts, many others had similar interests. Hsü Fu (11th century) and Kuo Yung (1091–1187), both of whom have biographies in the *Sung shih*, are examples of others later associated with this tradition of thought.[43]

Two aspects of Shao's concept of knowledge particularly reflect the influence of Ch'en's thought. Both are more closely associated with Taoism than with Confucianism and are characteristic of some Buddhist thought as well. These two aspects are a concern with esoteric truths about a mystical cosmic unity and the use of symbols to express what cannot be said adequately in words.

These aspects did not go unnoticed by other Chinese intellectuals. Ou-yang Fei (1047–1113), for instance, said that Shao had profound knowledge of the images and numbers, could see into the future, and knew things that cannot be put into words.[44] The Ming scholar Ch'en Chi-ju said, "K'ang-chieh's *hsien-t'ien* learning valued the images and did not value words."[45] Ou-yang and Ch'en thus clearly recognized Shao's emphasis on symbols, an emphasis that implies a recognition of the limitations of words. A similar view is found in the *Chuang Tzu* in regard to knowledge and the role of words.[46] Buddhism too, with its concept of *ch'uan-hsin* (transmitting the mind), places a high value on knowledge not contained in words.

Shao's concept of cosmic unity reflects a distinction between the primary emphases in *Yi* thought of ontological and mystical topics and of social and moral issues. Concepts deriving from the *Lao Tzu*, which became associated with the *Yi-ching* during the Han, contributed to the first emphasis, and the moral and political concerns of Mencius dominated the second. Distinguishing the learning of the images and numbers from that of moral principles, the Ch'ing scholar Hu Wei claimed that the former current of thought used the *Yi* of Lao Tzu rather than the *Yi* of the sages.[47]

Hu's comment indicates the explicit recognition that different traditions of knowledge used the *Yi-ching*. One tradition was judged to be Taoist in approach and another to be Confucian. Shao Yung himself described the distinction in saying: "Lao Tzu understood the essence of the *Yi*." And "people who are able to apply the *Yi* are those who understand the *Yi*. Such a person was Mencius. One can say that he was good at applying the *Yi*."[48] The point here is that Shao's use of the *Yi* in this context indicates his close ties to certain ideas from the *Lao Tzu* and the *Chuang Tzu*. Moreover, people from the Sung period on recognized this relationship.

It is important, however, not to separate Confucianism and Taoism rigidly. In the realm of thought, as opposed to specific behavior, the line between Confucianism and Taoism was often blurred because many ideas and attitudes that had originally belonged to one particular school had, over time, become part of the culture as a whole. Moreover, although both schools represented different views, they shared an interest in many similar problems. Han Confucianism itself was an eclectic mixture. As philosophical ideas combined, certain ones became epistemological imperatives of the culture, accepted by all. Their use did not make one an adherent of any particular early school of thought. In the realm of practices and behavior, however, it was far easier (although not necessarily accurate) to make distinctions regarding historical origins.

By the late eleventh century, there existed clear differences in judgment as to the contents of Shao's thought. Only two generations after Shao Yung, Yin T'un (Ho-ching; 1071–1142), a student of the Ch'engs, spoke of the lack of consensus. Yin said that Shao's learning was basically *ching-shih* (governing the world) learning (that is, cosmology and ontology), but most people knew only that Shao understood the *Yi* numbers and future events (predictive knowledge). Few knew of his emphasis on cosmological theory.[49] Although understanding that Shao's thought was not merely about numbers in the sense of prediction, fate, and foreknowledge, but also about the nature of the universe and human affairs, Yin omitted another aspect of Shao's thought, that concerned with the mystical experience of absolute reality. Yin's comment is important, however, because it indicates how some people were already, after only two generations, narrowing the scope of Shao's thought.

In the twelfth century opinion continued to be mixed. As the question of intellectual ties became increasingly important, philosophers examined the sources of ideas and made judgments about the relationship of one's thought to the *tao-t'ung*. Too close an association with ideas regarded as Taoist or as popular practices was a cause for criticism.

Chu Hsi, the great synthesizer of Neo-Confucian thought, was somewhat ambivalent about Shao Yung. Chu's comments about Shao's thought are important, nonetheless, because of his immense philosophical understanding and his influence on later scholars and philosophers.[50] Chu Hsi's interpretations of the classics were the orthodox Neo-Confucian view from the thirteenth through the nineteenth century. He wrote two books on the *Yi-ching*, and many of his ideas indirectly reflect the influence of Shao Yung. Although Chu's *Yi* learning combined the ideas of Shao Yung and Ch'eng Yi, particularly the numerical aspects, Shao Yung's thought clearly influenced Chu's *Yi-hsüeh ch'i-meng* (A guide to the study of the *Yi* learning).[51] Some of Chu Hsi's comments serve to explain or clarify Shao's ideas; others merely indicate Chu's opinion.[52]

In one passage, for example, Chu talked about Shao's alternating use of the numbers 12 and 30 to show the relationship of various periods of time.[53] In another passage, when asked if there was a difference between the *Yi* and Shao's *Huang-chi ching-shih shu*, Chu Hsi replied that the *Yi* was concerned with divination (*pu-shih*), whereas Shao's work had to do with casting horoscopes by the method of doubling of one to two, two to four, four to eight, and so on.[54] In another passage, Chu Hsi pointed out that Shao placed all things into one of four categories, each of which corresponded with other categories, such as sun, moon, stars, and zodiacal space, or water, fire, earth, and stone.[55]

These and other passages attempted to explain or to clarify Shao's ideas. Chu Hsi also, however, was not hesitant in giving his own opinion. When asked what he thought about Shao's *shu-hsüeh* (number learning), Chu Hsi said:

I do not yet necessarily comprehend the numbers, [but] from them there is this pattern [*li*]. If there is life, then there is death. If there is flourishing, there must be decline. This is like a flower. When it contains the stamens and pistils, it is about to open. When it has opened a little, it is exactly at its peak. When it is brilliant, it is declining.

Chu Hsi went on to say that Shao's "learning was based on understanding [this] pattern."[56]

Chu Hsi was referring in many passages to a topic that Shao discussed at length—the regularity of change in the world. In Shao's view, all things had to change, and many did so according to this particular pattern of development and decline. Only *t'ai-chi* did not change. In describing Shao's ideas on number, however, Chu Hsi failed to point out one of the important aspects of Shao's thinking. Shao was not interested just in describing the structure of the world. He also was interested in how this pattern of change was experienced and how it was conceptualized. Thus, Shao distinguished different observers' viewpoints. For example, viewed from outside the process, change was cyclical; viewed from within the process, change was developmental.

By the twelfth century, Shao Yung's ability to predict was regarded as a major aspect of his thought. In the *Yi* learning and in the popular culture, such matters were intimately tied to numbers and their manipulation. A question therefore arose on the relationship of Shao's ability to popular practices. The nature of Shao's abilities in these areas was not an obvious matter. Chu Hsi and others recognized that Shao differed from common diviners and fortune-tellers, and yet he was still described as having a similar ability.

Someone asked Chu Hsi the difference between Shao's thought and the common methods of divination. Chu replied that diviners are far from the *tao*, and their knowledge of K'ang-chieh's thought is practically nil.[57] Here Chu Hsi indicated that the difference between Shao and the others lay in Shao's closeness or fidelity to the *tao*. The implication is that Shao's foreknowledge was based on an understanding of universal principles, whereas the others simply based their predictions on the manipulation of numbers.

Another passage by Chu Hsi supports this view. When asked about Shao's method of foreknowledge, Chu Hsi quoted a poem from the *Shih-ching* that says that accordance with right is good fortune and following evil is bad fortune. Good and bad fortune do not concern tomorrow's weather.⁵⁸ In other words, from the Confucian viewpoint, foreknowledge is tied to the morality of one's acts, which are believed to be under one's control. The topic of good and bad fortune is not about uncontrollable matters of nature.

There was a certain lack of clarity about the basis for Shao's foreknowledge. On the one hand, in popular culture, numbers were basic to the method. However, Shao only sometimes used numbers, particularly in relation to the hexagrams. For example, the basis for Shao's prediction of the rise of Wang An-shih two years beforehand was *ch'i*.⁵⁹ Shao made another prediction on the basis of *wu-hsin* (having no mind), and yet another because of a dream.⁶⁰

Despite the accounts, Chu Hsi maintained that Shao Yung's learning was *shu-shu hsüeh* (divination based on numerical techniques), and its source was Ch'en T'uan.⁶¹ In contrast to "a sage [who] knows heaven-ordained destiny [*t'ien-ming*] through pattern [*li*], Shao knows it through techniques (*shu*). And yet, the essential points of *shu* that he has attained are not what *shu* should enable one to exhaust. But his beginning is just *shu*."⁶² This passage indicates that Chu Hsi believed that although assumptions pertaining to number were the starting point of Shao's thought, Shao's thought had more depth to it than numerological methods alone could provide. However, Chu did not attempt to resolve this apparent contradiction.

Twelfth-century scholars recognized not only the calendrical, cosmological, and predictive aspects of the *Yi* learning in Shao Yung's thought, but also the elements derived from Lao Tzu and Chuang Tzu. Chu Hsi, for instance, remarked that Shao Yung's poetry contained many ideas from Chuang and Lao.⁶³ Although Sung scholars seldom mentioned the pervasiveness of Taoist ideas in Shao's thought, Taoist ideas were not at all limited to Shao's poetry. It was not until the Ch'ing dynasty, however, that scholars widely acknowledged the fundamental importance of Taoist ideas to the *Yi* learning itself.⁶⁴

Chu Hsi spoke of other subjects found in Shao's thought, including Shao's interpretation of historical events and the ultimate aim of his philosophy. Chu Hsi said that the basis of Shao's learning lay in understanding principle (*ming li*). Moreover, quoting Ch'eng

Hao, Chu said, "Therefore [Ch'eng] Ming-tao said that after [Shao] contemplated the revolutions and changes of heaven and earth, he eased himself into complying with them; and with an all-embracing greatness, he returned [to the One]."[65] Here there is the recognition that Shao's cosmological knowledge was not an end in itself but was part of his ultimate goal of achieving a spiritual, mystical experience of oneness with the universe.

In some of his writings, Chu Hsi quoted Shao Yung frequently, and the selections chosen indicate that he understood the aim of Shao's thought. Chu mentioned such concepts as *tung* and *ching* (motion and rest), the triad of heaven and earth and humans, mind (*hsin*), and *yin* and *yang*. These concepts, important in Shao's thought, were related to questions about the nature and the experiencing of reality. According to Chu Hsi, Shao Yung once responded to a question by saying: "*Tao* is *t'ai-chi*.... *Hsin* [mind] is *t'ai-chi*. *Tao* is a term designating the natural principles of heaven and earth and all things. *Hsin* is a term designating this principle when humans have obtained it and regard it as the ruler of their whole selves." Chu Hsi commented: "This is so but *t'ai-chi* just is one and does not form a pair [with anything]."[66]

While fully recognizing the cosmological, ontological, and numerical elements of Shao's thought, Chu downplayed those epistemological aspects relating to the sage. However, Chu did not ignore the epistemological elements altogether. Although Chu expressed admiration for Shao, he did not condone those aspects of Shao's thought that he saw as being related to numerical techniques of divination and prediction.[67] Chu Hsi certainly recognized the complexity of Shao Yung's thought, but it is doubtful that he fully realized its great influence on his own thinking.

Despite his criticism of Shao, Chu Hsi did not try to ignore, change, or dismiss other people's favorable judgments of Shao Yung. Chu noted that even though their learning was not the same, the Ch'eng brothers still respected Shao very highly. Chu also pointed out that, Shao's beliefs to the contrary, his thought did contain Buddhist and Taoist influences and that Ch'eng Yi was wrong in saying that Shao's thought was not mixed. Chu Hsi commented that many admired Shao as a person, many were impressed by the wide scope of his learning, and some even recited his poetry.

In Chu's opinion, the bones and marrow of Shao's learning could be found in his *Huang-chi ching-shih*, but the flowers and grasses were his poems. To support his view, Chu quoted another's comment that Shao's poems speak of leisure, peacefulness, and pleasure.[68]

When Shao Yung's reputation took shape during the twelfth century, the distinction between the concepts of *hsüeh* (learning) and *shu* (techniques) had great importance. In the application of these concepts to the thought of Shao Yung, the opinion of Wei Liao-weng (Ho-shan; 1178–1237), a follower of Chu Hsi, is of interest. Wei said that the essence of Shao's *hsin-shu* (literally, mind method, also a Buddhist term for consciousness) could be found in his *Huang-chi ching-shih*. His feelings, however, were contained in his collection of poetry, the *Chi-jang chi*.[69] Wei was impressed by Shao and praised him highly. Perhaps more than others of his time, certainly more explicitly than others, he understood the structure of Shao's philosophy. Wei realized that Shao was interested in a comprehensive, intellectual understanding of all things and in an experiential understanding of the One. The intellectual understanding could be (and was) put into words and symbols (Shao's *hsien-t'ien hsüeh*). The experiential understanding involved the merging of the individual self into the whole. Since the latter depended on the former, probably both of these aspects of Shao's thought were what Wei meant by "mind method."

This brief sketch indicates the disagreements of Sung scholars over Shao Yung and their difficulty in evaluating and interpreting his philosophy. The disagreements existed during Shao's lifetime and continued into the generations immediately after him. On the one hand, his thought was praised as reaching to the essence of things, things that other people were not as capable of understanding. On the other hand, the possibility was raised that maybe Shao's thought was not so complicated after all; maybe it was just a method of doubling numbers. And if so, then perhaps it was ultimately peripheral to the main concerns of Confucianism.

The lack of a consensus seems to be closely related to the widespread phenomenon of equating an understanding of Shao's thought with the ability to identify its antecedents. Scholars recognized that a primary focus of Shao's thought was the forces and patterns of the universe. That Shao's thought in this area was based on ideas from the *Yi-ching* presented no problem, because the *Yi-ching* was a respected Confucian classic. That his thought dealt with regular divisions of time presented no difficulty, because the calendar and calendrical studies were recognized as a crucial governmental and Confucian matter.

Difficulty arose, however, over what people perceived to be missing from his thought—sufficient political and social emphases. Shao made great use of the charts and the accompanying body of knowledge, the *hsien-t'ien* learning, which dealt with the symbolic meanings of the charts. The charts, however, were associated with *wei-hsüeh*, apocryphal learning, and they were used in traditions of knowledge, at times called Taoist or identified with the *fang-shih*, that were clearly not Confucian. Furthermore, even though his well-known predictions do not seem to have been based on the numerical methods of popular diviners, some of Shao's interests seemed too similar to popular interests in prediction to be considered legitimate scholarly concerns.

Yang Shih's comment that Shao's kind of knowledge was not transmitted publicly indicates that Shao's knowledge was not a branch of learning generally pursued by intellectuals who identified as Confucian. Although Shao's ideas continued to be known, certainly their cohesiveness as a system was no longer a matter of any great interest. By the early twelfth century, the ideas were simply too far removed from the central Confucian core and its focus on moral and political philosophy.

Post-Sung Opinion

In the thirteenth century and afterward, opinions of Shao Yung's thought changed even further. In Neo-Confucianism, an opposition developed between the *li-hsüeh* of the Ch'eng-Chu school and the *hsin-hsüeh* of Lu Chiu-yüan (Hsiang-shan; 1139–93).[70] Later, with the contributions of Wang Yang-ming (Shou-jen; 1472–1529), *hsin-hsüeh* became known as the Lu-Wang school. Neo-Confucian orthodoxy, or adherence to the *li-hsüeh* of Ch'eng Yi and Chu Hsi was of primary importance; *hsin-hsüeh* was the only acceptable alternative. Philosophical thought that was judged outside either of these two schools had its classical and Confucian credentials questioned. As the separation between these two schools increased during the Yüan and Ming periods, with the Ch'eng-Chu orthodoxy being firmly established, Shao Yung's thought increasingly became a target of criticism.

Representing the orthodox Ch'eng-Chu position, Huang Chen (Tung-fa; 1213–80), for example, criticized Shao's numerical interpretation of the *Yi* as unclassical and unconcerned with human affairs.[71] Rather than recognize those aspects of Shao's thought that were close to the *hsin-hsüeh* of Lu Hsiang-shan, Huang focused on Shao's *hsien-t'ien hsüeh* and on those ideas concerned with the trigrams and hexagrams of the *Yi-ching*. Huang claimed that Shao used the *shu-hsüeh* (numerology) of Ch'en T'uan to construct *hsien-t'ien* charts, but moved the positions of the trigrams and hexagrams in the charts so that they were associated with directions different from those in the *Yi-ching*. Furthermore, the difference between the *hsien-t'ien* and *hou-t'ien* charts in Shao's thought was not based on the *Yi-ching*.[72] Huang found the ties between Shao's thought and *shu-hsüeh*, which he regarded as a non-Confucian tradition of learning, to be so objectionable that he ignored the Confucian elements of Shao's thought. Moreover, what was seen as a lack of political and social practicality in Shao's thought continued to be a source of disapproval.

Not all later philosophers, however, focused on Shao's *Yi* learning. Some, such as Liu Yin (1249–93) of the Yüan period, recognized Shao's commitment to Confucian moral principles.[73] This commitment was partly expressed by Shao's refusal to hold office. Because Liu Yin was responding to concerns different from those of Huang Chen, he saw Shao Yung and his thought in a different light. For Liu, the most important issue was not the purity of Shao's thought, but whether Shao put his ethical principles—that is, the *tao*—into practice. And certainly in Shao's own view, putting the *tao* into practice involved different acts in different periods.

The Ch'ing dynasty textual critics of the evidential research (*k'ao-cheng hsüeh*) school reassessed Shao's thought further. By the seventeenth and eighteenth centuries, many of Shao's assumptions were no longer accepted, and his thought came to be treated as part of the historical past, to be examined and criticized, but certainly not as a possible source of values and motivation. The question of orthodoxy still survived, however, and in that context, Shao's thought was excluded from the Ch'eng-Chu line of philosophical development.[74]

Ch'ing scholars were interested in recovering ancient texts and interpretations of the classics, particularly of the Han period. Thus they rejected the so-called Sung Learning. As a result of such works as the *Yi t'u ming pien* (A clarifying critique of the diagrams of the *yi-ching*) of Hu Wei and the *Yi-hsüeh hsiang-shu lun* (On the images and numbers of the *Yi* learning) of Huang Tsung-hsi (1610–95), many of the historical connections of the *Yi* learning were uncovered. Ch'ing scholars identified the ties between Han dynasty ideas and those of the Sung. Shao's ideas, for instance, were recognized as similar to those of K'ung An-kuo (ca. 156–ca. 74 B.C.), Ching Fang (79–37 B.C.), Liu Hsin (ca. 46 B.C.–A.D. 23), and Yü Fan (A.D. 164–233).[75] Connections between Sung thought and such works as the *Huai-nan Tzu*, *Li-chi*, and *Lü-shih ch'un-ch'iu* were made explicit. Also recognized was the central role of the *Lao Tzu* in the development of the *Yi* learning.[76] The Ch'ing scholars showed, beyond any doubt, that the *Yi* tradition, although not a monolithic and "pure" tradition, had developed with cohesion and continuity. In the Ch'ing, then, Shao's thought was seen as part of the *Yi* tradition, which had links not only to Confucian orthodoxy, but also to the alchemists and their secret transmission of knowledge. Shao Yung was regarded as the philosopher who made these heretofore esoteric ideas public.[77] This view of Shao's thought, however, emphasized only his *hsien-t'ien* learning.

In general, despite the disjunction in time, in knowledge, and in philosophical aim, Ch'ing scholars treated Shao Yung as a bad mathematical astronomer. According to Wang T'ing-hsiang (1474–1544) of the late Ming, Shao distorted the meaning of the *Yi-ching*, and his system did not agree with the purport of the sages or the structure of the universe. Huang Tsung-hsi criticized Shao for eliminating remainders, and in his supplement to the *Ch'ou-jen chuan* (Biographies of mathematicians and astronomers), Juan Yüan (1764–1849) similarly claimed that Shao had only round numbers and ignored remainders. Chang Hui-yen (1761–1802) criticized Shao for the Taoist origin of his thought, for his correlations, and for his view that the cosmos is orderly (thus ignoring anomalies). Both

Juan Yüan and Wang Fu-chih (1619–92) charged that Shao's cosmogony was an arbitrary account of the stages of cosmic evolution and beyond empirical investigation. The only important seventeenth-century thinker to view Shao favorably was Fang Yi-chih (1611–71).[78]

Such criticism was part of the Ch'ing movement to re-examine the past and re-evaluate traditional beliefs.[79] This movement spread across all areas of knowledge, and scarcely any past text or thinker was spared rigorous investigation. In terms of the evaluation of Shao Yung's thought, what is important about the evidential research movement is that, for the Ch'ing scholars, Shao's epistemological assumptions no longer held. Former categories of thought were not only gone; they were ridiculed. Just as the background against which Shao Yung's thought was seen changed, so too did scholars' understanding of the concerns of his philosophy.

Ch'ing scholars criticized Shao's view of the structure of the universe, but they did not critically discuss the philosophical purposes to which he put that view. Ch'ing critics ignored Shao's explanation of how people are able to know and experience things and implied (through omission) that Shao shared with the mathematical astronomers the aim of describing the structure of the universe, thus distorting the intentions of Shao's philosophy. By applying their standards to his thought, they found his thought severely deficient.

This dominant Ch'ing view of Shao's thought as defective astronomy may be said to have originated during the Sung period with the question of whether Shao's thought was *hsüeh* (learning or knowledge) or *shu* (methods or techniques). Whereas the first notion carries the implication of book learning, the second involves the idea of using a technique to manipulate something. People used both concepts in relation to Shao Yung's thought, in some cases understanding the same ideas in different ways, and in other cases referring to different aspects of Shao's thought.

Hsieh Liang-tso of the Sung, for instance, referred to Shao's learning (*hsüeh*) as one of *t'ien-jen ho-yi*, the unity of heaven and humans (in the tradition of the Han philosopher Tung Chung-shu). He also said that the two Ch'engs did not value Shao's methods (*shu*).[80] It is known from other sources that the Ch'engs respected some of Shao's thought but not his numerological concepts, and Hsieh was apparently distinguishing between the theoretical aspects of Shao's thought and his numerological techniques. That is, the Ch'engs viewed Shao's *Yi* learning more as a technique (*shu*) of numerical calculations than as knowledge (*hsüeh*) about basic principles. When speaking in general terms, however, the Ch'engs did refer to Shao's thought as *hsüeh*, as did Yin T'un and Ou-yang Fei.[81] Using the term *fa* (method) instead of *shu*, Chu Hsi spoke of Shao's *hsüeh* (learning), his *fa*, and his *shu-hsüeh* (number learning or numerology). Chu Hsi used the term *fa* in the context of saying that Shao used a method (*fa*) in regard to calendrical matters.[82]

The learning transmitted from Li Chih-ts'ai was called *hsüeh* or *hsien-t'ien hsüeh*, and it consisted of theories on the fundamental patterns or principles of the universe.[83] What made it *hsüeh*, in contrast to *shu*, was that it was knowledge in the form of statements or verbal claims. It did not necessarily have a practical side. However, Shao is also said to have learned Li Chih-ts'ai's method of prediction (*shu-fa*). In this use, *fa*, method, is similar to *shu*, method. Thus, in relation to Shao Yung's philosophy, people talked about four kinds of knowledge: the knowledge of the sage, knowledge of theoretical principles, knowledge of actual techniques for making predictions, and the foreknowledge gained from using the techniques. Unfortunately, these four kinds of knowledge were not always carefully distinguished.

When Wei Liao-weng characterized the contents of *Huang-chi ching-shih* as *hsin-shu* (mind method), the kind of knowledge to which he was referring may have been theoretical knowledge (Shao's *hsien-t'ien* learning). Certainly, Wei was also referring to Shao's ultimate aim as *hsin-shu*. This aim was to attain the knowledge of a sage, and it was to be an experience, not a description of one. Using the term *fa* in a way similar to *shu*, Shao himself spoke of his *hsien-t'ien hsüeh* as a *hsin-fa* (mind method), which is, as noted earlier, also a technical Buddhist term for consciousness.[84] Thus, the interchange of certain terms and concepts since Shao's time indicates that the theoretical and practical aspects of Shao's thought were closely related. Moreover, a lack of consistent differentiation between these two aspects contributed to a certain amount of ambiguity concerning Shao's thought.

In addition, other factors complicated the interpretation of Shao's thought. For example, for Shao, *hsin* (mind) referred not only to the individual person's mind, but also to *tao*, absolute reality, or the One. Thus, in a passage in which *hsin* is equivalent to *tao*, Shao said that Yang Hsiung made clear the mind of heaven and earth.[85] As for Shao's concept of *hsin-fa*, if *hsin* meant the *tao* of heaven and earth, then this concept was concerned with cosmology, astronomy, and theoretical principles. If, however, *hsin* meant the mind of humans, then this concept was a matter of a mystical experience. In actuality, both emphases were a part of Shao's philosophical system.

Thus, given the context of Shao's thought within Neo-Confucianism and the historically close relationship between the *Yi-ching* and astronomical ideas, it is understandable that by the Ch'ing period Shao's thought came to be seen as primarily outmoded astronomy and cosmology. Many concepts and terms in Shao's thought were used in different ways, making the perspective of the critic crucial.

Twentieth-century Opinion

In the course of Chinese intellectual history, Shao Yung's manner of theorizing and the way in which he treated philosophical questions have led to much disagreement and even confusion. From Shao Yung's time to this century, there has been no consensus regarding either the content or the significance of Shao's thought. Such an inability to reach substantial agreement concerning a philosopher's thought is not characteristic of Chinese intellectual history. The philosophical contributions of the other Neo-Confucian founders, for example, have been generally recognized and not greatly disputed. However, in the case of Shao Yung, cross-cultural judgments made in this century have been as diverse as the cross-temporal judgments within China from the Sung to the Ch'ing.

In this century, with the introduction of new categories and terms, the basis for critical judgment of traditional thought has expanded. On the one hand, there continue to be attempts to understand Shao in his historical context and to identify further the Taoist, Confucian, and Buddhist sources of Shao's thought. On the other hand, scholars are applying Western categories of knowledge and Western philosophical concepts. Depending on which aspects of his thought are emphasized, Shao Yung has been seen as a protoscientist, a mystic, a philosopher, a poet, a historian, a fortuneteller, even a political protester. The modern concern with epistemology and metaphysics, in particular, has entered into twentieth-century analyses of Shao's philosophical idealism. Chinese scholars, both Marxist and non-Marxist, from the 1920's to the present, have utilized a wide range of conceptual frameworks in their assessments of Shao Yung.

Discussions within the past twenty years have generally included an analysis both of the historical context and of Shao's epistemological and metaphysical positions. The diversity of opinions and comments has been considerable. Such breadth of opinion is not unwarranted, however, and contrary opinions are not even always contradictory. The reason for this paradoxical situation in part lies in the modern development of knowledge. Twentieth-century views about the nature of reality differ significantly from those held earlier. However, the same terms have continued in use, often with both their old and their new meanings. The word *objective* is an example of a term that has come to have several very different meanings. Those who describe Shao's method of *fan-kuan* (reflective perception) as one of objective observation, to use Needham's term, and those who say Shao's position is one of subjective idealism are referring to the same phenomenon. The perspective and the semantics vary, however. Differences in terminology reflect different backgrounds and different kinds of knowledge. Thus, no matter what label is applied, for modern scholars just as for traditional scholars, no single description adequately represents the complexity of Shao's thought.

A sampling of twentieth-century opinion will indicate the range of assessments of Shao Yung and perhaps give further insight into his philosophy. Writing in the period between the two world wars, when Chinese intellectuals were studying and advocating a variety of Western philosophical positions, including Marxism, liberalism, and pragmatism, Lü Ssu-mien emphasized traditional concerns for delineating the historical origins and context of Shao's thought.[86] Lü pointed out that Shao was concerned primarily with understanding the patterns of things and that his thought was based on the *Yi-ching* and on Taoism. He recognized that Shao's thought had elements in common with the (Taoist-related) traditions of fortune-telling and prognostication and commented that Shao's thought was descended from the learning associated with Wei Po-yang, the Han dynasty alchemist. Despite these associations, however, Lü was unwilling to place Shao in the tradition of the *fang-shih*, or those anomalous people with special skills or esoteric and nonorthodox kinds of knowledge.

Ch'en Chung-fan, a contemporary of Lü's, applied Western notions of philosophical idealism to traditional Chinese forms of idealism.[87] Implicitly applying the Marxist distinction between subjective and objective idealism, Ch'en believed that Shao's idealism contained contradictions, because Shao held that objective principles based on numerical relationships in the universe existed and that the universe was a matter of one's mind and things have no self-nature. In Ch'en's view Shao was both an idealist and not an idealist.

Ch'ien Mu, probably the most important non-Marxist Chinese intellectual historian of the twentieth century, continued the traditional stress on questions of historical context. In addition to the Confucian elements, he identified Buddhist and Taoist influences in Shao's thought and emphasized a mixture of sources for Shao's philosophical system.[88]

Wu K'ang, another mid-century traditional scholar, produced the first comprehensive study of Shao Yung in the twentieth century.[89] Although Wu dissected Shao's thought in terms of traditional categories emphasizing historical sources of ideas, he also initiated the analysis of Shao's thought from a philosophical, rather than simply historical, point of view. He saw Shao's thought as deterministic and mechanical and concluded that Shao was a strange figure in Chinese philosophy. Wu characterized Shao's thought as subjective idealism, or what he called "subjectivism." However, Wu observed that, unlike philosophical idealism in Western thought, Shao's idealism did not involve skepticism or doubt of the senses.

T'ang Chün-yi, an important, more recent Confucian scholar, has traced the historical origins of Shao's philosophy as well as the contemporary intellectual activities of Shao's peers.[90] In addition to their well-known philosophical activities, T'ang emphasized the significant historical studies of these Sung scholars. In assessing the content of Shao's thought, T'ang concentrated on three aspects: the *Yi* learning from the Han period, Shao's ideas on the observation of things and on human consciousness, and Shao's idealism. T'ang emphasized how close Shao's thinking was to traditional Taoism, but since many of Shao's major concepts derived from Confucianism, T'ang also insisted on Shao's Confucian identification. Moreover, T'ang acknowledged the influence of Buddhism. In utilizing traditional Chinese and modern Western types of analysis, T'ang concluded that Shao Yung's thought was a mixture of ideas that combined into a single philosophical system the study of the universe, the study of history, and the study of morality.

Other twentieth-century scholars have used modern and Western categories of knowledge and philosophy to analyze Shao's thought. From his special viewpoint of the history of science, Joseph Needham, for example, found two concepts in Shao's thought particularly interesting: "objective observation" and a "community of observers."[91] Further examination of Shao's thought has made Needham's interpretation questionable, however. For example, the concept in Shao's thought that Needham calls objective observation has little, if anything, to do with objectivity or observation from the perspective of science.

Yang Jung-kuo, a Marxist intellectual historian, emphasized Shao's subjective idealism; that is, the reality of the world is a matter of one's consciousness (in a Marxist sense).[92] Yang saw Shao as anticipating Immanuel Kant's (1724–1804) ideas on the *a priori* forms of consciousness. Yang noted the influence of Buddhism in the idealistic aspect of Shao's thought and claimed that other tendencies in Shao's thought were primarily a reflection of the society of the times, including a rich dialectical emphasis, a recognition that the entire world had processes of birth, growth, and decline, and a scientific-like understanding of natural phenomena.

Hou Wai-lu, the preeminent Chinese Marxist intellectual historian of this century, combined historical and philosophical considerations in his discussion of Shao Yung.[93] He noted that Shao's thought was infused with elements from three primary sources: the apocryphal learning of the Han; the thought of Lao Tzu, Chuang Tzu, and the *Yi-ching*; and Buddhism. Hou pointed out that Shao was an idealist, not a materialist, and claimed that Shao's theory of history was one of devolution or degeneration (a claim challenged in this study). In light of the views of others, perhaps most interesting is Hou's insistence that Shao was opposed to science. Hou said that Shao utilized scientific concepts and terms inappropriately and that his thought, in consequence, was of scant scientific value.

Although some scholars have seen scientific leanings in Shao's thought, Hou is not alone in recognizing an anti-science bias in Shao's thought. For example, Wei Cheng-t'ung, a traditional scholar who is not a Marxist, pointed out that Shao's attitude and goals were not those of science. However, Shao's thought did contain some scientific knowledge typical for his period.[94] This disagreement again raises the issue of perspective and the different meanings that certain terms have acquired.

The discussion in this chapter has focused on other philosophers' and scholars' understanding of Shao's philosophy. In general terms, others saw Shao's thought as part of that *Yi-ching* tradition of learning relating to the images and numbers. Specifically, Shao's areas of interest included knowledge concerning the nature of reality (its entities as well as the patterns of change), the ineffable knowledge of the whole gained from a personal mystical experience, and foreknowledge and prediction.

Some philosophers recognized the strong Confucian basis to Shao's ethical principles and conduct. Others deemed him a Taoist in poor disguise. In addition to elements from popular religion, particularly those pertaining to foreknowledge and prediction, his thought was further recognized as having Buddhist characteristics. Within a hundred years after his death, some Sung philosophers criticized him for not being concerned with human affairs. Seventeenth- and eighteenth-century critics, in addition, attacked him for the forced nature of his correlative and numerological ideas. These they saw as the core of his thought. Others, however, particularly later followers of the images and numbers learning, were sympathetic and regarded him as the possessor of great wisdom.[95]

The comments of critics indicate a recognition of a difference between the subject matter of his two major works, his philosophical treatise, *Huang-chi ching-shih*, and his collection of poetry, *Yi-ch'uan chi-jang chi*. Scholars believed that his poetry delved into areas of concern to early Taoism and the political and moral interests of Confucianism. On the other hand, Shao's philosophical treatise was seen as setting forth his philosophy based on the *Yi-ching*. (This analysis does not hold up under close examination, however.)

Moreover, despite the identification of Taoist influences on Shao and his Confucian shortcomings, he was not, in the end, rejected as a Confucian. He had interests in areas not usual for Confucians, and he had a corresponding lack of interest in some typically Confucian areas. However, along with Chou Tun-yi, Chang Tsai, and the Ch'eng brothers, he still was placed in the *Tao-hsüeh* section of biographies in the *Sung History*. Shao Yung and these four philosophers were officially regarded as the first generation of Neo-Confucians. This bibliographic categorization indicated that he was accepted as being in the continuing line of teaching from Confucius; that is, as part of the *tao-t'ung*.

During the late Ming and Ch'ing periods, when Shao was omitted from the orthodox Ch'eng-Chu line of teaching, this view changed. By then, however, it was clear that he fit into another category dating back to early Chinese history. This categorization resulted from society's making room for a certain unconventional, creative, politically sensitive, poetical, and somewhat "mad" intellect. Ch'ü Yüan is one example of someone in this category; the "seven sages of the bamboo grove" may be regarded as another example.[96] Shao Yung, too, was viewed as a conventionally eccentric heroic figure.

In this century, the old arguments over Shao's Confucian, Taoist, or Buddhist identification are significant only in a historical sense. Tracing the historical origins and ties of Shao's thought remains an important scholarly endeavor. Also of concern now are the efforts to understand Shao's thought according to the categories of Western philosophical analysis. A variety of approaches are being utilized in modern attempts to analyze Shao's philosophy. The combination of perspectives is fitting for someone whose sophisticated philosophical system drew on numerous sources.

10

The Threads Running Through

> *The road taken must be broad. If it is broad, then there are fewer obstacles.*
> —Shao Yung[1]

The preceding discussion of the philosophy of Shao Yung was shaped by two guiding principles. One aim was to suggest a theoretical approach for analyzing the implicit structure of Shao's thought. The approach offered here was to view his thought as explanatory theory. The other aim was to provide some insight into the historical and philosophical context of Shao's thought. Since there is an intimate relationship between ideas and the context in which they arise, and indeed the context is part of the meaning of ideas, the contextual aspect of Shao's thought could not be ignored.

Shao was interested in the abstract structure and the pattern of events in the universe, both those of nature and of the human world. He addressed such topics as the nature of the phenomenal and abstract realms of the universe, time and events-in-time, behavior and change, and reality and human consciousness. In part because this combination of theoretical interests was not typical, assessments of Shao have been far from uniform. Cross-temporal judgments have varied even more than cross-cultural ones. The fact that Shao's thought and lifestyle were at the same time both unusual and yet not actually foreign to Chinese culture certainly must be seen as another factor contributing to the lack of consensus about him.

The problem confronting modern Western scholars is to make realistic cross-temporal and cross-cultural judgments, a problem that clearly confronted premodern Chinese scholars as well. Chinese philosophers in the post-Sung period also had to make judgments from the perspective of vastly different conditions and times. In looking at Chinese assessments of Shao Yung, one cannot help but recognize Shao's complexity as a philosopher and as a person. One also cannot ignore the fact that this complexity was based in that of his culture.

How do the multiple aspects of Shao's thought fit within the varied intellectual traditions of China? Although specific ideas tend to be identified with given schools of thought, a particular person could, and usually did, embody elements from different traditions. In the intellectual and sociological reality of Chinese society, the various traditions of knowledge were not strictly separate. They were more like currents and subcurrents within a larger river. As they flowed together and developed over time, they mixed their waters, and yet in some places they still retained separate identities.

Historically, three basic areas of activity were integral to Confucianism. These areas received different emphases depending on the times. Liu Yi (1017–86) referred to them as substance (*t'i*), function (*yung*), and literary expression (*wen*), or the three aspects of the *tao*.[2] What Liu Yi referred to as *wen* was also called *ching-hsüeh*, classical learning. It consisted of textual commentary, particularly on the classics, but it also could refer to scholarship in a broader sense, including the writing of history. In general terms, activity in this area meant that one was involved with the search for the truth, as originally made manifest by the sages.

A second area of activity involved service in the bureaucracy.[3] Called *ching-shih* (governing the world) or *yung*, this aspect of Confucianism entailed a life of political action. A third emphasis, represented by *t'i*, was *hsiu-shen* (moral cultivation). Depending on one's assumptions about human nature, the cultivation of a moral life was seen as developing one's moral nature or as recovering one's moral nature. This aspect of Confucianism involved the implementation of moral philosophy on the personal level. It counterbalanced the implementation of political philosophy on the social level.

Taoism consisted of numerous subcurrents so varied that, in other contexts, they have been described as philosophy, religion, magic, science, and technology. In addition to certain attitudes and ideas, many of which were contradictory, subtraditions of Taoism specialized in various skills, techniques, and practices such as alchemy, geomancy, practices of nourishing life (*yang-sheng*), and techniques for predicting the future (ranging from physiognomy to the manipulation of sticks according to numerological theories).[4] Many of these practices were associated with the *Yi-ching*, and many had a numerological aspect. Ch'en Chi-ju of the Ming period was referring to this characteristic when he said, for instance, that Shao's learning was based on the numbers as much as were books on geomancy (*ti-li*), fortune-telling (*suan-ming*), Ma Yi's physiognomy (*Ma Yi hsiang-shu*), and divination by yarrow stalks (*pu-shih*).[5]

The differences between Confucianism and Taoism were significant for Shao's thought. First, since many Taoist areas of learning emphasized esoteric knowledge and secret transmission, symbols had great importance, just as they did in Shao's thought. The value given symbols in the esoteric traditions was comparable to that generally reserved for words in the highly literate Confucian culture. Second, in some subtraditions, theories of resonance and correspondence functioned as analogues of the Confucian emphases on moral action. Natural, almost mechanical, relationships between things and between categories of things were emphasized over more voluntary relationships. In terms of the functioning of nature, Shao certainly emphasized the natural, or nonvoluntary, aspect of relationships. Third, a mystical experience was identified more with Taoism than with Confucianism, which more typically stressed a state of perfect moral cultivation. In his philosophical thought, Shao Yung did not ignore states of moral cultivation, but his goal was more often religious or spiritual.

It is significant that Shao Yung's models embodied similar blends of the culture's intellectual currents. Ch'en T'uan, for example, received the Confucian *chin-shih* degree but afterward withdrew from official life to pursue esoteric knowledge and practices. Li Chih-ts'ai earned the *chin-shih* degree and held office but still pursued the learning of the images and numbers. Although neither a degreeholder nor an officeholder, Shao accepted Confucian morality and was concerned with Confucian political and historical thought. Yet he developed a philosophy based on the images and numbers, he had a reputation for being able to know the future, and he rejected a Confucian lifestyle of serving as an official in favor of a retired life that could be associated with Taoism. Withdrawal from active political life did not necessarily have to be only Taoist inspired, and in Shao's case, a Confucian connection is apparent.[6]

In addition to these openly recognized connections to particular traditions of knowledge, Shao's thought was linked to another intellectual current, not entirely explicitly acknowledged but still powerfully present. That current was Buddhism. Not only in certain of his ideas about knowledge and about the universe, but also in the very organizational structure of the *Huang-chi ching-shih*, there is evidence of the role that Buddhist ideas played in the formation of his thought. Since many eleventh-century literati, and later ones too, regarded Buddhism as a cultural threat and wanted to disavow its penetration of Chinese culture, it is not surprising that Shao's Buddhist ties tended to be largely ignored, or lamented if acknowledged. Moreover, Shao's occasional attacks on Buddhism most likely helped to maintain the view that Buddhism had minimal influence on him.[7]

Shao owed a debt to Buddhism primarily in the areas of cosmology and epistemology. Shao conceived of a universe that was divided into a succession of great cosmic time periods. Unlike the Buddhists, however, Shao did not believe that the universe was destroyed and then recreated.[8] Shao's view was more reminiscent of Han dynasty astronomy and Chuang Tzu's idea of the great transformation. Like most Buddhists, Shao believed that the pattern of development and decline in each period was reflected in the moral and political levels of human activity (but not in the length of people's lives, their physical height, or their attractiveness). Moreover, a division of things into four parts was characteristic of Buddhism. This quaternary division was also important in the *Yi* learning and so was not limited to Buddhism.

Some of Shao's epistemological concepts and terms are similar to Buddhist ones. For example, *fan-kuan* (reflective perception) has a remarkable similarity to Chih Yi's concept of *chih-kuan* (cessation and perception). Moreover, other of Shao's terms were employed in both Buddhist and non-Buddhist (either Taoist or Confucian) contexts, with the result that their use called forth multiple associations. Although Shao did not mention any Buddhist sutras by name, he did use such Buddhist terms as *shan* (to complete), *shou* (to receive sense perceptions), *wu-hsin* (having no mind), *wu-wo* (having no self), *wo* (self), and *hsin-fa* (literally mind-method, but a technical term in Buddhism meaning consciousness). Not only were these concepts important in Buddhism, but the two terms *no-mind* and *no-self* were important in Taoism and even appear in Confucian texts. In spite of these ties to Buddhism, a number of these and similar terms were part of the *Yi* learning. On the level of implicit and unspoken assumptions, evidence for further links with Buddhism is found in the structure of the *Huang-chi ching-shih*. As discussed in Chapter 1, its organization is similar to that more likely to be found in Buddhist works than in Confucian or Taoist works before the eleventh century.

It is clear that Shao Yung's thought was based on ideas drawn from different traditions of knowledge within Chinese society. His own writings and the statements of others indicate that he was familiar with a wide range of texts. However, this characteristic did not set him apart from the others of the six masters of the Northern Sung; an examination of the writings of Shao's contemporaries reveals that all had read widely. The variety and inclusiveness of Shao's philosophical ideas reflected the level of cultural literacy expected of an educated person in the eleventh century. Since Chinese high culture was a literary culture, knowledge of historical, classical, literary, and philosophical writings was essential to membership in that culture.[9] Despite the high standards of the educated class and the similar accomplishments of others, Shao Yung still managed to gain a reputation for his broad learning.

Although the diversity of his interests and his profound understanding earned him an almost universal reputation as a highly talented person, few people recognized Shao's contributions to the ongoing development of Chinese thought and culture. For instance, Shao Yung's ideas on the *Yi-ching*, along with those of Ch'eng Yi, formed the basis of Chu Hsi's philosophy relating to the *Yi-ching*, the dominant interpretation of that work from the fourteenth to the nineteenth centuries. Shao influenced the important historian

Hu Hung, and his ideas about the mind were a precursor to those of Ch'eng Hao, Lu Hsiang-shan, and Wang Yang-ming.[10] Shao became a cultural model for the virtuous and reclusive scholar and the patron saint of some physiognomists and fortune-tellers. Moreover, the binary system of numbers in his *Yi-ching*-related charts influenced Leibniz and Western philosophy and mathematics.

Shao's thought was certainly more than a mere synthesis, for he helped to change the way people thought. In my view, his development of a sophisticated idealist position should receive particular recognition. He recognized that human beings make and shape the reality they perceive and experience, that knowledge is a complex phenomenon, and that social reality cannot be adequately represented by a single point of view. At the same time, however, he also realized that some aspects of reality were independent of any human observer. Shao Yung thus was one of the most important predecessors of the great Ming philosopher Wang Yang-ming.

Much remains to be learned about the thought of Shao Yung. Research into the thought of his lesser known contemporaries will be important, for their thought may provide clues for the further understanding of Shao's ideas and his immediate historical context. The harsh judgments of Shao that led to a stereotyping of his thought must be reassessed. The views and values of cultural adjudicators are not inconsequential. Certainly, except for Social Darwinists, later judgments are not necessarily better ones. It will be no surprise if future research indicates that Shao Yung was a philosopher with much greater influence on the formation of Neo-Confucian thought than previously recognized.

Shao Yung wanted to keep the pathway to knowledge as broad as possible.[11] As a step in that direction, this study has been an attempt to examine the internal structure of Shao Yung's thought and to place his philosophy within the intellectual traditions of China. The goal has been to understand how Shao's philosophical system worked. One result has been to discover that his ideas did indeed fit together to form a coherent system. Despite his critics, Shao Yung knew that his thought, like that of Confucius, had one thread running through it all. Shao Yung's aim was to regain the state of original wholeness.

Appendixes

Appendix A

· · · · · ·

The Charts and Diagrams

The number and order of the charts and diagrams, as well as their names and content, vary in the different editions of the *Huang-chi ching-shih*. Shao Yung himself apparently developed four long charts, which are placed at the beginning of the *Huang-chi ching-shih*. These charts are listed below. The names are those used in the *Huang-chi ching-shih shu chieh* (*HCCSSC*), with Wang Chih's commentary.[1] Given in brackets are alternative names, used in the *Huang-chi ching-shih shu*, with Shao Po-wen's commentary. The first three charts consist of correlations involving numbers, the hexagrams, the stems and branches, and historical data. The fourth chart presents correlations involving musical tones and pitches, numbers, the images, and the two series of cycles, epochs, revolutions, generations, and years, months, days, hours.

1. "Yi yüan ching hui" 以元經會 (Regulating epochs with cycles)[2]
2. "Yi hui ching yün" 以會經運 (Regulating revolutions with epochs)[3]
3. "Yi yün ching shih" 以運經世 (Regulating generations with revolutions)[4]
4. "Sheng-yin ch'ang-ho: ssu-hsiang t'ien-ti chih shu t'u" 聲音唱和：四象天地之數圖 (The leading and following of tones and notes: chart of the numbers of the four images and heaven and earth)[5] ["Ching-shih ssu-hsiang t'i-yung chih shu t'u: wan-wu chih shu" 經世四象體用之數圖：萬物之數 Chart of the numbers of the forms and activities of the four images that rule the world: the numbers of the myriad things][6]

In the twelfth century, Ts'ai Yüan-ting attached the ten charts listed below to Shao's work. As with the charts mentioned above, the names are those used in the *HCCSSC*, with the alternative names given from the *Huang-chi ching-shih shu*. Since the ideas in these charts figure prominently in the *Huang-chi ching-shih*, Shao was most likely familiar with these charts or with versions of them. It is not known, however, whether Shao himself composed any of these charts. Certainly much of the material was part of the *Yi* tradition that Shao inherited.

1. "Fu Hsi shih hua pa-kua t'u: hsiao heng t'u" 伏羲始畫八卦圖：小橫圖

(Chart of the eight trigrams originally drawn by Fu Hsi: the small horizontal chart)[7] (see Fig. B1)

2. "Fu Hsi pa-kua ch'ung wei liu-shih-ssu kua t'u: heng t'u" 伏羲八卦重為六十四卦圖：橫圖 (Chart of the eight trigrams of Fu Hsi squared to become the 64 hexagrams: the horizontal chart)[8] ["Pa-kua ch'ung wei liu-shih-ssu kua t'u," Chart of the eight trigrams squared to become 64 hexagrams][9]

3. "Fu Hsi pa-kua fang-wei t'u: hsiao yüan t'u" 伏羲八卦方位圖：小圓圖 (Chart of the directional [square] positions of the eight trigrams of Fu Hsi: the small circular chart)[10] ["Pa-kua cheng-wei t'u" 八卦正位圖, Chart of the correct positions of the eight trigrams][11] (see Fig. B2)

4. "Fu Hsi liu-shih-ssu kua fang-wei t'u: yüan t'u fang t'u" 伏羲六十四卦方位圖：圓圖方圖 (Chart of the directional [square] positions of the 64 hexagrams of Fu Hsi: the circular chart and square chart)[12] ["Liu-shih-ssu kua fang yüan t'u" 六十四卦方圓圖, Square and circular chart of the 64 hexagrams][13] (see Fig. B3)

5. "Yang chiu yin liu yung shu t'u" 陽九陰六用數圖 (Chart of the activity numbers of *yang* nine and *yin* six);[14] Appended chart: "Pa-kua yin-yang yao shu t'u" 八卦陰陽爻數圖 (Chart of the lines and numbers of *yin* and *yang* of the eight trigrams)[15]

6. "Ching-shih yen-yi pa-kua t'u" 經世衍易八卦圖 (Chart of the eight trigrams that rule the world and illustrate change)[16] (see Fig. B4)

7. "Ching-shih t'ien-ti ssu-hsiang t'u" 經世天地四象圖 (Chart of the four images of heaven and earth that rule the world)[17] (see Fig. B5)

8. "Ching-shih liu-shih-ssu kua chih shu t'u: hsien-t'ien t'u" 經世六十四卦之數圖：先天圖 (Chart of the numbers of the 64 hexagrams that rule the world: the *hsien-t'ien* chart)[18] (see Fig. B6)

9. "Ching-shih t'ien-ti shih-chung chih shu t'u" 經世天地始終之數圖 (Chart of the numbers of the beginnings and ends of heaven and earth that rule the world)[19]

10. "Ching-shih yi-yüan hsiao-chang chih shu t'u" 經世一元消長之數圖 (Chart of the numbers of the waxing and waning of one cycle that rule the world);[20] Appended chart: "Yüan-hui-yün-shih nien-yüeh-jih-shih chih shu t'u" 元會運世年月日時之數圖 (Chart of the numbers of cycles, epochs, revolutions, generations, and years, months, days, hours)[21]

In addition to those listed above, other charts and diagrams were appended to Shao's work by various commentators and compilers.[22] Some of these related directly to Shao's own ideas, whereas others were part of the larger *Yi* tradition. Some charts, such as the *Ho T'u* (River chart) and *Lo Shu* (Lo writing), were developed before Shao Yung's time (see Fig. B7). Others were compiled later. In some cases, commentators enlarged Shao's charts with later historical data.[23]

Appendix B

· · · · · ·

Selected Charts

The following charts have been selected from the *Huang-chi ching-shih shu-chieh* (*HCCSSC*) for reproduction because of their importance in Shao Yung's thought as discussed in this study. Other charts are equally important but are too complicated to be presented here.

Fig. B1. "Fu Hsi shih hua pa-kua t'u" (Chart of the eight trigrams originally drawn by Fu Hsi; *HCCSSC*, shou-shang: 13b)

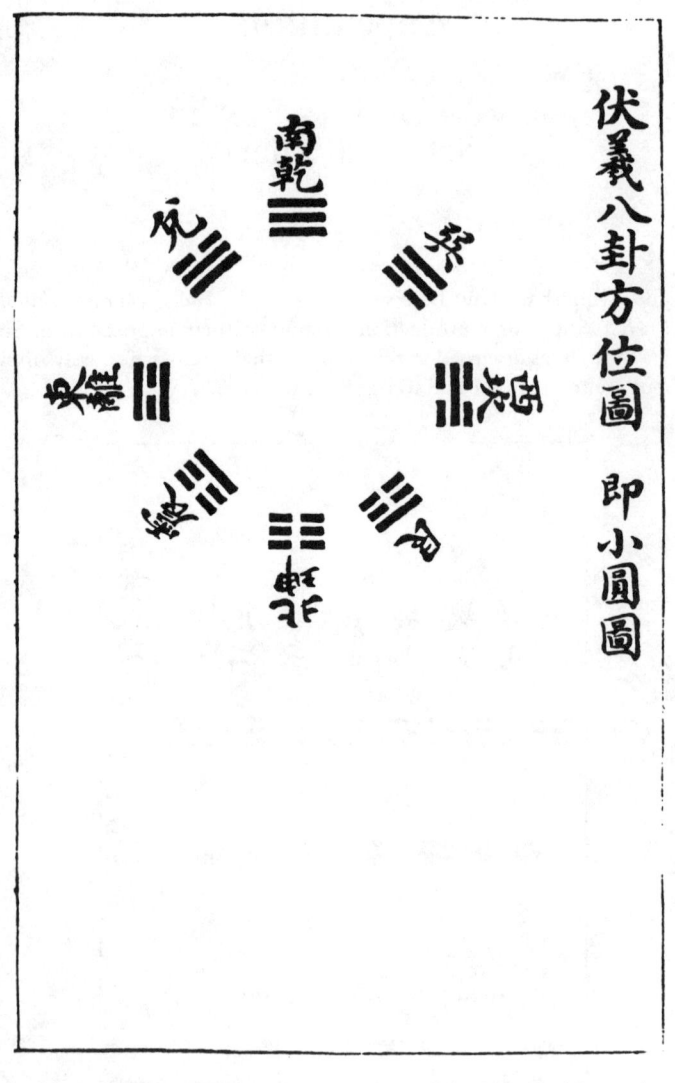

Fig. B2. "Fu Hsi pa-kua fang-wei t'u" (Chart of the directional [square] positions of the eight trigrams of Fu Hsi; HCCSSC, shou-shang: 26a)

Appendix B · 239

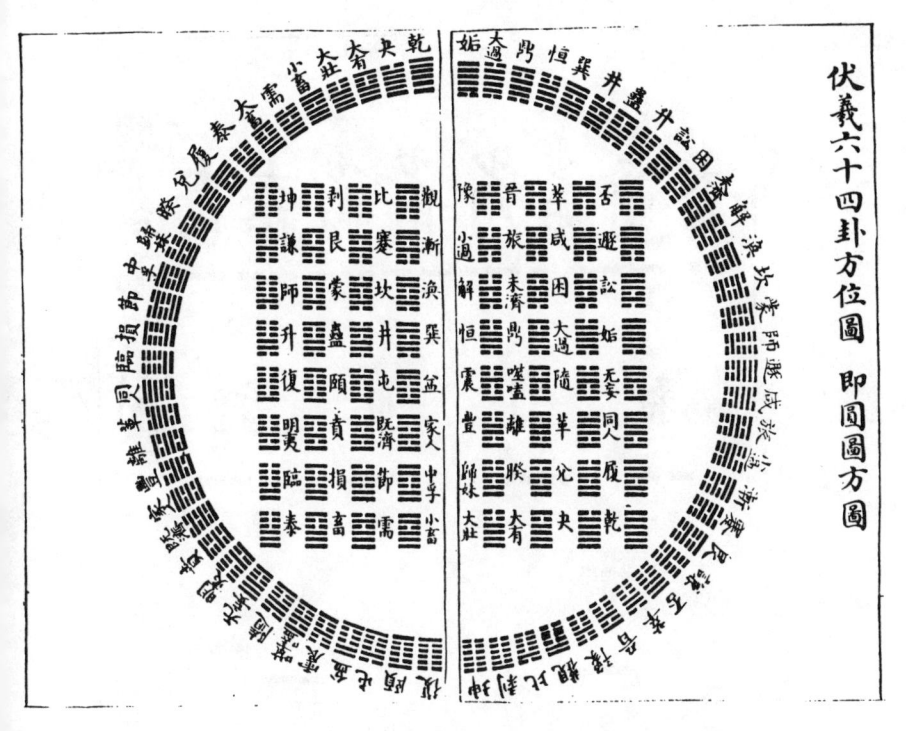

Fig. B3. "Fu Hsi liu-shih-ssu kua fang-wei t'u" (Chart of the directional [square] positions of the 64 hexagrams of Fu Hsi; *HCCSSC*, shou-shang: 27b–28a)

經世衍易八卦圖

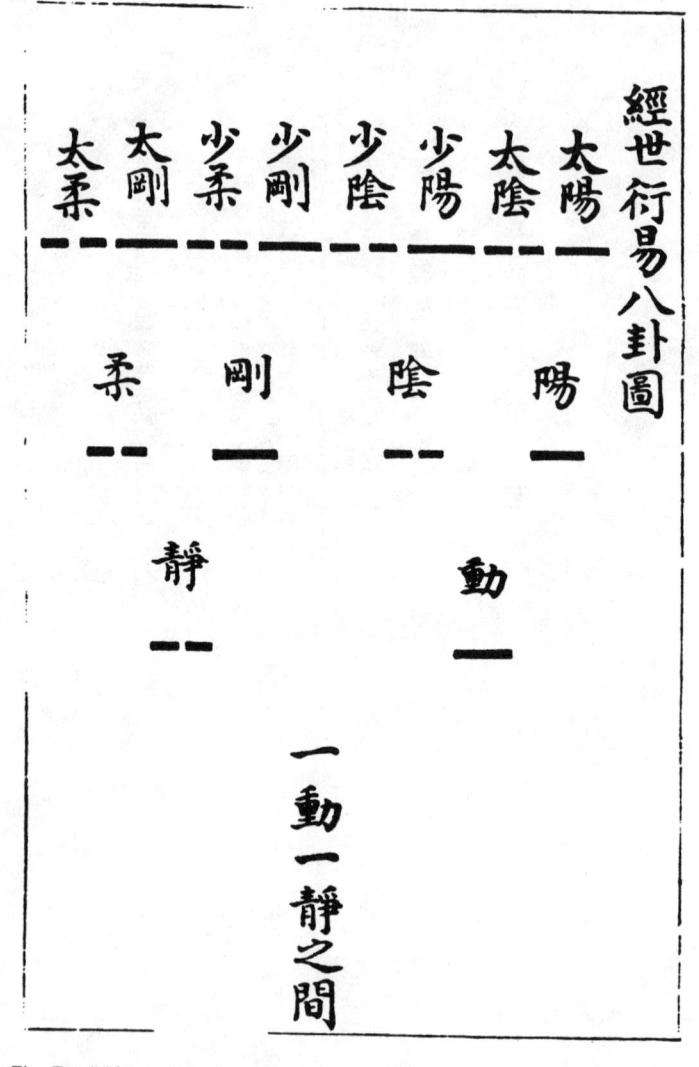

太陽　太陰　少陽　少陰　少剛　少柔　太剛　太柔

陽　陰　剛　柔

動　靜

一動一靜之間

Fig. B4. "Ching-shih yen-yi pa-kua t'u" (Chart of the eight trigrams that rule the world and illustrate change; *HCCSSC*, shou-shang: 38b)

Appendix B · 241

太陽乾	太陰兌	少陽離	少陰震	少剛巽	少柔坎	太剛艮	太柔坤
日 暑 性 ─ 附心	月 寒 情 ─ 膽	星 晝 形 ─ 脾	辰 夜 體 ─ 腎	石 雷 木 ─ 肺 骨	土 露 草 ─ 肝 肉	火 風 飛 ─ 胃 髓	水 雨 走 ─ 膀胱 血
目 元 皇	耳 會 帝	鼻 運 王	口 世 伯	色 歲 易	聲 月 書	氣 日 詩	味 辰 春秋

Fig. B5a. "Ching-shih t'ien-ti ssu-hsiang t'u" (Chart of the four images of heaven and earth that rule the world; *HCCSSC*, shou-hsia:1b–2a). For an English translation of this chart, see Fig. B5b overleaf.

Greater Jou (k'un)	Greater Kang (ken)	Lesser Jou (k'an)	Lesser Kang (sun)	Lesser Yin (chen)	Lesser Yang (li)	Greater Yin (tui)	Greater Yang (ch'ien)
flavors/water	odors/fire	sounds/earth	appearances/stone	mouth/zodiacal space	nose/stars	ears/moon	eyes/sun
hour/rain	day/wind	month/dew	year/thunder	generation/night	revolution/day	epoch/cold	cycle/heat
Ch'un-ch'iu/walking things	Shih/flying things	Shu/grassy things	Yi/woody things	hegemon/body	king/form	emperor/feelings	sage/nature
bladder	stomach	gall bladder	lungs	kidneys	spleen	liver	*Addendum* heart
blood	marrow	flesh	bones				

Fig. B5b. An English version of the chart given in Fig. B5a

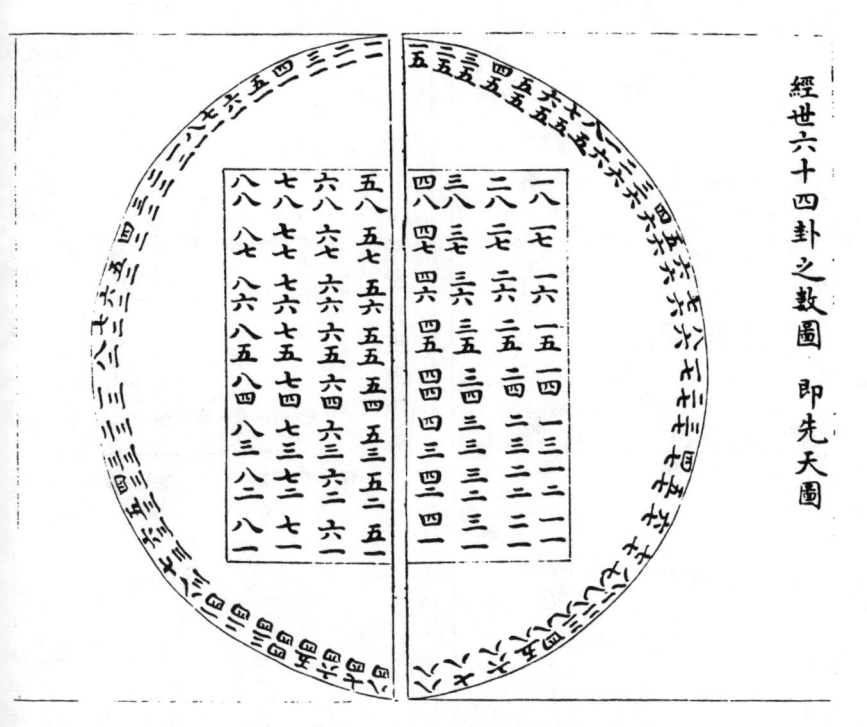

Fig. B6. "Ching-shih liu-shih-ssu kua chih shu t'u" (Chart of the numbers of the 64 hexagrams that rule the world; *HCCSSC*, shou-hsia:9ab)

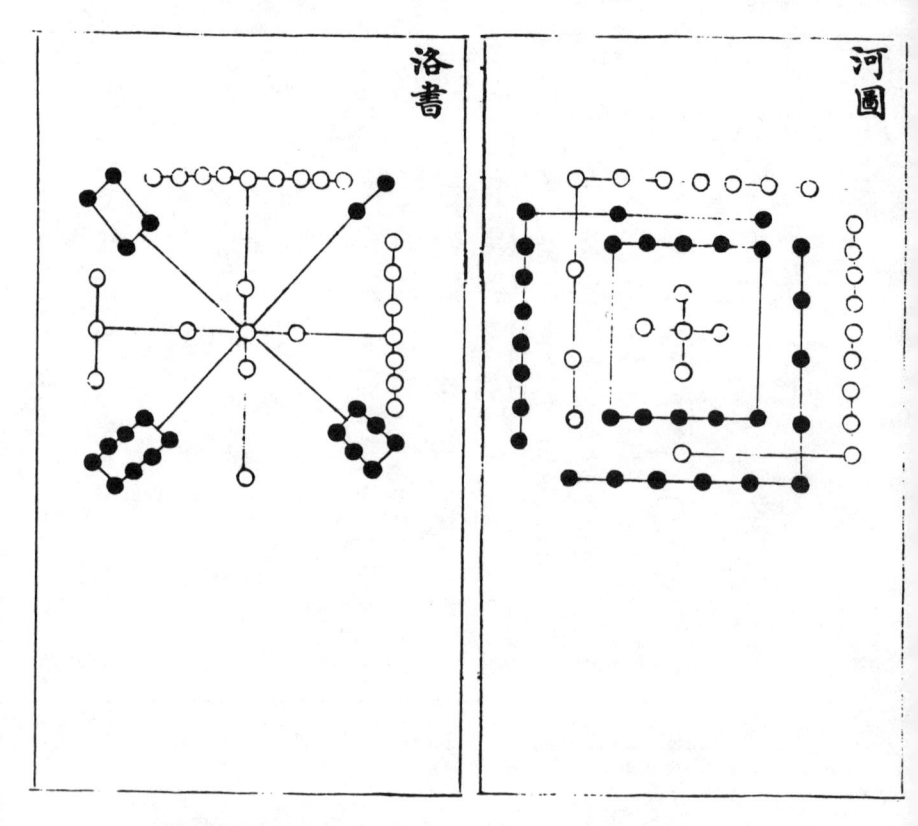

Fig. B7. "Ho T'u Lo Shu chih t'u" (The River chart [right] and the Lo writing [left]; *HCCSSC*, shou-hsia: 33ab)

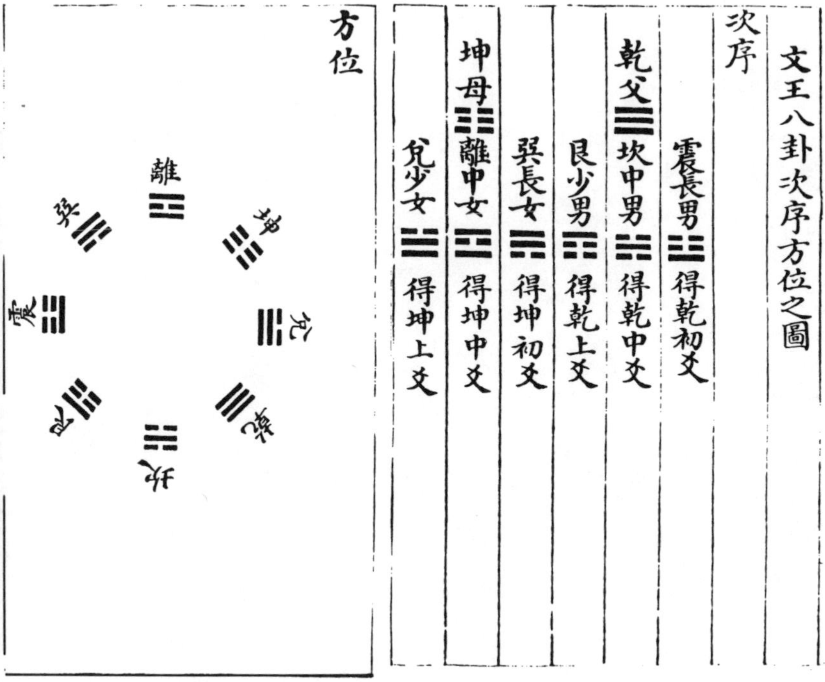

Appendix B · 245

文王八卦次序方位之圖

次序

乾父 ☰
震長男 ☳ 得乾初爻
坎中男 ☵ 得乾中爻
艮少男 ☶ 得乾上爻
坤母 ☷
巽長女 ☴ 得坤初爻
離中女 ☲ 得坤中爻
兌少女 ☱ 得坤上爻

方位

Fig. B8. "Wen Wang pa-kua tz'u-hsü fang-wei chih t'u" (Chart of the sequence and the directional [square] positions of the eight trigrams of King Wen; *HCCSSC*, shou-hsia: 37b–38a)

Appendix C

List of Chinese Characters

Personal names and titles of works listed in the Bibliography (pp. 291–307) are not given here.

an 安
An-le hsien-sheng 安樂先生
An-le wo 安樂窩

ch'a 差
Ch'an 禪
chang 長
Chang Chung-pin 張仲賓
Chang Heng 張衡
Chang Hui-yen 張惠言
Chang Hsüeh-ch'eng 章學誠
ch'ang 唱
chen 震
chen-chih 真知
chen-ti 眞諦
chen-wang 眞王
ch'en 辰
Ch'en 陳
Ch'en T'uan 陳摶 (Hsi-yi 希夷)
cheng (correct firmness) 貞
cheng (correctness) 正
cheng (struggle) 爭
cheng-ch'i 正氣
cheng-ming 正名
cheng tao 正道
cheng-t'ung 正統
ch'eng (fulfillment) 成
ch'eng (wholeness, sincerity) 誠

Cheng Tung-ch'ing 鄭東卿 (Shao-mei 少梅)
Ch'eng-Chu 程朱
chi (self) 己
Chi 姬 (surname)
chi (temporal regulators) 紀
chi (traces) 迹
chi-shu 極數
Chi-tsang 吉藏
ch'i 氣
Ch'i 齊
ch'i (arise) 起
ch'i (thing, utensil) 器
ch'i-hou 氣候
chiang-hsüeh 講學
Chiang Yü 姜愚
ch'iang-ming 強名
chiao 教
Ch'iao Ts'ai 喬柴
chien 兼
chien-ch'ieh 僭竊
ch'ien 乾
Ch'ien-hsü 潛虛
chih (disposition, matter) 質
chih (knowledge, understand) 知
chih (wisdom) 智
chih-cheng 至正
chih-ch'eng 至誠

chih-chung 至中
chih kuan 止觀
chih li 智力
chih ling 至靈
chih-pien 至變
chih-shu 植數
chih-ta 至大
Chih Yi 智顗
chih-yung 至用
Chin 晉 (ancient state)
chin (complete, exhaust) 盡
Chin-chou 晉州
Chin-hsien 晉縣
chin-shih 進士
Chin-ssu lu 近思錄
Ch'in 秦
ching (essence) 精
ching (stillness, rest) 靜
Ching Fang 京房
ching-hsüeh 經學
ching-shen 精神
ching-shih 經世
ch'ing 情
(Duke of) Chou 周公
Chou Ch'un-ming 周純明
Chou Yi chieh 周易解
Chu Chen 朱震
Ch'u 楚
ch'u-ju 出入
chü-hsi 巨細
chü-jen 舉人
ch'ü 去
Ch'ü Yüan 屈源
ch'uan-hsin 傳心
chüan 卷
ch'üan (adaptive behavior) 權
ch'üan (persuade) 勸
(King) Chuang 莊王
Ch'un-ch'iu 春秋
chün-tzu 君子
chung (ends) 終

chung (inside, center, within) 中
Chung Fang 种放 (Ming-yi 明逸)
chung-ho chih ch'i 中和之氣
Chung-ni (Confucius) 仲尼
chung-shih 終始
Chung-yung 中庸

en-hsin 恩信

fa (arise, release) 發
fa (method) 法
Fa Tsang 法藏
fan-kuan 反觀
fan-kuan tzu-hsin 反觀自心
fan-shen 反身
Fan-yang 范陽
fang-shih 方士
Fang Yi-chih 方以智
Fen-chou 汾州
Fu Hsi 伏羲
Fu Pi 富弼

Han Hsin 韓信
heng 亨
Heng-chang 衡漳
ho (following in harmony, harmonize with) 和
ho (harmonious fit) 合
Ho T'u 河圖
Ho-yang 河陽
Ho Yen 何晏
hou-t'ien 後天
hou-t'ien t'u 後天圖
hsi 翕
Hsi-tz'u chuan 繫辭傳
hsiang 象
(Duke) Hsiang 襄公
hsiang-shu hsüeh 象數學
hsiao-chang 消長
Hsieh Liang-tso 謝良左 (Shang-ts'ai 上蔡)

Appendix C · 249

hsien 賢
hsien-t'ien 先天
hsien-t'ien hsüeh 先天學
hsien-t'ien t'u 先天圖
hsin 心
hsin chih kuan 心之官
hsin-ch'uan 心傳
hsin-fa 心法
hsin-hsüeh (learning of the mind) 心學
hsin-hsüeh (new learning) 新學
hsin-shu 心術
hsing (forms, appearance) 形
hsing (nature) 性
hsing (stars) 星
hsing-ming 性命
hsiu-shen 修身
hsiu-ts'ai 秀才
hsü 虛
hsü ming 虛名
hsü-wei 虛位
(King) Hsüan 宣王
Hu Hung 胡宏
hua 化
Hua-shan 華山
hua-shu 化數
Hua-yen 華嚴
Huai-nan Tzu 淮南子
(Duke) Huan 桓公
huang 皇
Huang Chi 黃畿
Huang-t'ing ching 黃庭經
hui 會
Hui Ssu 慧思
Hui Tzu 惠子
hun-t'ien 渾天
"Hung fan" 洪範

jang 讓
jen (benevolence) 仁
jen (human being) 人

(Mr.) Jen 任先生
jih 日
jou 柔
ju 入
ju-shu 儒術
jun-shen 潤身

k'ai 開
kan 感
Kan Kung 甘公
kan-ying 感應
k'an 坎
kang 剛
k'ao-cheng hsüeh 考證學
ken 艮
kua 卦
kua ch'i 卦氣
kuai 夬
kuan 觀
kuan-hsin 觀心
Kuan-hsin lun 觀心論
Kuan Lu 管輅
kuan-pien 觀辨
kuan-wu 觀物
Kuan-wu nei-p'ien 觀物內篇
Kuan-wu wai-p'ien 觀物外篇
kuei chih 歸之
Kuei-ts'ang 歸藏
k'un 坤
kung 功
kung-cheng 公正
Kung-ch'eng 共城
K'ung An-kuo 孔安國
k'ung-chung lou-ke 空中樓閣
Kuo P'u 郭璞

lao 老
lei 類
li (advantageous gain) 利
li (etiquette) 禮
li (force) 力

li (inside, the hidden) 裏
li (mile) 里
li (one of the eight trigrams) 離
li (pattern, principle) 理
Li-chi 禮記
Li Chih-ts'ai 李之才 (Yen-chih 挺之)
li-hsüeh 理學
Liang 梁
liang-yi 兩儀
Lien-hsi 濂溪
Lien-shan 連山
ling 靈
ling yü wan-wu 靈於萬物
Liu Hsin 劉歆
liu-hsing chih yung 流行之用
Liu Mu 劉牧
liu-shih-ssu kua 六十四卦
Liu Yi 劉勢
Liu Yin 劉因
Lo Ch'in-shun 羅欽順
Lo-hsia Hung 洛下閎
Lo Shu 洛書
Loyang 洛陽
Lu (ancient state) 魯
Lu (surname) 陸
Lu Chiu-yüan 陸九淵 (Hsiang-shan 象山)
Lu-Wang 陸王
lü 履
Lü Kung-chu 呂公著 (Shen-kung 申公)
Lü-shih ch'un-ch'iu 呂氏春秋
Lung T'u 龍圖

Ma Yi 麻衣
Ma Yi hsiang shu 麻衣相書
min 民
ming (comprehend, clarify, bright) 明
ming (destiny, fate) 命
ming (names, fame) 名

Ming Chia 名家
ming li 明理
ming ts'un shih wang 名存實亡
mou 畝
(Duke) Mu 穆公
Mu Hsiu 穆修 (Po-chang 伯長)

nan 難
nien 年

Ou-yang Fei 歐陽棐

pa (po) 伯 or 霸
pa-kua 八卦
Pai-yüan 百原
pei 備
pen-t'i 本體
pi 閉
p'i 闢
piao 表
pieh-ming 別名
pien 變
pien-hua 變化
pien-shu 變數
p'ing 平
(King) P'ing 平王
po 剝
pu-shih 卜筮
pu yi wo kuan wu 不以我觀物

san-huang 三皇
San-lun 三論
san-ts'ai 三才
san-wang 三王
shan 善
shang 上
shao 少
(Duke) Shao 召公
Shao Chung-liang 邵仲良
Shao Fu 邵傅
shao-jou 少柔

shao-kang 少剛
Shao Ku 邵古 (T'ien-sou 天叟, Yi-ch'uan 伊川)
Shao Ling-chin 邵令進
Shao Mu 邵睦
Shao P'u 邵溥
Shao Te-hsin 邵德新
shao-yang 少陽
shao-yin 少陰
Shao Yung 邵雍 (Yao-fu 堯夫, K'ang-chieh 康節)
shen 神
Shen Hsiu 神秀
shen-ming 神明
sheng (birth) 生
sheng (flourish) 盛
sheng-hsien 聖賢
sheng-hsien chih shih-yeh 聖賢之事業
shih (beginnings) 始
shih (duties, affairs) 事
shih (generation) 世
shih (hour, season, time) 時
shih (reality) 實
shih (understanding) 識
Shih-ching 詩經
Shih Kung 石公
shih-yeh 事業
shou 收
shu (adepts, method) 術
shu (numbers) 數
Shu-ching 書經
shu-fa 數法
shu-hsüeh 數學
shu-shu hsüeh 術數學
shuai (decline) 衰
shuai (lead) 率
Shun 舜
ssu-fu 四府
ssu-hsiang 四象
Ssu-ma Kuang 司馬光

ssu-sheng 死生
Su-men Shan 蘇門山
suan-ming 算命
sui 歲
sun 巽
Sung (ancient state) 宋

Ta chuan 大傳
ta-hsin 大心
Ta-hsüeh 大學
ta hua 大化
Ta-yen 大衍
ta-yün 大運
t'ai-chi 太極
t'ai-ch'u 太初
t'ai-hsüan 太玄
t'ai-jou 太柔
t'ai-kang 太剛
t'ai-su 太素
t'ai-yang 太陽
T'ai-yi 太一
t'ai-yin 太陰
T'ang (ancient king) 湯
(Mr.) T'ang 湯氏
tao 道
tao-hsüeh 道學
tao-jen 道人
tao-li 道理
tao-lu 道路
Tao Te Ching 道德經
tao-t'ung 道統
te (attain) 得
te (virtue) 德
te-hsing chih chih 德性之知
teng-ch'a 等差
ti 帝
ti ching 地靜
ti-li 地理
t'i 體
t'i-shu 體數
ti-yung 體用

t'ien-jen ho-yi 天人合一
T'ien-ming 天命
T'ien-sou 天叟
T'ien-t'ai 天台
t'ien-ti 天地
t'ien-ti chih chung-shih 天地之終始
t'ien-ti chih t'i-yung 天地之體用
t'ien tung 天動
ting-ming 定名
t'ing 聽
ts'ai 才
Ts'ai Yüan-ting 蔡元定 (Hsi-shan 西山)
ts'ang 藏
Ts'ao Ts'ao 曹操
Tseng Tzu 曾子
Tso chuan 左傳
tsou lei 走類
Tsou Yen 騶衍
tu 度
t'u-shu p'ai 圖數派
tui 兌
tui-tai chih t'i 對待之體
tung (east) 東
tung (movement) 動
tung-ching 動靜
Tung Chung-shu 董仲舒
tung-shu 動數
t'ung 通
Tzu-chih t'ung-chien 資治通鑑
tzu-jan 自然
Tzu-kung 子貢
Tzu Ssu 子思
tz'u 辭

wan-wu 萬物
wan-wu chih kan-ying 萬物之感應
wang 王
Wang An-shih 王安石
wang chih 妄知
Wang Fu-chih 王夫之

Wang Kung-ch'en 王拱辰
Wang T'ing-hsiang 王廷相
Wang Yang-ming 王陽明 (Shou-jen 守仁)
wang yen 妄言
Wang Yün-hsiu 王允脩
wei-fa 未發
wei-hsüeh 緯學
Wei Liao-weng 魏了翁 (Ho-shan 鶴山)
wen 文
(Duke) Wen 文公
(King) Wen 文王
wen-chien chih chih 聞見之知
Wen Yen-po 文彥博
wo 我
Wu (ancient state) 吳
wu (enlightenment) 悟
wu (thing) 物
(King) Wu 武王
wu-hsin 無心
wu-hsing 五行
wu-li 物理
Wu-ming lun 無名論
wu-pa 五伯
wu-ti 五帝
wu-wei 無為
wu-wo 無我
wu-wo chih hsin 無我之心
wu-yu 無有

yang 陽
yang ch'i 陽氣
yang-sheng 養生
Yang Shih 楊時 (Kuei-shan 龜山)
(Emperor) Yao 堯
yeh 業
yeh tao 邪道
yen (word) 言
Yen (ancient place name) 燕
yi (ideas) 意

yi (one, identical) 一
yi (righteousness) 義
Yi 易 (the Yi learning; easy)
Yi-ching 易經
Yi-ch'uan 伊川
Yi-hsüeh 易學
Yi-hsüeh ch'i-meng 易學啓蒙
yi-li 義理
Yi-li 儀禮
yi-li hsüeh 義理學
yi tuan 一端
yi wu kuan wu 以物觀物
yin 陰
yin ch'i 陰氣
Yin fu ching 陰符經
yin-ke 因革
Yin T'un 尹焞 (Ho-ching 和靖)
ying 應
yu-wo chih hsin 有我之心
yu-wu 有無
Yü (dynasty of Emperor Shun) 虞
Yü (sage ruler) 禹
yü (stupidity) 愚
Yü Fan 虞翻
yüan 元
yüeh 月
yün 運
yung 用
yung-shu 用數

Reference Matter

Notes

Complete authors' names, titles, and publication data are given in the Bibliography, pp. 291–307. For the sake of simplicity, whenever possible I have used the Ssu-k'u ch'üan-shu edition of the *Huang-chi ching-shih*, with collected commentary by Wang Chih (*HCCSSC*). The following abbreviations are used in the Notes and Bibliography.

HCCSSC	Shao Yung, *Huang-chi ching-shih shu-chieh*.
HLTCS	*Hsing-li ta-ch'üan-shu*.
KWNP	*Kuan-wu nei-p'ien*, in Shao Yung, *Huang-chi ching-shih shu*.
KWWP	*Kuan-wu wai-p'ien*, in Shao Yung, *Huang-chi ching-shih shu*.
SKCS	*Ssu-k'u ch'üan-shu*.
SPPY	*Ssu-pu pei-yao*.
SYHA	Huang Tsung-hsi and Ch'üan Tsu-wang, *Sung Yüan hsüeh-an*.
TSCC	*Ts'ung-shu chi-ch'eng*.

Chapter 1

1. *HCCSSC*, 14:67a, *KWWP*, 12. This statement alludes to the attitude of Confucius. See *Lun-yü*, 1.1, 6.18; translated in Chan, *Source Book*, 18, 30.

2. See Chapter 9 of this study for a discussion of the range of opinions on Shao Yung and his thought that traditional and modern Chinese scholars have held.

3. For their biographies in the *Sung shih*, see 427:1a–3a (Chou Tun-yi), 427:10a–11b (Shao Yung), 427:8b–10a (Chang Tsai), 427:3a–5b (Ch'eng Hao), 427:5b–8b (Ch'eng Yi). There is also some disagreement over the extent to which the five founders influenced each other. See Graham, *Philosophers*, 152–78. I do not agree with Ira E. Kasoff's claim (and this study will show why) that Shao Yung was not part of the Confucian mainstream in the eleventh century. See Kasoff, 8.

4. As Hou Wai-lu (496) noted, Chu Hsi first identified six masters of the *tao* learning (see Chu Hsi, *Chu Tzu ta-ch'üan*, 85:9ab). In a later work (*Yüan-yüan lu*), however, apparently because of the influence of the followers of the Loyang learning, Chu omitted Ssu-ma Kuang from the orthodox line of transmission. On Shao Yung's omission from the *Chin-ssu lu*, see Chan, *Reflections*, xxxii–xxxiii.

5. Only when these cultural systems began to break down in the nineteenth century did the problem of separating traditional Chinese culture and its values from China as a modern political state become a major concern of Chinese intellectuals. See Schwartz, *Search*; and Levenson.

6. For a general history of this period, see Reischauer and Fairbank. For specialized studies, see Chaffee; Kracke, particularly 8–27; and J. T. C. Liu, *Reform*. On printing, see Carter; Chang Hsiu-min; Liu Chia-pi; and J. Needham et al., vol. 5.

7. For a general view of the development of Chinese philosophy, see Fung. On the development of Neo-Confucianism, see Bruce; Carsun Chang; and de Bary, "Reappraisal."

8. See Wei Cheng-t'ung, *Chung-kuo*; and Wu. For the earlier development of the *Yi* learning, see Mou Tsung-san, *Wei-Chin*.

9. See Guthrie, 1:146–340; and Philip. For a study concerning the possibility of Chinese influence on the Pythagorean school, see Swetz and Kao.

10. Quine.

11. In addition to Shao Yung, others followed the so-called *t'u-shu p'ai* (charts and diagrams branch) of the images and numbers learning. Shao Yung was the most famous, but Liu Mu (1011–64) and Chu Chen (1072–1138) were also important.

12. I agree with Graham's view (*Philosophers*, 153) that there is no evidence indicating that Shao Yung and Chou Tun-yi knew each other.

13. *Lun-yü*, 7.1; see Chan, *Source Book*, 31.

14. See Howard; Le Blanc; and Louton. As this study will show, Shao was greatly influenced by Han thought.

15. Tung and Yang represented different positions within Han thought, but both shared certain basic assumptions about the unity and correspondence of parts of the universe; see Fung, 2:7–150.

16. Wei Po-yang, a Han dynasty alchemist, wrote the *Chou Yi ts'an-t'ung-ch'i*, dated A.D. 142, which is considered to be the earliest book on theoretical alchemy. Kuan Lang (Tzu-ming; Wei dynasty) wrote the *Tung-chi chen-ching* and *Kuan shih Yi chuan*. During the Sung, Ts'ai Yüan-ting (1135–98) placed Shao's *Huang-chi ching-shih* in the tradition of Yang Hsiung's *T'ai-hsüan ching*, Kuan Lang's *Tung-chi chen-ching*, and Ssu-ma

Kuang's *Ch'ien-hsü*. See *HCCSSC*, shou-shang: 3b. For a discussion of alchemical ideas that indicate the necessary correlation of space and time, ideas similar to those of Shao Yung, see Sivin, "Alchemy and the Manipulation."

17. This claim does not apply to those Chinese philosophers who were part of the evidential research movement in the Ch'ing period (and even those who anticipated it before the Ch'ing), for they changed Chinese philosophy in fundamental ways. See Elman.

18. See Nakayama.

19. Graham, *Philosophers*, 161, quoting Ch'eng Yi. Nothing is known about Chou's ability to argue. Ch'eng's comment reflects the Chinese expectation that the reader should know enough to understand the remark.

20. See Hansen, *Language and Logic*; and Mou Jun-sun.

21. For examples of Buddhist styles of writing, see Willis; and Hakeda. The characterization I offer here does not apply to Ch'an Buddhist writings.

22. For their works, see Balazs, *Bibliography*.

23. See Watson, *Chuang Tzu*.

24. See Lau, 57; or Waley, 141; and Watson, *Chuang Tzu*, 32. Watson translates the phrase *wu ming* as "no fame." On Ho Yen's *Wu-ming lun*, see Mather.

25. The title of Shao's collection of poetry, in 20 *chüan*, alludes to several things. According to Chang Hsing-ch'eng ("Hsing chuang," 48), Shao Yung himself wrote the preface to this collection, which was dated Sung, Chih-p'ing period (1064–67), *ping-wu* year, the first day of *chung-ch'iu* (8th month). In the preface (3b) Shao explained the title: "If a determined man is in the fields, then he will talk about the fields. Therefore these poems are named *Yi-ch'uan chi-jang chi*." In other words, the contents of these poems consist of things that Shao Yung thought about. The collection was named shortly after Shao buried his father (whose courtesy name was Yi-ch'uan) by the banks of that river in 1064 (Ch'eng Hao, "Mu chieh ming," 45). The phrase "beating on the ground" is an allusion to an incident in the time of the sage-emperor Yao. Common belief held that it was a time when the world was at peace and the people had no troubles. Some old men were beating on the ground in the middle of the road and singing an old song: "We work when the sun comes up; we rest when the sun goes down; we drill a well and drink; we till the fields and eat; what power does the emperor have over us?" The title also alludes to a poem by Po Chü-yi and perhaps to one in the *Shih-ching*. See Legge, *She King*, 206. Okada (209n28) translates the title as *Poems of Striking an Earthen Instrument*. Bloom (*Knowledge*, 80n197) translates the title as *Strik-*

ing an Earthen Instrument in the I River. However, I would suggest that the title has the sense of striking the ground with some sort of utensil, just as Chuang Tzu pounded on a tub after his wife died. See Watson, *Chuang Tzu*, 191–92.

26. See Legge, *Shoo King*, 320–44. Emphasizing the political context, Legge (328) translates *huang-chi* as "royal perfection." In explaining the title *Huang-chi ching-shih*, Shao Po-wen said, "The extremely great [*chih-ta*] is called *huang*, the extreme center [*chih-chung*] is called *chi*, extreme correctness [*chih-cheng*] is called *ching*, and extreme change [*chih-pien*] is called *shih*." Since the *tao* cannot be seen, it can be understood only through the behavior of phenomenal things. Shao Po-wen thus indicated that the title referred to a concept of a supreme force in the universe, and this force may be thought of in such terms as the great equilibrium, the *tao*, the ultimate center, and the supreme principle. *HCCSSC*, 8:31a. Wang Chih disagreed with Shao Po-wen, however, and said that the title referred to the ultimate standards established by the three sage kings (Yao, Shun, Yü) for the regulation of society. *HCCSSC*, shou-shang:6b–12b, 8:38ab.

27. *HCCSSC*, shou-shang:1a–2b, 8:31a–38a.

28. Ibid., 3a–4a.

29. Ibid., 6b–12b, 8:38ab, 9:1a–9b.

30. In my view, Chu Hsi in part misrepresented Shao Yung's idea of pattern (*li*). Chu said that Shao's idea was one of birth (*sheng*) then death (*ssu*), flourishing (*sheng*) then decline (*shuai*), and Chu compared this pattern to that of a flower. However, Shao also emphasized the whole event, which was begun or born (*sheng*) and then completed (*ch'eng*). Shao was not looking only at the constituent parts, which were born and which died. See *HLTCS*, 13:26b–27a.

31. For example, J. Needham, 2:456, translates *fan-kuan* as "objective observation." By the term *objective*, he implies a kind of observation in which the limitations of the senses have been overcome. I now disagree with this interpretation and translate *fan-kuan* as "reflective perception." See note 5 to Chapter 8 below.

32. Levenson, 1:xxvii.

33. Ch'ien, *Sung Ming*, 38.

Chapter 2

1. Mannheim, 116.

2. Besides scattered comments in other works, my major sources of biographical information were (1) *Sung shih*, 427:10a–11b; (2) Shao Po-wen, *Ch'ien-lu*; (3) Shao Po; (4) Chu Hsi, *Yüan-yüan lu*; (5) Ch'en Chi-ju; (6) Ch'eng Hao and Ch'eng Yi, *Yi-shu*; and (7) *SYHA*, chüan 9–10.

3. Hou (510) points out that not only were the aristocratic great families of the Sung literati for generations, but also these *tao-hsüeh* followers had a kind of mystical *hsin-ch'uan* (transmission of the mind).

4. Ch'en Yi.

5. Chu Hsi, *Yüan-yüan lu*, 5:45; and Ch'en Yi.

6. *SYHA*, 9:57a, and Ch'en Yi. The *Sung shih* (427:10a), however, says that Shao Ku moved to Heng-chang.

7. Chu Hsi, *Yüan-yüan lu*, 5:45; and Ch'en Yi.

8. *SYHA*, 9:57a.

9. For Shao Ku's biography, see *SYHA*, 9:57a–58b; Ch'en Yi, a villager friend, wrote Shao's epitaph.

10. Ch'en Yi; Chu Hsi, *Yüan-yüan lu*, 5:48.

11. Chen Yi; Chu Hsi, *Yüan-yüan lu*, 5:45.

12. See W. Lo.

13. *SYHA*, 9:57b. The *Yi-ching* consists of a central text, the *Chou Yi*, and the so-called Ten Wings, appendixes attached to it during the Han dynasty. Other, earlier divination texts are thought to have existed: the *Lien-shan* of the Hsia dynasty (2205–1766 B.C.) and the *Kuei-ts'ang* of the Shang dynasty (1766–1122 B.C.).

14. See J. Needham, 2:216–345; and Fung, 2:7–132. For broader discussions of Chinese music, see DeWoskin, *Song*; and Hartner.

15. *SYHA*, 9:58b. These concepts are discussed in Chapters 3–8. The pairs of concepts convey the idea of a fundamental, complementary tension in nature.

16. *SYHA*, 9:58b. Passage quoted from Wang Ying-lin.

17. Ibid. Here, Wang is quoting Shao Yung; see *HCCSSC*, 14:3a–3b, *KWWP*, 10. Shao Ku's four sounds are similar to Shao Yung's concept of the four treasuries; see Chapter 6.

18. This chart is called either "Sheng-yin ch'ang-ho: ssu-hsiang t'ien-ti chih shu t'u," or "Ching-shih ssu-hsiang t'i-yung chih shu t'u: wan-wu chih shu." See Appendix A below. For the chart, see Shao Yung, *Huang-chi ching-shih*, 7–10, *Kuan-wu p'ien*, 35–50; *Huang-chi ching-shih shu*, 2, in *HLTCS*, 8:23a–44b; *Huang-chi ching-shih shu hsü-yen*, 4:3a–47b, *Kuan-wu p'ien*, 37–50; *SYHA*, 10:69b–89a; and *HCCSSC*, 4:1a–38a.

19. For *tao-hsüeh* followers' deliberately dressing and behaving in ways to indicate their beliefs, see J. T. C. Liu, "Neo-Confucian School," 497.

20. Shao Po-wen, *Ch'ien-lu*, 20:148.

21. *Sung shih*, 457:3a (biography of Ch'en T'uan).

22. For a recent discussion on how this emphasis affected the concept of truth in Chinese philosophy, see Hansen, "Chinese Language."

23. *Shuo fu*, 71:11b.

24. *HCCSSC*, 7:9b–11b, *KWNP*, 7. For a translation, see Chapter 7.
25. For the concept of a "hermit in town" (*shih yin*), see Bauer, 169. On the recluse, see also Li; and Mote, "Eremitism." McKnight (419) points out that "a recluse is not a hermit."
26. See Hou, 506.
27. See Schneider. This model was a widely known one. See Ching, *Wisdom*, 25–27.
28. Hou, 506. Hou based his views on those of Ma Yung-ch'ing of the Sung period found in his *Lan chen-tzu*, and of Shao Po-wen, *Ch'ien-lu*, 20:149. The accounts in English are not consistent as to whether Shao was wealthy, and whether he held office.
29. Ch'ao Yi-tao (1059–1129) quoted in *SYHA*, 10:25b; Wyatt, "Champion," 126–27.
30. Ch'en Chi-ju, 1:2.
31. Ibid.
32. For biographies of Shao Po-wen, see *Sung shih*, 433:1a–2b; *Sung shih hsin pien*, 161:12b; *Tung-tu shih-lüeh*, 118:6b; and *Sung-jen yi-shih hui-pien*, 4:9.
33. Shao Po-wen's most important works are his commentary on Shao Yung's *Huang-chi ching-shih*, several critical writings on the *Yi* learning, and his *Ch'ien-lu*. See *Sung shih*, 433:2b.
34. For a biography of Shao P'u, see *Sung shih yi*, 10:15a–16a; for biographies of Shao Po, see *Sung shih yi*, 10:16b–17a; and *Nan Sung kuan ke lu*, 8:2a.
35. See Schwartz, *World*.
36. *Sung shih*, 431:17b (biography of Li Chih-ts'ai); see also *SYHA*, 10:21a; Chu Hsi, *Yüan-yüan lu*, 5:46; and Shao Po-wen, *Ch'ien-lu*, 18:129.
37. *HCCSSC*, 14:47b, 55b, 62a–63a, *KWWP*, 12.
38. Shao Po, 5:29, 32.
39. Chu Hsi, *Yüan-yüan lu*, 5:47.
40. Shao Po-wen, *Ch'ien-lu*, 19:143. The sixth classic, the Classic of Music, was not extant in Shao's time.
41. See, e.g., *HCCSSC*, 11:40a, *KWWP*, 6. This significance of this passage is discussed in Chapter 4.
42. For example, see *HCCSSC*, 14:54a–65b, *KWWP*, 12; Shao Po-wen, *Ch'ien-lu*, 7:48; Shao Po, 6:36; and Shao Yung, *Chi-jang chi*, 12:8a. On Wang T'ung, a philosopher of the Sui period, see Wechsler.
43. Shao Po-wen, *Ch'ien-lu*, 19:143; also quoted in *SYHA*, 10:27b; for Shao Yung's actual quotes, see *HCCSSC*, 14:55b (reference to Mencius), and 14:62a, *KWWP*, 12 (reference to Lao Tzu).
44. *SYHA*, 9:58a.

45. Shao Po-wen, *Ch'ien-lu*, 18:129.
46. Ch'en Chi-ju, 1:3.
47. Ch'eng Hao and Ch'eng Yi, *Yi-shu*, 18:12a; *HLTCS*, 13:27a.
48. Ch'en Chi-ju, 1:3; Shao Po-wen, *Ch'ien-lu*, 19:142–43; Wyatt, "Champion," 35–36.
49. Chu Hsi, *Yüan-yüan lu*, 5:45.
50. Personal communication with Nathan Sivin, University of Pennsylvania.
51. Shao Po-wen, *Ch'ien-lu*, 19:143.
52. *HCCSSC*, 14:59b, *KWWP*, 12.
53. Nivison, *Life*, 99.
54. Hou, 506.
55. *Sung shih*, 431:17b.
56. On this phenomenon in Chinese alchemy, see, e.g., Sivin, *Preliminary Studies*, 11–80.
57. For a biography of Li Chih-ts'ai, see *Sung shih*, 431:17a–18a.
58. Shao Po-wen, *Ch'ien-lu*, 18:129.
59. Ibid.
60. *SYHA*, 9:45b.
61. *Sung shih*, 431:17b.
62. Ibid., 18a.
63. Chu Hsi, *Yüan-yüan lu*, 5:47.
64. Ch'en Chi-ju, 1:1; Chu Hsi, *Yüan-yüan lu*, 5:45; Shao Po, 5:30; *SYHA*, 10:23a.
65. Shao Po-wen, *Ch'ien-lu*, 18:129.
66. Ibid.; Chu Hsi, *Yüan-yüan lu*, 5:45. The *hsiu-ts'ai* degree was the lowest of the three major degrees and was followed by the *chü-jen* and *chin-shih*. For the development of the examination system during the Sung, see Chaffee.
67. Shao Po-wen, *Ch'ien-lu*, 18:129.
68. Chu Hsi, *Yüan-yüan lu*, 5:45.
69. The records differ on the details of when and where Shao traveled. See Chu Hsi, *Yüan-yüan lu*, 5:45, 47; and *Sung-shih*, 427:10a.
70. Wu, 2.
71. Shao Po-wen, *Ch'ien-lu*, 18:127–28; Chu Hsi, *Yüan-yüan lu*, 5:45; Ch'en Chi-ju, 1:1–2. *Mencius*, 4A:26; in Chan, *Source Book*, 75.
72. Many of Shao's poems in the *Yi-ch'uan chi-jang chi* and many passages in the *Huang-chi ching-shih* are concerned with Confucian morality.
73. Chu Hsi, *Yüan-yüan lu*, 5:47; *Sung shih*, 427:10b; Hou, 506; Shao Po-wen, *Ch'ien-lu*, 18:131.
74. Hou, 499.

75. Chu Hsi, *Yüan-yüan lu*, 5:47. It is perhaps not coincidental that Loyang was the home for many philosophers with similar interests in the *Yi* learning. For example, Chung Fang (biography in *Sung shih*, 457:3b–6b) was a native of Loyang (see Chapter 9 for Chung Fang's relationship to Shao's tradition of learning), and the ancestors of Kuo Yung (biography in *Sung shih*, 459:5a–6a) came from Loyang. Kuo Yung followed a slightly different branch of the *Yi* learning from Shao Yung.

76. Hou, 499, 506. For biographies, see *Sung shih*, 313:1a–6a (Fu Pi); 313:6a–10a (Wen Yen-po); 318:4a–6b (Wang Kung-ch'en); 336:1a–8a (Ssu-ma Kuang); 336:9a–12a (Lü Kung-chu).

77. *Sung shih*, 433:1a.

78. Shao Po, 9:57.

79. Shao Po-wen, *Ch'ien-lu*, 19:143.

80. See Hou, 506.

81. Shao Po-wen, *Ch'ien-lu*, 18:131–32, 19:144. Confucius also believed that he had a destiny or mission ordained by Heaven; see *Lun-yü*, 9.5; in Chan, *Source Book*, 35.

82. Chu Hsi, *Yüan-yüan lu*, 5:47.

83. J. T. C. Liu, "Neo-Confucian School," 490–91.

84. Ibid., 491. Also, the term *tao-hsüeh* was at first used pejoratively.

Chapter 3

1. Hao. Traditions of learning or schools of thought were conceived in a way similar to a lineage, with a founding ancestor and a recognized line of descendants.

2. McEvilly, 137.

3. Gaukroger, 144. For other works on theory, see Hanson; Hempel; and Kinoshita.

4. I disagree with Freeman (481) that the *Huang-chi ching-shih* "is not so much intended to be an interpretation as a manifestation of reality, that the cosmological charts are not theories about the universe but the universe itself set down on paper." As my discussion will show, many passages in Shao Yung's writings indicate that he clearly understood the difference between word and object, or theory and referent. For a discussion of how the charts were interpreted historically in Chinese culture, see Cammann, "Magic Square"; idem, "Symbols"; and Saso.

5. One faces this distinction with all *Yi-ching*-related thought. For an example concerning *pien* (to change), see T'ang Yung-t'ung, 145. See also Gaukroger, 17.

6. Cammann ("Symbols," 254) also makes the point that ideas were explained "by means other than written text."

7. *HCCSSC*, shou-shang: 1b–2b.
8. Chu Hsi, in *HLTCS*, 13:27a.
9. See Gaukroger, 3–79.
10. Cammann, "Symbols," 216.
11. For discussion of a view very close to that of Shao Yung, that of Chang Tsai, see Siu-chi Huang.
12. For discussion of the root metaphor, see Yü T'ung, 37–109; for three important metaphors in Sung thought, see Munro, "Family."
13. Han, 11:1b. Han Yü said, "Benevolence and righteousness are fixed terms [*ting-ming*], but *tao* and *te* are empty positions [*hsü-wei*]." This essay is translated in Chan, *Source Book*, 454–56.
14. On the distinction between part-whole structures and one-many structures, see Hansen, "Individualism."
15. For a discussion of the important ideas and assumptions found in the thought based on the *Yi-ching*, see Wilhelm, *Heaven*. See Hou, 256–76, for the influence particularly of the Hua-yen and Ch'an schools in the Northern period and later.
16. See Wilhelm and Baynes, 280–355; Legge, *I Ching*, 348–407; and Forke, *World-conception*. In the *Li-chi*, see *chüan* 5, "Yüeh ling," SPPY ed.; and in the *Huai-nan Tzu*, see *chüan* 3–5, "T'ien-wen hsün," "Chui-hsing hsün," and "Shih-tse hsün," respectively, SPPY ed.
17. I translate *t'ien-ti*, which refers to the realms of the sky and the earth or simply nature, as heaven and earth; *wan-wu*, literally the ten thousand things, as the myriad things; *shen* as spirit; and *hsin* as mind or heart/mind. The last is clumsy in long translations, and therefore I often shorten it simply to "mind." I usually do not translate *ch'i* and *tao*, and in those passages in which they are translated, the English word varies according to the context.
18. The concept of heaven differs from that of heaven and earth. See Forke, *World-conception*, 147–58, for seven meanings of the term *heaven*.
19. *HCCSSC*, 5:1b, *KWNP*, 1. Forke (*World-conception*, 50) quotes Chuang Tzu as saying that heaven and earth are the two largest bodies and *yin* and *yang* are the two greatest forces.
20. *HCCSSC*, 14:20a, *KWWP*, 10. Compare the difference in emphasis between Shao Yung's and Yang Chu's opinions on the differences among the myriad things. See the passage translated in de Bary, *Sources*, 1:250–51.
21. The concept of *ch'i* is discussed in most books on Chinese thought, but for a particularly detailed discussion of *ch'i* and related concepts, see Moran. Different states of *ch'i* were called by different terms.
22. *HCCSSC*, 10:14b–15a, *KWWP*, 2; *HCCSSC*, 14:36b, *KWWP*, 10.

23. *HCCSSC*, 5:2a, *KWNP*, 1; *HCCSSC*, 14:38b, *KWWP*, 10.
24. *HCCSSC*, 9:42a, *KWWP*, 1.
25. *HCCSSC*, 9:42b, *KWWP*, 1, commentary by Huang Chi.
26. *HCCSSC*, 9:49b, *KWWP*, 1.
27. *HCCSSC*, shou-shang:14a. Also translated in Fung, 1:384; and Legge, *I Ching*, 373.
28. See Moran, 319.
29. For discussion on the relationship between names and morality, see Mather.
30. Shao Yung, "Wu-ming," 13:20b. This passage indirectly refers to the opening passage of the *Lao Tzu*; see Lau, 57; and Waley, 141.
31. Shao Yung, *Yü-ch'iao*, 13:5a.
32. *HCCSSC*, 5:39a, *KWNP*, 4.
33. Shao Yung, *Yü-ch'iao*, 13:3b.
34. *HCCSSC*, 10:34a, *KWWP*, 2; *HCCSSC*, 11:39a, *KWWP*, 6; *HCCSSC*, 12:38a, *KWWP*, 7.
35. *HCCSSC*, 14:39b, *KWWP*, 10.
36. *HCCSSC*, 14:39b–40a, *KWWP*, 10.
37. *HCCSSC*, 11:44a, *KWWP*, 6.
38. However, in certain contexts, Shao also thought of this triad in the more traditional sense, as the three realms of heaven, earth, and humans, each with its own kind of activities.
39. Quoted in Welch, "Bellagio," 112.
40. Yü Ying-shih ("Morality," 229) borrows the term *unit-ideas* from Arthur O. Lovejoy for these pairs of polarized concepts.
41. *HCCSSC*, shou-shang:39a.
42. Ibid., 38b, "Ching-shih yen-yi pa-kua t'u" (Chart of the eight trigrams that illustrate change and rule the world, see Fig. B4).
43. Nivison, "Problem," 116–17.
44. *HCCSSC*, shou-shang:39a.
45. Ibid., 38b, "Ching-shih yen-yi pa-kua t'u" (see Fig. B4); ibid., 13b, "Fu Hsi shih hua pa-kua t'u" (Chart of the eight trigrams originally drawn by Fu Hsi, see Fig. B1).
46. Ibid., 26a, "Fu Hsi pa-kua fang-wei t'u" (Chart of the directional [square] positions of the eight trigrams of Fu Hsi, see Fig. B2); ibid., 38b, "Ching-shih yen-yi pa-kua t'u" (see Fig. B4). The square positions are the positions of earth, conceived of as square, as opposed to the positions of heaven, conceived of as round.
47. Ibid., 38b, "Ching-shih yen-yi pa-kua t'u" (see Fig. B4).
48. Ibid., 14:5a, *KWWP*, 10.
49. See Shaughnessy, 111.

50. *HCCSSC*, shou-shang:18a–22a, "Fu-hsi pa-kua ch'ung wei liu-shih-ssu kua t'u" (Chart of the eight trigrams of Fu Hsi squared to become the 64 hexagrams); shou-hsia:9ab, "Ching-shih liu-shih-ssu kua chih shu t'u" (Chart of the numbers of the 64 hexagrams that rule the world, see Fig. B6); shou-shang:27b–28a, "Fu Hsi liu-shih-ssu kua fang-wei t'u" (Chart of the directional [square] positions of the 64 hexagrams of Fu Hsi, see Fig. B3); and shou-hsia:11b–16a, "Ching-shih t'ien-ti shih-chung chih shu t'u" (Chart of the numbers of the beginnings and ends of heaven and earth that rule the world).
51. Ibid., shou-hsia:9ab.
52. See ibid., 11b–16a, "Ching-shih t'ien-ti shih-chung chih shu t'u."
53. Ibid., 16a. Slight variations in these numbers occur in different editions of *HCCS*. These figures are based on my calculations.
54. See Cammann, "Symbols," 253.
55. See Gaukroger, 72–77. Rodney Needham (31–37) makes the point that relations, which he calls "relational constants," are determined by the symbolic classification system. He refers not only to logical relations, but also to social and other kinds of relations.
56. For discussion of this kind of thinking, see J. Needham, 2:279–91.
57. Ibid., 336.

Chapter 4

1. Reichenbach, 4.
2. The concepts of the images and numbers developed along with the thought related to the *Yi-ching*. See Fung, 1:379–95; J. Needham, 2:304–35; Shaughnessy; Wilhelm, *Change*; and idem, *Heaven*.
3. *HCCSSC*, 5:7b, *KWNP*, 1.
4. As Moran (285) points out, relationships and not concrete instances are *li* (pattern, principle). In a comparable way, in Shao Yung's thought, the images are categories that represent relationships and so function as *li* does.
5. Hansen, *Language and Logic*, esp. Chap. 2.
6. *HCCSSC*, 6:2ab, *KWNP*, 5.
7. *HCCSSC*, 13:31b, *KWWP*, 9.
8. See, e.g., the correlations given in J. Needham, 2:312–21.
9. *HCCSSC*, 14:10b–39a, *KWWP*, 10–11. See the examples translated in Chapter 5 concerning the movements and responses of the myriad things.
10. *HCCSSC*, 8:18a, *KWNP*, 12.
11. *HCCSSC*, 14:3b, *KWWP*, 10.
12. *Shu* has a number of meanings, including notions of number,

numerology, regularities, calendar, calculation, fate, and prediction. See J. Needham, vol. 3; and Ho, *Li, Qi, and Shu*. Some philosophers recognized that numbers functioned in Shao Yung's thought in a way equivalent to principle (*li*). See Lo Ch'in-shun's comments in Bloom, *Knowledge*, 129–30.

13. See Gaukroger, 101.

14. For an explanation of this relationship, see Mungello, 147.

15. Shao Yung, *Huang-chi ching-shih shu*, 2, "Ts'uan-t'u chih-yao: hsia," in *HLTCS*, 8:52b–53a.

16. Ibid., 8:53b.

17. *Huang-chi ching-shih shu*, 4, *KWNP*, 10, in *HLTCS*, 10:22ab. Shao Po-wen emphasized that Shao Yung believed that the numbers are in front of us, in the activities of the world, and they are not to be found in books. Po-wen's commentary here (and in certain other places) is more extensive in the *Huang-chi ching-shih shu* than in *HCCSSC*, 7:34b, *KWNP*, 10.

18. *HCCSSC*, shou-hsia:12a, 8:5ab, *KWNP*, 11. The idea of cosmic periods has a long history in Chinese thought and did not originate with Shao Yung. See J. Needham, 3:390–408; and Sivin, "Cosmos."

19. *Ta-chuan*, 1.9.49. See Legge, *I Ching*, 365; and Wilhelm and Baynes, 308.

20. *HCCSSC*, 8:5b, *KWNP*, 11.

21. *HCCSSC*, 8:5b, 6a, *KWNP*, 11. Great Expansion (*Ta-yen*), a term used in the "Great Commentary" (Appendix 3) of the *Yi-ching* (Legge, *I Ching*, 365) in reference to matters of divination, the calendar, and astronomy, was also the name of a T'ang dynasty calendar. "Four" is a reference to the four seasons.

22. The number one was not associated with these concepts in all cases. Many times no numbers were associated with them. Sometimes *shen* (spirit) was seen as a second entity after *t'ai-chi*, as the activity (*tung*) of *t'ai-chi*, and hence was associated with the number two. Also, one was not always conceived of as a number, such as when it referred to the whole.

23. See also *HCCSSC*, shou-hsia:9a, "Ching-shih liu-shih-ssu kua chih shu t'u" (Fig. B6).

24. For discussion of the binary system inherent in Shao's so-called *hsien-t'ien* arrangement and the connection with Leibniz, see Wilhelm, *Heaven*, 6–11; and Ho, *Li, Qi, and Shu*, 46–51.

25. For discussion of the authorship of the "Great Commentary" (*Ta-chuan*), see Peterson. Yang Jung-kuo (67) points out that Shao Yung was influenced by Wang Pi, who was influenced by Chuang Tzu. Although many scholars note that Wang Pi represented the *yi-li* branch of the *Yi*

learning, as opposed to the *hsiang-shu* branch, Shao Yung's thought was so broad that his thought clearly encompassed characteristics that were once in opposition.

26. HCCSSC, 11:40a, KWWP, 6. This passage is an allusion to *Chuang Tzu*; see Watson, *Chuang Tzu*, 302.

27. Chuang Tzu's point was slightly different. "The fish trap exists because of the fish; once you've gotten the fish, you can forget the trap. The rabbit snare exists because of the rabbit; once you've gotten the rabbit, you can forget the snare. Words exist because of meaning; once you've gotten the meaning, you can forget the words. Where can I find a man who has forgotten words so I can have a word with him?" (Watson, *Chuang Tzu*, 302.)

28. Wang Pi, *Ming-hsing p'ien*, quoted in Hu Wei, 593–95. Parts of this passage are translated in Fung, 2:184; and in Shaughnessy, 4–5.

29. T'ang Yung-t'ung, 143.

30. Shaughnessy, 4.

31. Fung (2:185–86) notes Wang Pi's apparent inconsistency concerning the question of whether "words can completely express ideas."

32. For comparative purposes, see Gaukroger, 98–100, for a brief discussion of number in the thought of Plato and Aristotle.

33. HCCSSC, 14:43b, KWWP, 11.

34. HCCSSC, 14:44a, KWWP, 11.

35. HCCSSC, 11:41b, KWWP, 6.

36. Chang Hsing-ch'eng, *Yen-yi*, 2:7b. Chang says that one is not a number.

37. See Hou, 529. For Hou's discussion of the several meanings of *shen* in Shao Yung's thought, see 528–32.

38. HCCSSC, 11:41a, KWWP, 6.

39. HCCSSC, 11:41a, KWWP, 6. See *Ta-chuan*, 1.12.76, for an earlier textual source of some of these characteristics and entities; Legge, *I Ching*, 376–77.

40. Legge, *Ch'un Ts'eu*, pt. 2, 165. Tortoise shells and milfoil stalks were used in divination, the ideas and practices of which formed the earliest stage of the *Yi* learning.

41. *Ta-chuan*, 1.12.76; 1.8.38, and 1.12.79. See Legge, *I Ching*, 360, 376–78; Wilhelm and Baynes, 322.

42. HCCSSC, 11:41b, 42b, KWWP, 6.

43. Wang Pi, quoted in Hu Wei, 594.

44. HCCSSC, 11:43a, KWWP, 6.

45. These are Bodde's translations in Fung, 2:636.

46. For an interesting reordering of the hexagrams, see McKenna and

Mair. Shao Yung's ordering was a logical one in terms of mathematics but not in terms of the meanings of the hexagrams.

47. Chang Hsing-ch'eng (*So-yin*, "yuan-hsü," 1a) wrote: "The *hsien-t'ien* is the *Yi* of Fu Hsi, the *hou-t'ien* is the *Yi* of King Wen, the *T'ai-hsüan* [text: *T'ai-yüan*] is the *Yi* of Tzu-yün [Yang Hsiung] and is the pair with *hou-t'ien*, the *Huang-chi ching-shih* is the *Yi* of [Shao] K'ang-chieh and is the descendant of *hsien-t'ien*."

48. *HCCSSC*, 5:6b–7b, *KWNP*, 1.

49. For the "Hung Fan" (*shu* 5.4), see Legge, *Shoo King*, 320–44.

50. I agree with Yosida (82–83) that the Five Elements (five phases) represent the "functional aspect" and are part of *hou-t'ien*, but I disagree that the four images (which he calls "hypostases") represent an earlier stage. As I discuss, the evidence indicates that Shao Yung saw these two aspects as simultaneous.

51. *Ta-chuan*, 1.5.29; Legge, *I Ching*, 356.

52. Munro, "Family," 270.

53. *Huang-chi ching-shih shu*, 3, *KWNP*, 1, in *HLTCS*, 9:7ab. This commentary by Shao Po-wen is not quoted in *HCCSSC*.

54. *HLTCS*, 9:7b.

55. See W. N. Brown, 16–42.

56. *Wen Yen*, 1.34 (Appendix 4); trans. Legge, *I Ching*, 417.

57. These translations of *hsien-t'ien* are from the following: prior heaven and former heaven, Freeman, 482, where the latter term is mentioned but not used; pre-creation, Moran, 296–97; *a priori*, Yang Jung-kuo, 60; "what antedates Heaven," Fung, 2:460–61; Prior to Heaven, Mungello; and former celestial or sky [plan], Cammann, "Symbols," 249. Also, Wilhelm (*Heaven*, 10) has "Earlier Heaven."

58. *HCCSSC*, 11:24b, *KWWP*, 5.

59. *HCCSSC*, 11:24b, *KWWP*, 5.

60. *HCCSSC*, 13:28a, *KWWP*, 9. Textual (copyist's) error in SPPY ed., 8a:32b.

61. *HCCSSC*, shou-hsia:23ab.

62. *HCCSSC*, 13:26b, *KWWP*, 9.

63. See Schirokauer, 481.

64. See Cammann, "Symbols."

65. See Major.

66. *HCCSSC*, shou-shang:28b.

67. See Cammann, "Symbols," for a discussion of the historical development of the charts.

68. *HCCSSC*, 5:7b, *KWNP*, 1.

69. *HCCSSC*, shou-shang:26a, "Fu Hsi pa-kua fang wei t'u" (Chart

of the directional [square] positions of the eight trigrams of Fu Hsi; see Fig. B2). In this usage, *fang* (literally "square" and symbolic of earth) refers to the directions of the compass. See note 46 to Chapter 3. In *Huang-chi ching-shih shu*, 1, in *HLTCS*, 7:7a, this chart is called "Pa-kua cheng-wei t'u" (Chart of the correct positions of the eight trigrams), and different terms are used in it. Although both have the trigram lines and the cardinal directions, the first includes the names of the trigrams, whereas the second has the images of heaven, earth, fire, water, mountains, marshes, wind, and thunder (images from the *Ta-chuan*). On Chinese maps, south is at the top, north at the bottom, east on the left, and west on the right.

70. *HCCSSC*, shou-hsia: 38b.
71. *HCCSSC*, 5:7b, *KWNP*, 1.
72. Ch'iao, *t'u*, 13a.
73. Cammann, "Symbols," 249.
74. *HCCSSC*, 8:19a–21b, *KWNP*, 12.
75. *HCCSSC*, 8:19a–21b, *KWNP*, 12. In particular, see Wang Chih's commentary (8:21ab) and Shao Po-wen's commentary (8:22ab). Wang said that things (*wu*) have the differences (*teng-ch'a*) of the flying, walking, woody, and grassy categories; the people (*min*) have the differences of the social classes of scholar-official, farmer, artisan, and merchant; and numbers (*shu*) have the differences of the values of 1, 10, 100, and 1,000.
76. See, e.g., Watson, *Chuang Tzu*, 36–49; and idem, *Hsün Tzu*, 121–38.
77. Translated in Watson, *Chuang Tzu*, 43.
78. Translated in Watson, *Hsün Tzu*, 122.
79. *HCCSSC*, 8:19a–21b, *KWNP*, 12.
80. Concerning the topic of objectivity in relation to scientific method, see Popper, 652–57.
81. *HCCSSC*, 8:19b–21a, *KWNP*, 12.
82. *HCCSSC*, 8:19b–20a, 20b–21a, *KWNP*, 12.
83. *HCCSSC*, 8:19a–22b, *KWNP*, 12.
84. *HCCSSC*, 8:22b, *KWNP*, 12.
85. See Fung, vol. 2 *passim*; and J. Needham, vol. 2 *passim*. See also Moran, 307–12, for a discussion of turpid and pure *ch'i*, and the idea that humans have the most balanced (*cheng*) *ch'i* and so are the most spiritually responsive of things of the world. Moran is discussing the view of Chu Hsi here, a view not inconceivably derived in part from Shao Yung.
86. *HCCSSC*, 8:22a, *KWNP*, 12.
87. *HCCSSC*, 14:10b–13a, 26ab, *KWWP*, 10, and *passim*.
88. *HCCSSC*, 8:21b, *KWNP*, 12.

89. See Verdu. See also Moran, 296–305, on the different directions of the diagrams of Ch'en T'uan (returning to the one) and Chou Tun-yi (going out from the one). The idea of returning to the one was also an important aspect of the thought of Lao Tzu and Chuang Tzu.

90. Since the categories of thought and knowledge in traditional China differ greatly from those used today, modern disciplines and divisions of knowledge do not match those of the past. See Nakayama and Sivin, xii-xxx.

91. See Hansen, "Individualism," 36–38.

Chapter 5

1. *HCCSSC*, 6:15b, *KWNP*, 11.
2. *HCCSSC*, shou-shang: 3a–4a.
3. Some texts and philosophers substitute older (*lao*) and younger (*shao*) for greater (*t'ai*) and lesser (*shao*). For example, see the chart "Yang chiu yin liu yung-shu t'u" (Chart of the activity numbers of *yang* 9 and *yin* 6), ibid., 34b–36a.
4. *HCCSSC*, 14:38b, *KWWP*, 10. As noted above, Shao Yung's concept of *ch'i* was virtually identical to that of his contemporary Chang Tsai. *Chung* (centrality) and *ho* (harmony) are important concepts in the *Chung-yung*; see Legge, *Doctrine*, 384–85. Legge translates *chung* as equilibrium. *Ch'i* is not mentioned in this text.
5. *HCCSSC*, 14:28ab, *KWWP*, 10.
6. *HCCSSC*, 14:34a, 33b, *KWWP*, 10.
7. Shao Yung, *Huang-chi ching-shih shu*, 3, *KWNP*, 1, in *HLTCS*, 9:7ab, commentary by Shao Po-wen.
8. *HCCSSC*, 10:14b–15a, *KWWP*, 2.
9. *HCCSSC*, 5:6b, *KWNP*, 1, commentary by Shao Po-wen.
10. *HCCSSC*, 5:1a–2b, *KWNP*, 1.
11. *HCCSSC*, 5:2b, *KWNP*, 1.
12. See Ryle.
13. Although it is now a matter of dispute, according to Chan ("Patterns," 111), Wang Pi, in his commentary on the Lao Tzu, was the first Chinese philosopher to use the concept of *t'i* and *yung*. Shao's use of the concept was closer to the earlier than to the later usages, and hence it was closer to Wang Pi's usage than to that of later Neo-Confucianism. See Yü T'ung, 37–38; and Chan, "Patterns," 114.
14. *HCCSSC*, 5:3b, *KWNP*, 1.
15. *HCCSSC*, 5:4a, *KWNP*, 1.
16. *HCCSSC*, 5:4b, *KWNP*, 1.
17. *HCCSSC*, 5:4b, *KWNP*, 1.

18. Because Shao used *t'i-yung* both in his ontological and epistemological theory, we find different senses of the concept. See Lo Kuang, *Chung-kuo*, 206–9. The concept of *t'i-yung* had a variety of meanings as it developed in Chinese thought.
19. *HCCSSC*, 5:6a, *KWNP*, 1, commentary by Shao Po-wen.
20. Zodiacal space and earth were seen as comparable, for they were the places where the other images were located. See *HCCSSC*, 5:6b, *KWNP*, 1, commentary by Shao Po-wen.
21. *HCCSSC*, 5:6b, *KWNP*, 1.
22. *HCCSSC*, 5:6ab, *KWNP*, 1, commentary by Shao Po-wen.
23. *HCCSSC*, 5:6b, *KWNP* 1.
24. For a similar idea of Lao Tzu, see Lau, 103.
25. See Cammann, "Symbols," 240. See also Swanson, 70.
26. *HCCSSC*, 14:3a–4b, *KWWP*, 10. See also *Ta-chuan*, 1.11.69; Legge, *I Ching*, 372.
27. *HCCSSC*, 5:9b, *KWNP*, 1, commentary by Wang Chih. For a discussion of the different suggestions for the meaning of *pien* and *hua*, see Sivin, "*Pien, Hua*, and *T'ung*"; and Swanson.
28. *HCCSSC*, 12:27b, *KWWP*, 7.
29. *HCCSSC*, 5:8a, *KWNP*, 1.
30. *HCCSSC*, 5:8ab, *KWNP*, 1.
31. *HCCSSC*, 5:8b, *KWNP*, 1.
32. *HCCSSC*, 5:9a, *KWNP*, 1.
33. *HCCSSC*, 5:9a, *KWNP*, 1.
34. *HCCSSC*, 9:43a, *KWWP*, 1; *HCCSSC*, 12:34b, *KWWP*, 7.
35. *HCCSSC*, 9:49ab, *KWWP*, 1.
36. *HCCSSC*, 12:29a, *KWWP*, 7.
37. *HCCSSC*, 13:14a, *KWWP*, 8.
38. *HCCSSC*, 8:1a, *KWNP*, 11.
39. *HCCSSC*, 8:2b–3a, *KWNP*, 11.
40. *HCCSSC*, 8:4b–5a, *KWNP*, 11.
41. *HCCSSC*, 8:5ab; *KWNP*, 11.
42. See Hu Wei, 134–43.
43. *HCCSSC*, 12:34b, *KWWP*, 7.
44. A thorough examination of the role of the hexagrams and numbers is beyond the scope of this discussion. Shao presented many of his ideas on this topic in *HCCSSC, chüan* 12, *KWWP*, 7.
45. See Le Blanc; and Wallacker, Review.
46. *HCCSSC*, shou-hsia:1b–2a; and 14:26a, *KWWP*, 10.
47. *HCCSSC*, 5:9a, *KWNP*, 1, commentary of Huang Chi.
48. *HCCSSC*, 5:14b–15a, *KWNP*, 1.

49. *HCCSSC*, 5:16ab, *KWNP*, 1.

50. This problem began to be of great concern to Western philosophers from the seventeenth century on and was part of the argument between the empiricists and the idealists. See, e.g., Gilson and Langan.

51. *HCCSSC*, 9:30a, 47b, *KWWP*, 1 (these comments are similar to Chang Tsai's comments on *yin* and *yang* in his *Cheng meng*); *HCCSSC*, 9:48b, 61a, *KWWP*, 1.

52. Chu Hsi used a flower as an analogy to express this idea. See Chapter 9.

53. Yang Jung-kuo (69) mentions three poems by Shao from his *Yi-ch'uan chi-jang chi*: "Ch'uan-shang huai-chiu" (On the river cherishing the past), 3:6a; "Ssu tao yin" (Song on the four *tao*), 10:6b; "Kuan-wu yin" (Song on perceiving things), 14:6a.

54. *HCCSSC*, 14:23b, *KWWP*, 10. See also *HCCSSC*, 14:26b, *KWWP*, 10.

55. *HCCSSC*, 5:8b, *KWNP*, 1.

56. *HCCSSC*, 14:28ab, *KWWP*, 10. Wang Chih comments that the meaning is to lead and to follow.

57. *HCCSSC*, 5:10a, *KWNP*, 1.

58. *HCCSSC*, 5:10ab, *KWNP*, 1, commentary of Shao Po-wen.

59. *HCCSSC*, 5:9a, *KWNP*, 1.

60. *HCCSSC*, 5:10a, *KWNP*, 1.

61. *HCCSSC*, 14:31a–32b, 37a, *KWWP*, 10. Huang Chi commented here that "the *ch'i* of trees is received from stone. The image of stone is matched with [the image of] stars."

62. *HCCSSC*, 14:10b, *KWWP*, 10.

63. *HCCSSC*, 14:7b, *KWWP*, 10.

64. *HCCSSC*, 14:8b–9a, *KWWP*, 10.

65. *HCCSSC*, 14:10a, *KWWP*, 10.

66. *HCCSSC*, 5:10b, *KWNP*, 1.

67. *Ta-chuan*, 1.5.24; see Legge, *I Ching*, 355; and Wilhelm and Baynes, 297.

Chapter 6

1. *HCCSSC*, 6:8b, *KWNP*, 5. The remainder of the passage reads: "People all know that heaven and earth are heaven and earth, but they do not know why heaven and earth are heaven and earth. If they do not wish to know why heaven and earth are heaven and earth, then the matter is finished. If they must know why heaven and earth are heaven and earth, then aside from movement and stillness, what else is to be said?" (*HCCSSC*, 8b–9a, *KWNP*, 5.)

2. *HCCSSC*, shou-hsia: 1b–2a. As noted in Chapter 5, for the last three concepts of change, the four images associated with earth are arranged in reversed order in this chart.
3. Hou, 187–99.
4. *HCCSSC*, 5:16b–17a, 5:18b; *KWNP*, 1.
5. *HCCSSC*, 5:18b, *KWNP*, 1.
6. *HCCSSC*, 5:9a, *KWNP*, 1.
7. *HCCSSC*, 5:19ab, *KWNP*, 1.
8. *HCCSSC*, 5:21a, *KWNP*, 1, in a poem by Shao Yung quoted by Huang Chi, and *HCCSSC*, 8:11a, *KWNP*, 11. For Shao Po-wen, see *HCCSSC*, 5:20b, 8:1a. For Huang Chi, ibid., 8:12a. The last two commentaries link the idea of *pei* (to complete) with *ling* (consciousness).
9. Lo Kuang, *Chung-kuo*, 205–6.
10. See James. For an anthology of writings by idealist philosophers, see Ewing.
11. *HCCSSC*, 5:20a, *KWNP*, 1; *HCCSSC*, 8:11a, *KWNP*, 11.
12. *HCCSSC*, 7:28b, *KWNP*, 9.
13. *HCCSSC*, 8:11a, *KWNP*, 11.
14. *HCCSSC*, 5:20b, *KWNP*, 1.
15. *Mencius*, 7. A. 4; see Fung, 1:129; and Legge, *Mencius*, 450–51.
16. *HCCSSC*, 5:22a, *KWNP*, 2.
17. Hou, 187–99.
18. *HCCSSC*, 5:22b, *KWNP*, 2, commentary of Wang Chih. This concept of form (*hsing*) clearly is not limited to the sense of sight.
19. *HCCSSC*, 5:23a, *KWNP*, 2, commentary of Wang Chih.
20. See Legge, *Learning*, 357, paragraph 3; Chan, *Source Book*, 86.
21. *HCCSSC*, 14:18a, *KWWP*, 10. This passage was one reason physiognomists came to venerate Shao Yung. See Hou, 526.
22. *HCCSSC*, 14:18b, *KWWP*, 10, commentary of Wu Ch'eng.
23. *HCCSSC*, 13:26a, *KWWP*, 9.
24. *HCCSSC*, 13:26a, *KWWP*, 9.
25. *HCCSSC*, 5:31b–32a, *KWNP*, 3; *HCCSSC*, 5:33a, *KWNP*, 4. The first passage is partially translated in Chapter 7.
26. *HCCSSC*, 5:33ab, *KWNP*, 3.
27. *HCCSSC*, 5:33ab, *KWNP*, 3.
28. See Munro, "Family," 262.
29. *HCCSSC*, 11:31b–32b, *KWWP*, 6.
30. *HCCSSC*, 11:34ab, *KWWP*, 6.
31. *HCCSSC*, 5:34ab; *KWNP*, 3, commentary of Huang Chi.
32. *HCCSSC*, shou-hsia: 11b–16a. For an abbreviated version of this chart (with a slight change in terms), see "Yüan-hui-yün-shih nien-yüeh-

jih-shih chih shu t'u" (Chart of the numbers of cycles, epochs, revolutions, and generations, and years, months, days, and hours), ibid., 31b–32b. Although Shao was most likely influenced to some extent by Buddhist ideas of great periods of time, he was also continuing a tradition within Chinese astronomy from the Han period of an interest in cosmic cycles. On these cycles, see Sivin, "Cosmos."

33. *HCCSSC*, 7:33ab, *KWNP*, 10.
34. *HCCSSC*, 7:33ab, shou-hsia: 11b–16a.
35. *HCCSSC*, 7:33ab; *KWNP*, 10.
36. *HCCSSC*, 7:34ab, *KWNP*, 10.
37. Shao Yung, *Huang-chi ching-shih shu*, 4, *KWNP*, 10, in *HLTCS*, 10:22ab. Shao Po-wen's commentary is incomplete in *HCCSSC*, 7:34b, *KWNP*, 10.
38. See Sivin, "Cosmos," 8–22.
39. According to Ho Peng Yoke (*Li, Qi, and Shu*, 155), at times the Chinese for practical reasons worked in whole numbers of days per month in calculating the calendar even though they knew the lunar month was more than an even 29 days.
40. Shao Yung (*HCCSSC*, 7:36ab, *KWNP*, 10) correlated *yüan-hui-yün-shih* with the four seasons. Shao Po-wen (*HCCSSC*, 7:36b) then added, "Spring, summer, autumn, and winter are the revolution [*yün*] of one year [*sui*]. Their changes [*pien*] are like this. In the great revolution [*ta-yün*], it is also so. It is nothing more than the waxing and waning of *yin* and *yang*."
41. *HCCSSC*, 7:36a–41a, *KWNP*, 10.
42. *HCCSSC*, 7:36b, *KWNP*, 10.
43. *HCCSSC*, 7:39b, *KWNP*, 10.
44. *HCCSSC*, 7:37a, commentary of Wang Chih.
45. In the *Hun-t'ien* (spherical heavens) school of early Chinese cosmology, the circumference of the sphere of the sky was divided into 365.25 degrees. Shao's views appear to combine some features of all of the three major early cosmological schools. See Ho, *Li, Qi, and Shu*, 126–30. See also Yamada, "Shushi."
46. See, e.g., Cassirer.
47. See Henderson, 110–17. Moreover, neither Shao Yung nor any other of the founding Neo-Confucian philosophers appears in the *Ch'ou-jen chuan* (Biographies of mathematicians and astronomers) by Juan Yüan of the Ch'ing.
48. See Ho, *Li, Qi, and Shu*, 113–69.
49. See, e.g., *SYHA*, 10:26a, comment of Ch'ao Yi-tao.
50. Henderson, 111.
51. See Sivin, "Cosmos," on the development of this view.

52. *HCCSSC*, 12:39ab, *KWWP*, 7. See Ho, Li, Qi, and Shu, 125.
53. *HCCSSC*, 14:29b, *KWWP*, 10.
54. Discussed by Yamada, "Shushi." See also *HLTCS*, 27:1ab for the Ch'eng brothers' quote; 27:4a for Shen Kua's quote; and 5:17b for Chang Tsai's quote.
55. See Hu Wei, 136.
56. Ibid., 137.
57. Other works regarded as part of the same tradition as Shao Yung's *Huang-chi ching-shih* are the *Yi-ching*, *Chou Yi ts'an-t'ung-ch'i*, *T'ai-hsüan ching*, *Yin-fu ching*, and *Huang-t'ing ching*. See Hu Wei, 135–43. The *Yin-fu ching* is an early Taoist work of unknown authorship and date, but perhaps as early as the late Chou period. The *Huang-t'ing ching* is an early Taoist work, perhaps as early as the third century, and exists in a number of different versions.
58. Shao Yung shared with many others the belief that the classics were both history and a repository of principles. See, e.g., Levenson's (1:90–94) discussion of this debate during the Ch'ing period. Levenson quotes Su Hsün's (1009–66) view, which is very similar to that of Shao Yung.
59. *HCCSSC*, 5:38a, *KWNP*, 4.
60. *HCCSSC*, 5:38a, *KWNP*, 4.
61. *HCCSSC*, 13:29a, *KWWP*, 9.
62. *HCCSSC*, 13:28a, *KWWP*, 9. Although here Shao says "two emperors," in the other passages he says "five emperors."
63. In his correlations of sets of four entities, Shao omits one of the five hegemons (Duke Hsiang of Sung) and adds a fourth person, Duke Shao, to the three kings. See *HCCSSC*, 5:40b.
64. *HCCSSC*, 5:44b–48b, *KWNP*, 4.
65. *HCCSSC*, 13:27b, *KWWP*, 9.
66. *HCCSSC*, 13:26b, *KWWP*, 9.
67. *HCCSSC*, 5:39ab, *KWNP*, 4, commentary of Wang Chih.
68. According to the commentary of Huang Chi, from the Han through the Northern and Southern dynasties, the rulers were usurpers. He does not mention the Sui and T'ang dynasties. *HCCSSC*, 13:27b–28a, *KWWP*, 9.
69. *HCCSSC*, 5:39a, *KWNP*, 4.
70. Hou, 534–35.
71. Ibid., 535.
72. Lo Kuang, *Chung-kuo*, 267–68.
73. *HCCSSC*, 7:20b, *KWNP*, 9; see also *HCCSSC*, 5:54a, *KWNP*, 4, commentary of Wang Chih.
74. *HCCSSC*, 13:25a, *KWWP*, 9. See Shao Po-wen, *Ch'ien-lu*, 19:

142–43, for an account of an incident on a bridge in which Shao Yung predicted the appointment of a new prime minister (Wang An-shih) on the basis of the flow of *ch'i*.

75. *HCCSSC*, 13:25ab, *KWWP*, 9.
76. Lo Kuang, *Chung-kuo*, 265.
77. *HCCSSC*, 5:38b–39a, *KWNP*, 4.
78. *HCCSSC*, 5:39b–51a, *KWNP*, 4.
79. *HCCSSC*, 13:27b, *KWWP*, 9.
80. *HCCSSC*, 5:44b–48b, *KWNP*, 4.
81. *HCCSSC*, 13:36ab, *KWWP*, 9.
82. Hou, 524.
83. *HCCSSC*, 5:41b, *KWNP*, 4.
84. *HCCSSC*, 5:42b, 51a, 53a, *KWNP*, 4.
85. For a brief discussion of similar but not identical ideas, see Wei Cheng-t'ung, "Chu Hsi."
86. *HCCSSC*, 13:28b, *KWWP*, 9.
87. *HCCSSC*, 5:54a, *KWNP*, 4.
88. *HCCSSC*, 5:44b–48b, *KWNP*, 4.
89. *HCCSSC*, 5:48a, *KWNP*, 4.
90. *HCCSSC*, 5:48a, *KWNP*, 4. See also *HCCSSC*, 6:19b, *KWNP*, 6, on having no true king (*chen-wang*) but having an empty name (*hsü-ming*); and *HCCSSC*, 6:22b–23a, *KWNP*, 6, on the name continuing to exist after the reality is lost (*ming ts'un shih wang*).
91. *HCCSSC*, 6:1b, *KWNP*, 5.
92. *HCCSSC*, 6:3b, *KWNP*, 5.
93. Discussed throughout *HCCSSC*, *chüan* 6, *KWNP*, 5–6.
94. *HCCSSC*, 13:32a, *KWWP*, 9.
95. *HCCSSC*, 7:1ab, *KWNP*, 7. Quotation is from *HCCSSC*, 7:1b.
96. *HCCSSC*, 7:1b, *KWNP*, 7.
97. *HCCSSC*, 5:43a, 48b, *KWNP*, 4.
98. *HCCSSC*, 7:13ab, *KWNP*, 8.
99. *HCCSSC*, 7:22a, *KWNP*, 9.
100. *HCCSSC*, 7:23b, *KWNP*, 9.
101. *HCCSSC*, 7:24b–25a, *KWNP*, 9.
102. See *HCCSSC*, 6:19ab, *KWNP*, 6; and *HCCSSC*, 13:30a–31a, *KWWP*, 9.
103. *HCCSSC*, 13:31b, *KWWP*, 9. For another version, see *HCCSSC*, 6:22b–23a, *KWNP*, 6. Allusion is to the Confucian *Analects*, 3.17; see Chan, *Source Book*, 25.
104. See, e.g., Wright, "Sui Yang-ti."
105. See Hansen, "Chinese Language."

106. *HCCSSC*, 6:2ab, *KWNP*, 5; quoted in Chapter 4. The idealist schools of Buddhism stress the point that there is no absolute standpoint. See Hou, 239, for the relevant views of Fa Tsang of the Hua-yen school.

107. *HCCSSC*, 6:3ab, *KWNP*, 5.

108. Apparently, the word order of his concept "ends and beginnings" signifies that the cycle repeats without end. "Beginning(s) and end(s)" would imply only one cycle.

109. For a discussion of the problems involved, see R. Brown.

110. *HCCSSC*, 7:24b–25a, *KWNP*, 9.

111. Shao Yung (*HCCSSC*, 13:32a, *KWWP*, 9) said, "The *Ch'un-ch'iu* was written because the rulers were weak and the ministers were strong. Therefore it is called a book on names and duties." See also *HCCSSC*, 5:41b–42a, *KWNP*, 4, for Shao Po-wen's comment on what Shao Yung believed was the concern of each of the classics: "The *Yi* discusses *yin* and *yang*. The waxing and waning of *yin* and *yang* simply are the seasons. Therefore the sages, emperors, kings, and hegemons are regarded as the forms [*t'i*] of the *Yi*. The *Shu* discusses human affairs [*shih*]. The traces of emperors and kings are preserved in it. Therefore Yü, Hsia, Shang, and Chou are regarded as the forms of the *Shu*. The *Shih* discusses aims [*chih*]. It begins with the two odes of the south and ends with "[Ta]-Ya" and "[Chou]-Sung." Therefore Wen, Wu, Chou, and Shao are regarded as the forms of the *Shih*. The *Ch'un-ch'iu* discusses titles [names] and duties and reaches to the chaos of the titles and duties of the five hegemons. Confucius rectified titles and duties with the *Ch'un-ch'iu*. The *Ch'un-ch'iu* is entirely [about] the affairs of the five hegemons. Therefore Ch'in, Chin, Ch'i, and Ch'u are the forms of the *Ch'un-ch'iu*."

Chapter 7

1. *HCCSSC*, 14:67b, *KWWP*, 12.

2. In the thought of many other philosophers as well, the sage represented the ideal of returning to the original source. See, e.g., Chang Tsai, *Cheng meng*, *chüan* 6, in *HLTCS*, 5:36b. For discussion of Confucian ideas relating to the sage, see Tu, *Confucian Thought*; and idem, *Centrality*.

3. The Confucian position is represented, for instance, in the *Chung Yung*, 20:19–20; translated in Legge, *Doctrine*, 413; and Chan, *Source Book*, 107.

4. See Nivison, "Problem."

5. *HCCSSC*, 7:9b, *KWNP*, 7.

6. *HCCSSC*, 7:9b, *KWNP*, 7.

7. *HCCSSC*, 7:9b–10a, *KWNP*, 7.

8. *HCCSSC*, 7:10b–11a, *KWNP*, 7.

9. *HCCSSC*, 7:11ab, *KWNP*, 7.
10. See Hou, 180–82; K. Ch'en, 132–34; and Takakusu, 99.
11. See comments by Hansen, "Chinese Language," 504.
12. *HCCSSC*, 5:26b–27a, *KWNP*, 2.
13. See, e.g., Watson, *Chuang Tzu*, chap. 2.
14. *HCCSSC*, 5:27ab, *KWNP*, 2.
15. *HCCSSC*, 5:27b, *KWNP*, 2.
16. *HCCSSC*, 5:23a, *KWNP*, 2.
17. *HCCSSC*, 5:24b, *KWNP*, 2.
18. *HCCSSC*, 5:24b, *KWNP*, 2. Compare the description of the Buddha's experience of enlightenment (see Hamilton, 20–23). Shao, however, was not speaking of the particulars of existence, but of the patterns of things.
19. *HCCSSC*, 5:25a, *KWNP*, 2.
20. *HCCSSC*, 5:24b, *KWNP*, 2.
21. *HCCSSC*, 5:25b, *KWNP*, 2.
22. *HCCSSC*, 5:24b, *KWNP*, 2.
23. *HCCSSC*, 5:25b, *KWNP*, 2, commentary of Shao Po-wen.
24. *HCCSSC*, 5:24b–25a, *KWNP*, 2.
25. *HCCSSC*, 5:25a–26a, *KWNP*, 2, commentary of Shao Po-wen.
26. *HCCSSC*, 5:26a, *KWNP*, 2.
27. Thomas, *Life*, 66–68. See passage quoted in Hamilton, 21–23.
28. *HCCSSC*, 5:26b, *KWNP*, 2.
29. *HCCSSC*, 5:31b–32a, *KWNP*, 3.
30. *HCCSSC*, 5:30b, *KWNP*, 3.
31. *HCCSSC*, 5:30b–31b, *KWNP*, 3.
32. *HCCSSC*, 5:31b–32a, *KWNP*, 3. Translated more fully in Chapter 6.
33. *HCCSSC*, 5:33a, *KWNP*, 3.
34. *HCCSSC*, 5:44b–45a, *KWNP*, 4. Reference to *Lao Tzu*, chap. 57; see Waley, 211; or Lau, 118.
35. *HCCSSC*, 5:45b–46a, *KWNP*, 4.
36. Cf. the views of Chuang Tzu and Lao Tzu. See, e.g., Watson, *Chuang Tzu*, chap. 13; *Lao Tzu*, chaps. 1, 16, and 25; in Waley, 141, 162, and 174, and in Lau, 57, 72, and 82.
37. *HCCSSC*, 5:44b–48b, *KWNP*, 4.
38. *HCCSSC*, 5:50a, *KWNP*, 4.
39. *HCCSSC*, 14:48a, *KWWP*, 12.
40. *Lao Tzu*, chap. 1; see Lau, 57; and Waley, 141.
41. Respectively, *HCCSSC*, 9:61b, *KWWP*, 1; *HCCSSC*, 14:39b,

KWWP, 10 (cf. Watson, *Chuang Tzu*, chap. 5, for similarities with Chuang Tzu's ideas); *HCCSSC*, 11:44a, *KWWP*, 6; *HCCSSC*, 11:45a, *KWWP*, 6 (reference to the *Ta-chuan*, 1.5.24; see Legge, *I Ching*, 355); *HCCSSC*, 14:48a, *KWWP*, 12; *HCCSSC*, 10:39b, *KWWP*, 3; *HCCSSC*, 10:34a, *KWWP*, 3; *HCCSSC*, 10:44a, *KWWP*, 3.

42. *HCCSSC*, 8:32b, *KWNP*, 12.
43. *HCCSSC*, 11:39a, *KWWP*, 6.
44. For this type of activity in Buddhism, see Verdu.
45. Respectively, *HCCSSC*, 14:45b, 62b, 62a, 46a, 46b–47a, 51b, 54ab; all *KWWP*, 12. The concept of *ch'eng*, mentioned in the first passage translated here, is also translated "sincerity" or "integrity"; it derives from the *Chung-yung* and was also important in the thought of the other founders of Neo-Confucianism. The second passage contains an allusion to the *Chuang Tzu*, chap. 17; see Watson, *Chuang Tzu*, 188–89. Wang Chih's commentary on the last passage (*HCCSSC*, 14:54b) cites the *Chung-yung* as the source of the concept of the straight *tao* and the *Mencius* as the source of the idea of wholeness to the utmost (*chih-cheng*).

Chapter 8

1. *HCCSSC*, 14:67b, *KWWP*, 12.
2. In Western thought, too, perception and knowledge have been seen as closely related; see, e.g., Swartz.
3. *HCCSSC*, 7:28b, *KWNP*, 9.
4. Chang Tsai (*Cheng meng*, chüan 7) also made a distinction between two kinds of knowledge, which he called "knowledge from hearing and seeing" (*wen-chien chih chih*) and "knowledge from one's virtuous nature" (*te-hsing chih chih*). I discuss this topic in my article "Experiential Knowledge."
5. It is not easy to find a satisfactory English translation for *fan-kuan*. J. Needham (2:456) translated it as "objective observation," and Derk Bodde (Fung, 2:466n3) noted that it literally meant "to observe in a reversed manner." In a personal communication, N. Sivin suggested that the idea was more on the order of "reflective contemplation." Also, J. Ziemer (personal communication) has suggested that *fan* might retain a residual of its meaning of "turn [an object] over," with *kuan* functioning as the object of the verb, so that *fan-kuan* would mean something like "turning and re-turning one's observations." This would be analogous to picking up a stone and turning it over and over in one's hand to examine it from all angles. Similarly, *fan-kuan* would suggest turning one's observations over in one's mind, examining them from every angle, in order to understand the subsensorial level within the sensorial or the pattern with-

in the particular. As the discussion will indicate, because Shao Yung used *kuan* in several different meanings, none of these translations completely conveys the meaning of Shao's term. *Fan-kuan* means more than just observation and more than contemplation. Moreover, today, "objectivity" implies the use of a public method potentially available for anyone to use, but this was not Shao's idea. His was a subjective and mystical approach, with the goal of overcoming the limitations of the senses. For my earlier ideas on this topic, see my "Objective Observation."

6. Hou, 169, 266–70.
7. *HCCSSC*, 8:24ab, *KWNP*, 12.
8. See Takakusu, 126–32; and Fung, 2:299–359.
9. The term recalls the Buddhist term *chen-ti*, absolute truth; see Fung, 2:266.
10. *HCCSSC*, 8:21b, *KWNP*, 12. This term appears in the passage on the sages uniting with all things translated in Chapter 4.
11. For a discussion of this analogy, see Wayman.
12. *HCCSSC*, 11:47b, 48a, *KWWP*, 6.
13. *HCCSSC*, 11:47b, *KWWP*, 6.
14. *HCCSSC*, 8:26b–27a, *KWNP*, 12. Also translated in Chan, *Source Book*, 488.
15. *HCCSSC*, 8:24b, *KWNP*, 12.
16. *HCCSSC*, 8:24b–25a, *KWNP*, 12.
17. *HCCSSC*, 8:25a–26b, *KWNP*, 12.
18. See, e.g., Moran, 131–33, where he lists 40 meanings of the word *li* that he had discussed to that point.
19. For a general discussion of this topic, see T'ang Chün-yi, "Individual."
20. The use of *wo* for self was primarily Buddhist and was a translation of *atman*; see Fung, 2:300. *Chi* was the more common term for self. For concepts of the self, see also Munro, *Individualism and Holism*.
21. References to various related concepts are found in *HCCSSC*, *chüan* 14 *passim*, *KWWP*, 10–12. See Hou, 528–30.
22. See J. Needham's (2:56–83) discussion on similar views in Taoism.
23. Respectively, *HCCSSC*, 14:38b, *KWWP*, 10; *HCCSSC*, 14:49a, 49a, 49b, 51a, 51b, 51b, all *KWWP*, 12. In the last passage translated, the idea is similar to that in Ch'an Buddhism of keeping the mind still and whole and not making distinctions; see Hou, 269–70.
24. *HCCSSC*, 8:27b, *KWNP*, 12.
25. See Takakusu, chap. 6.
26. *HCCSSC*, 13:25a, *KWWP*, 9. I discuss Shao's concept of foreknowledge at greater length in my article "Foreknowledge."

27. Shao Po-wen, *Ch'ien-lu*, 19:144.
28. *HCCSSC*, 8:27ab, *KWNP*, 12.
29. On the T'ien-t'ai school, see Takakusu, chap. 9.
30. Yang Jung-kuo cites a number of Shao poems with this idea. See Shao Yung, *Chi-jang chi*, 15:1a ("Kuan-yi yin," Song on contemplating change); 15:2a ("Kuan san-huang yin," Song on contemplating the three sages); 16:11b ("Yü-chou yin," Song on the universe); 19:11b ("Le wu yin," Song on rejoicing in things).
31. *HCCSSC*, 8:27b–28a, *KWNP*, 12.
32. *HCCSSC*, 14:38b, *KWWP*, 10; discussed in Chapter 3.
33. Hou, 187.
34. *HCCSSC*, 8:28b–29b, *KWNP*, 12. The last line is from the *Ta-chuan*; see Legge, *I Ching*, 390, paragraph 34; and Wilhelm and Baynes, 338, paragraph 4.
35. *HCCSSC*, 8:30a–31a, *KWNP*, 12.
36. *HCCSSC*, 8:30a–31a, *KWNP*, 12.
37. *HCCSSC*, 14:58a, *KWWP*, 12. See the opening passage in the *Ta-hsüeh*; Chan, *Source Book*, 86–87. In describing this understanding, Shao was echoing *Chung-yung*, chap. 26; see Chan, *Source Book*, 109.
38. Translations from Watson, *Chuang Tzu*, 179, 43.
39. Watson, *Chuang Tzu*, 188–89. See *HCCSSC*, 14:62b, *KWWP*, 12; partially quoted in Chapter 7.
40. Watson, *Chuang Tzu*, 57–58.
41. *HCCSSC*, 14:38b, *KWWP*, 10. See Hou, 522. Translated more fully earlier in this chapter.
42. See Fung, 2:299–338, and Takakusu, chap. 5.
43. *HCCSSC*, 5:22a, *KWNP*, 2. Lo Kuang (*Chung-kuo*, 205–6) says *shan* means "to like." I question this because the commentators and Shao himself elsewhere use *pei* (to complete) as a substitute for *shan*.
44. *HCCSSC*, 14:38b, *KWWP*, 10. Pointed out by Hou, 522. See Watson, *Hsün Tzu*, 121–38. Translated more fully earlier in this chapter.
45. For a recent study of Chang Tsai, see Kasoff.
46. Chang Tsai, *Cheng meng ch'u-yi*, 7:2ab; translated in Fung, 2:491; and Chan, *Source Book*, 515, no. 59. Reference is to *Mencius*, 7.A.1; see Legge, *Mencius*, 448. For Ch'eng Yi's similar statement, see Yü Ying-shih, "Preliminary Observations," 110. See also discussion and translation in Bloom, "Matter," 308.
47. The origin of these terms is the *Chung-yung*, 27.6; see Legge, *Doctrine*, 422. *Wen-chien chih chih* is translated as "intellectual knowledge" by Yü, "Preliminary Observations," 106–10.
48. See Fung, 2:293–99.

Chapter 9

1. Wang Yang-ming, "On the Joy of Returning Home," translated in Ching, *Wisdom*, 231. Han Hsin (d. 196 B.C.) was one of the founders of the Han dynasty but was later killed as a result of an intrigue.

2. There are many passages in Shao Po-wen's *Ch'ien-lu* and Shao Po's *Hou-lu* that refer to particular concepts in Shao Yung's thought, but specific aspects of Buddhism, such as concepts, texts, or people, are not mentioned. One of the few references to Buddhism is in a passage discussing the early history of *Yi* learning in which Shao Po (5:30) said, "The images are based on Buddhist sutras." Another is the passage, quoted in Chapter 2, on Shao's views of past philosophers.

3. Ch'en Chi-ju, 3:24.

4. Ibid.; *SYHA*, 10:23a.

5. Quoted in *SYHA*, 10:23ab.

6. Ch'eng Hao and Ch'eng Yi, *Yi-shu*, 7:2a, 2a:14a; Chu Hsi, *Yüan-yüan lu*, 5:48.

7. Ch'eng Hao and Ch'eng Yi, *Yi-shu*, 2a:24ab. Quoted, with variations, in such works as Chu Hsi, *Yüan-yüan lu*, 5:48–49; and Hu Wei, 561–62.

8. Ch'en Chi-ju, 3:24.

9. On the shifting emphases of Neo-Confucianism in the Sung, see Yü Ying-shih, "Preliminary Observations," 122.

10. *SYHA*, 10:24a. Ch'eng is speaking about a state of mind similar to the Taoist concept of ataraxy.

11. Ch'eng Hao and Ch'eng Yi, *Yi-shu*, 7:1b; also quoted in Hu Wei, 562.

12. Ch'eng Hao and Ch'eng Yi, *Yi-shu*, 7:1b; also quoted in Chu Hsi, *Yüan-yüan lu*, 5:48; and Hu Wei, 562. For one account of the source of this phrase, see Weng (199), who says that Shen Kua (1031–95) mentioned a mirage of a city seen over the coastal waters off Shantung in his *Meng-ch'i pi-t'an* and that such conditions came to be called "castles in the air" (*k'ung-chung lou-ke*).

13. Chu Hsi, *Yüan-yüan lu*, 5:49; also quoted in Hu Wei, 562. *Ju*, as in *ju-shu*, may also be interpreted to mean "scholarly" or "of the scholars."

14. The thought of Mencius, who was a crucial link in the *tao-t'ung*, was still open to criticism in the eleventh century. Shao Po (*chüan* 11–13) recorded critical comments by such prominent people as Ssu-ma Kuang (1019–86), Su Tung-p'o (1036–1101), Li Kou (1009–59), Ch'en Tz'u-kung (11th century), Fu Yeh (1017–82), Liu Chung (1019–68), Chang Yü (11th century), Liu Tao-yüan (1032–78), and Ch'ao Yi-tao (1059–1129). Shao Po failed to mention another critic, Wang An-shih (1021–86).

15. Chu Hsi, *Yüan-yüan lu*, 5:48.
16. Hu Wei, 563.
17. Ch'eng Hao and Ch'eng Yi, *Yi-shu*, 7:1a.
18. *SYHA*, 10:25b–26a.
19. Chu Hsi, *Yüan-yüan lu*, 5:49.
20. Ch'eng Hao and Ch'eng Yi, *Yi-shu*, 18:12a; also quoted in Hu Wei, 563.
21. For Ch'ing criticisms of Shao Yung, see Henderson, 189–91. See also Hu Wei, 542, who notes the idea that Shao Yung began the practice of explaining the *Yi* with charts.
22. *SYHA*, 10:24a.
23. Chu Hsi, *Yüan-yüan lu*, 5:46.
24. *HLTCS*, 13:24b–25a.
25. Ibid., 13:25a.
26. Ibid., 13:25b.
27. Ibid., 13:23b–24a; also quoted in Hu Wei, 564–65, with some textual variation.
28. Chu Hsi, *Yüan-yüan lu*, 5:47.
29. *SYHA*, 10:26a. On Wei Po-yang, see J. Needham, 2:330–35.
30. *SYHA*, 10:28b–29a.
31. See Shao Yung's *Chi-jang chi*, 9:2b ("Hsieh Ning Ssu ch'eng hui Hsi-yi tsun"; Being grateful to the Ning temple door-gods for favoring the goblet of Hsi-yi) and 12:8b ("Kuan Ch'en Hsi-yi hsien-sheng chen chi mo chi"; Contemplating Mr. Ch'en Hsi-yi's portrait and writings).
32. Shao Po-wen, *Ch'ien-lu*, 7:47. This is similar to the Han view of Wang Ch'ung (A.D. 27–ca. 100), who regarded one's physiognomy and one's *ch'i* as the physical basis of one's fate (*ming*), but who was a famous skeptic and opposed the ideas of numerologists; see Forke, *Lun Heng*, 304–16.
33. Shao Po-wen, *Ch'ien-lu*, 7:47.
34. *SYHA*, 9:4b–6a.
35. *Sung shih*, 431:17a; also quoted in *SYHA*, 9:11b. For Mu Hsiu's biography, see *SYHA*, 9:11a–12a; for Chung Fang's biography, *Sung shih*, 457:3b–6b; and for Ch'en T'uan's biography, *Sung shih*, 457:2b–3b.
36. *Sung shih*, 431:17a.
37. For the biography of Chu Chen (1072–1138), see *Sung shih*, 435:2a–3a; see 2b–3a on the historical precedents.
38. For information on Ch'en T'uan, see *SYHA*, 9:1a–11a. For a study of Ch'en T'uan, see Knaul.
39. For a discussion of the historical development of the charts, see Cammann, "Symbols."

40. *Sung shih*, 457:3a.
41. On the *fang-shih*, see DeWoskin, *Doctors*; Ku; and Sivin, "Taoism and Science."
42. Hu Wei, 551.
43. See *Sung shih*, 457:10ab, 459:5a–6a, respectively, for biographies of Hsü Fu (11th century) and Kuo Yung (1091–1187).
44. *HLTCS*, 39:39a.
45. Ch'en Chi-ju, 4:29.
46. See Watson, *Chuang-tzu*, chap. 2.
47. Hu Wei, 446.
48. *HCCSSC*, 14:62a, 14:55b, *KWWP*, 12.
49. *HLTCS*, 39:36b. For Yin T'un's biography, see *Sung shih*, 428:2a–4b.
50. For a recent book on Chu Hsi's importance, see Chan, *Chu Hsi and Neo-Confucianism*. On Chu Hsi and Shao Yung, see Wyatt, "Chu Hsi's Critique."
51. Chang Liwen, esp. 292; Mao, esp. 510.
52. See Chu Hsi, *Yü-lei*, *chüan* 100, "Shao Tzu chih shu."
53. *HLTCS*, 13:25b.
54. Ibid., 13:26a.
55. Ibid.
56. Ibid., 13:26b, 13:27a.
57. Ibid., 13:27a.
58. Ibid., 39:42b.
59. Shao Po-wen, *Ch'ien-lu*, 19:142–43. For comparative purposes, see the discussion of Shang prediction and divination in Keightley.
60. Shao Po-wen, *Ch'ien-lu*, 19:144, 20:151.
61. *HLTCS*, 13:28b.
62. Ibid.
63. *SYHA*, 10:31b–32a.
64. For example, Hu Wei, *passim*; and Huang Tsung-hsi.
65. *HLTCS*, 13:26b–27a.
66. Ibid., 13:27b.
67. Ibid., 13:28b. In the view of Lo Ch'in-shun (1465–1547), a prominent follower of the Ch'eng-Chu school, Chu Hsi had praise for Shao Yung and recognized the depth of Shao's thought; see Bloom, *Knowledge*, 80.
68. *HLTCS*, 39:39b–40b.
69. Ibid., 13:31a.
70. For a discussion of the developments within Neo-Confucianism, see Fung, vol. 2, chap. 10–16; and de Bary, *Neo-Confucian Orthodoxy*.

71. See Henderson, 189.
72. *SYHA*, 86:15a–17a.
73. See Mote, "Eremitism."
74. Shao Yung was excluded from the *Tao-t'ung lu* by Chang Po-hsing (1651–1725). For a brief summary of how Shao was treated in the other anthologies of Neo-Confucianism, see Chan, *Source Book*, 482.
75. See Henderson, 125; Hu Wei, 136–40; and Huang Tsung-hsi. As indicated in Shao Po, 35, parts of this tradition of ideas were recognized in the Sung.
76. See T'ang Yung-t'ung, 124–61.
77. Hu Wei, 212–14.
78. Henderson, 189–91. Henderson (123), in referring to a particular series of numbers, says that Shao's system was not "based on any astronomical system" and "is only a highly schematized calendrical numerology." In my view, Henderson exaggerates here. Although Shao's thought is not identical to any known astronomical system, Shao's ideas of cycles clearly have similarities to Han cosmological systems. Moreover, the *Yi* tradition at least shared the same background as Han astronomical and cosmological thinking. Thus, although far removed from its foundation in astronomical and cosmological thought, Shao's system was based on earlier systems. Shao Yung was also not a mathematical astronomer, and so Henderson's statement is somewhat misleading. The question is the purpose of Shao's system. Attempts to understand him as an astronomer (in a modern sense) misinterpret the aim of his philosophical system. Although his ideas may have been somewhat hard to understand, the records indicate that he was part of the ongoing *Yi* tradition, and no Sung scholar suggested that his thought was part of the tradition of mathematical astronomy. Moreover, none of the people mentioned in the *Ch'ou-jen chuan* are people with whom Shao is known to have associated. Shao Yung himself was not included in it until the nineteenth century, with Juan Yüan's supplement to the *Ch'ou-jen chuan*.
79. See Elman, *Philosophy to Philology*.
80. *HLTCS*, 39:35a, 36a.
81. Ibid., 39:33b, 36b, 39a.
82. Ibid., 39:39b–40b, 13:26b.
83. Ibid., 39:33b, 13:25a.
84. For Wei, see *HLTCS*, 13:31a; for Shao, see *HCCSSC*, 10:34a, *KWWP*, 2; see also de Bary, *Neo-Confucian Orthodoxy*, 129.
85. *HCCSSC*, 12:38a, *KWWP*, 7. For an account of the debate by others over the human mind versus the moral mind, see Elman, "*Jen-hsin Tao-hsin* Debate."

86. Lü Ssu-mien, 48–65. Space limitations prevent discussion of twentieth-century Japanese and Western scholars.
87. Ch'en Chung-fan.
88. Ch'ien, *Sung Ming*, 32–39.
89. Wu; see esp. 2 and 82.
90. T'ang Chün-yi, *Chung-kuo*, 26–44.
91. J. Needham, 2:456.
92. Yang Jung-kuo, 59–74.
93. Hou, 521–35.
94. Wei Cheng-t'ung, *Chung-kuo*, 1045.
95. There continued to be followers of the charts and diagrams branch of the Yi learning well into the Ch'ing period. Representative works are *Chou Yi chi-chu* by Lai Chih-te (1525–1604), *Yi cho* by Tiao Pao (1609–69), *Yi ssu* by Ch'iao Ts'ai (1642–94), and *Chou Yi hsi-hsin* by Jen Ch'i-yün (1670–1744).
96. See Schneider, 208–11; and Balazs, *Civilization*, 213–54.

Chapter 10

1. *HCCSSC*, 14:60a, *KWWP*, 12.
2. Yü Ying-shih, "Preliminary Observations," 118–19; de Bary et al., *Sources*, 1:384.
3. See discussion in Wei Cheng-t'ung, *Chung-kuo*, 921–22.
4. See Sivin, "Word"; Welch, *Parting*; and Creel.
5. Ch'en Chi-ju, 26.
6. See *HCCSSC*, 14:56a–61b, *KWWP*, 12.
7. For instance, Shao (*HCCSSC*, 14:65b, *KWWP*, 12) said, "The Buddha rejected the way of ruler and minister, father and son, and husband and wife. How was this a natural principle?" During the Ming period, Lo Ch'in-shun recognized Shao Yung's anti-Buddhist bias; see Bloom, *Knowledge*, 107–8.
8. Shao also does not seem to have accepted the Buddhist notion that, as a concomitant to the idea of multiple existences, the time frame of history is illusory; see Bloom, "Matter," 306.
9. Wallacker makes the point of the importance of literacy as part of the Confucian tradition from the Han period on. See Wallacker, "Han Confucianism," 224.
10. Schirokauer, 481. Yang Jung-kuo (68) emphasizes Shao's influence on Lu Hsiang-shan and the idealistic position.
11. On his deathbed, Shao said to Ch'eng Yi that if the road is not broad, then there would no place for oneself, much less for anyone else; quoted by Wang Chih in *HCCSSC*, 14:60a, *KWWP*, 12.

Appendix A

1. For the following four charts, the Tao Tsang and SPPY editions of the *Huang-chi ching-shih* also use the same names as *HCCSSC*, except that the name for the fourth chart is omitted in the Tao Tsang edition. See *Huang-chi ching-shih*, 1–10, *Kuan-wu p'ien*, 1–50 (Tao Tsang ed.); and *Huang-chi ching-shih shu hsü-yen*, 1–4, *Kuan-wu p'ien* 1–50 (SPPY ed.).
2. *HCCSSC*, 1:1a–40b.
3. Ibid., 2:1a–72b.
4. Ibid., 3:1a–54a.
5. Ibid., 4:1a–41b.
6. *Huang-chi ching-shih shu*, 2, "Tsuan-t'u chih-yao" (Essentials of the collected charts), pt. 2, in *HLTCS*, 8:23a–44b.
7. *HCCSSC*, shou-shang:13b.
8. Ibid., 18a–22a.
9. *Huang-chi ching-shih shu*, 1, "Tsuan-t'u chih-yao," pt. 1, in *HLTCS*, 7:10a–14a.
10. *HCCSSC*, shou-shang:26a.
11. *Huang-chi ching-shih shu*, 1, "Tsuan-t'u chih-yao," pt. 1, in *HLTCS*, 7:7a.
12. *HCCSSC*, shou-shang:27b–28a.
13. *Huang-chi ching-shih shu*, 1, "Tsuan-t'u chih-yao," pt. 1, in *HLTCS*, 7:15ab.
14. *HCCSSC*, shou-shang:34b–36a.
15. Ibid., 37a–38a.
16. Ibid., 38b.
17. Ibid., shou-hsia:1a–2a.
18. Ibid., 9ab.
19. Ibid., 11b–16a.
20. Ibid., 23ab.
21. Ibid., 31b–32b.
22. In particular, see *HCCSSC* and the SPPY edition of the *Huang-chi ching-shih*. The SPPY edition provides the most comprehensive presentation of the supplemental material, in the form of both charts and commentary.
23. For example, in the SPPY edition, the chart "Yi hui ching yün" (Regulating revolutions with epochs) was expanded to include post-Sung historical items from the Yüan, Ming, and Ch'ing dynasties. See *Huang-chi ching-shih shu hsü-yen*, 2:1a–62a, *Kuan-wu p'ien* 13–26.

Bibliography

See p. 257 for a list of the abbreviations used in this bibliography.

Amore, Roy C. *Developments in Buddhist Thought: Canadian Contributions to Buddhist Studies.* Waterloo, Ontario: Wilfrid Laurier University Press, 1979.
Balazs, Etienne. *Chinese Civilization and Bureaucracy.* New Haven: Yale University Press, 1964.
———. Ed. by Yves Hervouet. *A Sung Bibliography.* Hong Kong: Chinese University Press, 1978.
Bauer, Wolfgang. "The Hidden Hero: Creation and Disintegration of the Ideal of Eremitism." In Donald J. Munro, ed., *Individualism and Holism: Studies in Confucian and Taoist Values,* 157–97.
Bennett, Steven J. "Patterns of the Sky and Earth: A Chinese Science of Applied Cosmology." *Chinese Science* 3 (Mar. 1978): 1–26.
Birdwhistell, Anne D. "The Concept of Experiential Knowledge in the Thought of Chang Tsai." *Philosophy East and West* 35, no. 1 (Jan. 1985): 37–60.
———. "The Philosophical Concept of Foreknowledge in the Thought of Shao Yung." *Philosophy East and West* 39, no. 1 (Jan. 1989).
———. "Shao Yung and His Concept of Objective Observation (*fan-kuan*)." *Journal of Chinese Philosophy* 9, no. 4 (Dec. 1982): 367–94.
Blofeld, John, trans. and ed. *I Ching (The Book of Change).* New York: E. P. Dutton & Co., 1968.
Bloom, Irene. "On the Matter of the Mind: The Metaphysical Basis of the Expanded Self." In Donald J. Munro, ed., *Individualism and Holism: Studies in Confucian and Taoist Values,* 293–330.
———, trans., ed., and intro. *Knowledge Painfully Acquired: The K'un-chih chi by Lo Ch'in-shun.* New York: Columbia University Press, 1987.
Bodde, Derk. "Harmony and Conflict in Chinese Philosophy." In Arthur F. Wright, ed., *Studies in Chinese Thought,* 19–80.
———. "Types of Chinese Categorical Thinking." *Journal of the American Oriental Society* 59 (1939): 200–219.

Brown, Roger. *Words and Things.* New York: Free Press, 1958.
Brown, W. Norman. *Man in the Universe: Some Cultural Continuities in India.* Berkeley: University of California Press, 1970.
Bruce, J. Percy. *Chu Hsi and His Masters.* London: Probsthain, 1923.
Cammann, Schuyler. "The Magic Square of Three in Old Chinese Philosophy and Religion." *History of Religions* 1 (1961): 37–80.
———. "Some Early Chinese Symbols of Duality." *History of Religions* 24, no. 3 (Feb. 1985): 215–54.
Carter, Thomas C. *The Invention of Printing in China and Its Spread Westward.* Rev. ed. New York: Columbia University Press, 1931.
Cassirer, Ernst. *The Problem of Knowledge: Philosophy, Science, and History Since Hegel.* New Haven: Yale University Press, 1950.
Chaffee, John W. *The Thorny Gates of Learning in Sung China.* London: Cambridge University Press, 1985.
Chan, Wing-tsit. "Patterns for Neo-Confucianism: Why Chu Hsi Differed from Ch'eng I." *Journal of Chinese Philosophy* 5, no. 2 (1978): 101–26.
———, ed. *Chu Hsi and Neo-Confucianism.* Honolulu: University of Hawaii Press, 1986.
———, trans. *Reflections on Things at Hand: The Neo-Confucian Anthology Compiled by Chu Hsi and Lü Tsu-ch'ien.* New York: Columbia University Press, 1967.
Chan, Wing-tsit, trans. and comp. *A Source Book in Chinese Philosophy.* Princeton: Princeton University Press, 1963.
———, trans. and intro. *The Platform Scripture.* New York: St. John's University Press, 1963.
Chang, Carsun. *The Development of Neo-Confucian Thought.* New York: Bookman Associates, 1957.
Chang Chung-yuan. *Creativity and Taoism: A Study of Chinese Philosophy, Art, and Poetry.* New York: Harper & Row, 1963.
Chang Hsing-ch'eng (Min) 張行成(㟁). "Hsing chuang lüeh" 行狀略 (Biographical outline). In Chu Hsi, *Yi-Lo yüan-yüan lu*, 46–48.
———. *Huang-chi ching-shih kuan-wu wai-p'ien yen-yi* 皇極經世觀物外篇衍義 (Explanation of the "Kuan-wu," outer chapters, of the *Huang-chi ching-shih*). SKCS 1st series. Taipei: Shang-wu yin-shu kuan, n.d..
———. *Huang-chi ching-shih so-yin* 皇極經世索隱 (Searches into the hidden meanings of the *Huang-chi ching-shih*). SKCS 1st series. Taipei: Shang-wu yin-shu kuan, n.d.
Chang Hsiu-min 張秀民. *Chung-kuo yin-shua shu te fa-ming chi ch'i ying-hsiang* 中國印刷術的發明及其影響 (The development of printing in China and its influence). Peking: Jen-min ch'u-pan she, 1958.

Chang Liwen. "An Analysis of Chu Hsi's System of Thought of *I*." In Wing-tsit Chan, ed., *Chu Hsi and Neo-Confucianism*, 292–311.

Chang Po-hsing 張伯行. *Tao-t'ung lu* 道統錄 (On the orthodox transmission of the way). In *Cheng-yi-t'ang ch'üan-shu* 正誼堂全書 (Complete library of the Hall of Rectification).

Chang Tsai 張載. *Cheng meng* 正蒙 (Correct discipline for beginners). In *HLTCS*, chüan 5–6.

———. *Cheng meng ch'u-yi* 正蒙初義 (Original meaning of the *Cheng meng*). Collected commentary by Wang Chih. SKCS ed. 2d series. Photoreprint of Wen Yüan Ko copy. Taipei: Shang-wu yin-shu kuan, 1971.

———. *Hsi ming* 西銘 (Western inscription). In *HLTCS*, chüan 4.

Chao Ling-ling 趙玲玲. *Shao K'ang-chieh kuan-wu nei-p'ien ti yen-chiu: T'ien-jen ho-yi li-nien te t'an-so* 邵康節觀物內篇的研究：天人合一理念的探索 (Researches on the "Kuan-wu," inner chapters, of Shao K'ang-chieh: Inquiry into the concept of the unity of heaven and humans). Taipei: Chia hsin shui-ni kung-ssu wen-hua chi-chin-hui, 1973.

Ch'ao Yi-tao 晁以道. Passage excerpted in *SYHA*, 10:25b–26a.

Ch'en Chi-ju 陳繼儒. *Shao K'ang-chieh hsien-sheng wai-chi* 邵康節先生外紀 (Informal records of Mr. Shao K'ang-chieh). TSCC ed.

Ch'en Chung-fan 陳鐘凡. *Liang Sung ssu-hsiang shu-p'ing* 兩宋思想述評 (A critical discussion of thought during the two Sung periods). Shanghai: Shang-wu yin-shu kuan, 1933.

Ch'en, Kenneth K. S. *Buddhism in China: A Historical Survey*. Princeton: Princeton University Press, 1964.

Ch'en Yi 陳繹. "Shao Ku mu ming" 邵古墓銘 (Epitaph of Shao Ku). In Lü Tsu-ch'ien, comp., *Sung wen chien*, 143:1891.

Ch'en Yü-fu 陳郁夫. "Shao K'ang-chieh te 'kuan-wu' lun" 邵康節的「觀物」論 (Shao K'ang-chieh's theory of "perceiving things"). *O-hu* 鵝湖 2, no. 1 (July 1965): 20–25.

Cheng, Chung-Ying. "Chu Hsi's Methodology and Theory of Understanding." In Wing-tsit Chan, ed., *Chu Hsi and Neo-Confucianism*, 169–96.

———. "Model of Causality in Chinese Philosophy: A Comparative Study." *Philosophy East and West* 26, no. 1 (Jan. 1976): 3–20.

Ch'eng Hao (Ming-tao) 程顥(明道). "Mu chieh ming" 墓誌銘 (Epitaph). In Chu Hsi, *Yi-Lo yüan-yüan lu*, 45–46.

——— and Ch'eng Yi (Yi-ch'uan) 程頤(明道). "Yi shih" 遺事 (Remembered events). In Chu Hsi, *Yi-Lo yüan-yüan lu*, 48–51.

———. *Ho-nan Ch'eng shih yi-shu* 河南程氏遺書 (Surviving works of the Ch'engs of Ho-nan). In *Erh-Ch'eng ch'üan-shu* 二程全書 (Complete works of the two Ch'engs). SPPY ed. Taiwan: Chung-hua shu-chü, 1966.

Ch'iao Ts'ai 喬萊. *Yi ssu* 易俟 (Continuations of the *Changes*). SKCS 4th series. Taipei: Shang-wu yin-shu kuan, 1973.

Ch'ien Mu. *Sung Ming li-hsüeh kai-shu* 宋明理學概述 (A general discussion of Neo-Confucianism during the Sung and Ming dynasties). Taipei: Chung-hua wen-hua ch'u-pan shih-yeh wei-yüan hui, 1953.

——, ed. *Chung-kuo hsüeh-shu shih lun chi* 中國學術史論集 (Collected articles on the history of Chinese scholarship). Taipei: Chung-hua wen-hua ch'u-pan shih-yeh wei-yüan hui, 1956.

Ching, Julia. "Chu Hsi on Personal Cultivation." In Wing-tsit Chan, ed., *Chu Hsi and Neo-Confucianism*, 273–91.

——. *To Acquire Wisdom: The Way of Wang Yang-ming*. New York: Columbia University Press, 1976.

Chou Lin-ching 周林靜. "Shao Yung *Yi*-hsüeh chih yen-chiu" 邵雍易學的研究 (Research on the *Yi* learning of Shao Yung). M. A. thesis, Chung-kuo wen-hua hsüeh-yüan, Taiwan, 1978.

Chou Tun-yi 周敦頤. *T'ai-chi t'u shuo* 太極圖說 (Diagram of the Supreme Ultimate explained). In *HLTCS*, chüan 1.

——. *T'ung shu* 通書 (Explanatory text). In *HLTCS*, chüan 2–3.

Chou Yi shu 周易述 (Chou changes with commentaries). SPPY ed.

Chu Hsi 朱熹. *Chu Tzu ta-ch'üan* 朱子大全 (Great collected writings of Master Chu). Comp. by Chu Tsai 朱在. SPPY ed. Shanghai.

——. *Chu Tzu yü-lei* 朱子語類 (Classified conversations of Master Chu). Copy of 1270 and 1473 ed. Taipei: Cheng-chung shu-chü, 1973.

——. *Yi-Lo yüan-yüan lu* 伊洛淵源錄 (Record of the origins of the schools of the two Ch'engs). TSCC ed.

Chu Pi 祝泌. *Huang-chi ching-shih chieh-ch'i shu chüeh* 皇極經世解起數訣 (Explaining the numerical secrets of the *Huang-chi ching-shih*). SKCS 1st series. Taipei: Shang-wu yin-shu-kuan, n.d.

——. *Kuan-wu p'ien chieh* 觀物篇解 (Explanation of the "Kuan-wu" chapters). SKCS 1st series. Taipei: Shang-wu yin-shu-kuan, n.d.

Chuang Tzu 莊子. SPPY ed.

Conze, Edward. *Buddhism: Its Essence and Development*. Oxford: Bruno Cassirer, 1951.

Curtis, James E., and Petras, John W., eds. *The Sociology of Knowledge: A Reader*. New York: Praeger Publishers, 1970.

Creel, Herrlee G. *What is Taoism? And Other Studies in Chinese Cultural History*. Chicago: University of Chicago Press, 1970.

Davison, Joanne L. [Birdwhistell, Anne D.] "The Thought and Environment of Li Yung: The Shaping of a Seventeenth-Century Confucian Philosopher." Ph. D. dissertation, Stanford University, 1974.

de Bary, W. Theodore. *Neo-Confucianism Orthodoxy and the Learning of the Mind-and-Heart*. New York: Columbia University Press, 1981.

———. "A Reappraisal of Neo-Confucianism." In Arthur F. Wright, ed., *Studies in Chinese Thought*, 81–111.

———, Wing-tsit Chan, and Burton Watson, comps. *Sources of Chinese Tradition*. 2 vols. New York: Columbia University Press, 1960.

——— et al. *Self and Society in Ming Thought*. New York: Columbia University, 1970.

——— et al. *The Unfolding of Neo-Confucianism*. New York: Columbia University Press, 1975.

DeWoskin, Kenneth J. *Doctors, Diviners, and Magicians of Ancient China: Biographies of Fang-shih*. New York: Columbia University Press, 1983.

———. *A Song for One or Two: Music and the Concept of Art in Early China*. Ann Arbor: University of Michigan, Center for Chinese Studies, 1982.

Elman, Benjamin A. *From Philosophy to Philology: Intellectual and Social Aspects of Change in Late Imperial China*. Cambridge, Mass.: Harvard University Press, 1984.

———. "Philosophy (*I-li*) Versus Philology (*K'ao-cheng*): The *Jen-hsin Tao-hsin* Debate." *T'oung Pao* 69, nos. 4–5 (1983): 175–222.

Ewing, A. C. *The Idealist Tradition: From Berkeley to Blanshard*. Glencoe, Ill.: Free Press, 1957.

Forke, Alfred. *The World-conception of the Chinese, Their Astronomical, Cosmological, and Physico-philosophical Speculations*. London: Probsthain, 1925.

———, trans. *Lun Heng*. 2 vols. New York: Paragon Book Gallery, 1907 [1962].

Foster, Lawrence, and Swanson, J. W., eds. *Experience and Theory*. Amherst: University of Massachusetts Press, 1970.

Franke, Herbert, ed. *Sung Biographies*. Weisbaden: Franz Steiner Verlag, 1976.

Freeman, Michael D. "From Adept to Worthy: The Philosophical Career of Shao Yung." *Journal of the American Oriental Society* 102 (1982): 477–91.

Fung Yu-lan. *A History of Chinese Philosophy*. 2 vols. Trans. Derk Bodde. Princeton: Princeton University Press, 1952–53.

Gardner, Daniel K. *Chu Hsi and the Ta-hsüeh: Neo-Confucian Reflection on the Confucian Canon*. Cambridge, Mass.: Harvard University Press, 1986.

Gaukroger, Stephen. *Explanatory Structures: Concepts of Explanation in Early Physics and Philosophy*. Atlantic Highlands, N.J.: Humanities Press, 1978.

Gilson, Etienne, and Thomas Langan. *Modern Philosophy: Descartes to Kant*. New York: Random House, 1963.

Graham, A. C. *Later Mohist Logic, Ethics, and Science*. Hong Kong: Chinese University Press, 1978.

———. *Two Chinese Philosophers: Ch'eng Ming-tao and Ch'eng Yi-ch'uan.* London: Lund Humphries, 1958.
Granet, Marcel. *La pensée chinoise.* Paris: Editions Albin Michel, 1950.
Guthrie, W. K. C. *A History of Greek Philosophy.* Vol. 1. Cambridge, Eng.: Cambridge University Press, 1962.
Hakeda, Yoshito S., trans. *The Awakening of Faith.* New York: Columbia University Press, 1967.
Hamilton, Clarence H., ed. *Buddhism: A Religion of Infinite Compassion.* Indianapolis: Bobbs-Merrill Company, 1952.
Han Yü 韓愈. "Yüan tao" 原道 (An inquiry on the Way). In *Ch'ang-li hsien-sheng chi* 昌黎先生集 (Collected works of Mr. Ch'ang-li): 11:1b. SPPY ed.
Hansen, Chad. "Chinese Language, Chinese Philosophy, and 'Truth.'" *Journal of Asian Studies* 44, no. 3 (May 1985): 491–519.
———. "Individualism in Chinese Thought." In Donald J. Munro, ed., *Individualism and Holism: Studies in Confucian and Taoist Values,* 35–55.
———. *Language and Logic in Ancient China.* Ann Arbor: University of Michigan Press, 1983.
Hanson, N. R. *Observation and Explanation.* New York: Harper & Row, 1971.
Hao Ling-ch'uan 郝陵川. *Chou Yi wai-chuan tzu-hsü* 周易外傳自序 (Preface to Outer commentaries on the *Chou Yi*). Excerpted in *SYHA,* 9:5b–6a.
Hartner, Willy. "Some Notes on Chinese Musical Art." In Nathan Sivin, ed., *Science and Technology in East Asia,* 32–54.
Hempel, C. G. *Aspects of Scientific Explanation.* New York: Free Press, 1965.
Henderson, John B. *The Development and Decline of Chinese Cosmology.* New York: Columbia University Press, 1984.
Ho Peng Yoke. *Li, Qi, and Shu: An Introduction to Science and Civilization in China.* Hong Kong: Hong Kong University Press, 1985.
———. "The System of the *Book of Changes* and Chinese Science." *Japanese Studies in the History of Science* 11 (1972): 23–39.
———. "Theories of Categories in Early Mediaeval Chinese Alchemy." *Journal of the Warburg and Courtauld Institute* 22 (1959): 173–210.
Hou Wai-lu 侯外廬. *Chung-kuo ssu-hsiang t'ung-shih* 中國思想通史 (A comprehensive history of Chinese thought). Vol. 4, pt. 1. Peking: Jen-min ch'u-pan she, 1959.
Howard, Jeffrey A. "Concepts of Comprehensiveness and Historical Change in the *Huai-nan-tzu.*" In Henry Rosemont, Jr., ed., *Explorations in Early Chinese Cosmology,* 119–31.
Hsing-li ta-ch'üan-shu 性理大全書 (Great collection on nature and principle).

Comp. by Hu Kuang 胡廣 et al. SKCS 5th series. Photoreprint of Wen Yüan Ko copy. Taipei: Shang-wu yin-shu kuan, 1974.

Hsü Fu-kuan 徐復觀. *Chung-kuo ssu-hsiang shih lun-chi* 中國思想史論集 (Collected discussions on the history of Chinese thought). Taichung: Tunghai University Press, 1959.

———. *Chung-kuo ssu-hsiang shih lun-chi hsü-p'ien* 中國思想史論集緒篇 (Supplement to *Chung-kuo ssu-hsiang shih lun-chi*). Taipei: China Times Publishing Co., 1982.

Hsün Tzu 荀子. SPPY ed.

Hu Shih. "The Scientific Spirit and Method in Chinese Philosophy." In Charles A. Moore, ed., *The Chinese Mind*, 104–31.

Hu Wei 胡渭. *Yi t'u ming pien* 易圖明辨 (A clarifying critique of the diagrams of the *Yi-ching*). Taipei: Kuang-wen shu-chü, 1976.

Huang Chen (Tung-fa) 黃震(東發). *Tung-fa jih-ch'ao* 東發日鈔 (Daily notes of Tung-fa). Excerpted in *SYHA*, 86:15a–17a.

Huang Kung-wei 黃公偉. "Shao Yung (K'ang-chieh) hsüeh-shuo kaikuan" 邵雍(康節)學說概觀 (General observations on Shao Yung [K'ang-chieh]'s learning). *Chung-yüan wen-hsien* 中原文獻 9, no. 6 (June 1966): 1–3.

Huang, Siu-chi. "Chang Tsai's Concept of *Ch'i*." *Philosophy East and West* 18, no. 4 (1968): 247–60.

Huang Tsung-hsi 黃宗羲. *Yi-hsüeh hsiang-shu lun* 易學象數論 (On the images and numbers of the *Yi* learning). SKCS 6th series. Taipei: Kuang-wen shu-chü, 1974.

——— and Ch'üan Tsu-wang 全祖望. *Sung Yüan hsüeh-an pu-yi* 宋元學案補遺 (Anthology of Sung and Yüan scholars with supplements). Comp. Wang Hsin-ts'ai 王梓材 and Feng Yun-hao 馮雲濠. Ssu-ming ts'ung-shu ed. 1937.

Hughes, E. R. "Epistemological Methods in Chinese Philosophy." In Charles A. Moore, ed., *The Chinese Mind*, 77–103.

James, William. *Essays in Radical Empiricism* and *A Pluralistic Universe*. New York: E. P. Dutton & Co., 1971.

Jen Ch'i-yün 任啟運. *Chou Yi hsi-hsin* 周易洗心 (Purifying the heart with the *Chou Yi*). SKCS 4th ed. Taipei: Shang-wu yin-shu-kuan, 1973.

Juan Yüan 阮元. *Ch'ou-jen chuan* 疇人傳 (Biographies of mathematicians and astronomers). Shanghai: Shang-wu yin-shu-kuan, 1935 [1955].

Kasoff, Ira E. *The Thought of Chang Tsai*. Cambridge, Eng.: Cambridge University Press, 1984.

Keightley, David N. "Late Shang Divination: The Magico-Religious Legacy." In Henry Rosemont, Jr., ed., *Explorations in Early Chinese Cosmology*, 11–34.

Kinoshita, Joyce. "Realms of Explanation: Theory and Illustrations." Ph.D. dissertation, Stanford University, 1983.

Knaul, Livia. *Lebun und Legende des Ch'en T'uan*. Frankfort am Main and Bern: Verlag Peter Lang, 1981.

Kracke, E. A., Jr. *Civil Service in Early Sung China, 960–1067*. Cambridge, Mass. Harvard University Press, 1959.

Ku Chieh-kang 顧頡剛. *Ch'in Han ti fang-shih yü ju-sheng* 秦漢的方士於儒生 (The *fang-shih* and Confucians of the Ch'in and Han periods). Shanghai: Jen-min ch'u-pan she, 1962.

Kuan Lang (Tzu-ming) 關朗(子明). *Tung-chi chen-ching* 洞極真經 (True classic of the concealed ultimate). Yü han shan fang chi yi shu ed.

Lai Chih-te 來知德. *Chou Yi chi-chu* 周易集註 (Collected commentaries of the *Chou Yi*). SKCS 4th series. Taipei: Shang-wu yin-shu-kuan. 1973.

Lamont, H. G. "An Early Ninth Century Debate on Heaven: Liu Tsung-yüan's *T'ien Shuo* and Liu Yü-hsi's *T'ien Lun*. An Annotated Translation and Introduction, Parts 1 and 2." *Asia Major* 18 (1973): 181–208; 19 (1974): 37–85.

Lao Tzu 老子. SPPY ed.

Lau, D. C., trans. *Lao Tzu: Tao Te Ching*. Baltimore: Penguin Books, 1963.

Le Blanc, Charles. *Huai-nan Tzu: Philosophical Synthesis in Early Han Thought*. Hong Kong: Hong Kong University Press, 1985.

Legge, James, trans. *The Chinese Classics*. Vol. 1: *Confucian Analects, The Great Learning, and The Doctrine of the Mean*; vol. 2: *The Works of Mencius*; vol. 3: *The Shoo King*; vol. 4: *The She King*; vol. 5: *The Ch'un Ts'eu with the Tso Chuen*. Oxford: Clarendon Press, 1893.

———. *I Ching: Book of Changes*. 1882. Ed., with intro., by Ch'u Chai with Winberg Chai. New Hyde Park, N.Y.: University Books, 1964.

Levenson, Joseph. *Confucian China and Its Modern Fate: A Trilogy*. 3 vols. Berkeley: University of California Press, 1972.

Li Chi. "The Changing Concept of the Recluse in Chinese Literature." *Harvard Journal of Asiatic Studies* 24 (1962–63): 234–47.

Liu Chia-pi (J.B.) 劉家壁. *Chung-kuo t'u-shu shih tzu-liao chi* 中國圖書史資料集 (Collection of materials on the history of Chinese books). Hong Kong: Lungmen Press, 1974.

Liu, James T. C. "How Did a Neo-Confucian School Become the State Orthodoxy?" *Philosophy East and West* 23, no. 4 (Oct. 1973): 483–505.

———. *Reform in Sung China: Wang An-shih (1021–1086) and His New Policies*. Cambridge, Mass.: Harvard University Press, 1959.

Liu, Shu-hsien. "The Use of Analogy and Symbolism in Traditional Chinese Philosophy." *Journal of Chinese Philosophy* 1 (June–Sept. 1974): 313–38.

Lo Kuang 羅光. *Chung-kuo che-hsüeh ssu-hsiang shih, Sung tai p'ien* 中國哲學思想史,宋代篇 (A history of Chinese philosophical thought, the Sung period). Taipei: Hsüeh-sheng shu-chü, 1980.

———. "Shao Yung te jen-shih lun" 邵雍的認識論 (Shao Yung's theory of consciousness). *Che-hsüeh yü wen-hua* 哲學與文化 4, no. 11 (Nov. 1966): 20–24.

Lo, Winston. "Philology, an Aspect of Sung Rationalism." *Chinese Culture* 17, no. 4 (Dec. 1976): 1–26.

Louton, John. "Concepts of Comprehensiveness and Historical Change in the *Lü-shih Ch'un-ch'iu*." In Henry Rosemont, Jr., ed., *Explorations in Early Chinese Cosmology*, 105–17.

Lü Ssu-mien 呂思勉. *Li-hsüeh kang-yao* 理學綱要 (A general outline of Neo-Confucianism). Shanghai: Shang-wu yin-shu kuan, 1931.

Lü Tsu-ch'ien 呂祖謙, comp. *Sung wen chien* 宋文鑑 (Sung literary mirror). Kuo-hsüeh chi-pen ts'ung-shu ed. Taipei: Shang-wu yin-shu kuan, 1968.

Lun-yü chu-shu 論語注疏 (Analects of Confucius, with commentary). SPPY ed.

Ma Yung-ch'ing 馬永卿. *Lan chen-tzu lu* 嬾真子錄 (Record of the Idle True Master). In *Shuo fu*, 9:17a–24a.

Major, John S. "Myth, Cosmology, and the Origins of Chinese Science." *Journal of Chinese Philosophy* 5, no. 1 (1978): 1–20.

Mannheim, Karl. "The Sociology of Knowledge." In James E. Curtis and John W. Petras, eds., *The Sociology of Knowledge: A Reader*, 109–30.

Mao Huaixin. "The Establishment of the School of Chu Hsi and Its Propagation in Fukien." In Wing-tsit Chan, ed., *Chu Hsi and Neo-Confucianism*, 503–20.

Mather, Richard B. "The Controversy over Conformity and Naturalness During the Six Dynasties." *History of Religions* 9 (1969–70): 160–80.

McEvilly, Wayne. "Synchronicity and the *I Ching*." *Philosophy East and West* 18, no. 4 (1968): 137–49.

McKenna, Stephen E., and Victor H. Mair. "A Reordering of the Hexagrams of the *I Ching*." *Philosophy East and West* 29, no. 4 (1979): 421–42.

McKnight, Brian. "Chu Hsi and His World." In Wing-tsit Chan, ed., *Chu Hsi and Neo-Confucianism*, 408–36.

Mei, Y. P. "Some Observations on the Problem of Knowledge Among the Ancient Chinese Logicians." *Tsing Hua Hsüeh Pao*, n.s. 1 (1956): 114–21.

Meng Tzu chu-shu 孟子注疏 (Mencius, with commentary). SPPY ed.

Moore, Charles. A., ed. *The Chinese Mind*. Honolulu: University of Hawaii Press, 1967.

Moran, Patrick E. "Explorations of Chinese Metaphysical Concepts: The

History of Some Key Terms from the Beginnings to Chu Hsi (1130–1200)." Ph. D. dissertation, University of Pennsylvania, 1983.
Mote, Frederick W. "The Arts and the 'Theorizing Mode' of the Civilization." In Christian Murck, ed., *Artists and Traditions: Uses of the Past in Chinese Culture*, 3–8.
———. "Confucian Eremitism in the Yüan Period." In Arthur F. Wright, ed., *The Confucian Persuasion*, 202–40.
Mou Jun-sun 牟潤孫. *Lun Wei-Chin yi-lai chih ch'ung-shang t'an pien chi ch'i ying-hsiang* 論魏晉以來崇尚談辯及其影響 (On the indulgence in "discourse and polemics" by scholars of the Wei and Chin periods and its influence in subsequent ages). Hong Kong: Chinese University Press, 1966.
Mou Tsung-san 牟宗三. *Chung-kuo che-hsüeh te t'e-hsing* 中國哲學的特性 (The special characteristics of Chinese philosophy). Hong Kong: Jen-sheng ch'u-pan she, 1963.
———. *Hsin-t'i yü hsing-t'i* 心體與性體 (The substance of mind and the substance of nature). 3 vols. Taipei: Cheng-chung shu-chü, 1968.
———. *Wei-Chin hsüan-hsüeh* 魏晉玄學 (The mysterious learning of the Wei and Chin periods). Taichung: Tung-hai University, Chung-yang shu-chü, 1962.
Mungello, David. *Leibniz and Confucianism: The Search for Accord*. Honolulu: University Press of Hawaii, 1977.
Munro, Donald J. "The Family Network, the Stream of Water, and the Plant." In idem, ed., *Individualism and Holism: Studies in Confucian and Taoist Values*, 259–91.
———, ed. *Individualism and Holism: Studies in Confucian and Taoist Values*. Ann Arbor: University of Michigan, Center for Chinese Studies, 1985.
Murck, Christian, ed. *Artists and Traditions: Uses of the Past in Chinese Culture*. Princeton: Princeton University Press, 1976.
Nakayama, Shigeru. *Academic and Scientific Traditions in China, Japan, and the West*. Trans. by Jerry Dusenbury. Tokyo: University of Tokyo Press, 1984.
Nakayama, Shigeru, and Nathan Sivin, eds. *Chinese Science: Explorations of an Ancient Tradition*. Cambridge, Mass.: MIT Press, 1973.
Nan Sung kuan ke lu 南宋館閣錄. Ed. Ch'en K'uei 陳騤. SKCS pieh-chi ed. Taipei: Shang-wu yin-shu-kuan, 1975.
Needham, Joseph, et al. *Science and Civilisation in China*, vol. 2, *History of Scientific Thought*; vol. 3, *Mathematics and the Sciences of the Heavens and the Earth*; vol. 5, *Chemistry and Chemical Technology*, pt. 1, *Paper and Printing*. Cambridge, Eng.: Cambridge University Press, 1954–85.
Needham, Rodney. *Symbolic Classification*. Santa Monica, Calif.: Goodyear Publishing Company, 1979.

Nivison, David S. *The Life and Thought of Chang Hsüeh-ch'eng (1738–1801)*. Stanford: Stanford University Press, 1966.

———. "The Problem of 'Knowledge' and 'Action' in Chinese Thought Since Wang Yang-ming." In Arthur F. Wright, ed., *Studies in Chinese Thought*, 112–45.

Ngo Van Xuyet. *Divination, magie, et politique dans la Chine ancienne: Essai suivi de la traduction des "Biographies de magiciens" tirées de l'* Histoire des Han postérieurs. Paris: Presses Universitaires de France, 1976.

Okada Takehiko. "Chu Hsi and Wisdom as Hidden and Stored." In Wing-tsit Chan, ed., *Chu Hsi and Neo-Confucianism*, 197–211.

Peterson, Willard J. "Making Connections: 'Commentary on the Attached Verbalizations' of the *Book of Change*." *Harvard Journal of Asiatic Studies* 42 (June 1982): 67–116.

Philip, J. A. *Pythagoras and Early Pythagoreanism*. Toronto: University of Toronto Press, 1966.

Popper, Karl. "The Sociology of Knowledge." In James E. Curtis and John W. Petras, eds., *The Sociology of Knowledge: A Reader*, 649–60.

Porkert, Manfred. *The Theoretical Foundations of Chinese Medicine: Systems of Correspondence*. Cambridge, Mass.: MIT Press, 1974.

Pulleyblank, E. G. "The Chinese Cyclical Signs as Phonograms." *Journal of the American Oriental Society* 99 (1979): 24–38.

Quine, W. V. "Grades of Theoreticity." In Lawrence Foster and J. W. Swanson, eds., *Experience and Theory*, 1–17.

Reichenbach, Hans. *Experience and Prediction: An Analysis of the Foundations and the Structure of Knowledge*. Chicago: University of Chicago Press, 1938 [1976].

Reischauer, Edwin O., and Fairbank, John K. *East Asia: The Great Tradition*. Cambridge, Mass.: Harvard University Press, 1958.

Rickett, W. Allyn. *Kuan-tzu: A Repository of Early Chinese Thought*. Hong Kong: Hong Kong University Press, 1965.

Rosemont, Henry, Jr., ed. *Explorations in Early Chinese Cosmology*. Journal of the American Academy of Religion Studies L (2). Chico, Calif.: Scholars Press, 1984.

Roy, David T., and Tsuen-hsuin Tsien, eds. *Ancient China: Studies in Early Civilization*. Hong Kong: Chinese University Press, 1978.

Rubin, Vitaly A. "The Concepts of Wu-hsing and Yin-yang." *Journal of Chinese Philosophy* 9 (June 1982): 131–57.

Russell, Bertrand. *A History of Western Philosophy*. New York: Simon & Schuster, 1945.

Ryle, Gilbert. *The Concept of Mind*. London: Hutchinson's University Library, 1949.

Saso, Michael. "What is the Ho T'u?" *History of Religions* 17 (1978): 339–416.
Schafer, Edward H. *Pacing the Void: T'ang Approaches to the Stars.* Berkeley: University of California Press, 1977.
Schirokauer, Conrad. "Chu Hsi and Hu Hung." In Wing-tsit Chan, ed., *Chu Hsi and Neo-Confucianism*, 480–502.
Schneider, Laurence A. *A Madman of Ch'u: The Chinese Myth of Loyalty and Dissent.* Berkeley: University of California Press, 1980.
Schwartz, Benjamin. *In Search of Wealth and Power: Yen Fu and the West.* Cambridge, Mass.: Harvard University Press, 1964.
———. "On the Absence of Reductionism in Chinese Thought." *Journal of Chinese Philosophy* 1 (Dec. 1973): 27–44.
———. *The World of Thought in Ancient China.* Cambridge, Mass.: Harvard University Press, 1985.
Shao Po 邵博. *Ho-nan Shao shih wen-chien hou-lu* 河南邵氏聞見後錄 (Later account of what has been heard and seen by Mr. Shao of Ho-nan). TSCC ed.
Shao Po-wen 邵伯溫. *Ho-nan Shao shih wen-chien ch'ien-lu* 前錄 (Former account of what has been heard and seen by Mr. Shao of Ho-nan). TSCC ed.
———. *Yi hsüeh pien huo* 易學辨惑 (Discussion of doubts about the *Yi* learning). SKCS 2d series. Taipei: Shang-wu yin-shu-kuan, 1971.
Shao Yung 邵雍. *Huang-chi ching-shih* 皇極經世 (Supreme principles that rule the world). Tao Tsang ed. Taipei: Yi-wen yin-shu kuan, 1962.
———. *Huang-chi ching-shih shu* 皇極經世書 (Book of the supreme principles that rule the world). Commentary by Shao Po-wen. In *HLTCS*, *chüan* 7–13.
———. *Huang-chi ching-shih shu-chieh* 皇極經世書解 (Commentary on the *Huang-chi ching-shih*). Collected commentary by Wang Chih 王植. SKCS 4th series. Taipei: Shang-wu yin-shu-kuan, 1973.
———. *Huang-chi ching-shih shu hsü-yen* 皇極經世書緒言 (Introduction to the *Huang-chi ching-shih*). Commentary by Huang Ao-chou (Chi) 黃粵洲(畿). SPPY ed. Shanghai: Chung-hua shu-chü, n.d.
———. "Wu-ming kung chuan" 無名公傳 (Biography of Mr. No Name). In *HLTCS*, 13:19a–22a.
———. *Yi-ch'uan chi-jang chi* 伊川擊壤集 (Collection of beating on the ground at Yi-ch'uan). Tao Tsang ed. Taipei: Yi-wen yin-shu kuan, 1962.
———. *Yü-ch'iao wen-tui* 漁樵問對 (Conversation between the fisherman and the woodcutter). In *HLTCS*, 13:1a–19a.
Shaughnessy, Edward L. "The Composition of the 'Zhouyi.'" Ph.D. dissertation, Stanford University, 1983.

Shchutskii, Iulian K. *Researches on the I Ching*. Princeton: Princeton University Press, 1979.
Shen Kua 沈括. *Meng-ch'i pi-t'an chiao-cheng* 夢溪筆談校證 (Dream Pool essays with corrections). Shanghai: Shang-hai ch'u-pan kung-ssu, 1956.
Shuo fu 說郛. Comp. T'ao Tsung-yi 陶宗儀. Shanghai: Shang-wu yin-shu kuan, 1927.
Sivin, Nathan. "Chinese Alchemy and the Manipulation of Time." In idem, ed., *Science and Technology in East Asia*, 108–22.
———. *Chinese Alchemy: Preliminary Studies*. Cambridge, Mass.: Harvard University Press, 1968.
———. "Cosmos and Computation in Early Chinese Mathematical Astronomy." *T'oung Pao* 55 (1969): 1–73.
———. "On the Word 'Taoist' as a Source of Perplexity: With Special Reference to the Relations of Science and Religion in Traditional China." *History of Religions* 17 (1978): 303–30.
———. "Preliminary Reflections on the Words *Pien*, *Hua*, and *T'ung* in the 'Great Commentary' to the *Book of Changes*." Unpublished paper.
———. "Taoism and Science." Unpublished paper.
———, ed., *Science and Technology in East Asia*. New York: Science History Publications, 1977.
Sung-jen yi-shih hui-pien 宋人軼事彙編 (Compilation on Sung notables). Comp. Ting Ch'uan-ching 丁傳靖. Beijing: Shang-wu yin-shu-kuan, 1958.
Sung shih 宋史 (History of the Sung Dynasty). 20 vols. SPPY ed. Taipei: Chung-hua shu-chü, 1966.
Sung shih hsin pien 宋史新編 (A new history of the Sung). Comp. K'o Wei-ch'i 柯維騏. Shanghai: Ta-kuang shu-chü, 1936.
Sung shih yi 宋史翼 (Addenda to the *Sung Shih*). Comp. Lu Hsin-yüan 陸心源. Taipei: Wen-hai ch'u-pan she, 1967.
Swanson, Gerald. "The Concept of Change in the *Great Treatise*." In Henry Rosemont, Jr., ed., *Explorations in Early Chinese Cosmology*, pp. 67–93.
Swartz, Robert J., ed. *Perceiving, Sensing, and Knowing: A Book of Readings from Twentieth Century Sources in the Philosophy of Perception*. Garden City, N.Y.: Doubleday & Company, 1965.
Swetz, Frank J., and Kao, T. I. *Was Pythagoras Chinese? An Examination of Right Triangle Theory in Ancient China*. University Park: Pennsylvania State University Press, 1977.
Takakusu, Junjiro. *The Essentials of Buddhist Philosophy*. Honolulu: University of Hawaii, 1947.
T'ang Chün-yi 唐君毅. *Chung-kuo che-hsüeh yüan-lun, yüan chiao p'ien, Sung-Ming ju-hsüeh ssu-hsiang chih fa-chan* 中國哲學原論,原教篇,宋明儒學思想之發展 (A discussion of Chinese philosophy, section on original

teachings, the development of Sung and Ming Confucian thought). Hong Kong: Hsin Ya yen-chiu so, 1975.

———. "The Individual and the World in Chinese Methodology." In Charles A. Moore, ed., *The Chinese Mind*, 264–85.

T'ang Yung-t'ung. "Wang Pi's New Interpretation of the *I Ching* and *Lun-yü*." Trans. by Walter Liebenthal. *Harvard Journal of Asiatic Studies* 10 (1947): 124–61.

Tazaki Masayoshi 田崎仁義. "Shō Kōsetsu no kō tei ō ha no ron" 邵康節の皇帝王霸の論 (Shao K'ang-chieh's theory of sages, emperors, kings, and hegemons). *Tōa keizai kenkyū* 東亞經濟研究 23, no. 3 (1939).

Thomas, Edward J. *The History of Buddhist Thought*. New York: Barnes & and Noble, 1951 [1967].

———. *The Life of Buddha as Legend and History*. New York: A.A. Knopf, 1927.

Tiao Pao 刁包. *Yi cho* 易酌 (Considerations of the *Changes*). SKCS 4th series. Taipei: Shang-wu yin-shu-kuan, 1973.

Tomoeda Ryūtarō 友枝龍太郎. "Shō Kōsetsu no shisō—sū yori ri e" 邵康節の思想—數より理へ (The thought of Shao K'ang-chieh—from numbers to principle). *Tōhō kodai kenkyū* 東方古代研究 1 (1952).

Ts'ai Te-an 蔡德安. *K'ang-chieh hsien-t'ien Yi-hsüeh p'ing-yi* 康節先天易學平議 (A critique of the *hsien-t'ien Yi* learning of K'ang-chieh). Taipei: Lung-ch'üan ch'u-pan she, 1973.

Tu, Wei-ming. *Centrality and Commonality: An Essay on "Chung-yung."* Honolulu: University Press of Hawaii, 1976.

———. *Confucian Thought: Selfhood as Creative Transformation*. Albany: State University of New York Press, 1985.

Tung-tu shih lüeh 東都事略. Comp. Wang Ch'eng 王稱. Taipei: Wen-hai ch'u-pan she, 1967.

Ueno Hideto 上野日出刀. *Isen Gekijō sho* 伊川擊瀼集 (Collection of beating on the ground at Yi-ch'uan). Tokyo: Meitoku shuppansha, 1979.

Verdu, Alfonso. *Dialectical Aspects in Buddhist Thought: Studies in Sino-Japanese Mahayana Idealism*. Lawrence: University of Kansas, Center for East Asian Studies, 1974.

Waley, Arthur. *The Way and Its Power: A Study of the Tao Te Ching and Its Place in Chinese Thought*. New York: Grove Press, 1958.

Wallacker, Benjamin E. "Han Confucianism and Confucius in Han." In David T. Roy and Tsuen-hsuin Tsien, eds., *Ancient China: Studies in Early Civilization*, 215–28.

———. *The Huai-nan Tzu, Book Eleven: Behavior, Culture and the Cosmos*. New Haven: American Oriental Society, 1962.

———. Review of *Huai-nan Tzu: Philosophical Synthesis in Early Han Thought*, by Charles Le Blanc. *Journal of Asian Studies* 46, no. 2 (May 1987): 398–99.

Wang Pi 王弼. *Chou Yi lüeh-li* 周易略例 (Outline of the system of the Chou Changes). TSCC ed.

Wang Shou-nan 王壽南, ed. *Chung-kuo li-tai ssu-hsiang chia* 中國歷代思想家 (Chinese thinkers through the ages). Taipei: Shang-wu yin-shu kuan, 1978.

Wang T'ung (Wen Chung-tzu) 王通(文中子). *Chung shuo* 中說 (Sayings on the center). Erh-shih-erh tzu ed.

———. Passages excerpted in *Shuo fu*, 71:9a–11b.

Wang Ying-lin 王應麟. *K'un-hsüeh chi-wen* 困學紀聞 (Record of what has been heard after arduous study). Excerpted in *SYHA*, 9:58a–b.

Ware, James, trans. *Alchemy and Medicine in the China of A.D. 320: The Nei-p'ien of Ko Hung's "Pao-p'u-tzu."* Cambridge, Mass.: MIT Press, 1966.

Watson, Burton, trans. *Basic Writings of Mo Tzu, Hsün Tzu, and Han Fei Tzu*. New York: Columbia University Press, 1963.

———, trans. *The Complete Works of Chuang Tzu*. New York: Columbia University Press, 1968.

Wayman, Alex. "The Mirror as a Pan-Buddhist Metaphor-Simile." *History of Religions* 13, no. 4 (May 1974): 251–69.

Weber, Max. *The Religion of China: Confucianism and Taoism*. Trans. and ed. Hans H. Gerth. Intro. C. K. Yang. New York: Macmillan, 1964.

Wechsler, Howard J. "The Confucian Teacher Wang T'ung 王通 (584?–617): One Thousand Years of Controversy." *T'oung Pao* 63 (1977): 225–72.

Wei Cheng-t'ung 韋政通. "Chu Hsi on the Standard and the Expedient." In Wing-tsit Chan, ed., *Chu Hsi and Neo-Confucianism*, 255–72.

———. *Chung-kuo ssu-hsiang shih* 中國思想史 (A history of Chinese thought). Taipei: Ta-lin ch'u-pan she, 1980.

Wei Po-yang 魏伯陽. *Chou Yi ts'an-t'ung-ch'i* 周易參同契 (Kinship of the three in the Chou *Changes*). Tao Tsang ed.

Welch, Holmes H. "The Bellagio Conference on Taoist Studies." *History of Religions* 9 (1969–79): 107–36.

———. *Taoism: The Parting of the Way*. Boston: Beacon Press, 1957; rev. ed., 1966.

Weng Ch'uan-yü 翁傳鈺, ed. *Ch'eng-yü ku-shih ta-ch'üan* 成語古書大全 (A great collection of the stories behind common sayings). Kaohsiung: Pai-ch'eng shu-tien, 1966.

Wilhelm, Hellmut. *Change: Eight Lectures on the I Ching*. Princeton: Princeton University Press, 1960.

———. *Heaven, Earth, and Man in the Book of Changes*. Seattle: University of Washington Press, 1977.

Wilhelm, Richard, and Cary F. Baynes, trans. *The I Ching or Book of Changes*. 3d ed. Princeton: Princeton University Press, 1967.

Willis, Janice Dean, trans. *On Knowing Reality: The Tattvartha Chapter of Asanga's Bodhisattvabhumi*. New York: Columbia University Press, 1979.

Wright, Arthur F. "Sui Yang-ti: Personality and Stereotype." In idem, ed., *The Confucian Persuasion*, 47–76.

———, ed. *The Confucian Persuasion*. Stanford: Stanford University Press, 1960.

———, ed. *Studies in Chinese Thought*. Chicago: University of Chicago Press, 1953.

Wu K'ang 吳康. *Shao Tzu Yi-hsüeh* 邵子易學 (The *Yi* learning of Master Shao). Taipei: Shang-wu yin-shu kuan, 1959.

Wyatt, Don J. "Chu Hsi's Critique of Shao Yung: One Instance of the Stand Against Fatalism." *Harvard Journal of Asiatic Studies* 45, no. 2 (Dec. 1985): 649–66.

———. "Shao Yung: Champion of Philosophical Syncretism in Early Sung China." Ph. D. dissertation, Harvard University, 1984.

Yabuuti, Kiyosi. "Chinese Astronomy: Development and Limiting Factors." In Shigeru Nakayama and Nathan Sivin, eds., *Chinese Science: Explorations of an Ancient Tradition*, 91–103.

Yamada Keiji 山田慶兒. "Shushi no uchūron josetsu" 朱子の宇宙論序說 (The antecedents of Chu Hsi's cosmology). *Tōhō gakuhō* 東方學報 36 (1964): 481–511.

———. ed. *Chūgoku no kagaku to kagakusha* 中國の科學と科學者 (Chinese science and scientists). Kyoto: Kyoto University, Institute for Humanistic Science, 1978.

Yampolsky, Philip B., trans. *The Platform Sutra of the Sixth Patriarch: The Text of the Tun-huang Manuscript with Translation, Introduction and Notes*. New York: Columbia University Press, 1967.

Yang Hsiung 揚雄. Passages excerpted in *Shuo fu*, 71:11b–14b.

———. *T'ai-hsüan ching* 太玄經 (Classic of the great mystery). SPPY ed.

Yang Jung-kuo 楊榮国. "Shao Yung ssu-hsiang p'i-p'an" 邵雍思想批判 (A critique of the thought of Shao Yung). *Li-shih yen-chiu* 歷史研究 1960, no. 5 (May): 59–74.

Yosida, Mitukuni. "The Chinese Concept of Nature." In Shigeru Nakayama and Nathan Sivin, eds., *Chinese Science: Explorations of an Ancient Tradition*, 71–89.

Yü T'ung 宇同. *Chung-kuo che-hsüeh wen-t'i shih* 中國哲學問題史 (A history of the problems in Chinese philosophy). Hong Kong: Lungmen Press, 1968.

Yü Ying-shih. "Morality and Knowledge in Chu Hsi's Philosophical System." In Wing-tsit Chan, ed., *Chu Hsi and Neo-Confucianism*, 228–54.

———. "Some Preliminary Observations on the Rise of Ch'ing Confucian Intellectualism." *Tsing Hua Hsüeh Pao*, n.s. 11 (Dec. 1975): 105–46.

Index

In this index an "f" after a number indicates a separate reference on the next page, and an "ff" indicates separate references on the next two pages. A continuous discussion over two or more pages is indicated by a span of page numbers, e.g., "57–59." *Passim* is used for a cluster of references in close but not consecutive sequence.

Absolute, the, 56–57, 175, 189. *See also* One, the
Action: vs. knowledge, 25, 163ff, 171; and images, 67, 70, 79f; part of larger whole, 96, 116, 121; and rhetoric, 163–64, 165; and sage, 168, 171
Activity number, 112f
Alchemy, 33, 207ff, 223, 259
Analects, 14, 163, 191
Analogical thought, 168
Appearance (image), 125–32 *passim*
Appearance images, 81
Appropriate names, 57, 167, 175
Argumentation: in Chinese philosophy, 7–10
Arithmetical processes: and mixtures of *ch'i*, 112–13
Artisans: knowledge possessed by, 12–13
Astronomy, 141–43, 218f, 221, 287

Behavior, 17, 96; and images, 67, 70; and *ch'i*, 70, 114–23 *passim*; historical patterns of, 144, 157
Benevolence (*jen*), 137
Birth (*sheng*), 83, 104, 107–8, 136ff, 144
Body (image), 115, 119, 125
Bouvet, Joachim, 75
Buddha, 30, 170, 174
Buddhism, 2, 5–6, 11, 14, 25, 163, 182, 196, 284; and Shao Yung, 29f, 59, 93, 128f, 132f, 155, 230–31,

276, 288; and Shao Yung's ideas on knowledge, 164, 166, 180, 183, 188–94 *passim*; and critiques of Shao Yung, 203, 209, 214, 222–26 *passim*

Ch'an Buddhism, 180, 202, 259, 282
Chang Chung-pin, 36
Chang Heng, 207
Chang Hsing-ch'eng, 29, 31, 206–7
Chang Hsüeh-ch'eng, 32
Chang Hui-yen, 218
Chang Po-hsing, 287
Chang Tsai, 3, 5, 54, 143, 202f, 226, 272, 281; *Cheng meng*, 11, 14, 41; views contrasted with Shao's, 194–96
Chang Yü, 284
Change, 15–16, 174f; explanation of, 48, 55, 62–63; and knowledge of *ch'i* categories, 70–71; and numbers and images, 71, 74ff; the six concepts of, 95–101, 107; and *sheng*, 107–8; and movement and response, 116–23; cyclical and regular, 133f, 136; temporal, 161; patterns of, and the sage, 169, 177; critiques of Shao's views on, 199, 212. *See also* Hua; Pien
Change number, 113
Changes and transformations of heaven and earth, 95, 97ff, 108–14, 115f, 119, 128f

310 · Index

Ch'ao Yi-tao, 203, 207, 284
Charts, 15, 62–63, 208, 216
Chen (trigram), 61, 87f, 127f
Ch'en Chi-ju, 209, 229
Ch'en Chung-fan, 223
Ch'en T'uan, 25, 30, 207–9, 213, 217, 229, 272
Ch'en Tz'u-kung, 284
Cheng (correct firmness), 81, 136
Cheng Hsüan, 142
Cheng Shao-mei, 207
Cheng-ming (rectification of names), 57
Ch'eng (sincerity, wholeness), 183, 281
Ch'eng brothers, 40, 143, 200–201, 214, 219–20, 226; Ch'eng Hao (Ming-tao), 3, 5, 96, 199–206 *passim*, 213–14, 232; Ch'eng Yi, 3, 5, 10, 39, 206, 211, 214, 231
Ch'eng-Chu school, 216f
Chi (self), 185
Chi-tsang, 166, 190, 196
Ch'i (primal substance), 50–55 *passim*, 70–71, 137, 140, 144, 150, 176, 190, 271f; as *t'ai-chi*, 58f; and images of heaven and earth, 67, 78–79, 88, 98f; and behavior, 70, 114–23 *passim*; and subsensorial world, 84, 127f, 133; quantities of, and quality, 92; and correlation of categories, 99, 101, 131, 133; and forms and activities of heaven and earth, 101, 104, 107; and *tung-ching*, 103; and *t'i*, 106; and *pien-hua*, 108–15 *passim*; and movements and responses, 114f, 116–23 *passim*; categories of, and perception, 116; and consciousness, 129–30; ultimate unity of, 189
Ch'i (vessel, utensil), 54
Chiang Yü, 27, 36
Ch'iao Ts'ai, 87f
Ch'ien (trigram, hexagram), 60, 62, 81, 87f, 106, 127, 136f
Ch'ien Mu, 223
Chih (matter), 54, 110
Chih Yi, 125, 132, 190, 193, 230
Chih-kuan (cessation and contemplation), 125, 190, 193, 230
Chinese classics, 28–29, 31ff, 172. See also *individual classics by name*; Four classics

Chinese philosophy: characteristics, 7–11, 25, 42–43
Ching Fang, 218
Ching-hsüeh (classical learning), 228
Ching-shih (governing the world), 228
"Ching-shih t'ien-ti ssu-hsiang t'u" chart, 98, 101, 105, 108, 114, 125, 128, 133, 138, 144
"Ching-shih yi-yüan hsiao-chang chih shu t'u" chart, 85–86
Chou Tun-yi, 2–3, 5, 11, 41, 203, 226, 258f, 272
Chou Yi, 23, 27, 30, 35. See also *Yi-ching*
Chu Chen, 208, 258
Chu Hsi, 3, 47–48, 208, 211–15, 220, 231, 258, 260, 286
Ch'ü Yüan, 26
Ch'uan-hsin (transmitting the mind), 33, 209
Ch'üan (adaptive behavior), 154, 156
Chuang Tzu, 30, 166f, 177, 180, 192–93, 196, 230, 268f, 272
Chuang Tzu, 12, 29, 77, 89f, 181n, 209f, 213, 225
Ch'un-ch'iu (Spring and Autumn Annals), 27–34 *passim*, 38, 40f, 135f, 204, 279; as image, 145ff, 153, 156, 161
Chung (center), 175
Chung Fang, 207f, 264
Chung-yung (Doctrine of the mean), 29, 40, 191
Classes, 68f, 89
Cold (image), 108–113 *passim*, 119f
Comprehensive systems, 6
Conceptual tools: Shao's, 49–63 *passim*
Confucianism, 5–6, 163f, 210, 228f; and Shao, 36–37, 229–30, 231, 263, 271; and critiques of Shao, 202ff, 205, 215–16, 222–26 *passim*
Confucius, 2, 5, 29
Consciousness (*ling*), 59, 95ff, 124–33, 179–85, 188, 193–96; of sage, 164–71 *passim*, 174–82 *passim*; critiques of Shao's views on, 226
Consciousness-Only school, 193
Correlation, 24, 28, 30, 72, 74; and six concepts of change, 96, 98f, 105, 109, 111, 115–23 *passim*, 125, 131, 133, 140; and history, 151–53

Index · 311

Correlative thinking, 49, 63–64
Cosmology, 210, 214, 218f, 221, 230, 287
Cultural pluralism, 6. *See also* Orthodoxy
Cycle (image), 62, 73, 133, 138, 140, 144
Cycles, 138–42 *passim*, 174, 276, 279

Day (image), 62, 108–13 *passim*, 119, 133, 138, 144
Death/being hidden (*ts'ang*), 136ff, 144
Destiny (*ming*), 25, 181, 183
Dew (image), 108–15 *passim*, 119
Disposition (*chih*), 79
Diurnal cycle, 111f, 114
Divination, 30, 203, 212–13
Divisions, 79; groups of two and four, 55, 67, 72ff, 93, 100–5 *passim*, 120, 131f, 134, 230; triadic, 59, 99–100
Double truth, 190, 196
Duke of Chou, 147f
Duties and accomplishments of the sages and worthies, 96f, 133, 144–61

Ears (image), 125–31 *passim*
Earth (*ti*), realm of, 70f, 78, 86, 88, 99–116 *passim*, 125, 133, 138, 145, 170
Earth (*t'u*, image), 67, 71, 101, 104f, 107, 109, 112f
Emperor (image), 145, 147, 152f, 156f, 173
Ends and beginnings of heaven and earth, 96f, 133–44
Enlightenment (*wu*), 190, 193
Entities, primary, 48
Epistemological imperatives, 51f, 210
Epistemology, 44–49, 125, 133, 162f, 207, 214, 219, 222, 230–31. *See also* Consciousness; Knowledge; Perception
Epoch (image), 62, 133, 138, 140, 144
Esoteric traditions, 4, 6–7, 207f, 229
Etiquette (*li*), 137
Events, 16–17, 96, 108–9
Evidence, 48–49
Evidential research movement (*k'ao-cheng hsüeh*), 217, 219, 259

Experience, 82, 85, 95, 180ff; and images and numbers, 66–73 *passim*, 77f, 80; and knowledge, 166ff, 181
Explanatory theories, 45–49
Eyes (image), 125–31 *passim*

Fa (method), 220
Fa Tsang, 193
Fan-kuan (reflective perception), 179ff, 184ff, 189, 192–96, 222, 230, 260, 281–82
Fan-kuan tzu-hsin (reflective perception of one's mind), 180
Fan-shen (introspection), 182
Fang Yi-chih, 219
Fang-shih (adepts), 208f, 216, 223
Feelings (image), 115, 119f, 125
Finite objects, 51, 53, 57, 101
Fire (image), 67, 71, 101, 104–9 *passim*, 112f
Five emperors, 146ff, 149, 173
Five hegemons, 146-50 *passim*, 155, 164, 173
Five phases, 51, 63, 82, 270
Fixed terms, 51
Flavors (image), 125–32 *passim*
Flying things (image), 115, 119, 125f
Forced names (*ch'iang-ming*), 57, 167, 175
Foreknowledge, 188, 212–13
Form (image), 115, 119, 125, 127
Former Chart of Heaven, 86f
Form number, 112
Forms (*hsing*), 79. *See also T'i*
Forms and activities of heaven and earth, 95, 97f, 101–8, 109, 111–12
Fortune-telling, 80, 204, 209f, 212–13, 220, 223
Four classics, 134ff, 137, 144–51 *passim*, 156f, 161
Four directions, 23, 30, 102f, 106f, 134
Four images, 24, 56, 60f, 63, 82ff, 270. *See also groups of images and individual images by name*
Four seasons, 23, 30, 102f, 109, 111, 134ff, 137, 140, 144; cycle of, 145f, 156f
Four stages of life cycle, 136f, 144; and history, 146, 148–56 *passim*
Four treasuries, 134–35, 137f, 144f, 172

Fractions, 89
Fu Hsi, 86f, 97, 147f
"Fu Hsi shih-hua pa-kua t'u" chart, 56
Fu Pi, 37f
Fu Yeh, 284

Generation (image), 62, 133, 138, 140, 144
Government, 146f, 152–58 passim, 173–74
Grades of theoreticity, 4, 74, 77–78
Grassy things (image), 115, 119, 125f
"Great Commentary" (Hsi-tz'u chuan), 52, 56, 74, 76, 80–81, 83, 88, 107f, 122
Growth (chang), 136ff, 144

Han Yü, 6, 30, 40, 51
Harmonious fit (ho), 126–28, 132
Heat (image), 108–15 passim, 119f
Heaven, 78, 86, 99f, 101ff, 135ff; four images of, 67, 88, 105–7, 113, 138; ch'i of, 70, 110f; and pien, 108–14 passim; and activity numbers, 112; and images of movement and response, 115; and images of consciousness, 125; and images of time, 133; cycles of, 138–40; and roundness, 140–41; and images of government, 145; human adaptations to changes in, 154–55; and sage, 169, 171–72, 174; august, 171–72
Hegemon (image), 145, 147, 152f, 156f
Hemilog, 59–60, 80, 100, 105
Heng (prosperous development), 81, 136
Hexagrams, 50, 56, 60ff, 76n, 80, 136ff, 150; Shao's arrangement of, 75, 270; and interaction of categories of ch'i, 114, 123
Hidden, the (li), 173
History, 145–57 passim, 160–61, 173, 225
Ho T'u (River Chart), 52, 86, 208
Ho Yen, 13
Hou Wai-lu, 26, 149, 153, 224–25
Hou-t'ien charts, 86–88
Hou-t'ien realm, 66, 68ff, 80–88 passim

Hour (image), 62, 133, 138, 144
Hsiang-shu hsüeh (images and numbers learning), 4f, 55, 59, 62, 74, 203, 210, 225, 258
Hsieh Liang-tso, 206, 219–20
Hsien-t'ien charts, 59, 62, 86–88, 106f, 150
Hsien-t'ien learning, 167, 176f, 205, 209, 216ff, 220
Hsien-t'ien realm, 66–71 passim, 80–89 passim, 93, 96ff, 141, 270
Hsin, see Mind
Hsin-fa, 220f, 231
Hsin-hsüeh, 216
Hsing (forms), 79. See also Nature
Hsiu-shen (moral cultivation), 228
Hsüeh (learning): and critique of Shao's views, 215, 219f
Hsün Tzu, 30, 89f, 180, 192, 194
Hsün Tzu, 29
Hu Hung, 86, 232
Hu Wei, 210, 218, 285
Hua (transformation), 108–15 passim. See also Change; Pien
Hua Yen school, 193
Huai-nan Tzu, 52, 218
Huang Chen, 217
Huang Chi, 70, 79, 91, 218; on ch'i, 110, 119, 127; on change in society, 164–65; on recognition of patterns, 167–68; on knowledge, 184, 187–89
Huang-chi ching-shih (Supreme principles that rule the world), 11f, 14–15, 82, 258ff, 264; organization of, 24, 46–47, 125, 230f; critiques of, 207, 215, 226
Hui Ssu, 180
Human realm, 23, 32, 59, 61, 90–91, 99–100, 180; and phenomenal world, 125–33 passim; cyclical patterns in, 140; and sage, 168–74 passim
"Hung Fan" (Great Plan), 82

Idealism, 223ff, 232
Ideas (yi), 76ff, 80, 173, 182, 201
Images (hsiang), 4, 40, 50, 67–81 passim, 98f, 128, 173. See also groups of images and individual images by name

Index · 313

Images and numbers, 52, 66–67, 76–89, 93
Images and numbers learning, see Hsiang-shu hsüeh
Infinite objects, 51, 56–57, 101
Intelligence, 130

James, William, 129
Juan Yüan, 218f

K'an (trigram), 61, 87f, 127
Kang-jou (hard/soft), 23f, 31, 54ff, 60f, 64, 67, 189; greater and lesser, 61, 98f, 104–11 passim, 115, 120, 127; and ch'i of earth, 70f; and hsien-t'ien realm, 88; and heaven and earth, 102f
Ken (trigram), 61, 87f, 127f
King (image), 145, 147f, 152f, 156f
Knowledge, 46f, 163–68, 209, 272; esoteric, 4, 6–7, 207f, 229; popular, 24–25; and action, 25, 163ff, 171; traditions of, 31, 207f, 229; sagely, 46, 163–71 passim, 174–78, 180–84, 189–91, 195; and patterns, 128, 168, 181; and action, 163ff, 171; and sense perception, 166, 176, 180–84, 194; path to, 181, 191–92; true, 181ff, 184, 189, 193; and self, 186f; critiques of Shao's views on, 220
Kuai (hexagram), 62
Kuan (perceive), 169, 184f, 191, 281–82
Kuan Lang, 6, 97, 207, 258
Kuan Lu, 209
Kuan-hsin (contemplating the mind), 180
Kuan-pien (observation and discrimination), 166
Kuan-wu (to observe), 179–85 passim, 192–96
Kuan-wu pien, 14, 24
K'un (hexagram, trigram), 60f, 81, 87f, 107, 127f, 136f
K'ung An-kuo, 218
Kuo P'u, 209
Kuo Yung, 264

Language, 163–64, 165, 167
Lao Tzu, 30, 73, 177, 272

Lao Tzu, 13, 29, 64, 107f, 172f, 175, 187, 196; and Yi learning, 209f, 218; and Shao, 210, 213, 215
Later Chart of Heaven, 86ff
Leibniz, Gottfried, 75, 232
Li, see Pattern
Li (advantageous gain), 81, 136
Li (trigram), 61, 87f, 127f
Li Chih-ts'ai, 30, 33ff, 36, 203f, 207f, 220, 229
Li Kou, 284
Li-chi (Book of Rites), 29, 40, 52, 218
Li-hsüeh, 216f
Liang-yi (two forces), 56, 59ff, 83f
Life cycle, 136f, 144
Life-styles, 24–27
Ling, see Consciousness
Ling yü wan-wu, 124, 130
Literati culture, 51–52
Liu Chung, 284
Liu Hsin, 218
Liu Mu, 258
Liu Tao-yüan, 284
Liu Yi, 228
Liu Yin, 217
Liu-shih-ssu kua (64 hexagrams), see Hexagrams
Living things, image categories of, 115, 121, 125–26
Lo Ch'in-shun, 286
Lo Kuang, 149
Lo Shu (Lo Writing), 52, 86, 208
Logic, 63–64
Lu Chiu-yüan (Hsiang-shan), 216f, 232, 288
Lu-Wang school, 216
Lü (hexagram), 62
Lü Kung-chu, 37f
Lü Ssu-mien, 223
Lü-shih ch'un-ch'iu, 52, 218

Manifest, the (piao), 173
Marxism: and critiques of Shao, 222ff
Maturity/harvest (shou), 136ff, 144
Medicine, 33
Mencius, 2, 29–30, 40, 131, 189, 195, 209f, 284
Mencius, 29, 181n, 189, 195
Metaphilosophy, 7–9
Mind (hsin), 52f, 56, 58, 102–3, 131f, 173–82 passim, 186ff, 221; and the

One, 59, 75, 175; and knowledge, 166; Chang Tsai on, 194–95; critiques of Shao's views on, 214, 232
Ming (to comprehend), 47
Mohism, 163
Month (image), 62, 133, 138, 144
Moon (image), 67, 70, 101, 104–13 *passim*, 138
Morality, 155–56, 165, 173f
Moral philosophy, *see Yi-li hsüeh*
Mouth (image), 125–31 *passim*
Movements and responses of the myriad things, 72, 95, 97, 114–24, 128f, 132–33
Moving observation point, 96, 115
Moving things number, 113
Mu Hsiu, 204, 207f
Music, 23–24, 30

Names, 17, 57, 68ff, 155–60 *passim*, 167, 175–76
Naturalists, school of, 64
Natural realm, 23f, 32, 34, 171–72
Nature (*hsing*), 92; as image, 115, 119f, 125; and knowledge, 181, 183, 187
Nature and destiny (*hsing-ming*), 34
Needham, Joseph, 224, 260
Neo-Confucianism, 2–3, 11, 24–25, 181n, 216–17, 226
"New learning" (*hsin-hsüeh*), 39
Night (image), 108–13 *passim*, 119
Nirvana, 190
No-mind (*wu-hsin*), 188, 231
Non-action (*wu-wei*), 172–73, 187
Non-being (*wu-yu*), 172–73
Nose (image), 125–31 *passim*
No-self (*wu-wo*), 188, 191, 195f, 231
Nouns, 68
Number images, 81
Numbers (*shu*), 4, 30, 40, 50, 71–81 *passim*, 173, 268; and hexagrams, 62; and comparisons, 89–94; and *ch'i*, 112–13; and cycles, 138–39, 144; critiques of Shao's views on, 203, 210ff, 213, 220
Numerology, 4

Objectivity, 90
Observation, 192–93
Odor (image), 125–32 *passim*
One, the, 51–58 *passim*, 79, 85, 162, 175ff, 182, 190
Ontology, 44; and explanatory theory, 45–49; concepts used to discuss, 50–63; critiques of Shao's views on, 210, 214. *See also* Ch'i; Reality
Order, natural, *see under* Reality; Universe
Order, social, 164f, 170
Orthodoxy, 40; and Shao, 26, 40, 201ff, 205, 215–16, 217f
Ou-yang Fei, 209, 220

Pa-kua, see Trigrams
Pattern (*li*), 17, 47f, 50, 56, 103, 122, 172; and images and numbers, 77–78, 79; and knowledge, 128, 168, 181; and sage, 169ff, 177, 181, 183, 187f, 191, 195; and the absolute, 175, 189; critique of Shao's views on, 200–201, 203
Perception, sense, 17, 128–29, 130, 132, 193; and *ch'i*, 116, 128; and knowledge, 166, 176, 180–84, 194; and sage, 169; and perceiving self, 180, 182, 186–87
Perspective, 17
Phenomenal world, 16, 67, 98, 100, 168; and images and numbers, 71–89 *passim*, 104, 107; and subsensorial *ch'i*, 111–12, 114, 119; and human beings, 125–33 *passim*; and knowledge, 166f, 169, 180
Physiognomy, 207f
P'i-hsi (opening and closing), 23
Pien (change), 108–14 *passim*, 121, 154. *See also* Change; *Hua*
Po (hexagram), 62
Profit, 164
Proof structure, 49, 64
Pu yi wo kuan wu (not perceiving things from the viewpoint of self), 195

Rain (image), 108–15 *passim*, 119
Reality: organization of, 17–18; divisions of, 44, 53, 59, 66; Shao's method of discussing, 45–49; Shao's assumptions regarding,

Index · 315

50–51; whole vs. parts, 51, 57, 59, 68–69, 75, 83–84, 94, 101f, 108–9; orderly nature of, 71, 93; and numbers, 72, 78; and human consciousness, 128–29, 130, 182; and names, 156f, 159, 175–76; and sage, 174, 177f, 182f, 188, 190–91, 195; and self, 189; critiques of Shao's views on, 214. *See also* Sensorial/subsensorial reality; Universe

Reclusion, 25–26, 28, 37, 39
Relativism, 68–69, 89–90, 96, 99f, 157–58, 192–93
Reflective perception, *see Fan-kuan*
Resonance, 114
Response (*ying*), 115, 121
Revolution (image), 62, 133, 138, 140, 144
Rhetoric, 163–64, 165, 173
Righteousness (*yi*), 137, 164
Root-and-branches metaphor, 50, 54

Sage, 92–93, 131, 135ff, 156, 279; knowledge of, 46, 163–71 *passim*, 174–78, 180–84, 189–91, 195f; characteristics of, 168–74; and subject-object distinction, 181–88 *passim*, 195; critiques of Shao's views on, 214, 220
Sage (image), 145, 147, 152f, 156f
San-lun (Three Treatise) school, 166
Science: and critiques of Shao's views, 225
Self, 177, 180, 182, 185–96 *passim*, 231, 282
Self-awareness, 187–88
Senses, 125–33 *passim*, 180. *See also* Perception, sense
Sensorial/subsensorial reality, 50–56 *passim*, 59, 84, 101, 104, 107, 111, 127f, 133
Sex distinctions, 137
Shan (to perfect), 128–29, 193f, 231
Shao Chung-liang, 27
Shao Fu, 27
Shao Ku, 22–24, 27, 30, 34f
Shao Ling-chin, 22
Shao Mu, 21f
Shao Po, 27, 29

Shao Po-wen, 15, 27, 115, 122, 126, 128, 260, 262, 284; on *tao*, 58, 102, 149; on numbers, 73f, 89, 113, 139, 268; on *t'ai-chi*, 83–84; on human nature, 92; on the sage, 92, 156, 171; on spontaneity, 105; on *t'i-yung*, 106; on images and *ch'i*, 109–10, 118; on the mind, 131; on time, 139f; on the One, 176; on *kuan*, 184, 191; on *fan-kuan*, 189; on Shao Yung's antecedents, 207
Shao P'u, 27
Shao Te-hsin, 22
Shao Yung, 2, 5, 7, 11, 115; writings, 11–15; family background, 21–24, 27–28; as "hermit in town," 24–25, 28, 37, 39; political protest, 26, 39, 202; descendants, 27, 36; education, 28–37; objects of study, 31–32; life in Loyang, 37–39; compared with contemporaries, 39–41; contemporary opinion on, 198–204; later Sung opinion on, 204–16; Yüan and Ming opinion on, 216–17; Ch'ing opinion on, 217–21; 20th-century opinion on, 221–26; and intellectual tradition, 228–32. *See also under subject headings*
Shen (spirit), 52–59 *passim*, 75, 78–79, 175, 268
Shen Hsiu, 180
Shen Kua, 143
Sheng, see Birth
Shih-ching (Book of Poetry), 29, 31f, 135f, 279; as image, 145ff, 148, 153, 156
Shou (to receive), 131, 193f, 231
Shu (number), 267–68. *See also* Numbers
Shu (techniques), 187, 213, 215, 219f
Shu-ching (Book of Documents), 29, 31f, 40, 82, 135f, 279; as image, 145ff, 153, 156
Shun, 147, 150, 165
Shunyata, 190
Sincerity (*ch'eng*), 183, 281
Sky Door, 107
Social groups, 51–52
Sound (image), 125–32 *passim*
Space, 53, 111

Speculation, 166, 168
Spontaneity (*tzu-jan*), 105, 172
Ssu-ma Kuang, 3, 5f, 27, 37f, 40–41, 97, 202, 258–59, 284
Stars (image), 67, 70, 101, 104–13 *passim*, 138
Stationary things number, 113
Stone (image), 67, 71, 101, 104f, 107, 109, 112f
Su Tung-p'o, 284
Subject-object distinction, 176f, 181–88 *passim*, 195f
Sun (image), 67, 70, 101, 104–12 *passim*, 115, 138
Sun (trigram), 61, 87f, 127
Superior man (*chün-tzu*), 168, 177, 187
Symbols, 16, 209. *See also* Images; Numbers

Ta-hsin (enlarging the mind), 194–95
Ta-hsüeh (Great Learning), 29, 40, 134, 191
T'ai-chi (Supreme Ultimate), 56–59, 83–84, 100, 104, 189f, 268; and number one, 75, 78f; and sage, 169; and the absolute, 175; critique of Shao's views on, 214
T'ai-ch'u (Great Beginning), 176
T'ai-hsüan (Great Mystery), 175
T'ai-su (Great Simplicity), 175
T'ai-yi (Great One), 107, 175–76
T'ang Chün-yi, 224
Tao, 52f, 56f, 85, 122, 190; and the One, 58f, 175; and number one, 75; of heaven and earth, 78, 102–3; of change, 117; of humans, 132, 148ff, 156–57; of cyclical time, 140; of history, 148ff, 156–57; relativity of, 157–58; and sage, 169, 171f, 178, 191; and observation, 192–93
Tao-hsüeh, 2, 39ff. *See also* Neo-Confucianism
Taoism, 2, 6, 12–13, 25, 209ff, 228–29; and Shao, 29f, 159, 183, 229f, 231; religious, 33; and knowledge, 163f, 183; and critiques of Shao's views, 203, 207, 209, 213f, 216, 218, 222ff, 225f
Tao-t'ung, 40, 202, 211, 226
Teachers, role of, 33–34
Techniques, *see Shu*

Theories: nature of, 44–45
Theory, realm of, 66, 95
Thought, 181f
Three kings, 146ff, 149, 164
Three realms, 99
Three sages, 146ff, 149, 155, 173
Thunder (image), 108–15 *passim*, 119
T'i (form, appearance), 55, 104, 106, 132, 228, 272
T'i-yung, 106, 153–54, 273
T'ien-t'ai school, 125, 180, 189, 193
T'ien-ti (heaven and earth), 52f, 60
Time, 17, 53, 73, 109ff, 114, 133f, 138–40, 143–44. *See also* Cycles
Transformation numbers, 113
Trigrams, 50, 56, 60f, 67, 80, 83f, 88; and charts, 87; and images, 104, 106–7; and categories of *ch'i*, 127f; and historical patterns, 150
Ts'ai Yüan-ting, 15, 56, 60, 86, 96ff, 105, 259
Tso Chuan, 80
Tsou Yen, 167
Tui (hexagram, trigram), 61f, 87f, 107, 127
Tung Chung-shu, 6, 258
Tung-ching (motion and rest), 56, 60, 67, 79, 103ff, 106, 121, 137, 214
Two forces (*liang-yi*), 56, 59ff, 83f

Unity, mystical, with universe, 162, 181–91 *passim*, 195f; critiques of Shao's views on, 209f, 214f
Universe: order in, 34, 50, 96, 99, 101, 105, 120, 131, 142; triadic division of, 59, 99–100; and six concepts of change, 95; and sage, 169f, 172, 174, 181–91 *passim*, 195f. *See also* Reality

Walking things (image), 115, 119, 125f
Wan-wu (the myriad things), 52f, 73–74, 115
Wang An-shih, 5, 37ff, 284
Wang Chih, 15, 67, 79, 154, 168, 170, 174, 184, 260
Wang Ch'ung, 285
Wang Fu-chih, 219
Wang Kung-ch'en, 37f
Wang Pi, 76ff, 80f, 268f, 272
Wang T'ing-hsiang, 218

Wang Yang-ming, 163, 216, 232
Wang Yün-hsiu, 27
Water (image), 67, 71, 101, 104f, 107, 109, 112f, 115
Wei Cheng-t'ung, 225
Wei Liao-weng, 215, 220
Wei Po-yang, 6, 143, 207, 209, 223, 258
Wen (literary expression), 228
Wen, King, 86f, 97, 147f, 150
Wen Chung-tzu (Wang T'ung), 30
Wen Yen-po, 38
Wind (image), 108–15 *passim*, 119
Wisdom, 90–91, 92, 137
Wo (self), 185, 193, 231, 282
Woody things, 115, 119, 125f
Word images, 81
Words, 76ff, 79f, 166ff, 173. *See also* Language; Rhetoric
Worthies, 108
Wu, King, 147f, 150
Wu K'ang, 223
Wu-hsing (five phases), 51, 63, 82, 270
"Wu-ming kung chuan" (Biography of Mr. No Name), 12f
Wu-wo chih hsin (a mind that does not possess a self), 187–88

Yang Hsiung, 6, 41, 74, 97, 120; influence on Shao, 25, 30, 141f, 205ff, 258
Yang Jung-kuo, 224
Yang Shih, 204–6, 216
Yang lines, 60, 76n, 81
Yao, 85f, 147f, 150, 165
Year (image), 62, 109, 111f, 114, 133, 137f, 144
Yi, see One, the
Yi-ching, 3f, 6, 16, 29f, 40, 52, 60, 136, 181n, 279; Shao Ku on, 23; and Shao Yung, 30f, 34f, 38, 45–46; and symbolic and phenomenal realms, 76; Shao's classification of images, 81; on *hsien-t'ien*, 84; and numbers, 113; and four treasuries, 135, 137; and Shao's views on knowledge, 183; used by Taoists and Confucianists, 209–10; Shao's influence on Chu Hsi's interpretation of, 211, 231. *See also* "Great Commentary"

Yi-ching (image), 145ff, 153, 156
Yi-ch'uan chi-jang chi (Collection of beating on the ground at Yi-ch'uan), 12ff, 23, 215, 226, 259–60
Yi learning, 3ff, 16, 40–41, 62ff; Shao Ku's interest in, 23; Shao Po-wen's interest in, 27; and Shao Yung, 30f, 34ff, 40; and evidence in Shao's thought, 49; and numbers, 74; and *hsien-t'ien* realm, 89; and six concepts of change, 95; and resonance, 114; and astronomy, 142ff; and critiques of Shao's thought, 203, 207f, 215–20 *passim*, 223ff; emphases, 209–10; and Taoism, 213, 218; in Ch'ing, 218, 288
Yi-li (Rites), 29
Yi-li hsüeh (moral philosophy), 4f, 34, 40, 77, 203f, 210
Yi wu kuan wu (seeing things as things), 194f
Yin T'un, 210, 220
Yin lines, 60, 76n, 81
Yin-yang, 23f, 31, 51–64 *passim*, 67, 189; greater and lesser, 60f, 98f, 104–11 *passim*, 115, 127; and heaven and earth, 70, 101f; and *hsien-t'ien* realm, 88; relativity of, 90, 99; and movement, 103, 105; and *t'i*, 106; and numbers, 112f; and behavior, 116–21 *passim*; and four seasons, 135, 137, 140, 144; and four treasuries, 137, 144; and *tao*, 175; critiques of Shao's views on, 199, 214
Yu-wo chih hsin (a mind that possesses a self), 187f
Yü, 147, 150
Yü Fan, 218
Yü Yen, 143
Yü-ch'iao wen-tui (Conversation between the fisherman and the woodcutter), 12
Yüan (originating growth), 81, 136
Yung (activity, function), 106, 132, 228, 272

Zodiacal space (image), 67, 70, 101, 104–13 *passim*, 138

Library of Congress Cataloging-in-Publication Data

Birdwhistell, Anne D.
　Transition to neo-Confucianism : Shao Yung on knowledge and symbols of reality/Anne D. Birdwhistell.
　　　p.　cm.
　Bibliography: p.
　Includes index.
　ISBN 0-8047-1550-5 (alk. paper):
　1. Shao, Yung, 1011–1077—Contributions in Neo-Confucianism.　2. Neo-Confucianism.　3. Shao, Yung, 1011–1077—Contributions in I ching.　4. I ching.　I. Title.
B128.S5B57　1989
181'.112—dc20
89-31272
CIP